Windows® 2000 Scripting Bible

Windows® 2000 Scripting Bible

William R. Stanek

Wiley Publishing, Inc.

Windows® 2000 Scripting Bible

Published by
Wiley Publishing, Inc.
909 Third Avenue
New York, NY 10022
www.wiley.com

Copyright ©2000 by Wiley Publishing, Inc.,
Indianapolis, Indiana

Published simultaneously in Canada

For general information on our other products and services or to obtain technical support, please contact our Customer Care Department within the U.S. at 800-762-2974, outside the U.S. at 317-572-3993, or fax 317-572-4002.

Wiley also publishes its books in a variety of electronic formats. Some content that appears in print may not be available in electronic books.

Library of Congress Cataloging-in-Publication Data:

Library of Congress Catalog Card Number: 00-101536

ISBN: 0-7645-4667-5

Manufactured in the United States of America
10 9 8 7 6 5 4 3...2

Credits

Acquisitions Editors
John Osborn
Sherri Morningstar

Project Editor
Matthew E. Lusher

Technical Editor
Chris Stone

Copy Editors
Amy Eoff
Lane Barnholtz

Project Coordinators
Linda Marousek
Danette Nurse
Joe Shines

Graphics and Production Specialists
Robert Bihlmayer
Jude Levinson
Michael Lewis
Dina F Quan
Ramses Ramirez
Victor Pérez-Varela

Proofreading and Indexing
York Production Services

Cover Design
Evan Deerfield

Illustrator
Shelley Norris

About the Author

William R. Stanek (win2000scripting@tvpress.com) has an MS degree in information systems and over 15 years' hands-on experience with advanced programming and development. He is a leading network technology expert and an award-winning author. He is also a regular contributor to leading publications like *PC Magazine*, in which you'll often find his work in the "Solutions" section. He has written, co-authored, or contributed to over 20 computer books. Current or upcoming books include *Windows NT Scripting Administrator's Guide*, *Microsoft Windows 2000 Administrator's Pocket Consultant*, *FrontPage 2000 Unleashed*, *Microsoft SQL Server 7.0 Administrator's Pocket Consultant*, and *Netscape Guide to the Mozilla Source Code*.

William is proud to have served in the Persian Gulf War as a combat crewmember on an electronic warfare aircraft. He flew on numerous combat missions into Iraq and was awarded nine medals for his wartime service, including one of the United States of America's highest flying honors, the Air Force Distinguished Flying Cross. Currently, he resides in the Pacific Northwest with his wife and three children.

Preface

If you've purchased *Windows 2000 Scripting Bible* or are thumbing through the book in a bookstore somewhere, you probably want to know how this book can help you. My goal in writing *Windows 2000 Scripting Bible* is to create the best resource available on scripting the Windows 2000 operating system.

As you'll learn in this book, Windows 2000 scripting involves many different technologies. These technologies include:

+ Windows 2000 Professional and Windows 2000 Server

+ Windows Script Host

+ Scripting languages, such as VBScript and JScript

+ ActiveX and COM (Component Object Model) components

+ Microsoft Active Directory

+ ADSI (Active Directory Services Interfaces)

I've tried to pack in as much information about these topics as possible, and to present the information in a way that is both clear and concise—and I hope you'll agree. I've also tried to present Windows 2000 scripting in a unique way, offering both VBScript and JScript solutions throughout the text. In this way, you can learn exactly how VBScript and JScript can be used with Windows 2000. With this approach, you gain insight into unique scripting techniques necessary to implement solutions in both VBScript and Jscript, and, if you prefer one scripting language over the other, there's no more guesswork.

Who Should Read This Book

If you are someone who is interested in any of the previously mentioned technologies, *Windows 2000 Scripting Bible* is definitely a book you should read. This comes with several caveats. This book is designed for:

+ Administrators who support Windows 2000 and pre-Windows 2000 systems

+ Developers who create scripts or programs for Windows 2000 and pre-Windows 2000 systems

+ Power users running Windows 2000, Windows 98, or Windows NT

To pack in as much information as possible, I had to assume that you have basic networking skills, a basic understanding of Windows 2000, and that Windows 2000 is already installed on your systems. With this in mind, I don't devote entire chapters to understanding, installing, or using Windows 2000. Beyond the introductory information in Chapters 1, 2, and 3, I don't cover scripting basics either. I do, however, cover every facet of Windows 2000 scripting, so if you want to learn Windows 2000 scripting inside and out — including techniques not published elsewhere — you've come to the right source.

Though the book highlights the latest and greatest features of Windows 2000, just about everything you learn in this book can also be applied to script Windows NT and Windows 98. Keep in mind that if you are using a pre-Windows 2000 system, however, you will need to install any necessary components. These components include Windows Script Host, Microsoft Script Engines version 5 or later, and Active Directory Services Interface extensions.

What You'll Learn from This Book

Every how-to book is supposed to teach its reader how to do something, and in the process convey some body of knowledge to the reader. *Windows 2000 Scripting Bible* is no exception. This book teaches you about Windows scripting and includes in-depth coverage of all related technologies.

Windows 2000 Scripting Bible isn't meant to be a do-everything guide to scripting. Rather, the book focuses on techniques you'll use to script Windows 2000 the operating system. Chapter by chapter, you learn how to create scripts. The detailed explanations provided are backed by hundreds of hands-on examples and over 250 complete source-code listings. This book also develops extensive utility libraries that you can use to quickly and efficiently perform complex tasks.

Special Formatting

As with most computer books, you'll see that some text is highlighted by special formatting or with special icons. Here's a field guide to the things you'll see.

Note
Notes provide additional details and often contain information that you should read before trying to implement a referenced technique.

    Notes look like this.

Cross-Reference

Cross-references tell you where you can find more information on a particular topic.

 More information is available, so look for it here.

Tip

Tips inform you of little factoids that may be useful to you as you work with Windows 2000 scripting. Tips provide helpful information that isn't always essential to getting things to work correctly. Rather, Tip material can be used to make things run better.

 Tips look like this.

Caution

Cautions provide a specific warning about things you should watch out for, or things you shouldn't do. You should pay particular attention to cautions when reading the text.

 Cautions look like this.

Source-Code Formatting

The text contains source-code listings as well as in-text references to objects, methods, properties, and other source-code elements. Source-code listings in this book have several formats. You'll find side-by-side code listings for VBScript and JScript, for example:

VBScript	*JScript*
| ```
Set fs = CreateObject
  ("Scripting.FileSystemObject")
Set f = fs.OpenTextFile
  (aFile, ForAppending)
f.WriteLine theLine
f.Close
``` | ```
var fs = new
  ActiveXObject
  ("Scripting.FileSystemObject");
var f = fs.OpenTextFile
  (aFile, ForAppending)
f.WriteLine(theLine)
f.Close()
``` |

You'll also find in-line code listings, like this:

VBScript
| ```
Set fs = CreateObject ("Scripting.FileSystemObject")
Set f = fs.OpenTextFile (aFile, ForAppending)
``` |
```

```
f.WriteLine theLine
f.Close
```

JScript

```
var fs = new ActiveXObject("Scripting.FileSystemObject");
var f = fs.OpenTextFile (aFile, ForAppending)
f.WriteLine(theLine)
f.Close()
```

Generally, I use side-by-side code listings when I want you to be able to directly compare VBScript and JScript scripting techniques (and the source-code lines are short enough to make this format work). On the other hand, when source-code lines are long or complex, I usually use in-line code listings where the VBScript example is followed by a JScript example.

In-text references to source-code elements are highlighted with a monospace font, as in the following sentence. The `OpenTextFile` method is used to open text files. Don't confuse monospace type with in-text elements printed in bold. When you see bold text in the middle of a paragraph, it means that this is something you should type in at the keyboard, such as type **cls** at the command prompt to clear the screen.

Support and Comments

Windows 2000 Scripting Bible is a work in progress, just like the Windows 2000 operating system itself and the body of work that's grown up around it. It's quite likely that errors will make themselves apparent after this book has gone to press and found its way onto your desktop. I very much appreciate the efforts of readers who go to the trouble of pointing out mistakes in the text so I can fix them in future editions. Even more, I am grateful for readers who offer their own hints, tricks, code, and ideas to me for inclusion in future editions of this book.

I truly hope you find that *Windows 2000 Scripting Bible* provides everything you need to perform essential scripting tasks. Through email, you can contact me at `win2000scripting@tvpress.com`. You're always welcome to write me with ideas, suggestions, improvements, or questions. If you provide an example that's used in a future edition of this book, I'll be especially grateful for your help and will credit you in that edition. I also have a Web site, which contains support material for this book, among other things. Point your browser to `http://www.tvpress.com/win2000scripting/` for corrections, enhancements, news, and additional thoughts. I'll post the source code from this book as well.

Thank you!

Acknowledgments

Writing *Windows 2000 Scripting Bible* took a lot of work and research. Much of the time was spent searching for undocumented features, resolving problems with poorly documented interfaces, and exploring uncharted areas of Windows 2000. Then, I had to write about the hidden features and the many interfaces I had discovered. I hope you'll agree that the result was worth all of the effort. The book contains over 250 code examples and dozens of working scripts all designed to provide a top-notch tutorial and reference.

Windows 2000 Scripting Bible wouldn't have been possible without a lot of help from others and, especially, the team at IDG Books. Thank you to John Osborn and Sherri Morningstar, who took the book through acquisitions; and Matt Lusher, who did the development work on the book. I'd also like to thank Christopher Stone for the technical review of the book. The task of copying editing went to Amy Eoff, and together with others on the editorial and production staff, like Lane Barnholtz and Linda Marousek, they did a good job.

A big thank you goes out to my close contacts and friends at Microsoft. Thanks also to Studio B literary agency and my agents, David Rogelberg and Neil Salkind. Neil has a terrific knack for helping me find projects that are both fun and challenging.

Hopefully, I haven't forgotten anyone but, if I have, it was an oversight. *Honest.* ;-)

Contents at a Glance

Contents

Part IV: Windows Scripting Libraries   453

Getting Started with Windows Scripting

◆ ◆ ◆ ◆

◆ ◆ ◆ ◆

Part I of the Windows 2000 Scripting Bible introduces you to the powerful administrative tool that is Windows scripting. You'll get an overview of Windows scripting and its potential, and an introduction to two languages you can use for Windows scripting: VBScript and JScript.

Introducing Windows Scripting

Windows scripting gives everyday users and administrators the ability to automate repetitive tasks, complete activities while away from the computer, and perform many other time-saving activities. Windows scripting accomplishes all of this by enabling you to create tools to automate tasks that would otherwise be handled manually, such as creating user accounts, generating log files, managing print queues, or examining system information. By eliminating manual processes, you can double, triple, or even quadruple your productivity and become more effective and efficient at your job. Best of all, scripts are easy to create and you can rapidly develop prototypes of applications, procedures, and utilities; and then enhance these prototypes to get exactly what you need, or just throw them away and begin again. This ease of use gives you the flexibility to create the kinds of tools you need without a lot of fuss.

Introducing Windows Scripting

You've heard the claims about scripting and now you're thinking, so what? What's in it for me? You may be an administrator rather than a developer. Or maybe you're a power user who helps other users from time to time. Either way, scripting will prove useful to your situation and needs. So in answer to the question, "What's in it for me?" consider the following:

- ✦ Would you like to have more free time? Windows scripting frees you from mundane and repetitive tasks, enabling you to focus on more interesting and challenging tasks.

✦ Would you like to be able to analyze trends and be proactive rather than reactive? You can use Windows scripting to extract and manipulate huge quantities of information and turn out easy-to-use reports.

✦ Would you like to be able to seize opportunities before they disappear? Windows scripting enables you to take advantage of opportunities and be more effective. You can solve problems quickly and efficiently.

✦ Would you like to be a top performer and receive the praise you deserve? Windows scripting enables you to accomplish in hours or days what would otherwise take weeks or months with traditional techniques. You'll be more successful and more productive at work.

✦ Would you like to be able to integrate activities and applications? Windows scripting enables you to integrate information from existing systems and applications, allowing you to kick off a series of tasks simply by starting a script.

✦ Would you like to have fun at work? Windows scripting can be fun, challenging, and rewarding. Give it a try and you'll see!

If Windows scripting can do so much, it must be terribly complex, right? On the contrary, it is its simplicity that enables you to do so much — not complexity. Most Windows scripts are only a few lines long and you can create them in a few minutes!

Taking a look at Windows Scripting

Windows Script Host is a core component of the Windows 2000 operating system and, as such, is installed by default when you install Windows 2000. Like other components, Windows Script Host can be uninstalled. It can also be upgraded through downloads or by installing service packs. To ensure that Windows Script Host is installed on your system, type **cscript** at a command prompt. You should see version information for Windows Script Host as well as usage details. If you don't see this information, Windows Script Host may not be installed and you'll need to install it as you would any other Windows component.

The key components of Windows Script host are the following:

✦ **WScript** — A Windows executable for the scripting host that is used when you execute scripts from the desktop. This executable has GUI controls for displaying output in pop-up dialog boxes.

✦ **CScript** — A command-line executable for the scripting host that is used when you execute scripts from the command line. This executable displays standard output at the command line.

✦ **WSH ActiveX Control** — An ActiveX control that provides the core object model for the scripting host.

✦ **Scripting Engines**—Scripting engines provide the core functions, objects, and methods for a particular scripting language. VBScript and JScript scripting engines are installed by default on Windows 2000.

A Windows script is a text file containing a series of commands. Unlike shell scripts, Windows script commands don't resemble commands that you'd type in at the keyboard. Instead, they follow the syntax for the scripting language you are using, such as VBScript or JScript.

Windows scripts can be created in Notepad. When you finish creating the script, save it with an extension appropriate for the scripting language (.VBS for VBScript, .JS for Jscript, or .WSF for batch scripts that combine scripts with markup). Once you create a Windows script, you run it with WScript or CScript.

Using and running scripts

Windows scripts can be run with either WScript or CScript, and most of the time the application you use depends on your personal preference. However, you'll find that WScript works best for scripts that interact with users, especially if the script displays results as standard text output. For tasks that you want to automate or run behind the scenes, you'll probably prefer CScript, with which you can suppress output and prompts for batch processing.

You can use WScript and CScript with scripts in several different ways. The easiest way is to set WScript as the default application for scripts and then run scripts by clicking their filename in Windows Explorer. Don't worry, you don't have to do anything fancy to set WScript as the default. The first time you click a Windows script, you'll be asked if you'd like to associate the file extension with WScript. Click Yes. Alternatively, you may see an Open With dialog box that asks which program you would like to use to open the file. Choose WScript, and then check the *Always use this program to open this file* checkbox.

You can also set CScript as the default interface. When you do this, clicking a Windows script runs CScript instead of WScript. Or, you could run scripts from the Run prompt just as you could when WScript was the default. To run scripts with CScript from the command line, enter **cscript** followed by the pathname of the script you want to execute. For now, don't worry about the details; you'll find detailed instructions in Chapter 4.

Windows Script Host Architecture

Windows Script Host (WSH) is a standard feature of Windows 98 and Windows 2000 and is available as an add-on for Windows NT 4.0. Windows Script Host provides architecture for building dynamic scripts that consists of a core object model, scripting hosts, and scripting engines—each of which is discussed in the sections that follow.

Core object model

The core object model and scripting hosts are packaged with WSH for Windows. Although the Windows Script Host is fairly new, several versions have already shipped, including WSH 1 and WSH 2. WSH 1 is standard on most versions of Windows 98, and comes with Service Pack 4 or 5 for Windows NT 4.0. WSH 2 ships with Windows 2000 and is available for Windows 98 and Windows NT 4.0. You can download the latest version online at the MSDN Web site (http://msdn.microsoft.com/scripting/).

Whether you install WSH on Windows NT 4.0 or work with WSH on Windows 98/2000, the core object model is implemented in the WSH.ocx ActiveX control. WSH.ocx provides the key functionality necessary for scripts to interact with the operating system. In WSH, objects are simply named containers that you'll use to interact with operating system components. For example, you'll use the WshNetwork object to access and configure network resources, like printers and drives.

Each object has properties and methods that are used to perform certain types of tasks. Properties are attributes of an object that you can access. Methods are procedures that you'll use to perform operations. As with other object-based programming languages, you can work with objects in a variety of ways. You can use built-in objects, create new objects based on the built-in objects, or you can define your own objects using unique methods and properties.

Table 1-1 provides a summary of the WSH object model. The WSH object hierarchy can be broken down into two broad categories: exposed objects and non-exposed objects. Exposed objects, like WScript, are the ones you'll work with in your scripts. Non-exposed objects, like WshCollection, are accessed through the methods or properties of other objects. These objects do the behind-the-scenes work.

Table 1-1
Core WSH Objects

Object Type	Object	Description
Exposed Object	WScript	Top-level object that provides access to core objects and other functionality such as object creation.
	WScript.WshNetwork	Automation object used to access and configure network resources, like printers and drives. Also provides user, domain, and computer information.
	WScript.WshShell	Automation object that provides access to the environment and file folders.

Object Type	Object	Description
Non-exposed Object	WshArguments	Accessed through WScript.Arguments. Obtains command-line arguments.
	WshCollection	Accessed through WshNetwork.EnumNetworkDrives or WshNetwork.EnumPrinterCollection. Used for iteration through a group of items, such as printers or drives.
	WshEnvironment	Accessed through WshShell.Environment. Allows you to work with environment variables.
	WshShortcut	Accessed through WshShell.CreateShortcut. Used to create and manage file shortcuts.
	WshSpecialFolders	Accessed through WshShell.Folder. Used to work with file folders.
	WshUrlShortcut	Accessed through WshShell.CreateShortcut method. Used to create and manage URL shortcuts.

Note Most of the Microsoft technical documentation refers to some objects using the wrong letter case. For example, WScript is referred to as Wscript for both VBScript and JScript. Unfortunately, the JScript scripting engine (through version 5.1) doesn't recognize this object unless you reference it as WScript, and since VBScript really doesn't care about letter case, either Wscript or WScript works just fine. For consistency's sake, I use WScript in both VBScript and JScript. If this conflict is resolved and the object name is changed to Wscript in future versions of the JScript scripting engine, you may need to change WScript references to Wscript.

More on scripting hosts

To execute Windows scripts, you'll use one of the two scripting hosts available, either WScript or CScript. WScript has GUI controls for displaying output in pop-up dialog boxes and is used primarily when you execute scripts from the desktop. CScript is the command-line executable for the scripting host that is used when you execute scripts from the command line. Although you can work with both of these hosts in much the same way, there are some features specific to each which I'll discuss later in Chapter 4. For now, let's focus on how the scripting hosts work.

Several file extensions are mapped for use with the scripting hosts. These file extensions are:

✦ .js — Designates scripts written in JScript.

✦ .vbs — Designates scripts written in VBScript.

✦ .wsf — Designates a Windows script file.

✦ .wsh — Designates a WSH properties file.

A limitation of .js and .vbs files is that they can only contain JScript or VBScript statements, respectively, and you cannot mix and match. This is where .wsf files come into the picture. You can use .wsf files to create WSH jobs, or what I call *batch* scripts. These batch scripts can combine multiple types of scripts and can also include type libraries containing constants.

Batch scripts contain markup tags that identify elements within the batch, such as individual jobs and the scripting language being used. These markup tags are defined as XML (Extensible Markup Language) elements. XML is structured much like HTML and uses plain text characters. You can use any text editor to create batch scripts and, because batch scripts contain XML, you can also use an XML editor.

Windows scripts can also use .wsh files. These files contain default settings for scripts, such as timeout values and script paths. Because of the introduction of .wsf files and direct in-script support for most script properties, .wsh files are rarely needed.

More on scripting engines

Scripting engines provide the core language functionality for Windows scripts and are packaged separately from the Windows Script Host itself. You can obtain scripting engines for JScript, VBScript, Perl, TCL, Python, and more. The official Microsoft scripting engines for VBScript and JScript are standard components on Windows 2000 and are the focus of this book.

With Windows scripting, many of the features available for scripting with Internet Explorer and the Web aren't available. Functions needed for Web scripting simply aren't needed for Windows scripting and vice versa. For example, in JScript, none of the window-related objects are available in WSH. The reason is that, in Windows, you normally don't need to access documents, forms, frames, applets, plug-ins, or any of those other browser-related features. The exception to this is if you create a script that starts a browser session; within the browser session, you can use the browser-related objects all you want.

Right now you may be wondering what exactly is and isn't supported by Windows scripts. In a nutshell, the scripting engines support core language and language run-time environments. The core language includes operators, statements, built-in objects, and built-in functions. Operators are used to perform arithmetic, comparisons, and more. Statements are used to make assignments, to conditionally execute code, and to control the flow within a script. For example, you can use `for` looping to execute a section of code for a specific count. These types of statements are all defined in the core language. Beyond this, the core language also defines the core functions and objects that perform common operations such as evaluating expressions, manipulating strings, and managing data.

The runtime environment adds objects to the core object model. These objects are used to work with the operating system and are available only with Windows Scripting. Table 1-2 provides a complete list of the available VBScript objects. The list is organized according to where the objects originate, either in the runtime environment or the core object model.

Table 1-2 VBScript Objects for Windows Scripting	
Runtime Objects	*Core Objects*
Dictionary **Object**	Class **Object**
Drive **Object**	Dictionary **Object**
Drives **Collection**	Err **Object**
File **Object**	FileSystemObject **Object**
Files **Collection**	Match **Object**
FileSystemObject **Object**	Matches **Collection**
Folder **Object**	RegExp **Object**
Folders **Collection**	
TextStream **Object**	

Table 1-3 provides a complete list of available JScript objects. Again, the list is organized according to where the objects originate.

Table 1-3 JScript Objects for Windows Scripting	
Runtime Objects	*Core Objects*
Dictionary **Object**	ActiveXObject **Object**
Drive **Object**	Array **Object**
Drives **Collection**	Boolean **Object**
File **Object**	Date **Object**
Files **Collection**	Dictionary **Object**
FileSystemObject **Object**	Enumerator **Object**
Folder **Object**	Error **Object**
Folders **Collection**	FileSystemObject **Object**
TextStream **Object**	Function **Object**
	Global **Object**
	Math **Object**
	Number **Object**
	Object **Object**
	RegExp **Object**
	Regular Expression **Object**
	String **Object**
	VBArray **Object**

Summary

Now that you've got a taste of what Windows scripting is all about, it's time to go to the next level. Chapters 2 and 3 provide essential scripting techniques for VBScript and JScript, respectively. If you don't know anything about VBScript or JScript, study these chapters before proceeding. You can also use these chapters to brush up on your VBScript and JScript knowledge.

✦   ✦   ✦

VBScript Essentials

Microsoft Visual Basic scripting edition (VBScript) has long been the favorite scripting language of Microsoft developers and soon it will be your favorite as well. VBScript is easy to learn and use, making the language a great choice, especially if you don't have a programming background.

Working with Variables

Variables are a part of most scripting languages, and VBScript is no exception. A variable is simply a placeholder for a value you want to work with.

Variable naming

You can create a variable by assigning the variable a name, which you can refer to in your code later. Variable names, like other VBScript structures, follow standard naming conventions. These naming rules are:

♦ Names must begin with an alphabetic character.

♦ Names cannot contain periods.

♦ Names must be less than 256 characters in length.

Variable names also have an additional property that isn't true of other structures in VBScript. They are case-sensitive, meaning `value1`, `Value1`, and `VALUE1` are all different variables. However, method, function, and object references in VBScript are not case-sensitive. For example, you can echo to the screen using any of the following commands:

```
wscript.echo "This is a test!"
Wscript.echo "This is a test!"
WScript.Echo "This is a test!"
```

But in reality the correct capitalization for this reference is WScript.Echo.

Declaring variables

In VBScript, variables are declared either explicitly or implicitly. To declare a variable explicitly, use the keyword Dim to tell VBScript that you are creating a variable and then specify the variable name, such as

```
Dim newString
```

You can then assign a value to the variable, such as

```
newString = "I really love VBScript!"
```

You can also declare multiple variables at the same time. You do this by separating the variable names with commas:

```
Dim firstName, lastName, middleInitial
```

To declare a variable implicitly, use the variable name without first declaring it; you don't need to use the Dim keyword. In this instance, VBScript creates the variable for you.

The problem with implicit variables is that any name is assumed to be valid, so you can mistakenly assign values to the wrong variable and you won't know it. Consider the following example, in which you assign a value to theTotal and later assign a value to a variable called theTotals:

```
theTotal = sumA + sumB + sumC

'working with the variable

'now you need to increase the total
theTotals = theTotals + 1
```

Tip   Everything following a single quotation mark is interpreted as a comment. You can use comments anywhere in a line of code.

In this example, I meant to increase `theTotal`, but increased `theTotals` instead. To avoid situations like this, set `Option Explicit`, which requires that all variables be declared explicitly with the `Dim` keyword and also ensures the validity of your variables. This option should be placed at the beginning of your script as shown in Listing 2-1.

Listing 2-1: **Using variables**

vars.vbs

```
Option Explicit
'Setting variables
Dim sumA, sumB, sumC
Dim theTotal

sumA = 100
sumB = 10*10
sumC = 1000/10

'Get the total
theTotal = sumA + sumB + sumC

'write total to command-line using WScript.Echo

  WScript.Echo "Total = ", theTotal
```

Output

```
300
```

Variable types

VBScript assigns all variables to the `variant` data type. Variants can hold numeric or string data and each is handled differently. The primary way in which VBScript determines if something is a number or a string is through the use of double quotation marks. In the previous code sample, `sumA`, `sumB`, and `sumC` are all handled as numbers. If you add double quotation marks to the values, they are treated as strings, as in the following example:

```
sumA = "100"
sumB = "10*10"
sumC = "1000/10"
```

The use of strings yields very different results when you add the values together, and as a result, the value of theTotal is:

```
10010*101000/10
```

The reason for this is that while numbers are summed, strings are concatenated so you get the literal sum of all characters in the string. To complicate things a bit more, VBScript also uses *variable subtypes*. Variable subtypes are summarized in Table 2-1. Subtypes enable you to put certain types of information into categories, which allows for better handling of dates, floating-point numbers, integers, and other types of variables. For example, if you are working with dates and you need to add two dates together, you wouldn't want the result to be an integer. Instead, you'd want the dates to be handled as dates and the result of any operations to be dates, which is exactly what subtypes offer.

Table 2-1
Variable Subtypes in VBScript

Subtype	Description
Boolean	A Boolean value that contains either True or False.
Byte	An integer byte value in the range 0 to 255.
Currency	A floating-point number in the range −922,337,203,685,477.5808 to 922,337,203,685,477.5807. Note the use of up to four decimal places.
Date (Time)	A number that represents a date between January 1, 100 to December 31, 9999.
Double	A double-precision, floating-point number in the range −1.79769313486232E308 to −4.94065645841247E−324 for negative values; 4.94065645841247E−324 to 1.79769313486232E308 for positive values.
Empty	An uninitialized variant. Value is 0 for numeric variables or an empty string ("") for string variables.
Error	An error number used with runtime errors.
Integer	An integer in the range −32,768 to 32,767.
Long	An integer in the range −2,147,483,648 to 2,147,483,647.
Null	A variant set to NULL that contains no valid data.
Object	An object reference.
Single	A single-precision, floating-point number in the range −3.402823E38 to −1.401298E-45 for negative values; 1.401298E-45 to 3.402823E38 for positive values.
String	A variable-length string.

Generally, if you use whole numbers, such as 3 or 5, with a variable, VBScript creates the variable as an `Integer`. Variables with values that use decimal points, such as 3.125 or 5.7, are generally assigned as `Doubles`, double-precision floating-point values. Variables with values entered with a mixture of alphabetical and numeric characters, such as Yeah! and Q3, are created as `Strings`.

Converting variable types

VBScript can automatically convert between some variable types, and this eliminates most variable conflict. However, if you try to add a string variable to a numeric variable type, you will get an error. Because of this, do not try to perform numeric calculations with alphanumeric data.

That said, VBScript includes many different functions for converting data from one subtype to another. These functions are summarized in Table 2-2.

Table 2-2
Functions for Converting Variable Subtypes

Function	Description
CBool(expression)	Converts any valid expression to a Boolean value. Returns either True or False.
CByte(expression)	Converts any valid expression to a Byte value.
CCur(expression)	Converts any valid expression to a Currency value.
CDate(date)	Converts any valid date string to a Date value. Returns a date value that can be used when adding dates and times.
CDbl(expression)	Converts any valid expression to a Double value.
CInt(expression)	Converts any valid expression to an Integer value.
CLng(expression)	Converts any valid expression to a Long value.
CSng(expression)	Converts any valid expression to a Single value.
CStr(expression)	Converts any valid expression to a String value.

Working with conversion functions is a lot easier than you may think. To convert a value, just pass the value to the conversion function, as follows:

```
stringA = "42"
stringB = "37"

intA = CInt(stringA) 'Set to integer value 42
intB = CInt(stringB) 'Set to integer value 37
```

The CBool(), CDate(), and CString() functions deserve a special note because they return output that is a bit different from what you might be used to. To learn more about these functions, take a look at Listing 2-2.

Listing 2-2: **Using conversion functions**

changetype.vbs

```
sumA = 30: sumB = 15        'Initialize variables

Test = CBool(sumA = sumB) 'Test contains false

sumB= sumB * 2              'Double value of sumB
Test = CBool(sumA = sumB) 'Test contains true

dateStr = "December 10, 2005" 'Define a date as a string
theDate = CDate(dateStr)       'Convert to Date data type

timeStr = "8:25:10 AM"       'Define a time as a string
theTime = CDate(timeStr)     'Convert to Date data type

aDouble = 715.255           'Define a numeric value
aString = CStr(aDouble)       'Convert to a string
```

Working with Arrays

Using arrays, you can group related sets of data together. The most common type of array you'll use is one-dimensional, but you can create arrays with up to 60 dimensions if you want to. While a one-dimensional array is like a column of tabular data, a two-dimensional array is like a spreadsheet with rows and columns, and a three-dimensional array is like a 3-D grid.

Initializing arrays

Arrays are declared much like regular variables except you follow the variable name with information describing the size and dimensions of the array. You can initialize an array with ten data elements as follows:

```
Dim bookArray(9)
```

Values in an array always begin at 0 and end at the number of data points in the array minus 1. This is the reason an array with 10 data points is initialized as bookArray(9). To access elements in an array, reference the element's index position within the array. For example, bookArray(0) references the first element, `bookArray(1)` references the second element, and so on. Use the index position to set values for the array as well, such as:

```
bookArray(0) = "A Tale Of Two Cities"
bookArray(1) = "Grapes Of Wrath"
```

Using arrays with multiple dimensions

Multiple dimensions are created by separating the size of each dimension with commas, such as `currentArray(3,3,3)` or `testArray(2,5,5,4)`. You can create a two-dimensional array with five columns each with four rows of data points as follows:

```
Dim myArray(4,3)
```

Then, if you want to obtain the value of a specific cell in the spreadsheet, you can use the following:

```
theValue = arrayName(columns -1, rows -1)
```

in which `columns` is the column position of the cell and `rows` is the row position of the cell. Following this, you can get the value of the cell in column 3, row 2 with this statement:

```
myValue = myArray(2,1)
```

Sizing arrays

Sizing arrays on the fly allows you to use input from users to drive the size of an array. You declare a dynamic array without specifying its dimensions, as follows:

```
Dim userArray()
```

Then size the array later using the `ReDim` function:

```
ReDim userArray(currValues - 1)
```

or

```
ReDim userArray(numColumns - 1, numRows - 1)
```

You can also use `ReDim` to change the size of an existing array. For example, you can increase the size of an array from 10 elements to 20 elements. However, when you change the size of an existing array, the array's data contents are destroyed. To prevent this, use the `Preserve` keyword, as follows:

```
ReDim Preserve userArray(numColumns - 1, numRows - 1)
```

VBScript Operators

Operators are used to perform mathematical operations, to make assignments, and to compare values. The two key types of operators you'll use in VBScript are arithmetic operators and comparison operators. As you'll see, VBScript supports fewer operators than the command line. While this may seem limiting, VBScript makes up for this by allowing you to use floating-point values and integers with high precision.

 Note VBScript also has logical operators such as AND, NOT, OR, and XOR. With the exception of NOT, these operators are rarely used.

Arithmetic operators

VBScript supports a standard set of arithmetic operators. These operators are summarized in Table 2-3.

Table 2-3	
Arithmetic Operators in VBScript	
Operator	**Operation**
+	Addition
=	Assignment
/	Division
^	Exponent
Mod	Modulus
*	Multiplication
-	Subtraction/Negation

As you can see in Table 2-3, there are few surprises when it comes to VBScript operators. Still, a few standouts are worth mentioning. In VBScript, you determine remainders using the Mod function versus the % for the command-line. But the syntax is essentially the same. With the expression:

    Answer = 9 Mod 3

Answer is set to 0. With the expression:

    Answer = 9 Mod 2

`Answer` is set to 1.

You can multiply by an exponent with the ^ operator. To achieve the same result as 8 *8 * 8 * 8, you would use:

    Answer = 8^4

You can negate a value using the – operator, such as:

    Answer = -6 * 2

If you mix operators, VBScript performs calculations using the same precedence order you learned in school. For example, multiplication and division in equations are carried out before subtraction and addition, which means:

7 + 2 * 2 = 11

and

5 / 5 + 6 = 7

Table 2-4 shows the complete precedence order for operators. As the table shows, exponents have the highest precedence order and are always calculated first.

Table 2-4		
Operator Precedence in VBScript		
Order	**Operation**	
1	Exponents (^)	
2	Negation (-)	
3	Multiplication (*) and Division (/)	
4	Remainders (Mod)	
5	Addition (+) and Subtraction (-)	

Comparison operators

When you perform comparisons, you check for certain conditions, such as whether A is greater than B or if A is equal to C. You primarily use comparison operators with conditional statements, such as `If Then` and `If Then Else`. The available operators are summarized in Table 2-5.

Table 2-5
Comparison Operators in VBScript

Operator	Description
=	Equality; evaluates to true if the values are equal.
<>	Inequality; evaluates to true if the values are not equal.
<	Less than; evaluates to true if value1 is less than value2.
<=	Less than or equal to; evaluates to true if value1 is less than or equal to value2.
>	Greater than; evaluates to true if value1 is greater than value2.
>=	Greater than or equal to; evaluates to true if value1 is greater than or equal to value2.

Listing 2-3 shows how you can use comparison operators in a script. Note that you can use these operators to compare numbers as well as strings and that there is no set precedence order for comparisons. Comparisons are always performed from left to right.

Listing 2-3: **Scripting with comparison operators**

checktotal.vbs

```
currTotal = 519
prevTotal = 321
if currTotal = 0 Then
  WScript.Echo "The total is zero."
End If
if currTotal = prevTotal Then
  WScript.Echo "The totals are equal."
End If
if currTotal <> 0 Then
  WScript.Echo "The total does NOT equal zero."
End If
if currTotal <> prevTotal Then
  WScript.Echo "The totals are NOT equal."
End If
if currTotal < 0 Then
  WScript.Echo "The total is less than zero."
End If
if currTotal > 0 Then
  WScript.Echo "The total is greater than zero."
End If
if currTotal <= prevTotal Then
```

```
    WScript.Echo "currTotal is less than or equal to prevTotal."
End If
if currTotal >= 0 Then
    WScript.Echo "The total is greater than or equal to zero."
End If
```

Output

```
The total does NOT equal zero.
The totals are NOT equal.
The total is greater than zero.
The total is greater than or equal to zero.
```

One other comparison operator you should learn about is the special operator Is. You use Is to compare objects, such as buttons. If the objects are of the same type, the result of the comparison is True. If the objects are not of the same type, the result of the comparison is False. You can test to see if the object theButton references the VBScript object Button as follows:

```
Answer = theButton Is Button
If Answer = True Then
    WScript.Echo "theButton is equivalent to Button."
Else
    WScript.Echo "theButton is NOT equivalent to Button."
End If
```

You can also perform the comparison directly in an If statement:

```
If theButton Is Button Then
    WScript.Echo "theButton is equivalent to Button."
Else
    WScript.Echo "theButton is NOT equivalent to Button."
End If
```

Performing operations on strings

The most common string operations you'll want to perform are assignment and concatenation. You assign values to strings using the equal sign, ensuring that the value is enclosed in double quotation marks, such as:

```
aString = "This is a String."
```

Concatenation is the technical term for adding strings together. Although you can use the + operator to concatenate strings, the normal operator for string concatenation is the & operator. Using the & operator, you can add strings together as follows:

```
custAddress = streetAdd & " " & cityState & " " & zipCode
```

Sometimes you may also want to display the value of a string in a message box. In such an instance, you will use the & operator as well. For example:

```
aString = "I get it!"
WScript.Echo "The string value is: " & aString
```

would display a dialog box with the message:

```
The string value is: I get it!
```

Conditional Statements

Traffic lights control the flow of traffic on the street. Conditional instructions control the flow of instructions in your code.

Using If ... Then

You use If statements to execute a set of instructions only when certain conditions are met. In VBScript, If...Then structures follow this syntax:

```
If condition = True Then
  'Handle the condition
End If
```

or

```
If condition Then
    'Handle the condition
End If
```

Note the use of the End If statement. This is what makes it possible to execute multiple commands when a condition exists, such as:

```
If sum > 25 Then
    WScript.Echo "The sum exceeds the expected Result"
    'Reset sum to zero
    sum = 0
End If
```

You can control the execution of instructions based on a false condition as follows:

```
If condition = False Then
  'The condition is false
End If
```

or

```
If Not condition  Then
  'The condition is false
End If
```

Using Else and ElseIf

You can extend the `If Then` condition with `Else` statements. The `Else` statement provides an alternative when a condition that you specified is not met. The structure of an `If Then Else` statement is as follows:

```
If checkValue = "Yes" Then
    WScript.Echo "The condition has been met."
Else
    WScript.Echo "The condition has not been met."
End If
```

To add more conditions, you can use `ElseIf` statements. Each additional condition you add to the code is then checked for validity. An example using `ElseIf` is shown in Listing 2-4.

Listing 2-4: **Working with ElseIf**

testvalue.vbs

```
If currValue < 0 Then
  WScript.Echo "The value is less than zero."
ElseIf currValue = 0 Then
  WScript.Echo "The value is equal to zero."
ElseIf currValue = 1 Then
  WScript.Echo "The value is equal to one."
ElseIf currValue = 2 Then
  WScript.Echo "The value is equal to two."
ElseIf currValue = 3 Then
  WScript.Echo "The value is equal to three."
ElseIf currValue = 4 Then
  WScript.Echo "The value is equal to four."
ElseIf currValue = 5 Then
  WScript.Echo "The value is equal to five."
Else
  WScript.Echo "Value doesn't match expected parameters."
End If
```

Select Case

Checking for multiple conditions using ElseIf is a lot of work for you and for the VB interpreter. To make things easier, use Select Case anytime you want to check more than three conditions. Using Select Case, you can rewrite Listing 2-4 in a way that is clearer and easier to understand, which you can see in Listing 2-5.

Listing 2-5: **Working with Select Case**

multicond.vbs

```
currValue = 9
Select Case currValue
   Case < 0
     WScript.Echo "The value is less than zero."
   Case 0
     WScript.Echo "The value is equal to zero."
   Case 1
     WScript.Echo "The value is equal to one."
   Case 2
     WScript.Echo "The value is equal to two."
   Case 3
     WScript.Echo "The value is equal to three."
   Case 4
     WScript.Echo "The value is equal to four."
   Case 5
     WScript.Echo "The value is equal to five."
   Case Else
     WScript.Echo "Value doesn't match expected parameters."
End Select
```

Output

```
Value doesn't match expected parameters.
```

If you compare the ElseIf example and the Select Case example, you will see that the Select Case example requires less code and has a simpler structure. You can apply this same structure anytime you want to check for multiple conditions. Start the structure with the name of the variable whose value you want to check. Here, you compare the value of userInput:

```
Select Case userInput
```

Afterward, you can check for specific conditions, such as:

```
Case < 0
 'less than zero
Case > 0
 'greater than zero
Case = 0
 'equal zero
```

or

```
Case "Yes"
 'value is yes
Case "No"
 'value is no
```

Use `Case Else` to specify statements that should be executed if no match is found in the specified `Case` statements, such as:

```
Case Else
    WScript.Echo "Value doesn't match expected parameters."
    WScript.Echo "Please check your input again."
```

Conditional controls and strings

When you perform string comparisons with conditional controls, pay particular attention to the letter case. VBScript automatically performs case-sensitive comparisons. Because of this, a comparison of "No" and "NO" returns false.

To avoid potential problems you should convert the string to upper- or lowercase for the comparison. Use `lcase()` to convert strings to lowercase. Use `ucase()` to convert strings to uppercase. Listing 2-6 shows how these functions can be used with `If...Then`. You can also use these functions with `Select Case`.

Listing 2-6: **Changing the case of a string**

changecase.vbs

```
'Setting variables
m = "No"
n = "NO"
If m = n Then
  WScript.Echo "Anything? Nope, I didn't think so."
End If
```

Continued

Listing 2-6 *(continued)*

```
If lcase(m) = lcase(n) Then
  WScript.Echo "Values are equal when converted to lowercase."
End If
if ucase(m) = ucase(n) Then
  WScript.Echo "Values are equal when converted to uppercase."
End If
```

Output

```
Values are equal when converted to lowercase.
Values are equal when converted to uppercase.
```

Control Loops

Sometimes you want to repeatedly execute a section of code. In VBScript, you can do this in several ways including:

✦ For Next **looping**

✦ For Each **looping**

✦ Do While **looping**

✦ Do Until **looping**

✦ While **looping**

For Next looping

VBScript For loops are very basic. You use VBScript For loops to execute a code segment for a specific count. The structure of For loops is as follows:

```
For Counter = startNum to endNum
    'add the code to repeat
Next
```

The following example uses a For loop to initialize an array of 10 elements:

```
For i = 0 to 9
    myArray(i) = "Placeholder"
Next
```

After the `For` loop is executed, all 10 elements in the array are initialized to the value `Placeholder`. Using the `Step` keyword, you can step through the counter at specific intervals. You can step by 2's as follows:

```
For i = 0 to 20 Step 2
    myArray(i) = "Even"
Next
```

When you use a negative step value, you reverse the normal order of the counter. So instead of going in ascending order, go in descending order, such as:

```
For i = 20 to 0 Step -1
    myArray(i) = "Unknown"
Next
```

For Each looping

With `For Each` loops, you iterate through each element in an object or array. `For Each` loops are very similar to standard `For` loops. The key difference is that the number of elements in an object or array determines the number of times you go through the loop. In Listing 2-7, you initialize an array using a regular `For` loop and then display its values using a `For Each` loop.

Listing 2-7: **Using For Each loops**

foreach.vbs
```
'initialize array
Dim myArray(10)

'set array values
For i = 0 to 9
   myArray(i) = "Placeholder" & i
Next

'display array values
For Each i IN myArray
  WScript.Echo i
Next
```
Output
```
Placeholder0
Placeholder1
Placeholder2
Placeholder3
```

Continued

Listing 2-7 *(continued)*

```
Placeholder4
Placeholder5
Placeholder6
Placeholder7
Placeholder8
Placeholder9
```

As you can see, the basic syntax of `For Each` loops is:

```
For Each element IN objArray
'add code to repeat
Next
```

where *element* is the counter for the loop and *objArray* is the object or array you want to examine.

Using Exit For

With `For` and `For Each` loops, you'll sometimes want to exit the loop before iterating through all of the possible values. To exit a `For` loop ahead of schedule, you can use the `Exit For` statement. The best place for this statement is within a `If Then` or `If Then Else` condition test, such as:

```
For Each i IN myArray
   WScript.Echo i

   If i = "Unknown" Then
      Exit For
   EndIf

Next
```

Using Do While loops

Sometimes you'll want to execute a code segment while a condition is met. To do this, you will use `Do While` looping. The structure of this loop is as follows:

```
Do While condition
    'add the code to repeat
Loop
```

With Do While, the loop is executed as long as the condition is met. This means to break out of the loop, you must change the condition at some point within the loop. Here is an example of a Do While loop that changes the status of the condition:

```
Do While continue = True
    y = y + 1
    If y < 10 Then
        WScript.Echo "Y is less than 10."
    ElseIf Y = 10 Then
        WScript.Echo "Y equals 10."
    Else
        WScript.Echo "Exiting the loop."
        continue = False
    EndIf
Loop
```

By placing the condition at the top of the loop, you ensure that the loop is only executed if the condition is met. In the previous example, the loop won't be executed at all if continue is set to False beforehand. However, sometimes you want to execute the loop at least once before you check the condition. To do this, you can place the condition test at the bottom of the loop, as in the following:

```
Do
    y = y + 1
    If y < 10 Then
        WScript.Echo "Y is less than 10."
    ElseIf Y = 10 Then
        WScript.Echo "Y equals 10."
    Else
        WScript.Echo "Exiting the loop."
        continue = False
    EndIf

Loop While continue = True
```

Using Do Until loops

Another form of control loop is a Do Until loop. With Do Until, you execute a loop *until* a condition is met instead of *while* a condition is met. As with Do While, you can place the condition test at the beginning or end of the loop. The following loop is executed zero or more times until the condition is met:

```
Do Until Answer = "No"
    'Add code to execute
    'Be sure to allow the condition to be changed
Loop
```

To ensure that the loop is executed at least once, use the following structure:

```
Do
    'Add code to execute
    'Be sure to allow the condition to be change
Loop Until Answer = "No"
```

Using Exit Do

Using Exit Do, you can exit a Do While and Do Until before a condition occurs. As with Exit For, the best place for Exit Do statement is within an If Then or If Then Else condition test, such as:

```
Do Until Answer = "No"
    'Add code to get answer
    'check to see if user wants to quit
    If Answer = "Quit" Then
        Exit Do
    End If
Loop
```

While ... WEnd loops

The final type of control loop available in VBScript is a While ... WEnd loop. With this type of loop, you can execute a loop while a condition is met, as in the following:

```
While x < 10
    'Execute this code
    x = x+1
    WScript.Echo x
WEnd
```

With While ... WEnd loop, the condition can only be placed at the beginning of the loop.

Using Procedures

Procedures are used to handle routine operations. You can pass in arguments and return values. You can even use Call to call a procedure if you want to. VBScript supports two types of procedures:

✦ **Functions**—procedures that return a value to the caller

✦ **Subroutines**—procedures that do not return a value to the caller

VBScript also supports a special type of subroutine called an event. Events occur when a certain condition exists, such as when a key is pressed, and can also be simulated in the code with method calls. I don't discuss events in this book. You just don't use them much with Windows scripting.

Working with functions

Many different built-in functions are available in VBScript. In earlier examples, you've seen `lcase()`, `ucase()`, and more. You can also create your own functions. These functions can perform many different types of tasks. Yet all functions have one thing in common: They are designed to return a value.

The basic structure of a function declaration is:

```
Function functionName(arg1, arg2, ..., argN)
    'Add your function code here.
End Function
```

As you can see, you declare the function, specify a name, and then set arguments that you want to pass to the function. Afterward, you add statements the function should execute and then end the function. When the function finishes executing, control returns to the caller and execution of the script continues from there.

You can call a function using several different techniques. You can use the `Call` statement, such as:

```
Call getTotal()
```

You can call a function directly in an assignment, such as:

```
value = getTotal()
```

You can also call a function within a statement:

```
WScript.Echo "The name you entered is: " & getUserName()
```

When there are no parameters to pass to the function, the parentheses are optional. This means you can use:

```
userName = getUserName
```

To return a value from a function, assign a value to a variable with the same name as the function. For example, if you create a function called `getSum`, you can return a value from the function as follows:

```
Call getSum(3,4,2)
Function getSum(varA, varB, varC)
```

```
      total = varA + varB + varC
      getSum = total / 2
End Function
```

Normally, all variables initialized within functions are temporary and exist only within the scope of the function. Thus, you can think of these variables as having a local scope. However, if you use a variable that is initialized outside the function, that variable has global scope. In the following example, you use a global variable in the function:

```
sample = "Placeholder"
WScript.Echo test
Function test()
    test = sample
End Function
```

The output is:

```
Placeholder
```

Listing 2-8 creates a function called getName(). The function accepts no parameters and so none are defined. A temporary variable called tempName is used to store input, and the function InputBox is used to display an input prompt to users. Once the user enters a name, the Do While loop is exited and the value the user entered is assigned to the function, allowing the value to be returned to the calling statement. The result is that the user input is echoed after the text "You entered:".

Listing 2-8: **Using functions in a script**

testfunction.vbs

```
WScript.Echo "You entered: " & getName()

Function getName()
   Dim tempName
   tempName = ""
   Do While tempName = ""
      tempName = InputBox("Enter your name:")
   Loop
   getName = tempName
End Function
```

Output

```
You entered: William Stanek
```

InputBox is a built-in function for getting user input. VBScript also supports message boxes with graphical buttons that can be selected. You'll learn about both of these features in Chapter 6.

You can break out of a function and return to the caller using the `Exit Function` statement. This statement is useful when a condition has been met and you want to return to the calling statement without finishing the execution of the function.

Working with subroutines

A *subroutine* is a procedure that does not return a value to the caller. Other than this, subroutines behave almost exactly like functions. Variables initialized within subroutines have local scope. You can call subroutines and pass in arguments. You can even exit the subroutine when a condition has been met, and you do this with `Exit Sub`.

Following this procedure, the basic structure of a subroutine is:

```
Sub subroutineName(argument1, argument2, ..., argumentN)
    'Add subroutine code here.
End Sub
```

You can use a subroutine in your code as follows:

```
Sub showError(errorMessage,title)
    MsgBox "Input Error: " & errorMessage,, title
End Sub
```

MsgBox is listed as a function in most documentation, but it is actually a built-in subroutine for displaying messages. Also, the double comma used in the example isn't a mistake. This is how you enter a null value for a parameter that you don't want to use. You'll learn about message boxes in Chapter 6.

In the example, showError is the name of the subroutine. The subroutine expects one parameter to be passed in, and this parameter holds an error message to display to the user. You can call this subroutine in several different ways. You can use a `Call` statement, such as:

```
Call showError "Input is invalid.","Error"
```

or you can call the subroutine directly:

```
showError "Input is invalid.","Error"
```

Cross-Reference When you call subroutines, you shouldn't use parentheses to enclose parameters. Parentheses are only used with functions.

When there are no parameters to pass to the subroutine, the parentheses are optional as well, such as:

```
Call mySub
```

However, subroutines cannot be used in expressions. For example, the following call causes an error:

```
test = showError()
Sub showError(errorMessage)
    MsgBox "Input Error: " & errorMessage
End Sub
```

Summary

As you've seen in this chapter, VBScript has much to offer programmers, administrators, and power users. VBScript provides extensive functions, procedures, control flow statements, and expressions. VBScript also provides top-notch array-handling capabilities and multidimensional arrays. Beyond the basics, you'll find good error-handling capabilities, routines for manipulating strings, and solid support for standard mathematical functions. All of these features make VBScript a good choice as your preferred scripting language.

✦　　✦　　✦

JScript Essentials

In This Chapter

Variable naming
conventions and
data types

Using strings, com-
ments, and arrays

Working with
operators

Using conditionals
and control loops

Creating and calling
functions

JScript is Microsoft's version of JavaScript. If you are familiar with Java or JavaScript, you'll be able to get right into
the swing of things with JScript. Many advanced programmers
prefer JScript to VBScript. JScript offers more features and
more control over many elements of your scripts. More features and controls also means that in some ways JScript is
more complex than VBScript.

Variables and Data Types

Like VBScript, JScript allows you to work with constants and
variables. Constants are distinguished from variables in that
their values do not change within the program.

Variables and naming conventions

JScript variable names are case-sensitive, which means
`valueA`, `ValueA`, and `VALUEA` all refer to different variables.
Variable names can include alphabetic and numeric characters as well as the underscore (_) character, but must begin
with an alphabetic character or the underscore character.
Further, variable names cannot include spaces or punctuation
characters. Using these variable-naming rules, the following
are all valid names for variables:

```
myvar
user_name
_varA
theAnswer
```

Unlike VBScript, the case-sensitivity rule applies to all objects in JScript. This means you can't call WScript using anything but `WScript` and that all of the following statements result in errors:

```
wscript.echo("This is a test!")
Wscript.echo("This is a test!")
WSCRIPT.echo("This is a test!")
```

As with VBScript, variables can have a global or local scope. By default, all variables have a global scope, meaning they can be accessed anywhere in the script. Variables declared within a function, however, cannot be accessed outside the function. This means the variables have a local scope.

In JScript, variables are generally initialized with the `var` keyword, such as:

```
var theAnswer = "Invalid"
```

But you don't have to use the `var` keyword all the time. The `var` keyword is optional for global variables but mandatory for local variables. I'll talk more about functions in the section titled "Using Functions".

Working with data types

Much like VBScript, JScript assigns a data type to variables based on their contents. This means you don't have to worry about assigning a specific data type. That said, you should learn how to use the basic data types shown in Table 3-1.

Table 3-1
Data Types in JScript

Data Type	Description	Example
Undefined	No value assigned; a variable that has been initialized but doesn't have a value has this data type	`Var resultA`
Boolean	A logical value; either true or false	`aBool = true`
Number	An integer or floating-point value	`theSum = 202.5`
String	Characters within single or double quotation marks	`theString = "Yes!"`
Null	The value of an undefined variable	`myVar = null`

JScript automatically converts between data types whenever possible, which eliminates most variable conflicts. However, if you try to add a string variable to a numeric variable type, you will usually have problems. You will also have problems if JScript expects a string and you reference a numeric value. You'll find solutions for these problems in the section titled "Using Strings".

With numerical data, JScript supports base 8, base 10, and base 16. Numbers with a leading zero are considered to be octal — base 8. Numbers with the 0x prefix are considered to be hexadecimal — base 16. All other number formats are considered to be standard decimal numbers — base 10. Examples of numbers in these formats include:

- ✦ Decimal — 12, 126, 8
- ✦ Octal — 032, 016, 061
- ✦ Hexadecimal — 0x3D, 0xEE, 0xA2

Note   JScript does not support base 2 (binary) but does support bitwise operators and functions that can perform binary operations.

Using Strings

Because JScript automatically types variables, you do not need to declare a variable as a string. Yet in order for JScript to recognize a variable as a string, you must use single or double quotation marks to enclose the value associated with the variable, such as:

```
myString = "This is a String."
```

When you work with strings, the two most common operations you'll perform are concatenation and conversion. These topics are covered in the sections that follow.

Concatenating strings

In your scripts, you will often need to add strings together. For example, if a user enters their full name as three separate variables representing their first, middle, and last names, you may want to add these strings together. To do this, you will use the + operator to concatenate the strings, such as:

```
userName = firstName + " " + middle + " " + lastName
```

Keep in mind that if you enclose numeric values within quotation marks, JScript still interprets the value as a string. This can lead to strange results when you try to add values together. As shown in the following example, if you add variables together that contain strings, you will not get the desired results:

```
varA = "25"
varB = "32"
varC = 8
total1 = varA + varB //the result is "2532" not 57.
total2 = varB + varC //the result is "328" not 40.
```

Now that you know not to enclose numeric values in quotation marks, you probably will not have problems with strings and variables in your code. However, this problem can also occur when you accept user input and try to perform calculations based on user input, because user input is interpreted as a string unless you tell JScript otherwise by converting the string to a number.

Converting to and from strings

As with VBScript, JScript supports built-in functionality for converting data types but this functionality isn't implemented in the same way. In JScript, you use method calls more often than function calls. Think of a method as a predefined function that is related to an object. Normally, to call a method, you reference the object by name followed by a period, and then the name of the method you are invoking. For example, to convert a number to a string, use the toString() method of a variable or object, such as:

```
varA = 900
varB = varA.toString() // varB is set to a string value of "900"
```

However, some built-in methods don't require an object reference. For example, to convert string values to numbers, you will use one of two built-in methods: parseInt() or parseFloat(). The parseInt() method converts a string to an integer. The parseFloat() method converts a string to a floating-point number. These methods can be used without referencing an object, as in the following:

```
varA = "27.5"
varB = "15"
theFloat = parseFloat(varA) //theFloat is set to 27.5
theInt = parseInt(varB) //theInt is set to 15
```

Using Comments

JScript supports two types of comments:

✦ Single-line comments that begin with a double slash (//):

```
//This is a comment
```

✦ Multiple-line comments that begin with the /* delimiter and end with the */ delimiter:

```
/* This is a comment */
```

If you have a begin-comment delimiter, you must have a matching end-comment delimiter. JScript interprets everything between the begin and end comment tags as a comment.

Using Arrays

Compared to VBScript, JScript arrays are very simple. JScript arrays can be only a single dimension and are initialized with the `new Array()` statement. As with VBScript, arrays always begin at 0 and end at the number of data points in the array minus 1. Following this, an array with six data points can be initialized as follows:

```
favBooks = new Array(5)
```

If the size of your array is determined by user input or otherwise subject to change, you can initialize the array without specifying its size, such as:

```
theArray = new Array()
```

Unlike VBScript, however, you don't have to set the size of the array before using it. You simply assign values to the array.

After you initialize an array, you can insert values for elements in the array. The most basic way to do this is with individual statements that reference the array element by its index. Listing 3-1 shows an example of setting values for the `cities` array.

Listing 3-1: **Creating an array and assigning values**

testarray.js

```
favBooks = new Array(5)
favBooks[0] = "Grapes Of Wrath"
favBooks[1] = "All Over But The Shouting"
favBooks[2] = "On Walden's Pond"
favBooks[3] = "Childhood's End"
favBooks[4] = "Life On the Mississippi"
favBooks[5] = "Dune"
```

After you set values for array elements, you access those values by referencing the element's index, such as:

```
theValue = favBooks[2]
```

Here, theValue is set to On Walden's Pond.

Another way to populate an array with values is to set the values directly in the array declaration. Following is how you would do this for the favBooks array:

```
favBooks = new Array("Grapes of Wrath",
"All over But the Shouting",
"On Walden's Pond",
"Childhood's End",
"Life on the Mississippi",
"Dune")
```

JScript Operators

JScript supports many different types of operators. You'll find arithmetic operators, comparison operators, assignment operators, and bitwise operators. You'll also find logical operators, such as && and ||.

Arithmetic operators

JScript's arithmetic operators are summarized in Table 3-2. The syntax is nearly identical in every case to VBScript, so there are few surprises.

Table 3-2 Arithmetic Operators	
Operator	*Operation*
*	Multiplication
/	Division
+	Addition
-	Subtraction
%	Modulus
=	Assignment
++	Increment
--	Decrement

You must pay special attention to the ++ and -- operators, which are called unary operators. Typically, if you want to increment a value by one, you can write out the statement as follows:

```
A = A + 1
```

Alternately, you can use the increment operator (++), as follows:

```
++A
```

The result of the previous statement is that A is incremented by one. Similarly, you can decrease the value of A using the decrement operator (--), such as:

```
--A
```

When using the increment or decrement operator in a statement, the placement of the operator is extremely important. The result of this statement is that A and B are set to 6:

```
B = 5
A = ++B
```

The JScript interpreter reads the statement as "add 1 to B and store the result in A." If you change the position of the increment operator as follows:

```
A = B++
```

the JScript interpreter reads the statement as "set A equal to B then add 1 to B." The result is that A is set to 5 and B is incremented to 6.

Table 3-3 lists the precedence order for operators in JScript. As the table shows, negation operators have the highest precedence order and are always calculated first.

Table 3-3	
Precedence of Arithmetic Operators	
Order	**Operation**
1	Negation (-)
2	Multiplication (*) and Division (/)
3	Modulus (%)
4	Addition (+) and Subtraction (-)

Comparison operators

Comparison operators are used to check for certain conditions, such as whether A is equal to B. Generally, you will use a control flow, such as conditional looping, in conjunction with your comparison. For example, if A is equal to B, then you will perform a specific task. If A is not equal to B, then you will perform a different task.

When performing comparisons, you are often comparing objects as well as numeric and textual data. To see if a variable is equal to another variable, you will use the comparison operator (==). This operator returns a result that is true if the objects are equivalent, false if they are not equivalent. Here is an example of code that checks for equality:

```
if (aValue == varA) {
    //The variables are equal
}
```

To see if variables are not equal, use the inequality operator. Here is an example of code that checks for inequality:

```
if (aValue != varA) {
    //The variables are not equal
}
```

To see if one variable is less than or greater than another variable, use the less than and greater than operators. You can check for values greater than or less than a variable as follows:

```
if (aValue < varA) {
    //aValue is less than varA
}
if (aValue > varA) {
    //aValue is greater than varA
}
```

Another type of comparison you can perform will tell you whether a variable is less than or equal to a value. Likewise, you can see whether a variable is greater than or equal to a value. Here is an example of this type of comparison:

```
if (theValue <= varA) {
    //theValue is less than or equal to varA
}
if (theValue >= 0) {
    //theValue is greater than or equal to varA
}
```

Table 3-4 summarizes the comparison operators available in JScript. As you've seen from the examples in this section, JScript and VBScript support a slightly different set of comparison operators. JScript uses a separate equality operator (==) and also has a different inequality operator (!=).

Table 3-4
Comparison Operators in JScript

Operator	Description
==	Equality; evaluates to true if the values or objects are equal.
!=	Inequality; evaluates to true if the values or objects are not equal.
<	Less than; evaluates to true if value1 is less than value2.
<=	Less than or equal to; evaluates to true if value1 is less than or equal to value2.
>	Greater than; evaluates to true if value1 is greater than value2.
>=	Greater than or equal to; evaluates to true if value1 is greater than or equal to value2.

Assignment operators

Assignment operators are useful for assigning a value to a named variable. Some assignment operators, such as the equal sign (=), are used in just about every statement you will write. Other assignment operators, such as divide by value, are used rarely — if at all.

Like the increment and decrement operators, you can use assignment operators to save some typing. Instead of typing

```
a = a + 3
```

you can type

```
a += 3
```

Although both statements perform the same operation, the second statement does so with less typing. Saving a few keystrokes becomes increasingly important in long scripts and in a series of repetitive statements. Assignment operators are summarized in Table 3-5.

Table 3-5 **Assignment Operators**	
Operator	*Descriptions*
+=	Increments (adds and assigns value)
-=	Decrements (subtracts and assigns value)
*=	Multiplies and assigns value
/=	Divides and assigns value
%=	Performs modulus arithmetic and assigns value

Logical operators

Logical operators are great for performing several comparisons within a control flow. For example, if you want to check whether A is greater than B, and C is less than B before you perform a calculation, you can use a logical operator.

Like comparison operators, logical operators return either true or false. Generally, if the operation returns true, you can perform a set of statements. Otherwise, you can skip the statements or perform other statements.

The most commonly used logical operators are logical And (&&) and logical Or (||). These operators compare two Boolean expressions, the results of comparison operators, or other logical expressions to produce a Boolean value, which can be true or false. The logical And returns a true value only when both expressions being compared return a true value. The logical Or returns a true value when either or both expressions return a true value.

Another logical operator available in JScript is Not (!). You will use the Not operator just as you do the keyword Not in VBScript. Listing 3-2 shows how logical operators can be used in your scripts.

Listing 3-2: **Using logical operators**

compare.js
```
varA = 12
varB = 5
varC = 6
varD = 2

if (varA > varC && varB < varD) {
    //evaluates when the results of both tests are true
```

```
    WScript.Echo("Both tests are true.")
}
if (varA > varB || varC < varB) {
    //evaluates when at least one side is true
    WScript.Echo("At least one side is true.")
}
if (!(varA <= varB)) {
    //evaluates when varB is less than varA
    WScript.Echo("Less than.")
}
```

Output

```
At least one side is true.
Less than.
```

Table 3-6 summarizes the available logical operators.

Table 3-6
Logical Operators

Operator	Operation
&&	Logical And
||	Logical Or
!	Logical Not

Bitwise operators

Bitwise operators are used to perform binary math. There is little use for binary math in JScript and you will probably never need to use JScript's bitwise operators. Just in case though, the bitwise operators are summarized in Table 3-7.

Table 3-7
Bitwise Operators

Operator	Description
&	Bitwise And; returns 1 if both bits compared are 1.
|	Bitwise Or; returns 1 if either bit compared is 1.
^	Bitwise Or; returns 1 only if one bit is 1.

Continued

Table 3-7 *(continued)*	
Operator	**Description**
~	Bitwise Not; turns zeros to ones and ones to zeros.
<<	Shift Left; shifts the values left the number of positions specified by the operand on the right.
>	Shift Right; shifts the values right the number of positions specified by the operand on the right.
>>	Zero Fill Shift Right; fills the values with zeros when shifts right.

Conditional Statements

When you want to execute a set of instructions only if a certain condition is met, you can use if or if...else structures. Unlike VBScript, JScript does not support elseif statements.

Using if

You can use if statements to control execution based on a true or false condition. The syntax for JScript if statements is a bit different than you are used to. Note the use of parentheses and curly brackets in the following example that tests for a true condition:

```
if (choice = "Y") {
    //then condition is true and choice equals Y
    //execute these statements
}
```

You can also control the execution of instructions based on a false condition. To do this, use the ! operator and add an extra set of parentheses, such as:

```
if (!(choice = "Y")) {
    //then condition is false and choice doesn't equal Y
    //execute these statements
}
```

Using if...else

You can extend if statements with the else statement. The else statement provides an alternative when a condition you specified is not met. The structure of an if...else condition is as follows:

```
if (choice="Y") {
    //condition is true and choice equals Y
```

```
    //execute these statements
}
else {
    //condition is false and choice doesn't equal Y
    //execute these statements
}
```

Control Flow with Looping

Sometimes you want to repeatedly execute a section of code. You can do this several ways in JScript. You can use:

- ✦ for and for in
- ✦ while and do while
- ✦ switch case

Using for loops

Using for loops in your code is easy. The following example uses this structure to initialize an array of 10 elements:

```
for (x = 0; x < 10; x++) {
    myArray(x) = "Test"
}
```

This for loop initializes a counter to zero, then sets the condition that the loop should continue as long as x is less than 10. During each iteration of the loop, the counter is incremented by 1. When the loop finishes, all 10 elements in the array are initialized to the value Placeholder. The structure of a for loop in JScript is as follows:

```
for (initialize counter; condition; update counter) {
    code to repeat
}
```

Using for in loops

JScript's for in loops work much like VBScript's For Each loops. Both looping techniques are designed to iterate through each element in an object or array. They differ only in the syntax used.

Listing 3-3 shows how you can examine the elements in an array using a for in loop. Note that with JScript, you have to index into the array even when you are in the for in loop.

Listing 3-3: **Checking values in an array**

arrayvalues.js

```
currArray = new Array()

for (x = 0; x < 10; x++) {
   currArray[x] = "Initial"
}

counter = 0
for (i in currArray) {
  WScript.Echo("Value " + counter + " equals: " + currArray[i])
  counter++

}
```

Output

```
Value 0 equals: Initial
Value 1 equals: Initial
Value 2 equals: Initial
Value 3 equals: Initial
Value 4 equals: Initial
Value 5 equals: Initial
Value 6 equals: Initial
Value 7 equals: Initial
Value 8 equals: Initial
Value 9 equals: Initial
```

Using while and do while loops

JScript's `while` loops are used much like the `While` loops in VBScript. To execute a code segment while a condition is met, you will use `while` looping. The structure of a loop that checks for a true condition is as follows:

```
while (condition) {
   //add code to repeat
}
```

The structure of a loop that checks for a false condition is as follows:

```
while (!condition) {
   /add code to repeat
}
```

As long as the condition is met, the loop is executed. This means to break out of the loop, you must change the condition at some point within the loop.

You can put the condition check at the bottom of the loop using a do while construct, such as:

```
do {
    //add code to repeat
} while (condition)
```

Using continue and break statements

When you are working with conditional looping, you will often want to break out of a loop or continue with the next iteration of the loop. In JScript, the break statement enables you to end the execution of a loop, and the continue statement enables you to begin the next iteration of a loop without executing subsequent statements. Whenever your script begins the next iteration of the loop, the condition is checked and the counter is updated as necessary in for loops.

Using switch case

JScript's switch case is the functional equivalent of VBScript's Select Case. To see how similar the structures are, compare Listing 3-4 with Listing 2-5. As you'll see, these listings check for similar information. However, JScript doesn't support the less-than operation used with VBScript, so I omitted this from the example. JScript doesn't support any other case either, such as VBScript's Case Else. Instead, JScript supports a default case.

Listing 3-4: **Working with switch case**

case1.js
```
currValue = 5
switch (currValue) {
    case 0 :
      WScript.Echo("The value is equal to zero.")
    case 1 :
      WScript.Echo("The value is equal to one.")
    case 2 :
      WScript.Echo("The value is equal to two.")
    case 3 :
      WScript.Echo("The value is equal to three.")
    case 4 :
      WScript.Echo("The value is equal to four.")
    case 5 :
      WScript.Echo("The value is equal to five.")
    default :
      WScript.Echo("Value doesn't match expected parameters.")
}
```

Continued

Listing 3-4 *(continued)*

Output

```
The value is equal to five.
Value doesn't match expected parameters.
```

If you run Listing 3-4, you learn another interesting fact concerning switch case—JScript can execute multiple case statements. In this case, the script executes case 5 and the default. To prevent JScript from executing multiple case statements, you need to exit the switch case using the break keyword as shown in Listing 3-5.

Listing 3-5: **Revised switch case example**

case2.js

```
currValue = 5
switch (currValue) {
    case 0 :
        WScript.Echo("The value is equal to zero.")
        break
    case 1 :
        WScript.Echo("The value is equal to one.")
        break
    case 2 :
        WScript.Echo("The value is equal to two.")
        break
    case 3 :
        WScript.Echo("The value is equal to three.")
        break
    case 4 :
        WScript.Echo("The value is equal to four.")
        break
    case 5 :
        WScript.Echo("The value is equal to five.")
        break
    default :
        WScript.Echo("Value doesn't match expected parameters.")
}
```

Output

```
The value is equal to five.
```

Using Functions

In JScript, functions are the key structure you use to create customizable procedures. JScript doesn't support subroutines or `goto`. As you will quickly discover, JScript functions work much like VBScript functions and, again, the main difference is syntax.

Function structure

In JScript, the basic structure of a function is:

```
function functionName(parameter1, parameter2, ..., parameterN)
{
    //Insert function code here.
}
```

You can use functions in your code as follows:

```
function getInput() {
    var userInput
    var timeOut = 10;    // set wait time
    var title = "Getting Input"; // set title
    var button = 4;          // Yes/No
    // create object
    var wshell = WScript.CreateObject("WScript.Shell");
    userInput = wshell.Popup ("Do you want to continue?",
                    timeOut,title,button)

    return userInput
}
```

Cross-Reference

Note the use of `Popup()` in the example. Unlike VBScript, none of the standard JScript dialog or input boxes are available in Windows Script Host and as a result, `Popup()` is the only way to display messages and get user input. For more information on `Popup()`s, see Chapter 6.

In the example, `getInput` is the name of the function. Because the function accepts no parameters, none are defined after the function name. A temporary local variable called `userInput` is created to store the user's input. Once the user enters a value, the `while` loop is exited. This value is then returned to the calling statement. Generally, all functions return one or more values using the `return` statement.

Calling functions

Calling a function in JScript is just like calling a function in VBScript. You can call a function as follows:

```
getInput()
```

or

```
Input = getInput()
```

When you call a function, you can pass in parameters as well. To better understand how parameters are used, I'll create a function that converts a time entry to seconds. This function called numseconds() accepts four parameters: xYears, xDays, xHours, and xMinutes. Because these parameters are passed directly to the function, you do not need to create temporary variables to hold their values within the function. The code for the function numSeconds() is as follows:

```
function numSeconds(xYears, xDays, xHours, xMinutes) {
    var count
    tempSeconds = ((365 * xYears + xDays) * 24 + xHours) * 3600
+ 60 * xMinutes
    return count
}
```

When you call this function, the parameters are expected and must be entered in the order defined. Here is a statement that calls the numSeconds() function:

```
theSeconds = numSeconds(5,25,10,30)
```

Summary

JScript provides an alternative to VBScript that is often preferred by people with a background in programming. In JScript, you'll find numerous functions, procedures, and control flow statements. You'll also find good support for arrays with access to multidimensional arrays through VBScript; extensive sets of ready-to-use objects with methods, properties, and events; strong support for mathematical functions (with many more functions supported than VBScript); and a very dynamic framework for handling errors.

✦   ✦   ✦

Windows Scripting Essentials

Part II gets you into the nuts and bolts of scripting: the Windows Script Host and the basic commands you can use in scripts. Part II also shows you how to run scripts, perform input and output, and handle errors. You'll learn how to work with the most common objects you can control with scripts: files and folders, drives and printers, and the applications themselves. Finally, you'll learn how to use scripts to work with the Windows Registry and event logs.

Creating Scripts and Scripting Files

Windows Script Host provides several different ways to work with Windows scripts. The easiest technique is to create scripts using only a single scripting language and then save the script using the appropriate extension for the scripting engine. If you use VBScript, you save the script with the .vbs extension. If you use JScript, you save the script with the .js extension. Unlike script files used with Web pages, WSH script files don't need to contain any special markup or any kind of instructions.

You can also combine multiple types of scripts in a batch script. With batch scripts, you can use a single file and save it with the .wsf file extension. Because batch scripts can use scripts written in multiple scripting languages, you must somehow identify the type of scripts you are using and other important aspects of these scripts. You do this using markup tags written in XML (Extensible Markup Language). Don't worry, you don't need to become an XML or HTML expert to work with batch scripts. However, you do need to learn a bit about the markup tags available to be used with WSH.

Running Scripts

You run scripts using the scripting hosts provided by WSH. These scripting hosts are:

+ **WScript** — WScript is a scripting host with GUI controls for displaying output in pop-up dialog boxes and is used primarily when you execute scripts from the desktop. The related executable is WScript.exe and it isn't related to the WScript object that is a part of the core object model.

✦ **CScript** — CScript is the command-line version of the scripting host. All output from CScript is displayed at the Windows command prompt unless you specify otherwise by using a pop-up box or dialog box. The related executable for CScript is CScript.exe.

The techniques you use to work with WScript and CScript are the same regardless of whether you are working with standard script files or batch script files.

Starting a Script

When you install WSH and the scripting engines on a system, several file types are mapped for use with the scripting hosts. These mappings allow you to run scripts like any other executable program. You can run scripts using any of the following techniques:

✦ Start Windows Explorer, and then browse until you find a script. Double-click on the script.

✦ Double-click on a desktop shortcut to a script.

✦ Enter a script name at the Run command on the Start Menu. Be sure to enter the full file extension, and path if necessary, such as C:\scripts\myscript.vbs.

✦ At the command-line prompt, type **wscript** followed by a script name, such as:

```
wscript myscript.vbs
```

✦ At the command-line prompt, type **cscript** followed by a script name, such as:

```
cscript myscript.js
```

Setting script properties

You can set script properties in Windows Explorer, or when you run scripts at the command-line. If you want to set properties for scripts in Windows Explorer, follow these steps:

1. Right-click a script file in Windows Explorer.

2. Select Properties on the shortcut menu.

3. Choose the Script tab as shown in Figure 4-1.

4. You can now set the default timeout value and determine whether a scripting logo is displayed when you execute WScript from the command line. Use the timeout value to stop execution of a script that has been running too long and to possibly prevent a runaway process from using up precious processor time.

5. Choose OK or Apply.

6. These properties are used with WScript.

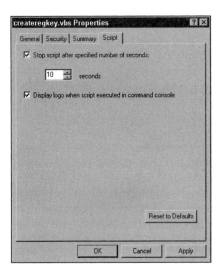

Figure 4-1: You can set script properties through the Script tab in Windows Explorer.

As I stated, you can also set script properties at the command line. You can do this only when you execute a script using CScript. I'll show you how to do this in the next section.

Command-line options for scripts

When you run scripts from the desktop or Windows Explorer, property settings can be applied as outlined in the previous section. These settings are for WScript. CScript, on the other hand, is a command-line executable, and like most command-line programs, can be configured using switches and modifiers.

The command-line syntax for Cscript is:

```
cscript [host_options] [script_name] [script_args]
```

in which *host_options* are options to set for CScript, *script_name* is the name of the script, and *script_args* are arguments to pass in to the script. The script name must include the file extension and any necessary path information, like the following:

```
cscript copyfiles.js
cscript c:\scripts\copyfiles.js
cscript c:\"my scripts"\copyfiles.js
```

Table 4-1 shows the available options for CScript. As you can see, options and arguments are differentiated using slashes. Host options are preceded with two slashes (//) and script arguments don't use slashes. For example, you can set a timeout for a script and pass in the script parameter "basic" as follows:

```
cscript //t:45 logon.vbs basic
```

<table>
<tr><td colspan="2">Table 4-1
Options for CScript</td></tr>
<tr><td>*Option*</td><td>*Description*</td></tr>
<tr><td>//?</td><td>Shows command usage.</td></tr>
<tr><td>//b</td><td>Sets Batch Mode, which suppresses command-line display of user prompts and script errors. (Opposite of //i.)</td></tr>
<tr><td>//d</td><td>Turns on the debugger.</td></tr>
<tr><td>//e:engine</td><td>Runs the script with the specified scripting engine.</td></tr>
<tr><td>//h:Cscript</td><td>Registers Cscript.exe as the default application for running scripts.</td></tr>
<tr><td>//h:Wscript</td><td>Registers Wscript.exe as the default application for running scripts. If not specified, Wscript.exe is assumed as the default.</td></tr>
<tr><td>//i</td><td>Sets Interactive Mode for scripts, which allows display of user prompts and script errors. Interactive mode is the default.</td></tr>
<tr><td>//Job:"Job Name"</td><td>Runs the specified job from a WSC file.</td></tr>
<tr><td>//logo</td><td>Displays CScript logo at runtime. This is the default setting.</td></tr>
<tr><td>//nologo</td><td>Turns off display of the CScript logo at runtime.</td></tr>
<tr><td>//s</td><td>Saves the current command-line options for the user logged on to the system.</td></tr>
<tr><td>//t:nn</td><td>Sets a timeout for the script, which is the maximum number of seconds (nn) the script can run. By default, scripts have no limit.</td></tr>
<tr><td>//x</td><td>Executes the program in the debugger.</td></tr>
</table>

As you can see from the table, scripts can be run in interactive mode or batch mode. In batch mode, scripts don't display prompts or errors, and this behavior is very useful when you want to schedule scripts to run with the Task Scheduler service. For example, if you want to run a Windows script every weekday at midnight, you would probably want to run in batch mode. For example:

```
AT 00:00 /every:M,T,W,Th,F "cscript //b backupdata.js"
```

Whether you run scripts from the command line or via the Task Scheduler, you'll often want to set more than one option. Having to retype scripting options each time you use a script isn't fun, which is why the //s option is provided. With this option, you can set default options to use each time you run CScript. For example, if you enter the following command:

```
cscript //b //nologo //t:30 //d //s
```

CScript is set to use batch mode, no logo, a timeout of 30 seconds, and debugging whenever you run scripts. The only way to override the default setup is to save a different set of options, like this:

```
cscript //i //s
```

As you work with WScript and CScript, you may find that you prefer one over the other. Don't worry, you can switch the default scripting host at any time. To use CScript as the default, enter the following command:

```
cscript //h:CScript
```

To use WScript as the default, enter:

```
cscript //h:WScript
```

Using drag and drop with scripts

Windows Script Host 2.0 and later supports drag and drop on Windows 98 and Windows 2000. Drag and drop allows you to drag one or more files onto a script file. The script is then automatically executed with the files as arguments.

When you drag files onto a WSH script, the filenames are translated into arguments on the command line. These filenames can be managed just like any other script arguments. The number of files you can drag onto a script is limited by the maximum command-line length your computer allows. If the total number of characters in all filenames (including the spaces added between filenames) exceeds this limit, the drag and drop operation will fail.

To give drag and drop a test run, create the script shown as Listing 4-1, then save the file to the Windows desktop. Afterward, start Windows Explorer. In Windows Explorer, select several files and then, while holding down the right mouse button, drag the files onto the script. The script displays the filenames in separate pop-up dialog boxes.

Listing 4-1: **Using drag and drop**

echoargs.vbs

```
Set objArgs = WScript.Arguments
For I = 0 to objArgs.Count - 1
  WScript.Echo "File " + CStr(I) + ": " + objArgs(I)
Next
```

Creating Batch Scripts

Batch scripts allow you to combine multiple scripts in a single file. These scripts can use the same scripting language or different scripting languages — it doesn't matter. The advantage of batch scripts is that they make it possible for scripts to interact. You can pass values back and forth between scripts. You can even call functions of scripts that aren't included in the file directly, which is the technique you'll use if you create utility libraries like those discussed in Part V of this book.

Batch scripts are saved in files with the .wsf file extension and make use of XML markup tags to tell the scripting host how to handle the batch scripts. As with HTML (Hypertext Markup Language), most XML markup tags have a begin tag and an end tag that, together, specify an element. An element that you may already be familiar with is script. The script element is used to specify the start and end of scripts in Web pages, as well as to specify information needed to locate and interpret scripts.

The scripting hosts support a special set of XML tags. These tags include:

- ✦ `<?job ?>` — sets special instructions for all scripts in the batch
- ✦ `<?XML ?>` — sets special instructions for parsing file as XML
- ✦ `<package>` — encloses multiple job definitions
- ✦ `<job>` — identifies the job (or script name)
- ✦ `<object>` — exposes objects for use in scripts
- ✦ `<reference>` — references an external-type library
- ✦ `<script>` — identifies the scripting language and source

The sections that follow examine each of these tags in turn. If you've never worked with markup tags before; don't worry, you don't need to know anything about XML or HTML, I promise.

Identifying the job name

Batch scripts are really designed to help administrators create scripting libraries with functions that can be easily accessed. Because you can potentially have dozens of scripts in a single library, you may need a container to be able to reference the script you want to run. You do this with the job element. As with most elements, the job element has a pair of markup tags associated with it. The `<job>` tag marks the beginning of the job element, and the `</job>` tag marks the end of the job element, like this:

```
<job>
  Insert body of job here
</job>
```

To identify the name of the job, you use the id *attribute*. An attribute is simply a property of an element that can be used to set values. Using the id attribute, you set the job name as follows:

```
<job id="WriteLogs">
</job>
```

The job element is a top-level element that can contain zero or more occurrences of these other elements: object, reference, and script. The job element itself can also be used more than once in a .wsf file, provided that you enclose the jobs within a package element. Enclosing multiple jobs is the only purpose of the package element and its use is mandatory when you have two or more jobs in a .wsf file.

When you use multiple jobs, you shouldn't nest job elements within job elements. Instead, you should start one job, end it, and then start another as shown in Listing 4-2.

Listing 4-2: **Using multiple jobs**

multijobs.wsf

```
<package>
<job id="WriteLogs">
  Insert body of job here
</job>
<job id="DeleteOldLogs">
  Insert body of job here
</job>
<job id="PublishLogs">
  Insert body of job here
</job>
</package>
```

Adding scripts and setting the scripting language

When you add scripts to the batch, you need to tell the scripting hosts about the script you are using. You do this with the `script` element. The `<script>` tag marks the beginning of a script and the `</script>` tag marks the end of a script. You always use the `script` element within a `job` element, like this:

```
<job id="WriteLogs">
<script>
 Insert script here
</script>
</job>
```

The scripting host also needs to know which language you are using. You specify the scripting language with the `language` attribute. Valid values for the `language` attribute include `VBScript`, `JScript`, `JavaScript`, and `PerlScript`. You can set the scripting language to `VBScript` as follows:

```
<script language="VBScript">
 'Insert VBScript here
</script>
```

WSH jobs can contain multiple scripts. When they do contain multiple scripts, you need to insert additional `script` elements. In Listing 4-3, the job uses scripts written in VBScript and JScript.

Listing 4-3: **Using multiple scripts within a single job**

multiscripts.wsf

```
<job id="WriteLogs">
<script language="VBScript">
 'Insert VBScript here
</script>
<script language="JScript">
 'Insert JScript here
</script>
</job>
```

Setting the script source

The source code for scripts doesn't have to be in the batch file. You can store the source code in separate .js, .vbs, and .pl files, and then reference the source file from within the batch. Source files that aren't located in the batch are referred to as external scripts, and their location is set with the `src` attribute.

The `src` attribute expects you to reference source locations using URLs (Universal Resource Locators). URLs are what you use when you browse the Web. However, while a typical Web URL looks like this: `http://www.centraldrive.com/index.html`, a typical file URL looks like this: `file://c:\working\myscript.vbs`. Where `http:` identifies the HyperText Transfer Protocol used on the Web, and `file:` identifies the file protocol used with file systems.

Source files can be referenced with *relative* file paths or *absolute* file paths. You access local files — files on your local system — using a relative file path. URLs with relative file paths generally do not name a protocol. When you use a relative path to locate a file, you locate the file in relation to the current batch script. You can use relative file paths in the following three key ways:

✦ To access a file in the current directory, such as:

```
<script language="JScript" src="test.js" />
```

✦ To access a file in a parent directory of the current directory, such as:

```
<script language="JScript" src="../test.js" />
```

✦ To access a file in a subdirectory of the current directory, such as:

```
<script language="JScript" src="scripts/test.js" />
```

Another way to access files is directly. You do this by specifying the complete path to the file you want to access, such as:

```
<script language="JScript" src="file://c:\scripts/test.js" />
```

As shown in the previous examples, you don't use an end script tag when you specify a script source. Instead, you tell the scripting host to end the element with the `/>` designator. A more complete example of using external scripts is shown in Listing 4-4.

Listing 4-4: Working with multiple jobs and external source files

multijobs2.wsf

```
<package>
<job id="WriteLogs">
  <script language="VBScript" src="fget.vbs" />
  <script language="JScript" src="fcreate.js" />
</job>
```

Continued

Listing 4-4: *(continued)*

```
<job id="DeleteOldLogs">
  <script LANGUAGE="VBScript" src="testfolder.vbs" />
  <script LANGUAGE="VBScript" src="delcreate.vbs" />
</job>
<job id="PublishLogs">
<script LANGUAGE="VBScript">
 'Insert VBScript here
</script>
<script language="JScript">
 'Insert JScript here
</script>
</job>
</package>
```

One of the primary reasons for placing multiple scripts in the same file is the ability to take advantage of the strengths of a particular scripting language. For example, VBScript features extensive support for arrays, while JScript doesn't. You can create a script that makes use of VBScript's arrays and then pass this information back to JScript where you can then take advantage of JScript's extensive mathematical functions to manipulate the data in the arrays.

Note   You'll find specific examples of combining scripting languages throughout this book. For specific pointers and helpful tips, see "Combining JScript and VBScript" in Chapter 5.

Referencing external objects and type libraries

External objects and type libraries enable you to extend the functionality of Windows scripts. With external objects, you can gain additional features. With type libraries, you can define sets of constants to use with scripts.

Windows scripts can use external objects and type libraries as long as those objects and libraries are defined appropriately for use with WSH. External objects must be defined as ActiveX objects and installed on the system that is running the script. Type libraries must be accessible for external calls and saved as .tlb, .olb, or .dll files.

When you use external objects in scripts, you need a way to tell your system about an object. You do this with the `classid` attribute of the `object` element. The `classid` attribute is a reference to the globally unique identifier (GUID) for the ActiveX object you want to use. Each ActiveX object has a GUID, and when the object is installed on a system, this value is stored in the Windows Registry. An ActiveX object has the same GUID on your system as it does on any other system.

The value {0002DF01-0000-0000-C000-000000000046} is the GUID for Internet Explorer. This value is also referred to as the CLSID or class ID for Internet Explorer. Your system accesses the appropriate object by looking up the class ID in the Windows Registry. Using the classid attribute, you reference controls by their CLSID value, such as:

```
<object classid="clsid:0002DF01-0000-0000-C000-000000000046" />
```

Note   In the previous example, the curly braces are removed from the CLSID. You must remove the curly braces from all CLSIDs before referencing them.

You are probably wondering how to obtain such a monstrous CLSID value. The easiest way to obtain the CLSID value is through the Registry Editor. You can run the Registry Editor by starting regedit.exe (or regedt32.exe).

As shown in Figure 4-2, the Registry Editor files entries by category into directories. For OLE and ActiveX objects, the directory you want to use is the HKEY_CLASSES_ROOT directory. Although the Registry Editor features a Find function under the Edit menu, this feature is only useful if you know the exact name of the object for which you are searching. Therefore, you will probably want to browse for the object you are looking for. To do this, select HKEY_CLASSES_ROOT on the local machine from the Window menu. With the HKEY_CLASSES_ROOT folder open, you will see folders for each registered item. Entries are listed by file extension, name, and GUID. The named entries are what you are looking for. Many ActiveX objects are filed beginning with the keyword "Internet."

When you find the entry you are looking for, click in its folder to view subfolders associated with the entry. The CLSID subfolder contains the CLSID you need , so click on the CLSID subfolder associated with the entry. Now, in the right pane of the Registry Editor, you should see the CLSID associated with the entry.

Double-click on the CLSID entry in the right pane to display the Edit String dialog box. With the CLSID highlighted, you can press Ctrl+C to copy the CLSID to the clipboard. When you are ready to use the CLSID, paste the value from the clipboard using Ctrl+V.

Before you can use the object, you need to create a reference to it. You do this by giving the object an identifier, such as IE for Internet Explorer. This identifier is assigned with the id attribute, such as:

```
<job id="WorkwithIE">
  <object ID="IE"
    classid="clsid:0002DF01-0000-0000-C000-000000000046" />
  <script language="VBScript" src="useie.vbs" />
</job>
```

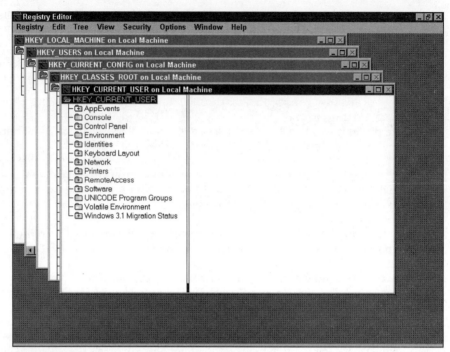

Figure 4-2: Working with the Windows Registry

Once you create an object reference, you can work with the object's methods and properties as you would any other object. The object is also available to multiple scripts associated with the current job.

The Reference element can also use CLSIDs to reference type libraries containing constants that you want to use in your scripts. With the Reference element, you set the CLSID with the guid attribute and should also specify the library version with the version attribute. If you do not specify a version, version 1.0 is assumed. Because you are referencing a GUID directly, you do not need the CLSID: prefix and you can use these attributes as follows:

```
<job id="WorkwithTypeLib">
  <reference guid="0002DF01-0000-0000-C000-000000000046"
           version=1.2/>
  <script language="VBScript" src="uselib.vbs" />
</job>
```

Rather than specifying the guid and version, you can specify a file location for the type library using the url attribute. When you do this, you set the relative or absolute location of the library file. In the source code, you must then create instances of the object class or classes that the library contains.

Cross-Reference If using CLSIDs and the Registry seems like a lot of work, that's because it is. In practice, you'll probably want to create instances of objects within scripts rather than reference external objects. To do this, you'll use the `CreateObject()` method of the `WScript` object. You'll learn more about `CreateObject()` in Chapter 9.

Setting job properties

Another element you may want to work with in a batch script is `<?job ?>`. This element sets error-handling instructions for the scripting host on a per-job basis. Each job in a .wsf file can have a separate `<?job ?>` element. The basic syntax for `<?job ?>` is:

```
<?job error="flag"
      debug="flag" ?>
```

where *flag* is a Boolean value, such as `True` or `False`. You can use the error and debug attributes as follows:

✦ `error` — Set to true to allow error messages for syntax or runtime errors. Default is false.

✦ `debug` — Set to true to enable debugging. When enabled, you can start the script debugger. Default is false. (This assumes a debugger is configured.)

Listing 4-5 shows an example of using error-handling in a script. Note that each job has a separate instruction.

Listing 4-5: **Setting special instructions in a batch script**

errorhandling.wsf

```
<package>
<job id="Backup">
<?job error="true" ?>
  <reference URL="file:c:\components\comp.lib">
  <script language="VBScript" src="backupset1.vbs" />
  <script language="VBScript" src="backupset2.vbs" />
  <script language="VBScript" src="backupset3.vbs" />
</job>
<job id="Restore">
<?job error="true" ?>
  <reference url="file:c:\components\comp.lib">
  <script language="VBScript" src="restore.vbs" />
</job>
</package>
```

Setting parsing instructions

The `<?XML ?>` element enables you to set parsing instructions for the .wsf file. If you use this element, the batch script is parsed as XML. The element has two attributes: `version` and `standalone`.

You use the `version` attribute to set the version of the XML specification to which the file conforms, such as 1.0. You use the `standalone` attribute to specify whether the file includes a reference to an external Document Type Definition (DTD). Normally, you want to set the value of `standalone` to `Yes`, which indicates that the batch script is a standalone document that does not use an external DTD.

If used, parsing instructions are set on the first line of the .wsf file; for example:

```
<?XML version="1.0" standalone="yes" ?>
<package>
<job id="job1">
</job>
<job id="job2">
</job>
</package>
```

Each file should have only one parsing instruction.

Summary

As you've seen in this chapter, the Windows Script Host provides a versatile environment for working with scripts. You can execute scripts from the command line, from the Windows desktop, and from Windows Explorer. In Windows 98 and Windows 2000, WSH also supports drag and drop. Both CScript and WScript support batch script files as well. With batch script files, you can combine multiple types of scripts in a single file.

✦   ✦   ✦

Scripting Basics

Now that you know a bit about creating script files and running scripts, you are ready to start working with the features Windows Script Host has to offer. You'll find that WSH structures are surprisingly powerful. You can perform many advanced tasks with only a few basic commands.

Key WSH Objects

As you learned in Chapter 1, the WSH object model contains exposed and nonexposed objects. Exposed objects are the ones you can access directly in your scripts and include `WScript`, `WScript.WshNetwork`, and `WScript.WshShell`. In this chapter you'll work with basic methods and properties of each of these objects.

Table 5-1 lists the methods and properties of `WScript`.

Table 5-1	
WScript Methods and Properties	
Methods	*Properties*
CreateObject	Application
DisconnectObject	Arguments
Echo	FullName
GetObject	Name
Quit	Path
Sleep	ScriptFullName
	ScriptName
	Version

WScript.WshNetwork is the object you'll use to manage network resources such as printers and network drives. The methods and properties of this object are listed in Table 5-2.

Table 5-2
WScript.WshNetwork Methods and Properties

Methods	Properties
AddPrinterConnection	ComputerName
EnumNetworkDrives	UserDomain
EnumPrinterConnection	UserName
MapNetworkDrive	
RemoveNetworkDrive	
RemovePrinterConnection	
SetDefaultPrinter	

Another important object is WScript.WshShell. You'll use this object to work with the environment and the operating system. Table 5-3 lists the methods and properties of this object.

Table 5-3
WScript.WshShell Methods and Properties

Methods	Properties
CreateShortcut	Environment
ExpandEnvironmentStrings	SpecialFolders
LogEvent	
Popup	
RegDelete	
RegRead	
RegWrite	
Run	

Displaying Text Strings

The first command you are going to learn about is Echo. You call Echo as a method of the WScript object. If you are using CScript and are in interactive mode, output from Echo is written to the command line. If you are using WScript and are in interactive mode, output from Echo is displayed in a pop-up dialog box.

Using Echo

You can use Echo in VBScript and JScript as shown in Listing 5-1. Note the difference in syntax between the two. With VBScript, you pass Echo strings and can use the standard concatenation rules to add strings together. You can also pass values in a comma-separated list. In JScript, you must use parentheses and can only pass values in a comma-separated list, which is then concatenated for you.

Listing 5-1: **Using Echo in VBScript and Jscript**

VBScript	*JScript*
echo.vbs	echo.js

```
theAnswer = "Yes"
WScript.Echo 1, 2, 3
WScript.Echo "Run, run, run!"
WScript.Echo "1: " + theAnswer
```

```
theAnswer = "Yes"
WScript.Echo(1, 2, 3)
WScript.Echo("Run, run, run!")
WScript.Echo("1: ", theAnswer)
```

Running the Echo script

You can run these scripts from the command line or from Windows Explorer. At the command line, change to the directory containing the scripts and then type:

```
cscript echo.vbs
```

or

```
cscript echo.js
```

The following output is then written to the command line:

```
1 2 3
Run, run, run!
1: Yes
```

With Windows Explorer, you access the directory containing the scripts and then double-click the script you want to run. Each call to Echo produces a separate pop-up dialog box. The first dialog box displays "1 2 3". When you click OK to close the first dialog box, a second dialog box displays "Run, run, run!". When you click OK to close the second pop-up, a third dialog box displays "1: Yes". Click OK again and then the script completes execution.

Examining Script Information

To accommodate a variety of user environments, your scripts will often need to test for version information before running. For example, if the user system is running the version 4 script engines, you don't want to try to run a version 5 script on the system because doing so could have unpredictable results. To prevent problems, you should at least check the script host version and the script engine version. Other scripting information you may want to check includes the location of the script hosts on the user's system, arguments passed in to the script at startup, and environment variables set on the system.

Last, with user scripts, you also may want to run other applications from within a script. For example, you may want to create a logon script that provides a menu for selecting the type of applications the user may want to start, such as Development Tools or Productivity Tools. Then, based on the response, you would start the related set of applications.

Getting script host information

When you want to examine information related to the script hosts (WScript or CScript), you'll use these properties of the WScript object:

✦ WScript.Fullname—Returns the full path to the current script host, such as:

C:\WIN2000\System32\cscript.exe

✦ WScript.Path—Returns the path to the script host, such as:

C:\WIN2000\System32

✦ WScript.Version—Returns the script host version, such as:

5.1

You can use these properties in VBScript and JScript as shown in Listing 5-2. Note the If Else condition used to call main() and error() functions. If the version is greater than or equal to 5, the main() function is executed. Otherwise, the error() function is executed.

Listing 5-2: **Validating script host information**

VBScript	JScript
wshinfo.vbs	**wsinfo.js**

```vbscript
vs = WScript.Version

If vs >= 5 Then
  main()
Else
  error()
End If

Function main
  WScript.Echo "Starting execution..."
End Function

Function error
  WScript.Echo "WSH version error!"
End Function
```

```jscript
vs = WScript.Version

if (vs >= 5) {
  main()
}
else {
  error()
}

function main() {
  WScript.Echo("Starting execution...")
}

function error() {
  WScript.Echo("WSH version error!")
}
```

If you use script host information to determine whether to run a script, you may want to use the Quit method. The Quit method quits execution of a script and returns an error code. For example, if you wanted to return an error code of 1 you would use:

VBScript	JScript
WScript.Quit 1	WScript.Quit(1)

Listing 5-3 shows how to rewrite the previous example using the Quit method. Here, you eliminate the error() method and replace the check for a version greater than or equal to 5 with a check for a version less than 5. If the version is less than 5, the script quits executing and returns an error code of 1.

Listing 5-3: **Ending script execution with an error code**

VBScript	*JScript*
wshquit.vbs	**wshquit.js**

```
vs = WScript.Version
```

```
vs = WScript.Version
```

```
If vs < 5 Then
 WScript.Quit 1
End If
```

```
if (vs < 5) {
 WScript.Quit(1)
}
```

```
Function main
WScript.Echo "Starting execution..."
End Function
```

```
function main() {
WScript.Echo("Starting execution...")
}
```

Getting scripting information

Just as you can examine information related to the script host, you can also examine information related to the script engine and the current script. To examine properties of the script engine, you use built-in functions available in VBScript and JScript. To examine script properties, you use properties of the WScript object. Following is a list of these functions and properties:

✦ ScriptEngine() — A built-in function that returns the script engine language, such as VBScript or JScript.

✦ ScriptEngineMajorVersion() — A built-in function that returns the script engine version, such as 5 or 6.

✦ ScriptEngineMinorVersion() — A built-in function that returns the revision number of the script engine, such as 1 or 2.

✦ ScriptEngineBuildVersion() — A built-in function that returns the build version of the script engine, such as 3715.

✦ ScriptFullName — A property of WScript that returns the full path to the current script, such as c:\scripts\createspreadsheet.vbs.

✦ ScriptName — A property of WScript that returns the file name of the current script, such as createspreadsheet.vbs.

Listing 5-4 shows an example of how you can use these functions and properties in a script. The listing builds the script information using two functions: GetSEInfo and GetScript. The GetSEInfo function returns script engine information. The GetScript function returns script path and name information.

Listing 5-4: Getting script information

VBScript	*JScript*

scriptinfo.vbs

```vbscript
WScript.Echo GetSEInfo()

WScript.Echo GetScript()

Function GetSEInfo
  Dim info
  info = ""
  info = ScriptEngine & " Version "
  info = info &
    ScriptEngineMajorVersion & "."
  info = info &
    ScriptEngineMinorVersion & "."

  info = info &
    ScriptEngineBuildVersion
  GetSEInfo = info
End Function
Function GetScript
  Dim info
  scr = "Name: "
  scr = WScript.ScriptName & " Full
    path: "
  scr = scr & WScript.ScriptFullName
  GetScript =  scr
End Function
```

scriptinfo.js

```jscript
se = GetSEInfo()
WScript.Echo(se)

sc = GetScript()
WScript.Echo(sc)

function GetSEInfo()
{
    var info;
    info = "";
    info += ScriptEngine() + " Version
       ";
    info += ScriptEngineMajorVersion()
       + ".";
    info += ScriptEngineMinorVersion()
       + ".";
    info += ScriptEngineBuildVersion();
    return(info);
}
function GetScript()
{
    var scr;
    scr = "Name: ";
    scr += WScript.ScriptName + " Full
       path: ";
    scr += WScript.ScriptFullName;
    return(scr);
}
```

Getting script arguments

Arguments set information needed by the script at runtime and are often needed with Windows scripts. WSH interprets any text following the script name as arguments. For example, if you typed:

```
cscript testarg.vbs Test Code 52
```

The first argument is Test, the second argument is Code, and the third argument is 52. As you can see, spaces are used to determine where one argument ends and another begins. This can cause some problems if you want to enter multiple words as a single argument. The workaround is to enclose the argument in double quotation marks, such as:

```
cscript testarg.vbs "Test Code 52"
```

Now the first argument is interpreted as Test Code 52.

Script arguments are placed in a container object called `WshArguments`. You can think of container objects as arrays with properties that are used to work with elements in the array. You need to create an instance of `WshArguments` before you can work with it. You do this with the WScript.Arguments property. For example:

VBScript	**JScript**
`Set theArgs = WScript.Arguments`	`var theArgs = WScript.Arguments`

Note   Note the use of `Set` and `var` in the example. In VBScript, you assign an object reference to a variable with the `Set` statement. In JScript, you do so with the `var` statement.

After you create the object instance, you can use the `Item` property of the `WshArguments` object to access arguments passed to a script according to their index position in the `WshArguments` object. The first script argument is at index position 0, the second at 1, and so on. You can assign argument 1 to a variable as follows:

VBScript	**JScript**
`arg1 = theArgs.Item(0)`	`arg1 = theArgs.Item(0)`

Both VBScript and JScript support a property for determining how many arguments were passed in as well. In VBScript, you use the `Count` property. In JScript, you use the corresponding `Count()` method or the `Length` property. If two arguments were passed to a script, these statements would return 2:

VBScript	**JScript**
`numArgs = theArgs.Count`	`numArgs = theArgs.Length`
	`numArgs = theArgs.Count()`

You can also use `For` loops to examine each argument in turn. When you do this, use the argument count to determine how many times to loop while examining the `WshArguments` object. Then use the `Item()` method to examine or display the value of each argument. An example of this technique is shown as Listing 5-5.

> ### Listing 5-5: **Examining script arguments using a loop**
>
> | **VBScript** | **JScript** |
> |---|---|
> | getargs.vbs | getargs.js |

```
Set theArgs = WScript.Arguments        var theArgs = WScript.Arguments
For I = 0 to theArgs.Count - 1         for (x = 0; x < theArgs.Length; x++)
  WScript.Echo theArgs(I)              {
Next                                       WScript.Echo(theArgs.Item(x))
For Each i IN theArgs                   }
  WScript.Echo i
Next
```

Working with Environment Variables

Environment variables play an important role in Windows scripting. In Windows scripts, you can access environment variables is several ways. In this section, I focus on two techniques. The first technique is one that you can rely on time and again, rather than the other techniques that may cause problems in your scripts.

Understanding environment variables

Environment variables come from many different sources. Just as you can look around and describe your personal surroundings, Windows looks around and describes what it sees in terms of processors, users, paths, and so on. Some variables are built into the operating system or derived from the system hardware during startup. These variables are called built-in system variables and are available to all Windows processes regardless of whether anyone is logged in interactively. System variables can also come from the Windows Registry. These variables are stored in the Registry's HKEY_LOCAL_MACHINE hive and are set when the system boots.

Other variables are set during logon and are called built-in user variables. The built-in user variables available are the same no matter who is logged on at the computer and, as you might expect, are only valid during an actual logon session. Because of this, shell scripts executed with the AT command cannot rely on user variables to be available. User variables can also come from the Windows NT Registry where they are stored in the Registry's HKEY_CURRENT_USER hive and are set during user login. These user variables are valid only for the current user and are not available for other users.

Table 5-4 lists the key built-in system and user variables you may want to work with in shell scripts. Additional variables can be created by users and the operating system.

Table 5-4
Built-in System and User Variables

Variable Name	Description	Sample Value
ALLUSERSPROFILE	Default profile for users.	F:\Documents and Settings\ All Users
APPDATA	Location of the current user's application data.	F:\Documents and Settings\wrstanek\ Application Data
COMMONPROGRAMFILES	Location of common program files on the computer.	F:\Program Files \Common Files
COMPUTERNAME	Computer account name.	Pluto
COMSPEC	Complete path to the current instance of CMD.EXE.	C:\WIN2000\system32\cmd.exe
HOMEDRIVE	Drive name on which the current user's profile resides.	C:
HOMEPATH	Location of the root directory on the home drive.	\
LOGONSERVER	UNC name of the logon domain controller.	\\Sun
NUMBER_OF_ PROCESSORS	Number of CPUs on the system.	3
OS	Operating system name.	Windows_NT
PATH	Executable path used by Windows.	Path=C:\;C:\WIN2000system32; C:\WIN2000
PATHEXT	Filename extensions for executable files.	.COM;.EXE;.BAT;.CMD;.VBS;.VBE;. JS;.VBE;.WSF;.WSH
PROCESSOR_ ARCHITECTURE	Architecture of the processors.	X86
PROMPT	Command prompt settings on the current machine.	PG
SYSTEMDRIVE	Drive name on which the operating system resides.	C:

Variable Name	Description	Sample Value
SYSTEMROOT	Path to the operating system.	C:\WIN2000
USERDOMAIN	Name of the logon domain.	WEBONE
USERNAME	Username of the current user.	WRSTANEK
USERPROFILE	Path to the current user's user profile.	F:\Documents and Settings\WRSTANEK

Accessing environment variables

Environment variables are accessed via the WScript.WshShell object, so you need to create an instance of WScript.WshShell before you can work with environment variables. Unfortunately, there isn't a property of the WScript object that you can use to return the WScript.WshShell object. Because of this, you must create the object instance yourself. You can do this with the CreateObject method of the WScript object. For example:

VBScript	JScript
Set ws = WScript.CreateObject ("WScript.Shell")	var ws = WScript.CreateObject ("WScript.Shell");

Next, as shown in Listing 5-6, use the ExpandEnvironmentStrings() method of WScript.Shell to specify the environment variable you want to work with. All of the environment variables described previously in Table 5-4 are available. You can use the paths returned by ExpandEvironmentStrings() to set file and directory locations.

Listing 5-6: **Using environment variables**

VBScript	JScript
envar.vbs	**envar.js**

Set WshShell = WScript.CreateObject
  ("WScript.Shell")
WScript.Echo
	var WshShell = WScript.CreateObject
	  ("WScript.Shell")
	WScript.Echo

Continued

Listing 5-6 *(continued)*

envar.vbs

```
WshShell.ExpandEnvironmentStrings
  ("%PATH%")
WScript.Echo
  WshShell.ExpandEnvironmentStrings
  ("%COMPUTERNAME%")
```

envar.js

```
(WshShell.ExpandEnvironmentStrings
  ("%PATH%"))
WScript.Echo
  (WshShell.ExpandEnvironmentStrings
  ("%COMPUTERNAME%"))
```

Working with environment variables: An alternative

In Windows scripts, you can access environment variables in several ways. In the previous section, I examined a technique that you can rely on time and again to get the job done. In this section, I examine an alternative technique that may or may not work in your particular circumstance.

With this technique, you access environment variables through `WshEnvironment`, then you use the `WshShell.Environment` method to specify which type of environment variables to work with. Following, environment variables are broken down into four possible classes:

- ✦ `System`—Refers to system environment variables
- ✦ `User`—Refers to user environment variables
- ✦ `Volatile`—Refers to temporary environment variables
- ✦ `Process`—Refers to process variables

You specify the type of environment variable you want to work with as follows:

VBScript	*JScript*
```Set ws = WScript.CreateObject ("WScript.Shell") Set sysEnv = ws.Environment ("SYSTEM")```	```var ws = WScript.CreateObject ("WScript.Shell"); var sysEnv = ws.Environment ("SYSTEM")```

Afterward, you can work with individual environment variables as shown in Listing 5-7. As you work with the environment variable classes, you'll often find that a variable you want to use isn't available in a particular class. If this happens, you'll have to use a different class. Rather than learning which variables are used with which classes, I recommend using the technique outlined in the previous section.

Listing 5-7: Working with environment variable classes

VBScript	JScript
sysenv.vbs	sysenv.js

```
VBScript                              JScript

sysenv.vbs                            sysenv.js
Set ws =                              var ws =
  WScript.CreateObject("WScript.Shell")   WScript.CreateObject("WScript.Shell");

Set sysEnv =                          var sysEnv =
  WshShell.Environment("SYSTEM")        WshShell.Environment("SYSTEM")
os = sysEnv("OS")                     os = sysEnv("OS")
thePath = sysEnv("PATH")              thePath = sysEnv("PATH")

Set usrEnv =                          var usrEnv =
  WshShell.Environment("USER")          WshShell.Environment("USER")
inc = usrEnv("INCLUDE")               inc = usrEnv("INCLUDE")
theLib = usrEnv("LIB")                theLib = usrEnv("LIB")

Set usrEnv =                          var usrEnv =
  WshShell.Environment("VOLATILE")      WshShell.Environment("VOLATILE")
lsvr = usrEnv("LOGONSERVER")          lsvr = usrEnv ("LOGONSERVER")
```

Running Programs from within Scripts

The Run() method of the WScript.Shell object lets you run programs. You can:

✦ Start Windows applications, such as Microsoft Word, Excel, or PowerPoint

✦ Run command-line programs, such as shutdown.exe or regedt32.exe

✦ Run command shell scripts

Tip   Not only can you run programs, you can also pass in arguments and keystrokes. You can activate program windows and pause programs temporarily as well. For complete details, see Chapter 18 "Creating and Scripting Objects".

Starting an application

To use the Run() method, create an instance of WScript.Shell and then access Run(). The following example starts the Windows Notepad in VBScript and JScript:

VBScript	JScript

```
VBScript                    JScript

Set ws =                    var ws =
  WScript.CreateObject        WScript.CreateObject
("WScript.Shell")           ("WScript.Shell");
ws.Run("notepad")           ws.Run("notepad")
```

The file path you pass to Run() is parsed by WSH. This allows you to use any available environment variable in the file path. However, you must tell WSH that you are using an environment variable that has a path that needs to be expanded. Do so by enclosing the variable name in percent signs (%). You can use %SystemRoot% for the SystemRoot environment variable, shown as follows:

VBScript	JScript
```Set ws = WScript.CreateObject ("WScript.Shell") ws.Run ("%SystemRoot%\ system32\notepad")```	```var ws = WScript.CreateObject ("WScript.Shell"); ws.Run ("%SystemRoot%\\ system32\\notepad")```

Tip   As you can see in the example, JScript file paths are referenced in a slightly different way than they are in VBScript. The reason is that JScript treats the slash character as a special character and, as a result, you must escape it with another slash character.

Passing arguments to an application

You can also pass in arguments to command-shell programs and to Windows applications that support command-line parameters. Simply follow the application name with the parameters you want to use. Be sure to add a space between the application name and the parameters. The following example starts Notepad with the active script accessed for editing:

VBScript	JScript
```Set ws = WScript.CreateObject ("WScript.Shell") ws.Run("notepad " & WScript.ScriptFullName)```	```var ws = WScript.CreateObject("WScript.Shell"); ws.Run("notepad " + WScript.ScriptFullName)```

Additional features for Run

The Run() method has more features than you'll probably ever use; but just in case, you can set additional features using the following syntax:

```
object.Run ("command", [winStyle], ["waitOnReturn"])
```

in which *command* is the program or shell script you want to run, *winStyle* is the window style, and *waitOnReturn* specifies whether the script should wait or continue execution. If *waitOnReturn* is not specified or set to False, the script continues execution without waiting on process termination. If waitOnReturn is set to True, script execution pauses until the application stops running or is exited — at which time, the Run() method returns any error code returned by the application, and script execution resumes.

If you want to track error codes, assign Run() to a variable and then check the error code returned by the application. Generally, a non-zero error code indicates an error of some kind. Listing 5-8 shows how you can run a shell script and check the error code the script returned. In this example, note that VBScript allows you to evaluate the error code as a number, but JScript treats the error code as a string.

Listing 5-8: **Checking for Run errors**

VBScript	*JScript*
runerrors.vbs	runerrors.js

```
Set ws =
  WScript.CreateObject
  ("WScript.Shell")
ret = ws.Run("log.bat",0,"TRUE")
If ret = 0 Then
  WScript.Echo "No error"
Else
  WScript.Echo "Error"
End If
```

```
var ws =
  WScript.CreateObject
  ("WScript.Shell");
ret = ws.Run("log.bat",0,"TRUE")
if (ret="0") {
  WScript.Echo("No error")
} else {
  WScript.Echo("Error")
}
```

Note If you specify an invalid program or script name, WSH won't report an error and an error code won't be set. In this case, ret would be a null string.

Table 5-5 shows the options you can use for window style. The most useful styles are 0 for running programs and scripts in the background, and 1 for displaying the window normally. You can use the other options to minimize or maximize the application.

Table 5-5
Window Style Options

Option	Description
0	Runs a program or script in the background.
1	Runs a program or script normally and displays a window if necessary. Generally, use this option before options 2–10.
2	Activates a program and displays it as a minimized window.
3	Activates a program and displays it as a maximized window.
4	Activates a program and displays it in its most recent size and position.

Continued

Table 5-5 *(continued)*

Option	Description
5	Activates a program and displays it in its current size and position.
6	Minimizes the specified window and activates the next top-level window in the Z order.
7	Minimizes the program window without activating it.
8	Displays the program window in its current state but doesn't activate it.
9	Activates and restores the window. If the window is minimized or maximized, the system restores it to its original size and position.
10	Sets the display state based on the state of the Windows script.

Combining JScript and VBScript

You'll often encounter situations in which you implement a script in one scripting language and then wish you could use features of another scripting language in the same script. Well, when you use batch scripts (.WSF files), you can combine scripts written in JScript and scripts written in VBScript in the same file. You can then call functions in one script from another script and return values to the caller.

In VBScript, you can:

    ✦ Call JScript functions and return values

In JScript, you can:

    ✦ Call VBScript subroutines to execute a section of code

    ✦ Call VBScript functions and return values

When the function or subroutine you've called finishes executing, control returns to the caller and execution of the original script continues from there. Listing 5-9 provides a detailed example of calling VBScript and JScript functions. You can use this technique in your own scripts as well.

Listing 5-9: **Combining functions of multiple scripting languages**

cfunctions.wsf

```
<!-- Author: William R. Stanek -->
<!-- Descr: Combined example for JScript and VBScript -->
```

```
<Job ID="MyJob">
<Script LANGUAGE="JScript">
function GetInfoJS()
{
    var info;
    info = "";
    info += ScriptEngine() + " Version ";
    info += ScriptEngineMajorVersion() + ".";
    info += ScriptEngineMinorVersion() + ".";
    info += ScriptEngineBuildVersion();
    return(info);
}

</Script>
<Script LANGUAGE="VBScript">
Function GetInfoVB
  Dim info
  info = ""
  info = ScriptEngine & " Version "
  info = info & ScriptEngineMajorVersion & "."
  info = info & ScriptEngineMinorVersion & "."
  info = info & ScriptEngineBuildVersion
  GetInfoVB =  info
End Function
</Script>

<Script LANGUAGE="VBScript">
WScript.Echo "VB2VB: " + GetInfoVB()
WScript.Echo "VB2JS: " + GetInfoJS()
</Script>

<Script LANGUAGE="JScript">
versionVB = GetInfoVB()
WScript.Echo("JS2VB: ", versionVB)

versionJS = GetInfoJS()
WScript.Echo("JS2JS: ", versionJS)
</Script>
</Job>
```

Output

```
VB2VB: VBScript Version 5.0.3715
VB2JS: JScript Version 5.0.3715
JS2VB:  VBScript Version 5.0.3715
JS2JS:  JScript Version 5.0.3715
```

You'll find additional examples of combining VBScript and JScript throughout this book. In particular, examine Part V, "Windows Scripting Libraries" where you'll find many advanced examples of working with multiple scripting languages.

Summary

In this chapter, you learned scripting basics such as displaying text strings and examining script information. You also learned how to access environment variables and run programs from within scripts. As you've seen, both VBScript and JScript can be used to perform these actions — though each scripting language has a different syntax. As we explore more of the features of Windows Script Host, I'll point out many additional areas where VBScript and JScript differ. If you are interested in using both scripting languages, be sure to keep track of these differences.

✦   ✦   ✦

Input, Output, and Error Handling

Displaying output to readers using WScript.Echo is useful but you often need to implement more powerful techniques in your scripts. For example, you may want to display a dialog box that allows users to make a selection, or you may want users to input a file path or directory name. In either case, you need to display a prompt that enables users to pass information to a script. This prompt can be an input box that allows users to type in text, a message box with clickable buttons, or a pop-up dialog box with clickable buttons.

As you work with input and output, you'll also need to learn error-handling techniques. If a user enters the wrong information, the script should handle the error appropriately. Some error-handling techniques are very basic, such as using control loops to ensure that users enter information. Other error-handling techniques are more advanced and usually involve the built-in error-detection capabilities of VBScript and JScript.

Input and Output Essentials

Chapter 5 discusses how you can use WScript.Arguments to access arguments passed to a script, and how you can display output with WScript.Echo. What that chapter doesn't discuss, however, is how Windows Script Host handles these standard input and output mechanisms. Basic I/O is handled through the standard input and standard output streams — much like I/O is handled in most programming languages. Errors are written to the standard error stream.

The WScript object has three special properties for working with the input, output, and error streams. These special properties are:

✦ StdIn—a read-only input stream

✦ StdOut—a write-only output stream

✦ StdErr—a write-only error stream

These properties return text stream objects. These objects are similar to the FileSystemObject.TextStream object, discussed in Chapter 8. The properties and methods for these streams are listed in Table 6-1.

Table 6-1
Methods and Properties of Input, Output, and Error Streams

Methods	Properties
StdIn Stream	
WScript.StdIn.Close()	WScript.StdIn.AtEndOfLine
WScript.StdIn.Read()	WScript.StdIn.AtEndOfStream
WScript.StdIn.ReadAll()	WScript.StdIn.Column
WScript.StdIn.ReadLine()	WScript.StdIn.Line
WScript.StdIn.Skip()	
WScript.StdIn.SkipLine()	
StdErr Stream	
WScript.StdErr.Close()	
WScript.StdErr.Write()	
WScript.StdErr.WriteBlankLines()	
WScript.StdErr.WriteLine()	
StdOut Stream	
WScript.StdOut.Close()	
WScript.StdOut.Write()	
WScript.StdOut.WriteBlankLines()	
WScript.StdOut.WriteLine()	

Windows Script Host exposes these streams whenever you run scripts using the command-line script host, CScript. Because of this, you can use the StdIn, StdOut, and StdErr streams in scripts that you intend to run from the command line. You cannot, however, use these streams in scripts that you run with the graphical script host, WScript.

Cross-Reference You'll find examples that use streams in Chapters 16, 17, and 18.

Using Input Boxes

Input boxes are only available in VBScript. You can think of input boxes as customizable dialog boxes that you can use to get input from users. This input can be any kind of text, such as a file path, the user's login name, or a response to a question.

Input box basics

To create input boxes, use the InputBox() function and add a prompt and title as necessary. In the example shown in Figure 6-1, InputBox() sets a display prompt and a title for the input box using the following statement:

```
Input = InputBox("Please enter the logon ID:",
                 "Setup Script")
```

Here, the Input variable holds the value of the user's response and can be used later in the script to test the validity of the input. As shown, the prompt and title you want to use are strings enclosed in double quotation marks and separated with a comma.

Figure 6-1: Input boxes are used to get user input. They can have titles and display prompts.

The order of elements in an input box must be exact. You cannot enter a title without entering a prompt — even if the prompt used is just an empty string, such as:

```
Input = InputBox("","Setup Script")
```

Input boxes have an OK button and a Cancel button. If the user types a value then clicks OK, or types a value and then presses Enter on the keyboard, the value is returned by the input function. The user can click OK or Cancel without entering a value, which will cause the function to return an empty string. To ensure the user enters text, you can use a control loop to examine the value entered.

In the following example, the script continues to loop until the user enters a value:

```
Do
theInput = InputBox("Enter your name:","Test Script")
Loop While theValue = ""
```

Setting default values for input boxes

If necessary, you can follow the prompt and the title with a default value for the input. This value is then used when the user clicks OK without entering a value. For example, with the logon example, you might want to set the default user to anonymous, like this:

```
Input = InputBox("Please enter the logon ID:",
                 "Setup Script",
                 "anonymous")
```

As stated before, the quotes around the default value aren't necessary when you use numeric values, though the order of input parameters is important. If you don't use a prompt or title, you must insert placeholder values; for example:

```
Input = InputBox("Please enter the logon ID:", "","anonymous")
```

Positioning input boxes

By default, input boxes are centered on the screen, but if you want, you can specify where you want it displayed as well. You do this by specifying the *x/y coordinate* for the upper-left corner of the input box. The *x* coordinate sets the horizontal distance in pixels from the left edge of the screen. The *y* coordinate sets the vertical distance in pixels from the top of the screen. The *x* and *y* coordinates follow the prompt and title in sequence. For example:

```
Input = InputBox("Please enter your login name:","Setup
Script",,300,300)
```

If you position an input box, you must always set both coordinates. In the examples for this section, the basic syntax for input boxes is:

```
varA = InputBox("prompt","title",defaultValue,X,Y)
```

where *prompt* is the text to display in the input box, *title* is the title for the input box, and *defaultValue* is the value to use when no input is entered.

Converting input values

Values entered into an input box are interpreted as strings provided they contain alphanumeric characters. If the value entered is a number, the value can be handled as a numeric value. This means you can perform arithmetic operations on the input; for example:

```
Dim theTotal: theTotal=0
For i = 1 to 3
 theTotal = theTotal + InputBox("Enter value " & i
                                ,"Compute Average")
Next
theAvg = theTotal/3
WScript.Echo theAvg
```

If you are looking for a particular type of numeric value such as an integer versus a real number, you can convert the value as necessary. In this example, the user could enter a value like 1.8 or 2.2, which you handle by converting the input to an integer:

```
Do
theValue = InputBox("Enter a value 1 to 100:",
                    "Setup Script",,300,300)
Loop While (theValue < 1 OR theValue > 100)
theValue = CInt(theValue)
```

Other conversion functions could also be used, such as CDbl() or CCur(). Conversion functions are listed in Table 2-2.

Using Message Boxes

Message boxes are only available in VBScript. You use message boxes to display information and to allow users to make selections. Because message boxes can have customized buttons and icons, they are a bit more complex than input boxes.

Message box basics

The most basic type of message box is one that calls the Msgbox function and displays a message, like this:

```
Msgbox "Time to run the scripts..."
```

When you use a basic message box, you get a plain dialog box with an OK button. To add pizzazz to message boxes, you can customize the dialog box with titles, icons, and multiple button styles. To add these elements to message boxes, use the following syntax:

```
Msgbox "Message to display", buttonType + iconType,
        "Message box title"
```

As with input boxes, message box parameters must be used in the order specified and you can't skip parameters. For example, if you want to add a title to a message box without specifying a button or icon type, you can use the following command:

```
Msgbox "Time to run the scripts...",,"User Alert!"
```

Adding buttons

As stated previously, the OK button is the default button for all message boxes. However, you can use many different buttons including Yes, No, Cancel, Retry, Ignore, and Abort. Use the following code to add Yes, No, and Cancel buttons to a message box:

```
dim vbYesNoCancel
vbYesNoCancel = 3
Msgbox "Do you want to continue?", vbYesNoCancel
```

where vbYesNoCancel represents the button types you want to add and 3 is the parameter value for this type of button. A message box with the Yes, No, and Cancel buttons is shown in Figure 6-2.

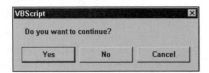

Figure 6-2: Message boxes can use Yes, No, and Cancel buttons. They can also use OK, Retry, Ignore, and Abort buttons.

If you want to, you can specify other types of buttons to use as well, such as vbOkCancel or vbAbortRetryIgnore. These button types are constants, which are variables whose values don't change. Because the script engine knows these values, you don't actually have to use the constant and you can refer to the value directly in the call to Msgbox. However, if you do this, you lose the advantage of being able to tell, at a glance, what types of buttons are used with a particular message box.

Table 6-2 provides a complete list of constants you can use to set button types and their corresponding values. These constants represent all of the available button combinations.

Table 6-2		
Buttons for Messages Boxes		
Constant	*Description*	*Value*
VbOkOnly	Displays the OK button	0
VbOkCancel	Displays OK and Cancel buttons	1
VbAbortRetryIgnore	Displays Abort, Retry, and Ignore buttons	2
VbYesNoCancel	Displays Yes, No, and Cancel buttons	3
VbYesNo	Displays Yes and No buttons	4
VbRetryCancel	Displays Retry and Cancel buttons	5

Adding icons

By default, message boxes use an information icon, but you can change this icon if you want to. Adding a unique icon to a message box is easy. Just keep in mind that buttons and icons are part of the same parameter, which is why you use the plus sign to separate the button types from the icon type. Following is an example message box with an icon:

```
Dim vbYesNo: vbYesNo=4
Dim vbQuestion: vbQuestion=32
Msgbox "Would you like to continue?", vbYesNo + vbQuestion
```

In this example, I've combined the initialization of the value with the actual declaration that sets the value. You can rewrite these statements on separate lines as follows:

```
Dim vbYesNo
vbYesNo=4
Dim vbQuestion
vbQuestion=32
Msgbox "Would you like to continue?", vbYesNo + vbQuestion
```

If you don't want to use constants to represent the numerical values you want to use, you can rewrite these statements as follows:

```
Msgbox "Error writing to disk", 36
```

where 36 is the sum of 4 + 32.

Table 6-3 shows a complete list of icons you can add to message boxes. As with buttons, the use of a constant is optional but makes it easier to work with the script.

Table 6-3
Icons for Messages Boxes

Constant	Description	Value
VbCritical	Displays an icon with an X, used for critical errors.	16
VbQuestion	Displays an icon with a question mark, used for questions.	32
VbExclamation	Displays an icon with an exclamation point, used for minor errors, cautions, and warnings.	48
VbInformation	Displays an icon with an I, used for informational messages (this is the default).	64

Evaluating button clicks

When you present users with multiple options, such as Yes/No or Retry/Cancel, you need a way to determine which button the user selected. You do this by storing the return value from MsgBox in a variable, like this:

```
returnValue = Msgbox ("Message to display", buttonType +
iconType, "Message box title.")
```

Note that the syntax has changed. You must now use parentheses after the function name.

Table 6-4 provides a summary of the status codes returned when message box buttons are pressed. Once you assign a variable to store the returned status code, you can use an `If Then` or `Select Case` structure to perform actions in response to the button click.

Table 6-4
Button Status Codes

Button	Constant	Return Value
OK	VbOk	1
Cancel	VbCancel	2
Abort	VbAbort	3
Retry	VbRetry	4
Ignore	VbIgnore	5

Button	Constant	Return Value
Yes	VbYes	6
No	VbNo	7

A script that evaluates button clicks in message boxes and then handles the result is shown in Listing 6-1. While the example uses an If Then loop to evaluate the button click, you can easily use a Select Case structure as well.

Listing 6-1: **Determining button selection in a script**

checkbuttons.vbs

```
Dim vbYesNoCancel: vbYesNoCancel=3
Dim vbQuestion: vbQuestion=32
Dim vbYes: vbYes=6
Dim vbNo: vbNo=7
Dim vbCancel: vbCancel=2

retry = Msgbox ("Write to log failed. Try again?",
                vbYesNoCancel + VBQuestion)

If retry = vbYes Then
    WScript.Echo "Yes"
ElseIf retry = vbNo Then
    WScript.Echo "No"
Else
    WScript.Echo "Cancel"
End If
```

Help files for message boxes

Windows help files can be used with message boxes. To do this, you need to specify the name of the help file to use as an additional parameter. Following the help file name, you can add a context identifier, which is a numerical value that points to a specific location in the help file. To specify a help file and context identifier, use the following syntax:

```
Msgbox "Message to display", buttonType + iconType,
       "Message box title", "helpFile", helpContextID
```

Here's an example:

```
Msgbox "Continue?", 4, "", "windows.hlp", 0
```

This message box will be displayed with Yes, No, and Help buttons. The Help button is added to allow users to access the Windows help files.

Using pop-up dialog boxes

JScript doesn't support InputBox() or Msgbox(). In the browser implementation of JScript, dialog and input boxes are associated with the window object. Unfortunately, the window object is not available in WSH (unless you start a browser instance). To work around this problem, the developers of WSH created the Popup() function. Popup() is essentially an implementation of the VBScript Msgbox() function that is available in both JScript and VBScript.

Everything you've learned about VBScript message boxes applies to pop-up dialog boxes. The only real difference is that these dialog boxes are accessed through the Popup() method of the Shell object and they have a timeout mechanism. The basic syntax for Popup() is:

VBScript	JScript

answ = object.Popup("*msg*",
                ["*title*"],
                [*wait*],
                [*type*])
	answ = object.Popup(*msg*,
	                [*wait*],
	                ["*title*"],
	                [*type*])

These options are used in the following ways:

- ✦ *msg*—the message you want to display.
- ✦ *wait*—the number of seconds to wait before closing the pop-up.
- ✦ *title*—the title for the pop-up.
- ✦ *type*—the value representing the button and icon types to use. These values are the same as those listed previously in Table 6-1 and Table 6-2.

Because the Popup() method is accessed through the Shell object, you must create an instance of Shell and then reference the Popup() method of this object. You create instances of objects using the CreateObject method of the WScript object. Creating an object instance is a bit different in VBScript and JScript. In VBScript, you create an object reference using the Set keyword. In JScript, you create an object reference using the var keyword. The object reference is then used in the code to access methods and properties of the object you instantiated.

The following code creates an object instance in both VBScript and JScript:

VBScript	JScript
`Set w = WScript.CreateObject("WScript.Shell")`	`var w = WScript.CreateObject("WScript.Shell");`

Listing 6-2 shows how you can use `CreateObject()` and `Popup()` in a script. As discussed, you create an instance of `Shell` and then reference its `Popup()` method. Note that the value for the buttons (4) comes from Table 6-1. You can also set icons for the popup using values in Table 6-2. When you use both icons and buttons, you add the values together and then assign this value in the type property.

Listing 6-2: **Displaying a pop-up dialog box.**

VBScript	JScript
popup.vbs	**popup.js**

```
popup.vbs
answer = getResponse()

function getResponse()
Dim answ
timeOut = 10
title = "Error!"
button = 2
'create object
Set w =
  WScript.CreateObject("WScript.Shell")
getResponse = w.Popup ("Write failure.
  Try again?",timeOut,title,button)

End Function
```

```
popup.js
answer = getResponse()

function getResponse() {
    var answ
    var timeOut = 10;
    var title = "Error!"
    var button = 2
    //create object
    var w =
WScript.CreateObject("WScript.Shell");
    answ = w.Popup ("Write failure.
    Try again?", timeOut, title, button)
    return answ
}
```

The return value from `Popup` tells you which button the user selected. Return values are the same as those listed previously in Table 6-3 with one important addition. If the user doesn't press a button and the timeout interval elapses, the method returns –1.

Listing 6-3 shows how you can handle user selections and errors in both VBScript and JScript. Note that the primary difference between the two is syntax.

Listing 6-3: **Checking the user selection and handling a timeout error**

VBScript	JScript

usersel.vbs

```
function getInput()
Dim answ
timeOut = 30
title = "Write Failure!"
btype = 2
'create object
Set w =
WScript.CreateObject("WScript.Shell")

getInput = w.Popup ("Error writing to
   the drive. Try
   again?",timeOut,title,btype)

End Function

answer = getInput()
Select Case answer
  Case 3
    WScript.Echo "You selected Abort."

  Case 4
    WScript.Echo "You selected Retry."

  Case 5
    WScript.Echo "You selected Ignore."

  Case Else
    WScript.Echo "No selection in the
       time allowed. "

End Select
```

usersel.js

```
function getInput() {
   var answ;
   var timeOut = 30;
   var title = "Write Failure!";
   var type = 2;
   //create object
   var w =
WScript.CreateObject("WScript.Shell");

   answ = w.Popup ("Error writing to
      the drive. Try
      again?",timeOut,title,type);
   return answ;
}

answer = getInput()
switch (answer) {
  case 3 :
    WScript.Echo("You selected
       Abort.")
    break
  case 4 :
    WScript.Echo("You selected
       Retry.")
    break
  case 5 :
    WScript.Echo("You selected
       Ignore.")

    break
  default :
WScript.Echo("No selection in the time
   allowed.")
    break
}
```

ERROR HANDLING

d Handling

)f reasons. The user may have entered the wrong
not be able to find a necessary file, directory, or
've handled errors using basic techniques, such as
the error detection and handling functionality that's

Handling runtime errors in VBScript

The most common type of error you'll encounter is a runtime error. Runtime errors occur while a script is running and are the result of the script trying to perform an invalid operation, such as dividing by zero. The sections that follow examine techniques you can use to handle runtime errors in VBScript.

Preventing runtime errors from halting script execution

In VBScript, any runtime error that occurs is fatal. This means that an error message is displayed and execution of the script stops. To prevent runtime errors from halting script execution, you need to add an On Error Resume Next statement to the script. This statement tells VBScript that execution should continue with the statement that immediately follows the statement that causes an error.

To see how On Error Resume Next works, consider the example shown in Listing 6-4. The user is asked to enter the number of values to total. If the user doesn't enter a value or enters zero, a "Type Mismatch Error" occurs on line 5 but script execution isn't halted. Instead, an error number, its description, and source are pushed onto the current error stack and script execution continues on line 6. Line 7 will again generate a "Type Mismatch Error". The related error number, its description, and source are pushed onto the error stack. This error replaces the previous error and script execution continues. Line 8 generates a "For Loop Not Initialized Error" and then line 9 generates a "Type Mismatch Error".

Listing 6-4: **Computing the average value**

resume.vbs

```
On Error Resume Next
Dim theTotal: theTotal=0
Dim vals: vals=0
vals = InputBox("Number of values to total:"," Average")
vals = CInt(vals)
```

Continued

Listing 6-4 *(continued)*

```
For i = 1 to vals
 theTotal = theTotal + InputBox("Enter value " & i," Average")
Next
theAvg = theTotal/vals
WScript.Echo theAvg
```

Table 6-5 shows other common runtime errors that you may see. These errors are listed by error number and description. Both error values are set by the runtime environment.

Table 6-5
Common Runtime Errors in VBScript

Error Number	Error Description
5	Invalid procedure call or argument
6	Overflow
7	Out of memory
9	Subscript out of range
10	Array fixed or temporarily locked
11	Division by zero
13	Type mismatch
14	Out of string space
28	Out of stack space
35	Sub or Function not defined
48	Error in loading DLL
51	Internal error
53	File not found
57	Device I/O error
58	File already exists
61	Disk full
67	Too many files

Error Number	Error Description
70	Permission denied
75	Path/File access error
76	Path not found
91	Object variable or With block variable not set
92	For loop not initialized
94	Invalid use of Null
322	Can't create necessary temporary file
424	Object required
429	ActiveX component can't create object
438	Object doesn't support this property or method
440	Automation error
445	Object doesn't support this action
446	Object doesn't support named arguments
447	Object doesn't support current locale setting
448	Named argument not found
449	Argument not optional
450	Wrong number of arguments or invalid property assignment
451	Object not a collection
500	Variable is undefined
501	Illegal assignment

Checking for and catching errors in VBScript

While the `On Error Resume Next` statement prevents VBScript from halting execution on an error, it doesn't actually handle the error. To handle the error, you need to add statements to the script that check for an error condition and then handle an error if it occurs. Generally, you'll want to check for errors at key places within your code. For example, in Listing 6-5 you would check for errors after line 4 and line 8. These are places where the user enters values that can affect the execution of the code.

You may also be thinking that you could have prevented an error by checking to see if the user entered a value or by checking for a range of values, such as you see in Listing 6-5.

Listing 6-5: **Computing the average value**

alternative1.vbs

```
On Error Resume Next
Dim theTotal: theTotal=0
Dim vals: vals=0
Do
 vals = InputBox("Number of values to total:"," Average")
Loop While vals = ""
vals = CInt(vals)
For i = 1 to vals
 Do
   theTotal = theTotal + InputBox("Enter value " & i," Average")
 Loop While theTotal = 0
Next
theAvg = theTotal/vals
WScript.Echo theAvg
```

Unfortunately, you can't always predict the values users may enter or the results of operations that are based on user input. The previous example assumes that the user enters numerical values and this may not be the case. The example also has a logic flaw in that it allows the user to enter no value on the second and subsequent iterations of the For loop.

Obviously, you need basic controls such as those provided in Listing 6-6. You also need to look at other ways to manage errors; this is where the Err object comes into the picture. The Err object has methods and properties for displaying and setting information about the current error. These methods and properties are listed in Table 6-6.

Table 6-6
Methods and Properties of the Err Object

Methods	Properties
Clear	Description
Raise	HelpContext
	HelpFile
	Number
	Source

The error number is your most valuable tool in determining if an error has occurred. When a script is executing normally, the error number is set to zero. This means that no error has occurred. When a runtime error occurs, the runtime environment sets a nonzero error number, description, and source. The source of a runtime error is set as "Microsoft VBScript runtime error" instead of "Microsoft VBScript compilation error".

One way to detect an error is to use an `If Then` conditional that checks for an error number other than zero, such as this:

```
If Err.Number <> 0 Then
   'An error has occurred.
   WScript.Echo Err.Number & " "
      & Err.Description & " " & Err.Source
End If
```

As you've seen, the error number, description, and source are set automatically. Values that you can configure when an error occurs are the name of a Windows help file and the context identifier within the help file that can be used to provide detailed help for the user. You set the filename of a help file with the `HelpFile` property and the context identifier with the `HelpContext` property, like this:

```
Err.Helpfile = "myHelpFile.hlp"
Err.HelpContext = 0
```

After handling an error, you should clear the error from the error stack using the `Clear` method. The `Clear` method resets the error code, description, and source to allow normal execution to continue. If you want to catch each individual error, you'll need to add error detection and handling code wherever errors may occur, in the code.

Listing 6-6 shows how you could use the `Clear` method and some other techniques discussed in this section to handle an error. If a runtime error occurs, a message box similar to the one shown in Figure 6-3 is displayed. Note that a Help button is displayed to allow users to access online help files, as well as the additional parameters specified for the message box in the script.

Listing 6-6: **Detecting and handling errors**

alternative2.vbs

```
On Error Resume Next
Dim Msg
Err.HelpFile = "myHelpFile.hlp"
```

Continued

Listing 6-6 *(continued)*

```
Err.HelpContext = 0

Dim theTotal: theTotal=0
Dim vals: vals=0
Do
 vals = InputBox("Number of values to total:"," Average")
Loop While vals = ""

vals = CInt(vals)
For i = 1 to vals
 Do
  theTotal = theTotal + InputBox("Enter value " & i," Average")
 Loop While theTotal = 0
Next
theAvg = theTotal/vals
WScript.Echo theAvg
If Err.Number <> 0 Then
 Msg = "Press F1 or click Help to view a help file."
 MsgBox Msg,1, Err.Description, Err.Helpfile, Err.HelpContext
 Err.Clear
End If
```

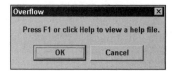

Figure 6-3: Message boxes have a special format and syntax for Windows help.

Manually generating runtime errors

In advanced scripts, there are times when you may want to generate a runtime error. For example, a user enters a file path and your script checks the file path before using it. If the file path isn't valid, the script generates a runtime error and displays a message box that enables the user to access help on setting file paths.

You can use the Raise method of the Err object to generate runtime errors. The complete syntax for the method is:

```
Err.Raise(number, "source", "description", "helpfile",
helpcontext)
```

The arguments for the `Raise` method are used much like the related property values for the `Err` object. If you wanted to generate a "Path Not Found error", you could use the following code:

```
On Error Resume Next
Err.Raise 76
MsgBox "Error " & Err.Number & ": " & Err.Description
Err.Clear
```

You can also set custom errors. When you do this, you should use an error code above 50,000, which is the range set aside for user-defined errors. This example sets a custom error designated as error number 50001:

```
On Error Resume Next
Err.Raise 50001,,"Not a valid choice"
MsgBox "Error " & Err.Number & ": " & Err.Description
Err.Clear
```

You can also generate an error with an associated help file, like this:

```
On Error Resume Next
Dim Msg
Err.Raise 50001,,"Not a valid choice","usage.hlp",0
Msg = "Error " & Err.Number & ": " & Err.Description
MsgBox Msg,1, Err.Description, Err.Helpfile, Err.HelpContext
Err.Clear
```

Handling runtime errors in JScript

JScript takes a different approach to error handling. In many ways, this approach is more intuitive and more powerful than the VBScript approach, so let's take a look.

Checking for and catching errors in JScript

The core mechanisms for error handling are `try catch` statements. Use a `try` statement to identify a section of code where an error may occur and a `catch` statement to handle any resulting errors. The basic syntax for `try catch` is:

```
try {
  //code where an error might occur
}
catch(exception) {
  //catch errors that may occur
}
```

If an error occurs within the `try` statement, control is passed to the `catch` statement and the value of `exception` is set to the value of the error that occurred. You may be wondering why the developers of JScript decided to use the keywords `try` `catch` rather than `detect handle` or something else. Primarily this is because errors that occur in scripts are said to be thrown by the runtime environment and thus, the `catch` statement catches them so they don't cause problems in the script.

As with VBScript, errors can be generated both automatically and manually. For example, if you call a function that doesn't exist, an object error occurs which you can handle in the following way:

```
try {
  nosuchfunction()
}
catch(e) {
  if (e == "[object Error]")
    WScript.Echo(e)
}
```

If you want to manually set error values, you can throw errors as well, which we will discuss next.

Throwing errors

You manually generate errors using the `throw` statement. The `throw` statement expects a single argument, which is an expression that yields a string, number, or object. This argument sets the error value. If you pass `throw` the following string:

```
throw "division by zero"
```

the error value is set to:

```
division by zero
```

You can use `throw` with `try` and `catch` as follows:

```
try {
  if (x < 0)
    throw "value less than zero";
  else if (x == 0)
    throw "value equals zero";
  }
  catch(e) {
    WScript.Echo("Error: " + e)
}
```

This example sets error values based on the value of x. If x is less than zero, the error value is set to "value less than zero". If x equals zero, the error value is set to "value equals zero". The `catch` statement is used to detect and handle an error if it occurs. If an error occurs, the script displays an error statement.

So far, we've been looking at how you can handle localized errors directly. Unfortunately, you may not want to handle errors directly. Instead, you may want to detect one or more errors locally and then pass unresolved errors to a higher context to handle them globally, like this:

```
try {
  if (x < 0)
    throw "value less than zero";
  else if (x == 0)
    throw "value equals zero";
  }
  catch(e) {
    if (e == "value less than zero")
      return("Error handled locally.");
    else
      throw e; //error not handled locally, pass exception on.
}
```

Listing 6-7 shows a more complete example of handling errors locally and globally. The first call to the `tryTest` function passes in a value of -1. This causes the script to throw an exception and set the error value to "value less than zero". The `catch` statement uses `If Else` to determine whether to handle the error. Here, the error value matches the value expected by the `If` statement, and the error is handled locally. The subsequent call to `tryTest`, however, sets x to 0, and this error isn't handled locally. Instead, the error is thrown to a higher context and then handled globally.

Listing 6-7: **Throwing an error**

throwerror.js

```
function tryTest(x)
{
 try {
  if (x < 0)
    throw "value less than zero";
  else if (x == 0)
    throw "value equals zero";
  }
  catch(e) {
    if (e == "value less than zero")
      return("Error handled locally.");
    else
      throw e;
  }
}
```

Continued

Listing 6-7 *(continued)*

```
try {
 WScript.Echo("Result A: " + tryTest(-1))
}
catch(e) {
 WScript.Echo("Error passed to higher context. Handled globally.");
}
try {
 WScript.Echo("Result B: " + tryTest(0))
}
catch(e) {
 WScript.Echo("Error passed to higher context. Handled globally.");
}
```

Output

```
Result A: Error handled locally.
Error passed to higher context. Handled globally.
```

Other error-handling techniques

As with VBScript, you can examine error codes and descriptions in JScript.
Table 6-7 shows the common errors by error code and description.

Table 6-7
Common Runtime Errors in JScript

Error Code	Error Description
5	Invalid procedure call or argument
6	Overflow
7	Out of memory
9	Subscript out of range
10	This array is fixed or temporarily locked
11	Division by zero
13	Type mismatch
14	Out of string space
17	Can't perform requested operation

Error Code	Error Description
28	Out of stack space
35	Sub or Function not defined
48	Error in loading DLL
51	Internal error
52	Bad file name or number
53	File not found
54	Bad file mode
55	File already open
57	Device I/O error
58	File already exists
61	Disk full
62	Input past end of file
67	Too many files
68	Device unavailable
70	Permission denied
71	Disk not ready
74	Can't rename with different drive
75	Path/File access error
76	Path not found
91	Object variable or With block variable not set
92	For loop not initialized
93	Invalid pattern string
94	Invalid use of Null
322	Can't create necessary temporary file
424	Object required

To access the error code and description, use the Error object. The Error object is created automatically by the catch statement and has two properties: Description and Number. The Description property returns or sets the error message. The Number property returns or sets the error number associated with the error.

You access the `Description` property directly through the `Error` object, like this:

```
try {
  nosuchfunction()
}
catch(e) {
  WScript.Echo(e.description)
}
```

On the other hand, the `Number` property is accessed through a 32-bit value. The upper 16-bit word from this value is a facility code, which you won't use in most cases. The lower 16-bit word is the actual error code. You can examine both codes as follows:

```
try {
  nosuchfunction()
}
catch(e) {
  WScript.Echo("Facility Code: " + e.number>16 & Ox1FFF)
  WScript.Echo("Error Code: " + e.number & OxFFFF)
}
```

Again, the error code is the value you'll want to use in your scripts.

Summary

Input, output, and error handling are important parts of any script. The most common techniques for displaying output and gathering input are dialog boxes. In the runtime environment, three types of dialog boxes are available: input boxes, message boxes, and pop-up dialog boxes. While VBScript supports all three types of dialog boxes, JScript only supports pop-ups. This support for VBScript and JScript is different from what you may be used to if you've worked with browser-based scripting, and it is something you should keep in mind whenever you work with Windows scripts.

✦   ✦   ✦

Working with Files and Folders

The file system is one of the most important parts of any operating system and Windows is no exception. Your scripts will often need to manage files and folders. For example, before you can extract information from a log file you must learn how to find files, how to check for a file's existence, and how to read files. This chapter examines high-level techniques for working with files and folders. You'll learn how to create files and folders, how to examine file and folder properties, and how to move and delete files and folders. Reading and writing files is the subject of Chapter 8.

Understanding the FileSystemObject

The top-level object for working with the Windows desktop and file systems is the FileSystemObject (FSO). It is through FSO that you access most of the other file-system-related objects. Because this object is so complex, lets take a step-by-step look at its components including related objects, methods, and properties.

FSO objects and collections

The FileSystemObject is implemented in the scripting run-time library (Scrrun.dll) and as such, it is an extension of the JScript and VBScript scripting engines rather than a part of the Windows Script Host object model. This distinction is important if you plan to use Windows Script Host with other scripting engines. For example, if you plan to use the PerlScript scripting engine, you will use PerlScript's file system objects, or you can define file system functions in VBScript and JScript and access them from PerlScript as part of a batch script job.

Many different objects and collections are accessed through the `FileSystemObject`. These elements are summarized in Table 7-1. As you already know, objects are containers for related sets of methods and properties. Collections, on the other hand, may be new to you. *Collections* are containers for groups of related items, such as the `Drives` collection that contains references for all the drives on a particular system. Normally, collections are accessed through the properties and methods of other objects. For example, to examine drives on a system, you'll use the `Drives` property of the `FileSystemObject`.

Table 7-1
Objects and Collections Accessed through FileSystemObject

Object/Collection	Description
`Drive` **Object**	Used to examine information on storage devices, including disk drives, CD-ROM drives, RAM disks, and network drives.
`Drives` **Collection**	Provides a list of physical and logical drives on the system.
`File` **Object**	Used to examine and manipulate files.
`Files` **Collection**	Provides a list of files in a folder.
`Folder` **Object**	Used to examine and manipulate folders.
`Folders` **Collection**	Provides a list of subfolders in a folder.
`TextStream` **Object**	Used to read and write text files.

FSO methods and properties

As shown in Table 7-2, the `FileSystemObject` provides many different methods for working with file systems. These methods sometimes provide the same functionality as the methods of lower-level objects. For example, the `FileSystemObject`'s `CopyFile` method is identical to the `File` object's `Copy` method. They both expect the same arguments and have the same syntax.

Table 7-2
Methods of FileSystemObject

Method	Description
`BuildPath`	Appends file path information to an existing file path.
`CopyFile`	Copies files from one location to another.
`CopyFolder`	Copies folders and their contents from one location to another.

Method	Description
CreateFolder	Creates a folder.
CreateTextFile	Creates a text file and returns a TextStream object.
DeleteFile	Deletes a file.
DeleteFolder	Deletes a folder and all of its contents.
DriveExists	Determines if a drive exists.
FileExists	Determines if a file exists.
FolderExists	Determines if a folder exists.
GetAbsolutePathName	Returns the full path to a file or folder.
GetBaseName	Returns the base name of a file or folder.
GetDrive	Returns a Drive object.
GetDriveName	Returns a drive name.
GetExtensionName	Returns a file extension from a path.
GetFile	Returns a File object.
GetFileName	Returns a filename from a path.
GetFolder	Returns a Folder object.
GetParentFolderName	Returns the parent folder name from a path.
GetSpecialFolder	Returns an object pointer to a special folder.
GetTempName	Returns a randomly generated file or folder name that can be used with CreateTextFile.
MoveFile	Moves files from one location to another.
MoveFolder	Moves folders and their contents from one location to another.
OpenTextFile	Opens an existing text file and returns a TextStream object.

The only property of the FileSystemObject is Drives. This property returns a Drives collection that contains a list of all physical and logical drives on the system.

Using the FileSystemObject

As stated earlier, the FileSystemObject isn't a part of the Windows Script Host object model and is instead a part of the scripting type library. Because of this, you access the FileSystemObject via the Scripting object, like this:

VBScript	**JScript**
```Set fs = WScript.CreateObject ("Scripting.FileSystemObject ")```	```fs = new ActiveXObject ("Scripting.FileSystemObject");```

In these examples, note that you create the `FileSystemObject` in JScript using the `ActiveXObject` method rather than the `CreateObject` method. `ActiveXObject` is a JScript method designed to return references to ActiveX Automation objects.

Once you create an instance of the `FileSystemObject` you can use its objects, methods, and properties. You need only one instance of the `FileSystemObject` in a script, and when you are finished using it, you may want to destroy the object instance and free up the memory it uses. To do this, you can set the reference variable to null, like this:

VBScript	**JScript**
```Set fs = Nothing```	```fs = ""```

Note   `Nothing` is a reserved keyword in VBScript. You use `Nothing` in an assignment to null the object (free the memory associated with the object).

Working with Folders

Folders are an important part of the file system, and whether you want to access existing folders or create new folders, you can use Windows scripts to get the job done. Often, the way you work with folders depends on the tasks you want to perform. For example, if you want to examine folder properties, you first need to create a `Folder` object and then you can work with the `Folder` object. The sections that follow examine key folder administration tasks, including:

✦ Viewing folder contents

✦ Examining and working with folder properties

✦ Checking for and creating folders

✦ Deleting, copying, and moving folders

✦ Working with special folders

Checking folder contents

Before you can view the contents of a folder, you must create a reference to the folder you want to work with. You do this with the `GetFolder` method of the `FileSystemObject`. You pass the `GetFolder` method the path of the folder you want to work with and the method returns a `Folder` object that you can use in your scripts. The following example shows how you can call `GetFolder`:

VBScript	JScript

`Set fs = CreateObject`
`   ("Scripting.FileSystemObject")`
`Set f = fs.GetFolder("C:\Win2000")`
	`fs = new ActiveXObject`
	`   ("Scripting.FileSystemObject");`
	`var f = fs.GetFolder("C:\\Win2000")`

 Tip   Don't forget that you must use escape directory paths in JScript. If you forget to use double slashes, your scripts may not work.

After calling `GetFolder`, you can use the `Subfolders` and `Files` properties of the `File` object to examine the elements contained in the specified folder. These properties return `Folder` and `File` collections respectively, which you can iterate through with a `For` loop.

Listing 7-1 shows an example using `GetFolder`. The example displays a pop-up dialog box that contains a list of all subfolders under the C:\WIN2000 directory.

Listing 7-1: **Examining collections of subfolders and files**

VBScript	JScript
viewfolder.vbs	**viewfolder.js**

```
viewfolder.vbs
Set w = WScript.CreateObject
  ("WScript.Shell")
w.Popup ShowFolders("C:\WIN2000")
Function ShowFolders(folderName)

Dim fs, f, f1, fc, s
s = ""
Set fs = CreateObject
  ("Scripting.FileSystemObject")
Set f = fs.GetFolder(folderName)
Set fc = f.SubFolders
For Each f1 in fc

s = s & f1.name
s = s &  (Chr(13) & Chr(10))
Next
  ShowFolders = s
End Function
```

```
viewfolder.js
var w = WScript.CreateObject
  ("WScript.Shell");
w.Popup (ShowFolders("C:\\WIN2000"))
function ShowFolders(folderName)
{
var fs, f, fc, s;
s = ""
fs = new ActiveXObject
  ("Scripting.FileSystemObject");
f = fs.GetFolder(folderName);
  fc = new Enumerator(f.SubFolders);
  for (; !fc.atEnd(); fc.moveNext())
  {
    s += fc.item();
    s += "\r\n"
  }
  return(s);
}
```

As Listing 7-1 shows, the techniques you use to examine collections in VBScript and JScript differ. In VBScript, you can use a simple For Each structure to examine the contents of the collection. The structure of the For Each loop isn't really any different from structures I've used in past examples. You start out by obtaining a Folder object:

```
Set fs = CreateObject("Scripting.FileSystemObject")
Set f = fs.GetFolder(folderName)
```

Next, you obtain the SubFolders collection within the folder:

```
Set fc = f.SubFolders
```

Then, you examine each item in the collection using a For Each loop:

```
For Each fl in fc
s = s & fl.name
s = s &  (Chr(13) & Chr(10))
Next
```

You use the s variable to hold the list of folder names, placing the names on separate lines by combining Chr(13) and Chr(10). Chr(13) is a carriage return and Chr(10) is a line feed.

With JScript, on the other hand, accessing collections requires some new techniques. You start out by obtaining a pointer to a Folder object:

```
fs = new ActiveXObject("Scripting.FileSystemObject");
f = fs.GetFolder(folderName);
```

Next, because the items in a collection aren't directly accessible in JScript, you use the Enumerator() method to obtain the SubFolders collection within the specified folder:

```
fc = new Enumerator(f.SubFolders);
```

Enumerator() provides access to special methods for working with collections. These methods are:

✦ atEnd—Returns True if the current item is the last in the collection. Otherwise, returns False.

✦ item—Returns an item in a collection.

✦ moveFirst—Resets the collection pointer to the beginning of the collection. Returns undefined if there aren't any items.

✦ moveNext—Advances to the next item in the collection. Returns undefined if the pointer is at the end of the collection.

In the example below, these methods are used to move through the collection. The following For loop iterates through the available items:

```
for (; !fc.atEnd(); fc.moveNext())
  {
    s += fc.item();
    s += "\r\n"
  }
```

You use the s variable to hold the list of folder names, placing the names on separate lines by combining \r and \n. The special character \r is a carriage return and \n is a line feed.

Examining folder properties

When you work with folders, you often want to examine their properties, such as the creation date or the date last modified. You can use these properties to view folder attributes, to display folder information to users, and more. Before you can examine folder properties, you must reference the folder through its Folder object. You can then work with any of the folder properties available. The following example shows how you can examine the creation date of a specified folder:

VBScript	JScript
Set fs = CreateObject ("Scripting.FileSystemObject") Set f = fs.GetFolder("C:\WIN2000") creDate = f.DateCreated	fs = new ActiveXObject ("Scripting.FileSystemObject"); var f = fs.GetFolder("C:\\WIN2000") creDate = f.DateCreated

A complete list of folder properties is shown in Table 7-3. All folder properties are read-only, except for the Attributes property. This means you can read the properties but you can't change their values.

Table 7-3
Properties of the Folder Object

Property	Description	Sample Return Value
Attributes	Sets or returns folder properties. See the section titled, "Examining and Working with File Properties" for complete details.	16

Continued

Table 7-3 *(continued)*

Property	Description	Sample Return Value
DateCreated	Returns the folder creation date and time.	10/15/00 6:11:21 PM
DateLastAccessed	Returns the date the folder was last accessed.	10/21/00
DateLastModified	Returns the date and time the folder was last modified.	10/21/00 6:52:12 PM
Drive	Returns the drive letter on which the folder resides.	C:
Files	Returns a Files collection.	-
IsRootFolder	Returns 1 (True) if the folder is the root folder, such as C:\ or D:\. Otherwise, returns zero.	0
Name	Returns the folder name.	Win2000
ParentFolder	Returns the Folder object of the parent folder.	C:\
Path	Returns the path to the folder.	C:\WIN2000
ShortName	Returns the MS DOS-compliant name of the folder.	Win2000
ShortPath	Returns the MS DOS-compliant path to the folder.	C:\WIN2000
Size	Returns the byte size of all files and subfolders in the folder.	1576524
SubFolders	Returns a SubFolders collection.	-
Type	Returns the folder type.	File Folder

Most of the folder properties have fairly obvious uses. For example, you use the CreationDate property when you want to display the folder's creation date to a user, or perform a calculation based on the creation date.

Some properties are more useful than you might imagine. For example, you can use IsRootFolder and ParentFolder to move through directory structures. You create an instance of a folder and set it to a path, like this: C:\WIN2000\System32\LogFiles. Then use the ParentFolder property to move through each of the parent folders, stopping when you reach the root folder C:\. An example that uses this technique is shown in Listing 7-2.

Listing 7-2: **Using IsRootFolder and ParentFolder**

VBScript	JScript
checkfolder.vbs	**checkfolder.js**

```
folderP = CheckFolders
  ("C:\WIN2000\System32\LogFiles")
Set w = WScript.CreateObject
  ("WScript.Shell")
w.Popup folderP
Function CheckFolders(folderPath)

Dim fs, f, n, s
s = ""
n = 0
Set fs = CreateObject
("Scripting.FileSystemObject")
Set f = fs.GetFolder(folderPath)
If f.IsRootFolder Then
  s = "This is the root folder."
Else
  Do Until f.IsRootFolder
    Set f = f.ParentFolder
      n = n + 1
  Loop
End If
'Work with folder
s = "Folder is nested " & n & "
  levels deep."

CheckFolders = s
End Function
```

```
folderP = CheckFolders
  ("C:\\WIN2000\\System32\\LogFiles")
var w = WScript.CreateObject
  ("WScript.Shell");
w.Popup (folderP)
function CheckFolders(folderPath)
{
  var fs, f, n, s;
  s = "";
  n = 0;
  fs = new ActiveXObject
  ("Scripting.FileSystemObject");
  f = fs.GetFolder(folderPath);
  if (f.IsRootFolder)
    s = "Root folder."
    else {
      do {
        f = f.ParentFolder;
        n++;
      }
    while (!f.IsRootFolder)
  //Work with folder
  s = "Folder is nested " + n + "
    levels deep."
  }
  return(s);
}
```

Output
```
Folder is nested three levels deep.
```

Output
```
Folder is nested three levels deep.
```

As shown, the ParentFolder property returns a Folder object that you can manipulate. If you just want the name of the parent folder, use the GetParent FolderName method instead. This method returns a string containing the name of the parent folder and can be used as follows:

VBScript	JScript

```
Set fs = CreateObject
("Scripting.FileSystemObject")
par = f.GetParentFolderName
  folderpath
```

```
fs = new ActiveXObject
("Scripting.FileSystemObject");
par = f.GetParentFolderName
  (folderpath)
```

Here, if the folder path is C:\WIN2000\System32, the par variable is set to C:\WIN2000. Note that if the folder path is a root folder, such as C:\, the GetParentFolderName method returns an empty string. The reason for this is that root folders don't have parent folders.

Creating folders

In the previous examples, we've assumed that the folder exists on the user's system. As this may not always be the case, you may want to test for a folder's existence before you try to work with it. To do this, you can use the FolderExists method of FileSystemObject. This method returns True if the folder exists and can be used as shown in Listing 7-3.

Listing 7-3: **Using FolderExists**

VBScript	*JScript*
checkfolder2.vbs	**checkfolder2.js**

```
WScript.Echo(CheckFolder("C:\WIN2000"))
Function CheckFolder(foldr)
Dim fs, s
  Set fs = CreateObject
    ("Scripting.FileSystemObject")
  If (fs.FolderExists(foldr)) Then
    s = foldr & " is available."
  Else
    s = foldr & " doesn't exist."
  End If
  CheckFolder = s
End Function
```

```
WScript.Echo(CheckFolder("C:\\WIN2000"))
function CheckFolder(foldr)
{
var fs, s = foldr;
fs = new ActiveXObject
  ("Scripting.FileSystemObject");
  if (fs.FolderExists(foldr))
    s += " is available.";
  else
    s += " doesn't exist.";
  return(s);
}
```

Output

```
C:\WIN2000 is available.
```

Output

```
C:\WIN2000 is available.
```

After checking for a folder's existence, one of the most common tasks you'll want to perform is the creation of a necessary folder. You can create folders with the CreateFolder method of the FileSystemObject. The main argument for this method is a string containing the path to the folder you want to create, such as:

VBScript	*JScript*

```
Set fs = CreateObject
  ("Scripting.FileSystemObject")
Set foldr = fs.CreateFolder
  ("d:\data")
```

```
var fs = new ActiveXObject
  ("Scripting.FileSystemObject");
var foldr = fs.CreateFolder
  ("d:\\data");
```

Copying, moving, and deleting folders

With Windows scripts, there are two different ways to copy, move, and delete files. You can use methods of `FileSystemObject` to work with multiple folders or you can use methods of the `Folder` object to work with individual folders.

Issues for multiple folders

Using `FileSystemObject`, the methods for copying, moving, and deleting folders are:

✦ `DeleteFolder`

✦ `CopyFolder`

✦ `MoveFolder`

Using DeleteFolder

The `DeleteFolder` method is used to delete a folder and all of its contents, which can include subfolders and files. When you use the method, specify the path to the folder you want to delete and optionally force the method to delete read-only files. For example, you can delete a working directory in C:\working\data as follows:

VBScript	JScript

Set fs = CreateObject
  ("Scripting.FileSystemObject")
fs.DeleteFolder("C:\working\data")
	var fs = new ActiveXObject
	  ("Scripting.FileSystemObject");
	fs.DeleteFolder("C:\\working\\data");

Caution   The `DeleteFolder` **method can be very dangerous. It allows you to specify the root folder for deletion, which will delete all contents on an entire drive.**

If the directory contains read-only files that you want to delete, an error occurs and the delete operation is cancelled. To prevent this from happening, you must set the force flag to True. For example:

VBScript	JScript

fs.DeleteFolder
  "C:\working\data",True
	fs.DeleteFolder
	  ("C:\\working\\data", "True");

You can also use wildcards when deleting folders. To do this, specify the wildcard as the last element of the path. For example, you can delete the folders C:\working\test and C:\working\test2 as follows:

VBScript	JScript
fs.DeleteFolder "C:\working\tes*"	fs.DeleteFolder("C:\\working\\tes*");

Using CopyFolder

The CopyFolder method copies a folder and all of its contents — which can include subfolders and files — to a new location. Using CopyFolder, you specify the source path of the folder you want to copy and the destination path for the folder. For example, you can copy C:\working to D:\data as follows:

VBScript	JScript
```Set fs = CreateObject ("Scripting.FileSystemObject") fs.CopyFolder "C:\working", "D:\data" ```	```var fs = new ActiveXObject ("Scripting.FileSystemObject"); fs.CopyFolder ("C:\\working", "D:\\data"); ```

You can also use CopyFolder to copy between existing folders. For example if both C:\working and D:\data exist, you can copy files and subfolders from C:\working to D:\data. However, when you do this, there are several rules you must follow. If the destination directory already exists and any files are overwritten during the copy, an error occurs and the copy operation stops. To force the method to overwrite existing files, you must set the overwrite flag to True, like this:

VBScript	JScript
```fs.CopyFolder "C:\working", "D:\data", True ```	```fs.CopyFolder ("C:\\working", "D:\\data", "True"); ```

If the destination directory already exists and you want to copy specific files and folders, use a wildcard as the final element of the source folder name. The following example copies the C:\Working\test and C:\Working\test2 folders to D:\data\test and D:\data\test2:

VBScript	JScript
```fs.CopyFolder "C:\working\tes*", "D:\data" ```	```fs.CopyFolder("C:\\working\\tes*", "D:\\data"); ```

Tip   Normally, you don't want to specify the last element of the destination path as a folder separator (\). If you do, the CopyFolder method assumes the destination folder exists and will not create it if it is necessary to do so.

Using MoveFolder

If you want to move a folder and all of its contents to a new location, use MoveFolder. When you use the MoveFolder method, you specify the source path of the folder you want to move and the destination path. For example, you can move C:\data to D:\work\data as follows:

VBScript	JScript
| ```
Set fs = CreateObject
  ("Scripting.FileSystemObject")
fs.MoveFolder "C:\data",
  "D:\work\data"
``` | ```
var fs = new ActiveXObject
  ("Scripting.FileSystemObject");
fs.MoveFolder("C:\\data",
  "D:\\work\\data");
``` |

You can also use `MoveFolder` to move files and subfolders between existing folders. For example if both C:\working and D:\data exist, you can move files and subfolders from C:\working to D:\data. To do this, use wildcards to match subfolders and file contents, like this:

VBScript	JScript
| ```
fs.MoveFolder "C:\working\tes*",
  "D:\data"
``` | ```
fs.MoveFolder("C:\\working\\tes*",
  "D:\\data");
``` |

Note
If you specify the last element of the destination path as a folder separator (\), the `MoveFolder` method assumes that the destination folder exists and will not create it if it is necessary to do so. Also, the move operation will not overwrite existing files or folders. In such a case, the move fails the first time it tries to overwrite.

Issues for individual folders

With the `Folder` object, the methods for copying, moving, and deleting folders are:

✦ `Delete`

✦ `Copy`

✦ `Move`

Note
You cannot use wildcards when copying, moving, or deleting individual folders.

Using Delete

The `Delete` method of the `Folder` object works almost the same as the `DeleteFolder` method discussed previously. The method deletes a folder and all of its contents, which can include subfolders and files, and can also force the deletion of read-only contents. The `Delete` method works with a specific `Folder` object reference and, as a result, can delete a folder just by calling the method, like this:

VBScript	JScript
| ```
Set fs = CreateObject
  ("Scripting.FileSystemObject")
Set f = fs.GetFolder("C:\working")
f.Delete
``` | ```
var fs = new ActiveXObject
  ("Scripting.FileSystemObject");
var f = fs.GetFolder("C:\\working");
f.Delete()
``` |

If the folder contains read-only subfolders and files that you want to delete, you must set the force flag to True, like this:

VBScript	JScript
`f.Delete True`	`f.Delete("True")`

Using Copy

The `Copy` method copies a folder and all of its contents to a new location. With `Copy`, you obtain a `Folder` object and then set the destination path for the folder in the `Copy` method. For example, you can copy C:\working to D:\data as follows:

VBScript	JScript
| ```
Set fs = CreateObject
  ("Scripting.FileSystemObject")
Set f = fs.GetFolder("C:\working")
f.Copy "D:\data"
``` | ```
var fs = new ActiveXObject
  ("Scripting.FileSystemObject");
var f = fs.GetFolder("C:\\working");
f.Copy("D:\\data");
``` |

As with `CopyFolder`, you can also use the `Copy` method to copy between existing folders. For example if both C:\working and D:\data exist, you can copy files and subfolders from C:\working to D:\data. In this case, you may want to force the method to overwrite existing files, which you do by setting the overwrite flag to True, like this:

VBScript	JScript
`f.Copy "D:\data", True`	`f.Copy("D:\\data", "True");`

If you try to overwrite existing files and don't set the overwrite flag, an error occurs and the `Copy` operation stops.

Using Move

The `Move` method moves a folder and all of its contents to a new location. Before you use `Move`, you must first obtain a `Folder` object and then you can set the destination path for the folder in the `Move` method. For example, you can move C:\data to D:\work\data like this:

VBScript	JScript
```Set fs = CreateObject ("Scripting.FileSystemObject") Set f = fs.GetFolder("C:\data") f.Move "D:\work\data"```	```var fs = new ActiveXObject ("Scripting.FileSystemObject"); var f = fs.GetFolder("C:\\data"); f.Move("D:\\work\\data");```

You can also use `Move` to move files and subfolders between existing folders. For example if both C:\data and D:\backups\data exist, you can move files and subfolders from C:\data to D:\backups\data. However, the `Move` method will not overwrite existing files. If you try to do this, an error occurs and the operation stops.

Using Special Folders

Entering a specific value for folder paths works in many cases, but there are times when you'll need to work with certain folders in a way that isn't specific to a particular system. For example, if you create a login script, users may log in from Windows 98, Windows NT, or Windows 2000. These operating system files are installed in different locations by default and can be set to just about any directory name during installation.

So, if you want to create a script that works with operating system files, you shouldn't enter a precise path. Instead, you should work with environment variables that act as pointers to the location of the operating system files, `SystemRoot` for example. As discussed in Chapter 9, you can use the `ExpandEnvironmentStrings` method of the `Shell` object to obtain a string representation of the `SystemRoot` environment variable. You can then assign this value to a method that uses the path information. An example is shown in Listing 7-4.

Listing 7-4: **Working with paths and environment variables**

VBScript	JScript

envpaths.vbs

```
Set fs = CreateObject
  ("Scripting.FileSystemObject")
Set WshShell = WScript.CreateObject
  ("WScript.Shell")
osdir =
  WshShell.ExpandEnvironmentStrings
  ("%SystemRoot%")
Set f = fs.GetFolder(osdir)
WScript.Echo f
```

envpaths.js

```
var fs = new ActiveXObject
  ("Scripting.FileSystemObject");
var WshShell = WScript.CreateObject
  ("WScript.Shell")
osdir =
  WshShell.ExpandEnvironmentStrings
  ("%SystemRoot%")
var f = fs.GetFolder(osdir);
WScript.Echo(f)
```

Output

```
C:\WIN2000
```

Output

```
C:\WIN2000
```

Accessing environment variables before working with folders requires a few extra steps that can be avoided by using the `GetSpecialFolder` method of `File SystemObject`. With this method, you can directly obtain one of three folders: the Windows folder, the System folder, or the Temp folder. The method accepts a value that represents the folder you want to work with. The three values are listed below:

✦ 0 — For the Windows folder, such as C:\WIN2000. Associated constant is `WindowsFolder`.

✦ 1 — For the System folder, such as C:\WIN2000\System32. Associated constant is `SystemFolder`.

✦ 2 — For the Temp folder, such as C:\TEMP. Associated constant is `TemporaryFolder`.

An example using `GetSpecialFolder` is shown in Listing 7-5.

Listing 7-5: **Working with special folders**

VBScript	JScript

specialfolder.vbs

```
Set fs = CreateObject
  ("Scripting.FileSystemObject")
'Get the Windows folder
```

specialfolder.js

```
var fs = CreateObject
  ("Scripting.FileSystemObject")
//Get the Windows folder
```

```
Set wfolder = fs.GetSpecialFolder(0)      var wfolder = fs.GetSpecialFolder(0)
'Get the System folder                    //Get the System folder
Set sfolder = fs.GetSpecialFolder(1)      var sfolder = fs.GetSpecialFolder(1)
'Get the Temp folder                      //Get the Temp folder
Set tfolder = fs.GetSpecialFolder(2)      var tfolder = fs.GetSpecialFolder(2)
```

Working with Files

Many of the tasks you perform in Windows scripts will relate to files. You can use scripts to copy, move, and delete files. You can also use scripts to create, read, and write text files. The types of text files you can work with include HTML, XML, scripts, and other types of files containing standard ASCII or Unicode text. The sections that follow examine key file administration tasks, including:

✦ Examining and working with file properties

✦ Copying, moving, and deleting files

✦ Checking for and creating files

✦ Reading and writing files

Examining file properties

Files have many different properties. Some of these properties can only be read. Others are read/write, which means you can change their values. A complete list of folder properties is shown as Table 7-4.

Table 7-4
Properties of the File Object

Property	Description	Sample Return Value
Attributes	Sets or returns file properties.	32
DateCreated	Returns the file creation date and time.	7/15/00 12:05:11 AM
DateLastAccessed	Returns the date the file was last accessed.	9/10/00
DateLastModified	Returns the date and time the file was last modified.	9/10/00 8:26:35 PM
Drive	Returns the drive letter on which the file resides.	D:

Continued

Table 7-4 *(continued)*

Property	Description	Sample Return Value
Name	Returns the filename.	index.html
ParentFolder	Returns the Folder object of the parent folder.	C:\working
Path	Returns the path to the file.	C:\working\ index.html
ShortName	Returns the MS DOS-compliant name of the file.	index.htm
ShortPath	Returns the MS DOS-compliant path to the file.	C:\working\ index.htm
Size	Returns the byte size of the file.	45225
Type	Returns the file type.	Netscape Hypertext Document

Before you can examine file properties, you must reference the file through its related File object. You can then work with any of the file properties available. The following example shows how you can examine the size of a file:

VBScript	JScript
| ```
Set fs = CreateObject
  ("Scripting.FileSystemObject")
Set f = fs.GetFile("D:\index.htm")
fileSize = f.size
``` | ```
fs = new ActiveXObject
  ("Scripting.FileSystemObject");
var f = fs.GetFile("D:\\index.htm")
fileSize = f.size
``` |

One of the key properties you'll work with is Attributes. The value that is returned by the Attributes property is the combination of the related values for all the flags set for the file or folder. You can change file properties by setting Attributes to a new value or by adding and subtracting from its current value. With folders, however, you can only display attribute values.

Table 7-5 provides a complete list of Attribute values that can be used with files and folders. While read-only values cannot be changed, read/write values can be combined to set multiple attributes.

	Table 7-5 **Attribute Values for Files and Folders**	
Constant	**Value**	**Description**
Normal	0	A normal file with no attributes set.
ReadOnly	1	A read-only file. Attribute is read/write.
Hidden	2	A hidden file. Attribute is read/write.
System	4	A system file. Attribute is read/write.
Volume	8	A disk drive volume label. Attribute is read-only.
Directory	16	A folder or directory. Attribute is read-only.
Archive	32	A file with the archive bit set (meaning it has changed since last backup). Attribute is read/write.
Alias	64	A link or shortcut. Attribute is read-only.
Compressed	128	A compressed file. Attribute is read-only.

Changing read/write file attributes is easy. The following example sets the read-only flag for a file named log.txt:

VBScript	**JScript**

```
Set fs = CreateObject                  fs = new ActiveXObject
  ("Scripting.FileSystemObject")         ("Scripting.FileSystemObject");
Set f = fs.GetFile("D:\log.txt")       var f = fs.GetFile("D:\\log.txt")
f.Attributes = f.Attributes + 1        f.Attributes += 1
```

Now you may be wondering what would happen if the file was read-only already and you added one to its value. The result is unpredictable, but a hidden, read-only file (value 3) would become a system file (value 4). To ensure that you only set a particular flag—that is, if it's not set already—you can use an AND test. In Listing 7-6, the file is changed to read-only, but only if this flag isn't already set:

Listing 7-6: **Checking for attributes before making changes**

VBScript	JScript
attribs.vbs	**attribs.js**

```
Set f = fs.GetFile("D:\log.txt")
If f.Attributes and 1 Then


f.Attributes = f.Attributes + 1
End If
```

```
var f = fs.GetFile("D:\\log.txt")
if (f.Attributes && 1)
{
f.Attributes += 1
}
```

Creating files

So far, we've assumed that the file we want to work with exists on the user's system. However, this may not always be the case, so you may want to test for a file's existence before you try to work with it. To do this, use the `FileExists` method of `FileSystemObject`. This method returns True if the folder exists and False if not.

Listing 7-7 shows how you can test for a file's existence.

Listing 7-7: **Using FileExists**

VBScript	JScript
testfile.vbs	**testfile.js**

```
WScript.Echo
  CheckFile("C:\data.txt")
Function CheckFile(aFile)
Dim fs, s
  Set fs = CreateObject
("Scripting.FileSystemObject")
  If (fs.FileExists(aFile)) Then
    s = aFile & " is available."
  Else
    s = aFile & " doesn't exist."
  End If
CheckFile = s
End Function
```

```
WScript.Echo
  (CheckFile("C:\\data.txt"))
function CheckFile(aFile)
{
var fs, s = aFile;
fs = new ActiveXObject
  ("Scripting.FileSystemObject");
  if (fs.FileExists(aFile))
    s += " is available.";
  else
    s += " doesn't exist.";
  return(s);
}
```

VBScript	JScript
Output	Output
`C:\data.txt is available.`	`C:\data.txt is available.`

If a file you want to write to doesn't exist, you may want to create it. To do this, you can use the CreateTextFile method of the FileSystemObject. The main argument for this method is a string containing the path to the file you want to create:

VBScript	JScript

<pre>Set fs = CreateObject
  ("Scripting.FileSystemObject")
Set aFile = fs.CreateTextFile
  ("d:\data\data.txt")</pre>
	<pre>var fs = new ActiveXObject
	  ("Scripting.FileSystemObject");
	var aFile = fs.CreateTextFile
	  ("d:\\data\\data.txt");</pre>

The Folder object also has a CreateTextFile method. With the Folder object, you specify only the filename rather than a complete path, like this:

VBScript	JScript

<pre>Set fs = CreateObject
  ("Scripting.FileSystemObject")
Set f = fs.GetFolder("D:\data")
Set aFile =
  f.CreateTextFile("data.txt")</pre>
	<pre>var fs = new ActiveXObject
	  ("Scripting.FileSystemObject");
	var f = fs.GetFolder("D:\\data")
	var aFile =
	  f.CreateTextFile("data.txt");</pre>

The CreateTextFile method returns a TextStream object that you can use to work with the newly created file. If you try to create a file with the same name and path as an existing file, an error occurs. By default, CreateTextFile won't overwrite an existing file. You can change this behavior by setting the overwrite flag, like this:

VBScript	JScript

<pre>Set aFile = f.CreateTextFile
  ("data.txt", True)</pre>
	<pre>var aFile = f.CreateTextFile
	  ("data.txt", "True");</pre>

Another default behavior of the CreateTextFile method is to create files in ASCII text mode. You can also set Unicode mode and to do this, you need to set the Unicode flag to True, like this:

VBScript	JScript
```Set aFile = f.CreateTextFile ("data.txt", False, True)```	```var aFile = f.CreateTextFile ("data.txt", "False", "True");```

Tip   You cannot skip the overwrite flag when you set the Unicode flag. Instead, set the overwrite flag to True or False explicitly and then set the Unicode flag.

Copying, moving, and deleting files

You can manage files using methods of FileSystemObject or methods of the File object. Use FileSystemObject methods when you want to work with multiple files. Use the File object when you want to work with individual files.

Issues for multiple files

FileSystemObject methods for copying, moving, and deleting files are:

✦ DeleteFile

✦ CopyFile

✦ MoveFile

Using DeleteFile

You can use the DeleteFile method to delete one or more files. When you use this method, specify the path to the file you want to delete and optionally force the method to delete read-only files. Delete one file by specifying an absolute path, such as C:\working\data.txt. Delete multiple files by using wildcards in the file-name. For example, you can delete all .txt files in C:\working as follows:

VBScript	JScript
```Set fs = CreateObject ("Scripting.FileSystemObject") fs.DeleteFile "C:\working*.txt"```	```var fs = new ActiveXObject ("Scripting.FileSystemObject"); fs.DeleteFile("C:\\working*.txt");```

The `DeleteFile` method deletes only read-only files when you set the force flag to True, like this:

VBScript	JScript
```fs.DeleteFile "C:\working\data.txt",True```	```fs.DeleteFile ("C:\\working\\data.txt", "True");```

Note

If `DeleteFile` encounters a read-only file and you haven't set the force flag, the operation stops and no other files are deleted.

Using CopyFile

The `CopyFile` method copies one or more files to a new location. To copy a single file, specify the absolute path to the file you want to copy and then the destination path. For example, you can copy C:\working\data.txt to D:\backup\data.txt as follows:

VBScript	JScript
```Set fs = CreateObject ("Scripting.FileSystemObject") fs.CopyFile "C:\working\data.txt", "D:\backup\data.txt"```	```var fs = new ActiveXObject ("Scripting.FileSystemObject"); fs.CopyFile("C:\\working\\data.txt", "D:\\backup\\data.txt");```

You can copy multiple files by using wildcards in the file name as well. For example, to copy all .html files from C:\working to D:\webdata you can use the following code:

VBScript	JScript
```Set fs = CreateObject ("Scripting.FileSystemObject") fs.CopyFile "C:\working*.html", "D:\webdata"```	```var fs = new ActiveXObject ("Scripting.FileSystemObject"); fs.CopyFile("C:\\working*.html", "D:\\webdata");```

You can also use `CopyFile` to copy files between directories that already exist. For example if both C:\working and D:\data exist, you can copy files from C:\working to D:\data. However, when you do this, there are several rules you must follow. If the files you are copying exist at the destination, an error occurs and the copy operation stops. To force the method to overwrite existing files, set the overwrite flag to True, like this:

VBScript	JScript
```fs.CopyFile "C:\working*.txt", "D:\data", True```	```fs.CopyFile("C:\\working*.txt", "D:\\data", "True");```

CopyFile will not write into a read-only directory and it will not write over read-only files either. You cannot change this behavior with the overwrite flag.

Using MoveFile

If you want to move one or more files to a new location, use MoveFile. To move a single file, specify the absolute path to the file as the source and then set the destination path. For example, you can move C:\data.txt to D:\work\data.txt as follows:

VBScript	JScript
| ```
Set fs = CreateObject
    ("Scripting.FileSystemObject")
fs.MoveFile "C:\data.txt",
    "D:\work\data.txt"
``` | ```
var fs = new ActiveXObject
    ("Scripting.FileSystemObject");
fs.MoveFile("C:\\data.txt",
    "D:\\work\\data.txt");
``` |

To move multiple files, you can use wildcards. For example, if you want to move all .txt files from C:\working to D:\backup, you can use the following code:

VBScript	JScript
| ```
Set fs = CreateObject
    ("Scripting.FileSystemObject")
fs.MoveFile "C:\working\*.txt",
    "D:\backup"
``` | ```
var fs = new ActiveXObject
    ("Scripting.FileSystemObject");
fs.MoveFile("C:\\working\\*.txt",
    "D:\\backup");
``` |

You can also use MoveFile to move files to an existing directory. For example if both C:\working and D:\data exist, you can move all .html files from C:\working to D:\data, like this:

VBScript	JScript
| ```
fs.MoveFile "C:\working\*.HTML",
    "D:\data"
``` | ```
fs.MoveFile("C:\\working\\*.HTML",
    "D:\\data");
``` |

Note   If you specify the last element of the destination path as a folder separator (\), the MoveFile method assumes the destination folder exists and will not create it if it is necessary to do so. Also, the move operation will not overwrite existing files. In such a case, the move fails the first time it tries to overwrite.

Issues for individual files

With the File object, the methods for copying, moving, and deleting files are:

✦ Delete

✦ Copy

✦ Move

Note You cannot use wildcards when copying, moving, or deleting individual files.

Using Delete

The Delete method of the File object deletes a file and can also force the deletion of a read-only file. This method works with a specific File object reference and, as a result, you can delete a file just by calling the method, like this:

VBScript	*JScript*
Set fs = CreateObject ("Scripting.FileSystemObject") Set f = fs.GetFile ("C:\working\data.txt") f.Delete	var fs = new ActiveXObject ("Scripting.FileSystemObject"); var f = fs.GetFile ("C:\\working\\data.txt"); f.Delete()

If the file is read-only, you must set the force flag to True, like this:

VBScript	*JScript*
f.Delete True	f.Delete("True")

Using Copy

The Copy method copies a file to a new location. With Copy, you must obtain a File object and then set the destination path for the file in the Copy method. For example, you can copy C:\data.txt to D:\data\data.txt as follows:

VBScript	*JScript*
Set fs = CreateObject ("Scripting.FileSystemObject") Set f = fs.GetFile("C:\data.txt") f.Copy "D:\data\data.txt"	var fs = new ActiveXObject ("Scripting.FileSystemObject"); var f = fs.GetFile("C:\\data.txt"); f.Copy("D:\\data\\data.txt");

As with `CopyFile`, you can also use the `Copy` method to copy over an existing file. To do this, you must set the overwrite flag to True, like this:

VBScript	JScript
`f.Copy "D:\data\data.txt", True`	`f.Copy("D:\\data\\data.txt", "True");`

Note   If you try to overwrite a file and don't set the overwrite flag to True, an error occurs and the copy operation fails.

Using Move

Use the `Move` method to move a file to a new location. Before you use `Move`, you must first obtain a `File` object and then you can set the destination path for the file in the `Move` method. You can move C:\data.txt to D:\work\data.txt as follows:

VBScript	JScript

`Set fs = CreateObject`
`  ("Scripting.FileSystemObject")`
`Set f = fs.GetFile("C:\data.txt")`
`f.Move "D:\work\data.txt "`
	`var fs = new ActiveXObject`
	`  ("Scripting.FileSystemObject");`
	`var f = fs.GetFile("C:\\data.txt");`
	`f.Move("D:\\work\\data.txt");`

Note   You cannot use `Move` to overwrite an existing file.

Summary

As you've seen in this chapter, the `FileSystemObject` is used to manipulate files and folders. File and folder operations you can perform include create, copy, move, and delete. You can examine folder and file information as well. In the next chapter, you learn how to read and write files.

✦   ✦   ✦

Reading and Writing Files

Now that you know how to manage files and folders, you're ready to take a closer look at manipulating the contents of files. Many different methods and properties are available for working with files. But before you can work with a file, you need to open it for reading, writing, or appending.

Opening Files

Two methods are provided for opening files. You can use the OpenTextFile method of FileSystemObject or the OpenAsTextStream method of the File object. While both methods return a TextStream object, they are used in slightly different ways.

Using OpenTextFile

The OpenTextFile method expects to be passed the full path to the file you want to open, such as:

VBScript	JScript
```Set fs = CreateObject ("Scripting. FileSystemObject") Set ts = fs.OpenTextFile ("D:\data\log.txt")```	```var fs = new ActiveXObject ("Scripting. FileSystemObject"); var ts = fs.OpenTextFile ("D:\\data\\log.txt")```

If you plan to work with the file, you should set the access mode as well. Three access modes are provided:

✦ 1 — Opens a file for reading. Associated constant is ForReading.

✦ 2 — Opens a file for writing to the beginning of the file. Associated constant is ForWriting.

✦ 8 — Opens a file for appending (writing to the end of the file). Associated constant is ForAppending.

As you can see, the access modes are designed for specific tasks, such as reading, writing, or appending. You must use the appropriate mode for the task you want to perform and then close the file before performing a different task. For example, if you want to write to a file, you must open it in ForWriting mode. Later, if you want to read from the file, you must close it and then open it in ForReading mode.

Beyond access modes, you can also specify that you want to create the referenced file if it doesn't already exist and set the file's format mode. To create a file if it doesn't exist, set the create flag to True. Otherwise, the file isn't created and an error may occur. To set a file's format mode, use one of these values:

✦ -2 — Opens the file using the system default. Associated constant is TristateUseDefault.

✦ -1 — Opens the file as Unicode. Associated constant is TristateTrue.

✦ 0 — Opens the file as ASCII. Associated constant is TristateFalse.

Listing 8-1 opens a file in ForWriting mode. If the file doesn't exist, it is created automatically, which is handy, as you don't have to test for the file with FileExists. The file is also set to ASCII text mode, which is the default mode on most systems. The listing also creates an extensive set of constants for working with files. Use constants when you want your scripts to be easy to read.

Using OpenAsTextStream

The OpenAsTextStream method is used much like OpenTextFile. The key differences are that you already have a file reference, so you don't have to set a file path, and you cannot set a create flag. Other than that, the methods are identical. Listing 8-2 shows how you can open an ASCII text file in ForReading mode.

Reading Text Files

You can read from a text file only when you open it in the ForReading access mode. Once you open the file for reading, you can read information for the file in several different ways. You can read the entire contents of the file, character strings from the file, or you can read lines of information from the file.

Listing 8-1: **Using OpenTextFile**

VBScript	JScript
usefile.vbs	**usefile.js**

```
Const ForReading = 1                ForReading = 1
Const ForWriting = 2                ForWriting = 2
Const ForAppending = 8              ForAppending = 8
Const TristateUseDefault = -2       TristateUseDefault = -2
Const TristateTrue = -1             TristateTrue = -1
Const TristateFalse = 0             TristateFalse = 0

Set fs = CreateObject               var fs = new ActiveXObject
  ("Scripting.FileSystemObject")      ("Scripting.FileSystemObject");
Set ts = fs.OpenTextFile            var ts = fs.OpenTextFile
  ("D:\data\log.txt", ForWriting,     ("D:\\data\\log.txt",ForWriting,
   True, TristateFalse)                "True", TristateFalse)
```

Listing 8-2: **Using OpenAsTextStream**

VBScript	JScript
usestream.vbs	**usestream.js**

```
Const ForReading = 1                ForReading = 1
Const TristateFalse = 0             TristateFalse = 0

Set fs = CreateObject               var fs = new ActiveXObject
  ("Scripting.FileSystemObject")      ("Scripting.FileSystemObject");
Set f =                             var f =
  fs.GetFile("D:\data\log.txt")       fs.GetFile("D:\\data\\log.txt");
Set ts =                            var ts =
  f.OpenAsTextStream                  f.OpenAsTextStream
    (ForReading, TristateFalse)          (ForReading, TristateFalse)
```

Preparing to read

Just because you can open a file doesn't mean it contains any information. There-fore, before you try to read the file, you should verify that it contains information. To do this, you can use the AtEndOfStream property of the TextStream object. The AtEndOfStream property returns True when you are at the end of a file and False otherwise. If the file exists but is empty, the AtEndOfStream property returns True immediately after you open the file.

You should also use the AtEndOfStream property to test for the end-of-file marker prior to reading additional information from a file. One way to test for an empty file and to check for the end-of-file marker prior to reading it is to use a Do While loop as shown in Listing 8-3.

Listing 8-3: **Using AtEndOfStream**

VBScript	JScript
checkeos.vbs	checkeos.js

```
Const ForReading = 1
Const TristateFalse = 0

Set fs = CreateObject
  ("Scripting.FileSystemObject")
Set f =
  fs.GetFile("D:\data\log.txt")
Set ts = f.OpenAsTextStream
  (ForReading, TristateFalse)
Do While theFile.AtEndOfStream <> True
  'Read from the file
Loop
```

```
ForReading = 1
TristateFalse = 0

var fs = new ActiveXObject
  ("Scripting.FileSystemObject");
var f =
  fs.GetFile("D:\\data\\log.txt");
var ts = f.OpenAsTextStream
  (ForReading, TristateFalse)
while (!f.AtEndOfStream) {
  //Read from the file
}
```

Another helpful property is AtEndOfLine, which returns True if you've reached an end-of-line marker. This property is useful if you are reading characters from files where fields or data records are stored on individual lines. Here, you read from the file until the end of line is reached, at which point you know you've reached the end of a field or record. An example using AtEndOfLine is shown here:

VBScript	JScript

```
Do While theFile.AtEndOfLine <> True
  'Read characters from the file
Loop
```

```
while (!f.AtEndOfLine) {
  //Read characters from the file
}
```

Your window into text files is gained through column and line pointers. The column pointer indicates the current column position within a file. The line pointer indicates the current line position within a file. To check the value of these pointers, use the Column and Line properties of the TextStream object, respectively.

After opening a file, the column and line pointers are both set to 1. This means you are at column 1, line 1. If you then read in a line from the file, you are at column 1, line 2. If you read 10 characters from a file without advancing to the next line, you are at column 11, line 1. Being able to check the column and line position is very useful when you work with fixed-length records or you want to examine specific lines of data.

Listing 8-4 shows how you could check the column and line position at various stages of reading a file. You'll find more pointers for using these properties later in this chapter.

Listing 8-4: **Using the Column and Line properties**

VBScript	**JScript**
fpointers.vbs	**fpointers.js**

```
Const ForReading = 1
Const TristateFalse = 0

Set fs = CreateObject
  ("Scripting.FileSystemObject")
Set f =
  fs.GetFile("D:\data\log.txt")
Set ts = f.OpenAsTextStream
  (ForReading, TristateFalse)
currColumn = f.Column
currLine = f.Line

WScript.Echo "Position is: Column " &
  currColumn & " Line " & currLine
```

```
ForReading = 1
TristateFalse = 0

var fs = new ActiveXObject
  ("Scripting.FileSystemObject");
var f =
  fs.GetFile("D:\\data\\log.txt");
var ts = f.OpenAsTextStream
  (ForReading, TristateFalse)
currColumn = f.Column
currLine = f.Line

WScript.Echo("Position is: Column " +
  currColumn + " Line " + currLine)
```

You can read from a file using any of these three methods:

✦ Read(x) — Reads x number of characters from a file.

✦ ReadLine — Reads a line of text from a file.

✦ ReadAll — Reads the entire contents of a file.

Whether you read in a file all at once, a few characters at a time, or line by line depends on the type of information the file contains. If the file contains fixed-length records or is written as a single line of data, you'll usually want to use Read or ReadAll. If the file contains lines of data and each line ends with an end-of-line marker, you'll usually want to use ReadLine or ReadAll.

Reading characters

You use the Read method to read a specific number of characters from a file. The read begins at the current column position and continues until the number of characters specified is reached. Because you want to maintain the information returned from Read, assign the return value to a variable. Listing 8-5 shows how you can open a file and read 20 characters.

Listing 8-5: **Reading characters from a file**

VBScript	*JScript*
readchars.vbs	**readchars.js**

```
Const ForReading = 1
Const TristateFalse = 0

Set fs = CreateObject
   ("Scripting.FileSystemObject")
Set f = fs.OpenTextFile
   ("D:\data\log.txt",
   ForReading, True)
returnValue = f.Read(20)
```

```
ForReading = 1
TristateFalse = 0

var fs = new ActiveXObject
   ("Scripting.FileSystemObject");
var f = fs.OpenTextFile
   ("D:\\data\\log.txt",
   ForReading, "True")
returnValue = f.Read(20)
```

The Read method doesn't stop at end-of-line markers. Instead, the method reads the individual characters that make up this marker as one or two characters (either carriage return, or carriage return and line feed). To have the Read method stop when the end of the line is reached, you should read one character at a time and test for the end-of-line before each successive read, like this:

VBScript	*JScript*

```
Do While theFile.AtEndOfLine <> True
val = val + theFile.Read(1)
Loop
```

```
while (!theFile.AtEndOfLine)    {
val += theFile.Read(1);
}
```

Reading lines

For files written using lines, you can use the ReadLine method to read a line from the file. As with the Read method, you store the value returned by the ReadLine method in a variable so you can use the results. An example is shown as Listing 8-6.

Note When you read files that include end-of-line designators, you normally use `ReadLine` rather than `Read`. If, however, you read the first 20 characters in a line without reaching the end-of-line designator and then issued a `ReadLine` command, the `ReadLine` method would read from the current pointer position to the end of the current line.

Listing 8-6: **Using ReadLine**

VBScript	*JScript*
readlines.vbs	readlines.js

```
Const ForReading = 1
Const TristateFalse = 0

Set fs = CreateObject
  ("Scripting.FileSystemObject")
Set f = fs.OpenTextFile
  ("D:\data\log.txt", ForReading,
  True)
theLine = f.ReadLine
```

```
ForReading = 1
TristateFalse = 0

var fs = new ActiveXObject
  ("Scripting.FileSystemObject");
var f = fs.OpenTextFile
  ("D:\\data\\log.txt", ForReading,
  "True")
theLine = f.ReadLine()
```

Unless you know that each line of a file has a fixed length, you probably won't use the `Column` pointer in conjunction with the `ReadLine` method. Instead, you'll use the individual lines of data to move around within the file. Let's say you want to extract data from a file five lines at a time. To do this, you can open the file for reading and then use a loop to advance through the file as is shown in Listing 8-7.

Listing 8-7: **Reading data sets with ReadLine**

VBScript	*JScript*
readdatasets.vbs	readdatasets.js

```
Const TristateFalse = 0
count = 5
dataSet = 0

Set fs = CreateObject
  ("Scripting.FileSystemObject")
Set f = fs.OpenTextFile
  ("D:\data.txt", ForReading, True)
```

```
TristateFalse = 0
count = 5
dataSet = 0

var fs = new ActiveXObject
  ("Scripting.FileSystemObject");
var f = fs.OpenTextFile
  ("D:\\data.txt", ForReading, "True")
```

Continued

Listing 8-7 *(continued)*

VBScript	JScript
| ```
Do While f.AtEndOfStream <> True
 data = ""
 For a = 1 to count
  If f.AtEndOfStream <> True Then
   data = data + f.ReadLine
  End If
 Next
 dataSet = dataSet + 1
 WScript.Echo "Data Set " & dataSet
   & ": " & data
Loop
``` | ```
while (!f.AtEndOfStream) {
 var data = ""
 for (a = 0; a < count; a++) {
  if (!f.AtEndOfStream) {
   data += f.ReadLine()
  }
 }
 dataSet++
 WScript.Echo("Data Set " + dataSet +
   ": " + data)
}
``` |

Reading an entire file

The ReadAll method allows you to read in the entire contents of a file and is useful if you want to manipulate the file contents all at once, or display the contents to a user. Listing 8-8 shows how you can read in the contents of a file and display the results in a pop-up dialog box.

Listing 8-8: **Using ReadAll**

VBScript	JScript
readfile.vbs	**readfile.js**
| ```
Const ForReading = 1

Set fs = CreateObject
  ("Scripting.FileSystemObject")
Set f = fs.OpenTextFile
  ("D:\data.txt", ForReading, True)
fContents = f.ReadAll
f.Close

Set w = WScript.CreateObject
  ("WScript.Shell")
a = w.Popup
  (fContents,60,"Display File",1)
``` | ```
ForReading = 1

var fs = new ActiveXObject
  ("Scripting.FileSystemObject");
var f = fs.OpenTextFile
  ("D:\\data.txt", ForReading, "True")
fContents = f.ReadAll()
f.Close()

var w = WScript.CreateObject
  ("WScript.Shell");
a = w.Popup
  (fContents,60,"Display File",1)
``` |

Skipping Lines in a File

Skipping characters and lines are common tasks you'll want to perform when you read from a file. To do this, you can use these methods:

✦ Skip(*x*) — Skips *x* number of characters.

✦ SkipLine — Skips one line of text.

You cannot skip characters in a file you open to write in or append. In the ForWriting mode, the file is initialized and any existing contents are deleted. In the ForAppending mode, the file pointer is set to the end of the file, so there are no characters to skip.

Skipping characters

In a file you are reading, you can set the number of characters to skip when you call the Skip method. In Listing 8-9, you skip the first 30 characters and then read the next 30 characters.

Listing 8-9: **Working with Skip**

VBScript	JScript
skipchars.vbs	**skipchars.js**

```
Const ForReading = 1

Set fs = CreateObject
  ("Scripting.FileSystemObject")
Set f = fs.OpenTextFile
  ("D:\data.txt", ForReading, True)
f.Skip(30)
record = f.Read(30)
```

```
ForReading = 1

var fs = new ActiveXObject
  ("Scripting.FileSystemObject");
var f = fs.OpenTextFile
  ("D:\\data.txt", ForReading, "True")
f.Skip(30)
record = f.Read(30)
```

Note
The SkipLine method looks for the end-of-line designator to determine when it has reached the end of a line. So if you called the method after reading part of a line with the Read method, but before reaching the end of the line, SkipLine would find the end-of-line designator for the current line and then set the pointer to the beginning of the next line.

Skipping lines

The SkipLine method is also pretty straightforward. Each time you call the method, it skips one line in a file. It does this by looking for the next occurrence of the end-of-line designator. If you know the first three lines of a file have comments that you don't want to use in a data set, you can skip them as follows:

VBScript	JScript
| ```
For a = 1 to 3
  If f.AtEndOfStream <> True Then
    f.SkipLine
  End If
Next
``` | ```
for (a = 0; a < 3; a++) {
  if (!f.AtEndOfStream) {
    f.SkipLine()
  }
}
``` |

Writing to a File

You can write to text files using the ForWriting and the ForAppending modes. The access mode determines the initial position of the pointer within the file. With the ForWriting mode, the file is initialized, erasing any existing data. The pointer is then set at the beginning of the file. With ForAppending mode, the pointer is set to the end of the file and any data you write is added to the existing data in the file.

Preparing to write

While you may want to overwrite temporary data files, you probably don't want to inadvertently overwrite other types of files. If you have any doubts about whether a file exists, you should use the FileExists method to check for the file before trying to access it in ForWriting mode. The FileExists method returns True if the file exists and False if it does not exist. As shown in Listing 8-10, you can use the results of the FileExists test to determine whether you open a file in the ForWriting mode or the ForAppending mode.

Listing 8-10: **Setting mode based on FileExists**

VBScript	JScript
setmode.vbs	setmode.js
| ```
Const ForWriting = 2
Const ForAppending = 8

aFile = "C:\data.txt"
Set fs = CreateObject
  ("Scripting.FileSystemObject")
``` | ```
ForWriting = 2
ForAppending = 8

aFile = "C:\\data.txt"
var fs = new ActiveXObject
  ("Scripting.FileSystemObject");
``` |

```
If (fs.FileExists(aFile)) Then        if (fs.FileExists(aFile))
   Set f = fs.OpenTextFile              var f = fs.OpenTextFile
     (aFile, ForAppending)                 (aFile, ForAppending)
Else                                  else
   Set f = fs.OpenTextFile              var f = fs.OpenTextFile
     (aFile, ForWriting, True)             (aFile, ForWriting, "True")
End If
```

When you are finished writing to a file, you should close the file by calling the
Close method. Close writes the end-of-file marker to the file and releases the file.
You are then free to open the file in a different mode, such as ForReading. You
close a file as follows:

VBScript	**JScript**
f.Close	f.Close()

Caution

Closing a file after a write is essential. If you forget to do this, the end-of-file
marker may not be written to the file and this may cause problems when trying to
read the file later.

Writing to a new file or appending data to the end of an existing file is fairly easy.
You start by creating a TextStream object. Afterward, you open the file for writing
or appending, then write to the file. Regardless of which write-related method you use,
the write begins at the pointer position set when the file was opened (which is either
the beginning or end of the file). You can write to a file using any of these methods:

✦ Write(x) — Writes x number of characters to a file.

✦ WriteLine — Writes a line of text to a file.

✦ WriteBlankLines(n) — Writes n blank lines to a file.

Writing characters

The Write method writes strings to a file. You set the string to write when you call
the Write method, like this:

VBScript	**JScript**
Set fs = CreateObject ("Scripting.FileSystemObject") Set f = fs.OpenTextFile (aFile, ForAppending) f.Write theData f.Close	var fs = new ActiveXObject ("Scripting.FileSystemObject"); var f = fs.OpenTextFile (aFile, ForAppending) f.Write(theData) f.Close()

Writing lines

The `WriteLine` method is used to write lines of data to a file. The runtime engine terminates lines with an end-of-line marker (the carriage return and line-feed characters). You can use the `WriteLine` method as follows:

VBScript	JScript
```Set fs = CreateObject ("Scripting.FileSystemObject") Set f = fs.OpenTextFile (aFile, ForAppending) f.WriteLine theLine f.Close```	```var fs = new ActiveXObject ("Scripting.FileSystemObject"); var f = fs.OpenTextFile (aFile, ForAppending) f.WriteLine(theLine) f.Close()```

Writing blank lines

The `WriteBlankLines` method is used to write blank lines to a file. The only contents on a blank line are end-of-line markers (the carriage return and line-feed characters). When you call the `WriteBlankLines` method, you set the number of blank lines to add to the file, such as 3 or 5.

Normally, you'll use this method in conjunction with `WriteLine`, like this:

VBScript	JScript
```Set fs = CreateObject ("Scripting.FileSystemObject") Set f = fs.OpenTextFile (aFile, ForAppending) f.WriteLine theHeaderLine f.WriteBlankLines 1 f.WriteLine theDataLine f.WriteBlankLines 1 f.WriteLine theFooterLine```	```var fs = new ActiveXObject ("Scripting.FileSystemObject"); var f = fs.OpenTextFile (aFile, ForAppending) f.WriteLine(theHeaderLine) f.WriteBlankLines(1) f.WriteLine(theDataLine) f.WriteBlankLines(1) f.WriteLine(theFooterLine)```

Writing a blank line to a file is useful when you are managing text files, such as logs or flat-file databases in which multiple blank lines serve as record separators. But keep in mind that blank lines usually aren't shown in HTML documents. To create a blank line in an HTML document, you'll need to insert an empty paragraph element. You'll learn more about using scripts to create HTML documents in other chapters. Using Internet Explorer with scripts is covered in Chapter 19.

Summary

Reading and writing files is one of the fundamental tasks that you'll need to master. As you set out to create your own scripts to read and write files, don't forget the essential lessons learned from this chapter. You open files for reading, writing, and appending using `ForReading`, `ForWriting`, and `ForAppending`. Then, once you have the file open in the appropriate mode, you can read, write, or skip within the file.

✦   ✦   ✦

Managing Drives and Printers

This chapter completes our look at managing the file system and then moves on to examine managing network resources. You'll learn how to work with drives and how to examine drive properties. You'll also learn how to map network drives and configure network printer connections.

Managing Drives

Two different ways of working with drives are available. You can work with a specific drive, such as the C: drive, or you can work with drive collections. *Drive collections* are containers for all of the local and network drives on a particular system.

Obtaining Drive Information

Most functions that work with drives allow you to reference drive paths in any of these ways:

✦ By drive letter, such as C or D

✦ By drive path, such as C:\ or D:\

✦ By network share path, such as \\PLUTO\MYSHARE or \\SATURN\DATA

Most network drives have a drive designator associated with them as well as a path. For example, the network drive \\PLUTO\MYSHARE may be mapped on the system as the H: drive. You can obtain a drive designator for a network drive using the GetDriveName method of FileSystemObject. This method expects to be passed a drive path and can be used as follows:

VBScript	JScript
| ```
Set fs = CreateObject
  ("Scripting.FileSystemObject")
d = fs.GetDriveName ("\\PLUTO\DATA")
WScript.Echo d
``` | ```
fs = new ActiveXObject
  ("Scripting.FileSystemObject");
d = fs.GetDriveName("\\PLUTO\\DATA")
WScript.Echo (d)
``` |

Checking for a drive

You'll usually want to test for a drive's existence before you try to work with it. To do this, you can use the DriveExists method of FileSystemObject. This method returns True if a drive exists and can be used (shown in Listing 9-1).

Listing 9-1: **Checking for a drive**

VBScript	JScript
testdrive.vbs	**testdrive.js**
| ```
WScript.Echo CheckDrive("C")
Function CheckDrive(drv)

Dim fs, s
  Set fs = CreateObject
    ("Scripting.FileSystemObject")
  If (fs.DriveExists(drv)) Then
    s = drv & " is available."
  Else
    s = drv & " doesn't exist."
  End If
 CheckDrive = s
End Function
``` | ```
WScript.Echo (CheckDrive("C"))
function CheckDrive(drv)
{
var fs, s = drv;
fs = new ActiveXObject
  ("Scripting.FileSystemObject");
  if (fs.DriveExists(drv))
    s += " is available.";
  else
    s += " doesn't exist.";

  return(s);
}
``` |
| **Output** | **Output** |
| `C is available.` | `C is available.` |

Using the Drive object

After checking for a drive's existence, one of the most common tasks you'll want to perform is to obtain a Drive object. You can then use this object to check drive properties.

To obtain a `Drive` object, use the `GetDrive` method of `FileSystemObject`. The main argument for this method is a string containing the path to the drive you want to work with, such as:

VBScript	JScript

`Set fs = CreateObject`
  `("Scripting.FileSystemObject")`
`Set drv = fs.GetDrive("D")`
	`var fs = new ActiveXObject`
	  `("Scripting.FileSystemObject");`
	`var drv = fs.GetDrive("D")`

Once you have a `Drive` object, you can examine its properties. To do this, use the `Drive` object properties summarized in Table 9-1.

Table 9-1
Properties of the Drive Object

Property	Description	Sample Value
AvailableSpace	Returns the amount of available space on the drive in bytes. This is a per-user value that can be affected by quotas.	632116580
DriveLetter	Returns the drive letter without a colon.	C
DriveType	Returns the drive type as an integer value. 0 for Unknown, 1 for Removable, 2 for Fixed, 3 for Network, 4 for CD-ROM, and 5 for RAM Disk.	2
FileSystem	Returns the file system type such as FAT, FAT32, NFTS, or CDFS.	NTFS
FreeSpace	Returns the total amount of free space on the drive.	1275478
IsReady	For removable-media drives and CD-ROM drives, returns `True` if the drive is ready.	True
Path	Returns the drive path.	C:\
RootFolder	Returns a `Folder` object containing the root folder on the specified drive.	-
SerialNumber	With removable media, returns the serial number of the media.	329941809
ShareName	With network drives, returns the network share name.	work
TotalSize	Returns the total size of the drive in bytes.	128282853399
VolumeName	Returns the volume name of the drive.	Primary

One of the most useful drive properties is `FreeSpace`. You can use this property to help you keep track of system resources throughout the network. For example, you can create a script that runs as a periodically scheduled job on your key servers, such as your email and file servers. When the script runs, it logs the free space on system drives. If any of the drives has less free space than is desirable, you can log a warning that the drive is getting low on space as well.

Cross-Reference Because the DriveInfo.js script may run through the Task scheduler, you'll need to map the drives you want to use to the network. Mapping network drives is covered later in this chapter.

Listing 9-2 shows an example script for displaying drive information. You can use this script to obtain summary information for a specific drive. Using the `Drive` collection, you could extend the script to obtain a report for all drives on a system.

Listing 9-2: **Obtaining drive information**

driveinfo.js

```
drvpath = "C"
WScript.Echo(GetDriveInfo(drvpath))

function GetDriveInfo(drvpath)
{
  var fs, d, s, t, wnet, cname;

  wNet = WScript.CreateObject ("WScript.Network");
  cname = wNet.ComputerName;

  fs = new ActiveXObject("Scripting.FileSystemObject");
  d = fs.GetDrive(drvpath);
  switch (d.DriveType)
  {
    case 0: t = "Unknown"; break;
    case 1: t = "Removable"; break;
    case 2: t = "Fixed"; break;
    case 3: t = "Network"; break;
    case 4: t = "CD-ROM"; break;
    case 5: t = "RAM Disk"; break;
  }
  s = "==========================" + "\r\n";
  s += cname + "\r\n";
  s += "==========================" + "\r\n";
  s += "Drive " + d.DriveLetter + ": - " + t;
  s += " - " + d.FileSystem + "\r\n";
  if (d.VolumeName)
```

```
  s += "Volume: " + d.VolumeName + "\r\n"
 if (d.ShareName)
  s += " Share: " + d.ShareName + "\r\n"
 s += "Total space " + Math.round(d.TotalSize/1048576)
 s += " Mbytes" + "\r\n";
 s += "Free Space: " + Math.round(d.FreeSpace/1048576)
 s += " Mbytes" + "\r\n";
 s += "=========================" + "\r\n";
 return(s);
}
```

Output

```
=========================
PLUTO
=========================
Drive C: - Fixed - FAT
Volume: Primary
Total space 2047 Mbytes
Free Space: 557 Mbytes
=========================
```

The drive information script uses a few new techniques. First of all, a `Switch Case` structure is used to convert the integer value returned by `DriveType` to a string:

```
switch (d.DriveType)
   {
     case 0: t = "Unknown"; break;
     case 1: t = "Removable"; break;
     case 2: t = "Fixed"; break;
     case 3: t = "Network"; break;
     case 4: t = "CD-ROM"; break;
     case 5: t = "RAM Disk"; break;
   }
```

Next, the script builds the output by concatenating a series of strings. Tucked away in these strings is a function that converts the byte values returned by `TotalSize` and `FreeSpace` to a value in megabytes. The bytes to megabytes conversion is handled by dividing the return value by 1,048,576, which is the number of bytes in a megabyte. The result is then rounded to the nearest integer value using the `Math.round()` method. In the script, this results in:

```
s += "Total space " + Math.round(d.TotalSize/1048576)
s += " Mbytes" + "\r\n";
s += "Free Space: " + Math.round(d.FreeSpace/1048576)
```

Examining all drives on a system

The easiest way to examine all drives on a system is to use the Drives collection. You work with the Drives collection much like any other collection discussed in this book. In VBScript, you obtain the collection, then use a For Each loop to examine its contents. In JScript, you obtain the collection through an Enumerator object and then use the methods of the Enumerator object to examine each drive in turn.

Listing 9-3 shows a sample script that works with the Drives collection. The output provided is a partial listing of drives from my system. Note that the A: drive is a floppy drive. Because the drive didn't contain a disk when checked, the drive wasn't ready for certain tasks, such as reading the volume name or obtaining the amount of free space.

Listing 9-3: **Working with the Drives collection**

VBScript

checkdrives.vbs

```vbscript
WScript.Echo GetDriveList()

Function GetDriveList
'Initialize variables
Dim fs, d, dc, s, n, CRLF
'Specify EOL designator
  CRLF = Chr(13) & Chr(10)
  Set fs = CreateObject
    ("Scripting.FileSystemObject")
  Set dc = fs.Drives

  For Each d in dc

    n = ""
    s = s & d.DriveLetter & " - "
    If d.DriveType = Remote Then
      n = d.ShareName
    ElseIf d.IsReady Then
      n = d.VolumeName
    End If

    s = s & n & CRLF
  Next
  GetDriveList = s
End Function
```

JScript

checkdrives.js

```jscript
WScript.Echo(GetDriveList())

function GetDriveList()
{
\\Initialize variables
  var fs, s, n, e, d;

  fs = new ActiveXObject
    ("Scripting.FileSystemObject");
  e = new Enumerator(fs.Drives);
  s = "";
  for (; !e.atEnd(); e.moveNext())
  {
    d = e.item();
    s = s + d.DriveLetter + " - " ;
    if (d.DriveType == 3)
      n = d.ShareName;
    else if (d.IsReady)
      n = d.VolumeName;
    else
      n = "(Drive not ready)";
    s +=  n + "\r\n";
  }
  return(s);
}
```

VBScript	JScript

Output	Output
| ```
A - (Drive Not Ready)
C - PRIMARY
D - SECONDARY
E - MICRON
``` | ```
A - (Drive Not Ready)
C - PRIMARY
D - SECONDARY
E - MICRON
``` |

Mapping Network Drives

Network drives allow users and scripts to access remote resources on the network. If you are using a script to configure network drives for a particular user, you should log in as this user and then run the script, or have the user log in and then run the script. This ensures that the network drives are configured as necessary in the user's profile. On the other hand, if you are using a network drive in a script, such as a script that runs as a scheduled job, you should connect to the drive, use the drive, and then disconnect from the drive.

Connecting to a network share

Network shares aren't automatically available to users or to scripts. You must specifically map a network share to a network drive before it is available. In Windows scripts, you map network drives using the MapNetworkDrive method of the Network object. The basic structure for this method requires the drive letter to map the name of the network share to the local system, like this:

VBScript	JScript
| ```
Set wn = WScript.CreateObject
  ("WScript.Network")
wn.MapNetworkDrive "H:",
  "\\Saturn\data"
``` | ```
var wn = WScript.CreateObject
  ("WScript.Network")
wn.MapNetworkDrive("H:",
  "\\\\Saturn\\data")
``` |

Note   The four backslashes used with JScript aren't typos. Remember, in JScript you must escape each slash in a directory path with a slash.

By default, the network drive mapping isn't permanent, and the next time the user logs on, the drive isn't mapped. To change this behavior, you can specify that the drive is persistent by setting the optional persistent flag to True. This updates the user profile to ensure the drive is automatically mapped in subsequent user sessions. You can set the persistent flag like this:

VBScript	JScript

``Set wn = WScript.CreateObject``
``  ("WScript.Network")``
``wn.MapNetworkDrive "H:",``
``  "\\Saturn\data", True``
	``var wn = WScript.CreateObject``
	``  ("WScript.Network")``
	``wn.MapNetworkDrive("H:",``
	``  "\\\\Saturn\\data", "True")``

When mapping a network drive for use by scripts that run as scheduled jobs, you may need to set a username and password in order to establish the connection. You do this by supplying the username and password as the final parameters. In this example, `scriptAdmin` is the username and `gorilla` is the password:

VBScript	JScript

``Set wn = WScript.CreateObject``
``  ("WScript.Network")``
``wn.MapNetworkDrive "H:",``
``  "\\Saturn\data", True,``
``  "scriptAdmin", "gorilla"``
	``var wn = WScript.CreateObject``
	``  ("WScript.Network")``
	``wn.MapNetworkDrive("H:",``
	``  "\\\\Saturn\\data", "True",``
	``  "scriptAdmin", "gorilla")``

Caution   Placing passwords in a script isn't a sound security practice. If you are going to set passwords in scripts, you should A) place the scripts in a directory with very limited access, and B) create a special account that is used only for scripts and has limited permissions.

Disconnecting from a network share

When you are finished working with a network drive, you may want to disconnect the associated drive. To do this, you can use the `RemoveNetworkDrive` method of the `Network` object. Specify the designator of the network drive you want to disconnect, like this:

VBScript	JScript

``Set wn = WScript.CreateObject``
``  ("WScript.Network")``
``wn.RemoveNetworkDrive "H:"``
	``var wn = WScript.CreateObject``
	``  ("WScript.Network")``
	``wn.RemoveNetworkDrive("H:")``

If a drive is still in use, it won't be disconnected. You can force the drive to disconnect by setting the optional force flag to `True`, like this:

VBScript	Jscript
```Set wn = WScript.CreateObject ("WScript.Network") wn.RemoveNetworkDrive "H:", True```	```var wn = WScript.CreateObject ("WScript.Network") wn.RemoveNetworkDrive("H:", "True")```

The third and final parameter for `RemoveNetworkDrive` removes the persistent mapping for the drive. If you want to remove the persistent mapping for the drive in the user's profile, set this flag to `True`, like this:

VBScript	JScript
```Set wn = WScript.CreateObject ("WScript.Network") wn.RemoveNetworkDrive "H:", True, True```	```var wn = WScript.CreateObject ("WScript.Network") wn.RemoveNetworkDrive ("H:", "True", "True")```

Managing Network Printers

Windows scripts can configure default printers, as well as add and remove network printers. A network printer is a shared printer that is accessible to other systems on the network. If you are using a script to configure printers for a particular user, you should log in as the user and run the script, or have the user log in and then run the script. This ensures that the printers are configured as necessary in the user's profile. If you are using a printer in a script, such as one that runs in a scheduled job, you should connect to the printer, use the printer, and then disconnect from the printer.

Setting a default printer

The default printer is the primary printer for a user. This printer is used whenever a user prints a document and doesn't select a specific destination printer. You can set a default printer using the `SetDefaultPrinter` method of the `Network` object. This method automatically updates the user's profile to use the default printer in the current session as well as subsequent sessions.

When you use `SetDefaultPrinter`, you must specify the network share for the printer to use as the default, such as \\NPSERVER\SW12. The network share path is the only parameter for `SetDefaultPrinter`. You can use the method in a script as follows:

VBScript	JScript
```Set wn = WScript.CreateObject ("WScript.Network") wn.SetDefaultPrinter "\\NPSERVER\SW12"```	```var wn = WScript.CreateObject ("WScript.Network") wn.SetDefaultPrinter ("\\\\NPSERVER\\SW12")```

Adding printer connections

Windows scripts manage connections to network printers much like they manage connections to network drives. You map printer connections using `AddPrinterConnection` or `AddWindowsPrinterConnection`. You remove printer connections using `RemovePrinterConnection`.

The basic structure for `AddPrinterConnection` requires a local resource name for the printer, and the path to the network printer name. For example, if you work in an office building, you may want to map to the printer in the southwest corner of the 12th floor. If the printer is shared as \\NPSERVER\SW12, you can map the printer to the local LPT1 port as follows:

VBScript	JScript
```Set wn = WScript.CreateObject ("WScript.Network") wn.AddPrinterConnection "LPT1", "\\NPSERVER\SW12"```	```var wn = WScript.CreateObject ("WScript.Network") wn.AddPrinterConnection ("LPT1", "\\\\NPSERVER\\SW12")```

The port is used with Windows 95/98 and ignored on Windows NT/2000. So for Windows 2000, you can enter "" for the port parameter, for example:

VBScript	JScript
```Set wn = WScript.CreateObject ("WScript.Network") wn.AddPrinterConnection "", "\\NPSERVER\SW12"```	```var wn = WScript.CreateObject ("WScript.Network") wn.AddPrinterConnection ("", "\\\\NPSERVER\\SW12")```

If you just need to use the printer temporarily, you probably don't want to update the user's profile to maintain the printer connection in subsequent user sessions. On the other hand, if you are configuring printers that will be used regularly, you can set the optional persistent flag to `True`. This updates the user profile to ensure that the printer is automatically connected to in subsequent user sessions. You can set the persistent flag as follows:

VBScript	**JScript**
| ```
Set wn = WScript.CreateObject
  ("WScript.Network")
wn.AddPrinterConnection
  "LPT1", "\\NPSERVER\SW12",
  True
``` | ```
var wn = WScript.CreateObject
  ("WScript.Network")
wn.AddPrinterConnection
  ("LPT1", "\\\\NPSERVER\\SW12",
  "True")
``` |

When mapping a network printer for use by scripts that run as scheduled jobs, you may need to set a username and password in order to establish the connection. You do this by supplying the username and password as the final parameters. In this example, prUser is the user name and gorilla is the password:

VBScript	**JScript**
| ```
Set wn = WScript.CreateObject
  ("WScript.Network")
wn.AddPrinterConnection "LPT1",
  "\\NPSERVER\SW12", False,
  "prUser", "gorilla"
``` | ```
var wn = WScript.CreateObject
  ("WScript.Network")
wn.AddPrinterConnection("LPT1",
  "\\\\NPSERVER\\SW12", "False",
  "prUser", "gorilla")
``` |

An alternative to AddPrinterConnection is AddWindowsPrinterConnection. On Windows NT/2000, the AddWindowsPrinterConnection method expects to be passed the path to the network printer, such as:

VBScript	**JScript**
| ```
Set wn = WScript.CreateObject
  ("WScript.Network")
wn.AddWindowsPrinterConnection
  "\\NPSERVER\SW12"
``` | ```
var wn = WScript.CreateObject
  ("WScript.Network")
wn.AddWindowsPrinterConnection(
  "\\\\NPSERVER\\SW12")
``` |

On Windows 95/98, the AddWindowsPrinterConnection method expects to be passed the path to the network printer and the name of the printer driver to use, such as:

VBScript	**JScript**
| ```
Set wn = WScript.CreateObject
  ("WScript.Network")
wn.AddWindowsPrinterConnection
  "\\NPSERVER\SW12", "HP DeskJet"
``` | ```
var wn = WScript.CreateObject
  ("WScript.Network")
wn.AddWindowsPrinterConnection(
  "\\\\NPSERVER\\SW12", "HP DeskJet")
``` |

An optional third parameter is the port to use. If you don't specify the port on Windows 95/98, the LPT1 port is used by default. Windows NT/2000 ignores the device driver and port information if specified.

Note Rather than using both AddPrinterConnection and AddWindowsPrinterConnection, I recommend choosing the one that makes the most sense for your network environment and sticking with it. AddPrinterConnection usually meets most needs.

Removing printer connections

When you are finished working with a network printer, you may want to remove the connection. To do this, you can use the RemovePrinterConnection method of the Network object. Specify the local designator of the printer you want to disconnect, like this:

VBScript	*JScript*
```Set wn = WScript.CreateObject ("WScript.Network") wn.RemovePrinterConnection "PrinterSW12"```	```var wn = WScript.CreateObject ("WScript.Network") wn.RemovePrinterConnection ("PrinterSW12")```

You can force the printer to disconnect by setting the optional force flag to True, like this:

VBScript	*JScript*
```Set wn = WScript.CreateObject ("WScript.Network") wn.RemovePrinterConnection "PrinterSW12", True```	```var wn = WScript.CreateObject ("WScript.Network") wn.RemovePrinterConnection ("PrinterSW12", "True")```

You can also remove the persistent mapping for a printer in the user's profile. To do this, set the third and final parameter to True, like this:

VBScript	*JScript*
```Set wn = WScript.CreateObject ("WScript.Network") wn.RemovePrinterConnection "PrinterSW12", True, True```	```var wn = WScript.CreateObject ("WScript.Network") wn.RemovePrinterConnection ("PrinterSW12", "True", "True")```

If you create a printer connection for a script, you'll usually want to remove the connection before the script exits. On other hand, if you create a connection in a user logon script, you usually won't remove the printer connection.

Summary

As you've seen, you can create scripts to manage drives and to create reports detailing drive information. Drive reports can be extremely useful when you want to track drive usage and free space on enterprise servers. Windows scripts can also be used to map network drives and network printers — essential tasks that you may need to implement in logon scripts.

✦　　✦　　✦

Configuring Menus, Shortcuts, and Startup Applications

Shortcuts, menu options, and startup applications are items that most people don't give much thought. After all, menu options are configured when you add and remove programs. Startup applications are configured based on desktop configuration, and you can create shortcuts without a whole lot of thought. In Windows 2000, you can move items around the menu simply by clicking on them and dragging them to a new location. So you may be wondering, why in the world would you need to do this with a script?

Well, have you ever tried to track down a startup application that you didn't want to start any more? If you have, you know that you have to browse several different folders to determine where the startup application is defined. You then have to delete the reference to the startup application and hope that you didn't miss another reference somewhere else. To make this process easier, you can use a script to examine all startup application definitions and then delete the unnecessary ones. The script takes care of the dirty work for you and can be used on one system or a thousand quite easily. Starting to see how scripts can be useful in this area?

Working with Menus, Desktops, and Startup Applications

In the Windows operating system, menus, desktops, and startup applications are all configured with shortcuts and it is the location of the shortcut that determines how the shortcut is used. For example, if you want to add a menu option for a user, you add a shortcut to the user's Programs or Start folder. These shortcuts then appear on the user's menu. If you want to configure startup applications for all users, you add shortcuts to the `AllUsersStartup` folder. These applications then automatically start when a user logs in to the system locally.

In Chapter 7, I talked about special folders that you may want to use when managing files and folders. There's also a set of special folders that you may want to use when configuring menus, desktops, and startup applications, for example, Programs, Start, and AllUsersStartup.

Table 10-1 provides a summary of special folders you can use with shortcuts. Keep in mind that these folders aren't available on all Windows systems. For example, Windows 95 systems can't use any of the global user folders. (These folders are AllUsersDesktop, AllUsersPrograms, AllUsersStartMenu, and AllUsersStartup).

Table 10-1
Special Folders for Use with Shortcuts

Special Folder	Usage
AllUsersDesktop	Desktop shortcuts for all users.
AllUsersPrograms	Programs menu options for all users.
AllUsersStartMenu	Start menu options for all users.
AllUsersStartup	Startup applications for all users.
Desktop	Desktop shortcuts for the current user.
Favorites	Favorites menu shortcuts for the current user.
Fonts	Fonts folder shortcuts for the current user.
MyDocuments	My Documents menu shortcuts for the current user.
NetHood	Network Neighborhood shortcuts for the current user.
Printers	Printers folder shortcuts for the current user.
Programs	Programs menu options for the current user.
Recent	Recently used document shortcuts for the current user.
SendTo	SendTo menu shortcuts for the current user.

Special Folder	Usage
StartMenu	Start menu shortcuts for the current user.
Startup	Startup applications for the current user.
Templates	Templates folder shortcuts for the current user.

Before you can work with a special folder, you need to obtain a `Folder` object that references the special folder. The easiest way to do this is to use the `SpecialFolders` method of the `WScript.WshShell` object. This method expects a single parameter, which is a string containing the name of the special folder you want to work with. For example, if you want to add or remove desktop shortcuts, you can obtain the Desktop folder like this:

VBScript	JScript
| ```
Set ws = WScript.CreateObject
  ("WScript.Shell")
dsktop = ws.SpecialFolders("Desktop")
``` | ```
var ws = WScript.CreateObject
  ("WScript.Shell")
dsktop = ws.SpecialFolders("Desktop")
``` |

Creating Shortcuts and Menu Options

Creating a shortcut is a very different process from most other administrative tasks we've looked at so far. In fact, you don't really *create* a shortcut — rather, you *build* shortcuts. The process goes like this:

1. Obtain a target folder for the shortcut.

2. Obtain a shortcut object.

3. Set properties for the shortcut.

4. Save the shortcut, which writes it to the target folder or menu.

Each of these steps is examined in the sections that follow.

Obtaining a target folder for the shortcut

Previously, I covered how to obtain a special folder for a shortcut. You aren't limited to creating shortcuts for special folders, however. You can create shortcuts in any type of folder.

With a standard folder, you can obtain a pointer to the folder you want to use with the `GetFolder` method or any other method that returns a `Folder` object. If you want to create a shortcut in the C:\Data folder, you can do so like this:

VBScript	*JScript*
| ```
Set fs = CreateObject
   ("Scripting.FileSystemObject")
Set f = fs.GetFolder("C:\Data")
``` | ```
fs = new ActiveXObject
   ("Scripting.FileSystemObject");
var f = fs.GetFolder("C:\\Data");
``` |

Obtaining a shortcut object

Shortcuts can point to local and network files as well as remote Internet resources. With local or network files, the shortcut name must end with .lnk, which stands for link. With remote Internet resources, the shortcut must end with .url, which indicates a Universal Resource Locator. For brevity, I'll refer to these shortcuts as *link shortcuts* and *URL shortcuts*.

Regardless of type, you can obtain the necessary object for working with a shortcut via the `CreateShortcut` method of the `Shell` object. For link shortcuts, the method returns a `WshShortcut` object. For URL shortcuts, the method returns a `WshUrlShortcut` object. These objects have different sets of properties, which I examine later in this chapter.

The name of the shortcut is the text that immediately precedes the file extension. For example, if you want to create a shortcut to Microsoft Word, you can name the shortcut MS Word using the following designator:

```
MS Word.lnk
```

Listing 10-1 shows how you can create a link shortcut named Notes. The shortcut is set to execute the Notepad text editor along the path %WINDIR%\notepad.exe. Then the shortcut is saved to the Windows desktop with the `Save` method. `Save` is the only method for shortcut-related objects.

Listing 10-1: **Creating a link shortcut**

VBScript	*JScript*
links.vbs	**links.js**
| ```
Set ws = WScript.CreateObject
   ("WScript.Shell")
``` | ```
var ws = WScript.CreateObject
   ("WScript.Shell")
``` |

```
dsktop = ws.SpecialFolders("Desktop")          dsktop = ws.SpecialFolders("Desktop")

Set scut = ws.CreateShortcut                    var scut = ws.CreateShortcut
  (dsktop & "\Notes.lnk")                          (dsktop + "\\Notes.lnk")
scut.TargetPath =                               scut.TargetPath =
  "%windir%\notepad.exe"                           "%windir%\\notepad.exe"
scut.Save                                       scut.Save()
```

As you examine the previous listing, note how the folder path and the link path are concatenated. In VBScript, you add the paths together using:

```
dsktop & "\Notes.lnk"
```

in JScript, you use:

```
dsktop + "\\Notes.lnk"
```

Listing 10-2 shows how you can create a URL shortcut named IDG BOOKS. This shortcut is set to access the URL http://www.idgbooks.com/. Then the shortcut is saved with the Save method. The shortcut is created without a folder path and, as a result, is created in the current working directory.

Listing 10-2: **Creating a URL shortcut**

VBScript	**JScript**
urls.vbs	**urls.js**
| ```
Set ws = WScript.CreateObject
  ("WScript.Shell")
Set scut = ws.CreateShortcut
  ("IDG BOOKS.URL")
scut.TargetPath =
  "http://www.idgbooks.com/"
scut.Save
``` | ```
var ws = WScript.CreateObject
  ("WScript.Shell")
var scut = ws.CreateShortcut
  ("IDG BOOKS.URL")
scut.TargetPath =
  "http://www.idgbooks.com/"
scut.Save()
``` |

Note   The forward slash is not a special character in JScript. Thus, the forward slash doesn't need to be escaped.

Setting properties for link shortcuts

Link shortcuts are usually used to start applications or open documents rather than access a URL in a browser. Because of this, link shortcuts have different properties than URL shortcuts. The properties are summarized in Table 10-2. At first glance, it seems like a truckload of options, but you can work through the properties one step at a time.

Table 10-2 — Properties of WshShortcut		
Property	**Description**	**Sample VBScript Value**
Arguments	Arguments to pass to an application started through the shortcut.	"C:\data\log.txt"
Description	Sets a description for the shortcut.	"Starts Notepad"
Hotkey	Sets a hotkey sequence that activates the shortcut. Can only be used with desktop shortcuts and Start menu options.	"ALT+SHIFT+Z"
IconLocation	Sets the location of an icon for the shortcut. If not set, a default icon is used. The zero indicates the index position of the icon. Few applications have multiple icons indexed, so the index is almost always zero.	"netscape.exe, 0"
TargetPath	Sets the path of the file to execute.	"%windir%\notepad.exe"
WindowStyle	Sets the window style of the application started by the shortcut. The default style is 1. The available styles are the same as options 0-6 discussed in Chapter 9, Table 9-4.	1
WorkingDirectory	Sets the working directory of the application started by the shortcut.	"C:\Working"

Caution   If you set any property incorrectly or set a property that isn't supported by a linked application, the shortcut may not be created. In this case, you'll need to correct the problem and try to create the shortcut again.

Setting shortcut Arguments

One of the most valuable options is the `Arguments` property. You can use this property to set arguments to pass in to an application you are starting. Using this property, you can create a shortcut that starts Microsoft Word and loads in a document at C:\Data\Todo.doc as shown in Listing 10-3.

Listing 10-3: **Setting Arguments for link shortcuts**

VBScript	JScript
largs.vbs	**largs.js**

```
Set ws = WScript.CreateObject
  ("WScript.Shell")
Set scut = ws.CreateShortcut
  ("To-do List.lnk")
scut.TargetPath = "C:\Program Files
  \Microsoft Office
  \OFFICE\WINWORD.EXE"
scut.Arguments = "C:\Data\Todo.doc"
scut.Save
```

```
var ws = WScript.CreateObject
  ("WScript.Shell")
var scut = ws.CreateShortcut
  ("To-do List.lnk")
scut.TargetPath = "C:\\Program Files
  \\Microsoft Office
  \\OFFICE\\WINWORD.EXE"
scut.Arguments = "C:\\Data\\Todo.doc"
scut.Save()
```

Setting shortcut hotkeys

When you add shortcuts to the Windows desktop or the Start menu, you can set a hotkey sequence that activates the shortcut. The hotkey sequence must be specified with at least one modifier key and a key designator. The following modifier keys are available:

- ✦ `ALT` — The Alt key

- ✦ `CTRL` — The Ctrl key

- ✦ `SHIFT` — The Shift key

- ✦ `EXT` — The Windows key

Modifier keys can be combined in any combination, such as `ALT+CTRL` or `ALT+SHIFT+CTRL`, but shouldn't duplicate existing key combinations used by other shortcuts. Key designators include alphabetic characters (A–Z) and numeric characters (0–9) as well as `Back`, `Clear`, `Delete`, `Escape`, `End`, `Home`, `Return`, `Space`, and `Tab`.

Listing 10-4 creates a shortcut for the Start menu. The shortcut uses the hotkey ALT+SHIFT+E.

Listing 10-4: Setting hotkeys for link shortcuts

VBScript	JScript
lkeys.vbs	**lkeys.js**

```
Set ws = WScript.CreateObject
  ("WScript.Shell")
smenu = ws.SpecialFolders("StartMenu")

Set scut = ws.CreateShortcut
  (smenu & "\Internet Explorer.LNK")
scut.TargetPath = "C:\Program Files
  \Plus!\Microsoft Internet
  \IEXPLORE.EXE"
scut.Hotkey = "ALT+SHIFT+E"
scut.Save
```

```
var ws = WScript.CreateObject
  ("WScript.Shell")
smenu = ws.SpecialFolders("StartMenu")

var scut = ws.CreateShortcut
  (smenu + "\\Internet Explorer.LNK")
scut.TargetPath = "C:\\Program Files
  \\Plus!\\Microsoft Internet
  \\IEXPLORE.EXE"
scut.Hotkey = "ALT+SHIFT+E"
scut.Save()
```

Setting icon locations

When you create shortcuts for applications, the applications normally have a default icon that is displayed with the shortcut. For example, if you create a shortcut for Internet Explorer, the default icon is a large E. When you create shortcuts to document files, the Windows default icon is used in most cases.

If you want to use an icon other than the default, you can use the IconLocation property. This property expects to be passed an icon location and an icon index. Normally, the icon location equates to an application name, such as iexplore.exe or notepad.exe, and the icon index is set to 0. Listing 10-5 adds an option to the Programs menu for all users. The icon for this option is the Internet Explorer icon.

Listing 10-5: Setting icons for link shortcuts

VBScript	JScript
licons.vbs	**licons.js**

```
Set ws = WScript.CreateObject
  ("WScript.Shell")
pmenu = ws.SpecialFolders
  ("AllUsersPrograms")
```

```
var ws = WScript.CreateObject
  ("WScript.Shell")
pmenu = ws.SpecialFolders
  ("AllUsersPrograms")
```

```
Set scut = ws.CreateShortcut          var scut = ws.CreateShortcut
  (pmenu & "\Current Script.LNK")        (pmenu + "\\Current Script.LNK")
scut.TargetPath =                      scut.TargetPath =
  "%windir%\notepad.exe"                 "%windir%\\notepad.exe "
  "%windir%\notepad.exe"                 "%windir%\\notepad.exe "
scut.Arguments =                       scut.Arguments =
  "C:\data\curr.vbs"                     "C:\\data\\curr.vbs"
scut.IconLocation = "iexplore.exe, 0"  scut.IconLocation = "iexplore.exe, 0"
scut.Save                              scut.Save()
```

Tip Windows has to be able to find the executable. If the executable can't be found in the path, the icon can't be set. In this case, enter the full path to the executable, like this:

```
scut.IconLocation = "C:\\Program Files\\Plus!\\Microsoft
Internet\\IEXPLORE.EXE, 0"
```

Setting working directories

The working directory sets the default directory for an application. This directory is used the first time you open or save files. Listing 10-6 creates a Start menu shortcut for Windows Notepad. The default directory is set to D:\working.

Listing 10-6: **Setting a working directory for link shortcuts**

VBScript	JScript
workingdir.vbs	**workingdir.js**

```
Set ws = WScript.CreateObject          var ws = WScript.CreateObject
  ("WScript.Shell")                      ("WScript.Shell")
smenu = ws.SpecialFolders("StartMenu") smenu = ws.SpecialFolders("StartMenu")

Set scut = ws.CreateShortcut          var scut = ws.CreateShortcut
  (smenu & "\Notepad for Working.LNK")   (smenu + "\\Notepad for Working.LNK")
scut.TargetPath =                      scut.TargetPath =
  "%windir%\notepad.exe"                 "%windir%\\notepad.exe"
scut.WorkingDirectory = "C:\working"   scut.WorkingDirectory = "C:\\working"
scut.Save                              scut.Save()
```

Setting properties for URL shortcuts

URL shortcuts open Internet documents in the appropriate application. For example, Web pages are opened in the default browser, such as Internet Explorer. With URL shortcuts, the only property you can use is `TargetPath`, which sets the URL you want to use. Listing 10-7 creates a URL shortcut on the Start menu.

Listing 10-7: **Setting the target path for URL shortcuts**

VBScript	JScript
urlshortcut.vbs	urlshortcut.js

```
Set ws = WScript.CreateObject
  ("WScript.Shell")
smenu = ws.SpecialFolders("StartMenu")
Set scut = ws.CreateShortcut
  (smenu & "\Cool Web Site.URL")
scut.TargetPath =
  "http://www.centraldrive.com/"
scut.Save
```

```
var ws = WScript.CreateObject
  ("WScript.Shell")
smenu = ws.SpecialFolders("StartMenu")
var scut = ws.CreateShortcut
  (smenu + "\\Cool Web Site.URL")
scut.TargetPath =
  "http://www.centraldrive.com/"
scut.Save()
```

Managing Shortcuts and Menus

As you've seen, creating shortcuts isn't that difficult. Now let's extend what you've learned to new areas, such as creating, updating, and deleting menus.

Creating menus

Windows scripts can also create new menus. When you create menus, you add folders to existing special folders, such as Start or Programs. Start by obtaining a reference to the menu you want to add onto, like this:

VBScript	JScript

```
Set ws = WScript.CreateObject
  ("WScript.Shell")
pmenu = ws.SpecialFolders ("Programs")
```

```
var ws = WScript.CreateObject
  ("WScript.Shell")
pmenu = ws.SpecialFolders ("Programs")
```

Then create a new menu by adding a folder to the special menu. The following example creates a submenu called Work Files under the Programs menu:

VBScript	JScript
| ```
Set fs = CreateObject
  ("Scripting.FileSystemObject")
Set foldr = fs.CreateFolder
  (pmenu & "\Work Files")
``` | ```
fs = new ActiveXObject
  ("Scripting.FileSystemObject");
var foldr = fs.CreateFolder
  (pmenu + "\\Work Files")
``` |

After you create the menu, you can add options to it. You do this by creating shortcuts that point to a location in the new menu. The following example creates a URL shortcut in the Work Files menu:

VBScript	JScript
| ```
Set ws = WScript.CreateObject
  ("WScript.Shell")
Set scut = ws.CreateShortcut (pmenu
  & "\Work Files\CentralDrive.URL")
scut.TargetPath =
  "http://www.centraldrive.com/"
scut.Save
``` | ```
var ws = WScript.CreateObject
  ("WScript.Shell")
var scut = ws.CreateShortcut (pmenu
  + "\\Work Files\\CentralDrive.URL")
scut.TargetPath =
  "http://www.centraldrive.com/"
scut.Save()
``` |

Accessing and listing menu options

When you manage menus, you'll often find that you need to display or manipulate all of the available options on a particular menu. Unfortunately, accessing a complete list of menu options is a bit more complex than one would imagine. For starters, you need to obtain a WshShell object and then you use this object to access the special folder you want to work with, like this:

VBScript	JScript
| ```
Set ws = WScript.CreateObject
("WScript.Shell")
 smenu = ws.SpecialFolders(mname)
``` | ```
var ws = WScript.CreateObject
  ("WScript.Shell")
smenu = ws.SpecialFolders(mname)
``` |

Afterward, you need to access the file collection associated with the special folder. You do this through the FileSystemObject, like this:

VBScript	JScript
| ```
Set fs = WScript.CreateObject
  ("Scripting.FileSystemObject")
Set f = fs.GetFolder(smenu)
Set fc = f.Files
``` | ```
fs = new ActiveXObject
  ("Scripting.FileSystemObject");
f = fs.GetFolder(smenu);
fc = new Enumerator(f.Files);
``` |

Once you have the file collection, you can use For looping to examine the contents of the collection. This example places the full name and path for menu options on separate lines:

VBScript	JScript
```For Each f1 in fc s = s & f1 s = s & Chr(10) & Chr(13) Next CheckMenu = s End Function }```	```for (; !fc.atEnd(); fc.moveNext()) { f1 = fs.GetFile(fc.item()); s += f1 + "\r\n" } return (s)```

If you want to display only the option name, you can use the name property of the File object, like this:

VBScript	JScript
```For Each f1 in fc s = s & f1.name s = s & Chr(10) & Chr(13) Next CheckMenu = s End Function }```	```for (; !fc.atEnd(); fc.moveNext()) { f1 = fs.GetFile(fc.item()); s += f1.name + "\r\n" } return (s)```

Listing 10-8 shows how these procedures could come together in an actual script. This example displays all of the options on the current user's Programs menu.

Listing 10-8: **Viewing menu options**

VBScript	JScript
viewoptions.vbs	**viewoptions.js**
```Function CheckMenu(mname) Dim fs, f, f1, fc, s, smenu, ws Set ws = WScript.CreateObject ("WScript.Shell") smenu = ws.SpecialFolders(mname) Set fs = WScript.CreateObject ("Scripting.FileSystemObject") Set f = fs.GetFolder(smenu)```	```function CheckMenu(mname) { var fs, f, fc, s; var ws = WScript.CreateObject ("WScript.Shell") smenu = ws.SpecialFolders(mname) fs = new ActiveXObject ("Scripting.FileSystemObject"); f = fs.GetFolder(smenu);```

```
  Set fc = f.Files                    fc = new Enumerator(f.Files);
                                      s = "";
   For Each fl in fc                  for (; !fc.atEnd(); fc.moveNext())
                                      {
   s = s & fl.name                    fl = fs.GetFile(fc.item());
   s = s & Chr(10) & Chr(13)          s += fl.name + "\r\n"
   Next                               }
   CheckMenu = s                      return (s)
 End Function                         }

 WScript.Echo CheckMenu("Programs")   WScript.Echo(CheckMenu("Programs"))
```

Updating current shortcuts and menu options

Through Windows scripts, you can update the properties of any shortcut or menu option. You do this by creating a new shortcut with the exact same name as the old shortcut. For example, if you created a Start menu shortcut named Notes.lnk, you can update its settings by creating a new shortcut named Notes.lnk.

In most cases, only the options you specifically set for the shortcut are overwritten. If necessary, you can clear an existing option by setting its value to an empty string. For example, Listing 10-5 creates a shortcut for Notepad. This shortcut sets an argument that opens a document called curr.vbs. If you delete curr.vbs and don't want to use it anymore, you can update the shortcut as shown in Listing 10-9.

Listing 10-9: **Updating a shortcut**

VBScript	*JScript*

update.vbs

```
Set ws = WScript.CreateObject
  ("WScript.Shell")
pmenu = ws.SpecialFolders
  ("AllUsersPrograms")

Set scut = ws.CreateShortcut
  (pmenu & "\Web Script.LNK")
scut.TargetPath =
  "%windir%\notepad.exe"
scut.Arguments = ""
scut.IconLocation = "iexplore.exe, 0"
scut.Save
```

update.js

```
var ws = WScript.CreateObject
  ("WScript.Shell")
pmenu = ws.SpecialFolders
  ("AllUsersPrograms")

var scut = ws.CreateShortcut
  (pmenu + "\\Web Script.LNK")
scut.TargetPath =
  "%windir%\\notepad.exe "
scut.Arguments = ""
scut.IconLocation = "iexplore.exe, 0"
scut.Save()
```

Deleting shortcuts and menu options

Shortcuts and menu options are specified in files. You can delete them as you would any system file. If a shortcut called Notes.LNK is in the current working directory, you can delete it as follows:

VBScript	*JScript*
| ```
Dim fs
Set fs = CreateObject
  ("Scripting.FileSystemObject")
fs.DeleteFile "Notes.LNK"
``` | ```
var fs
fs = new ActiveXObject
  ("Scripting.FileSystemObject");
fs.DeleteFile("Notes.LNK")
``` |

If a shortcut is in a special folder, such as the Start menu folder, you need to obtain the related folder object before trying to delete the shortcut. Use the path to the folder to retrieve the shortcut using the `GetFile` method of `FileSystemObject`. Afterward, call the `Delete` method of the `File` object. This removes the shortcut. Listing 10-10 shows an example of deleting a shortcut from the Start menu.

Listing 10-10: **Deleting start menu options**

VBScript	*JScript*
deleteoption.vbs	**deleteoption.js**
| ```
Dim ws, fs, f, smenu
Set ws = WScript.CreateObject
  ("WScript.Shell")
Set smenu = ws.SpecialFolders
  ("StartMenu")

Set fs = CreateObject
  ("Scripting.FileSystemObject")
Set f = fs.GetFile(smenu &
  "\Notes.LNK")
f.Delete
``` | ```
var ws = WScript.CreateObject
  ("WScript.Shell")
smenu = ws.SpecialFolders
  ("StartMenu")

fs = new ActiveXObject
  ("Scripting.FileSystemObject");
f = fs.GetFile(smenu +
  "\\Notes.LNK")
f.Delete();
``` |

Deleting menus

You delete menus in much the same way as you delete menu options. However, you normally delete submenus of special folders rather than the special folders themselves. Also, when you create a menu for all users, you must delete the menu via the related special folder. For example, if you create a submenu of `AllUsersStartMenu`, you must delete the submenu via the `AllUsersStartMenu` special folder.

The first step in deleting a menu is to obtain a reference to the appropriate special folder, for example:

VBScript	**JScript**
| ```
Set ws = WScript.CreateObject
  ("WScript.Shell")
pmenu = ws.SpecialFolders ("Programs")
``` | ```
var ws = WScript.CreateObject
  ("WScript.Shell")
pmenu = ws.SpecialFolders ("Programs")
``` |

Afterward, use the `DeleteFolder` method to delete the submenu. Listing 10-11 shows how you can delete a submenu called Work Files under the Programs menu.

Listing 10-11: **Deleting a menu**

VBScript	**JScript**
deletemenu.vbs	**deletemenu.js**
| ```
Set ws = WScript.CreateObject
  ("WScript.Shell")
pmenu = ws.SpecialFolders ("Programs")
Set fs = CreateObject
  ("Scripting.FileSystemObject")
fs.DeleteFolder(pmenu & "\Work Files")
``` | ```
var ws = WScript.CreateObject
  ("WScript.Shell")
pmenu = ws.SpecialFolders ("Programs")
fs = new ActiveXObject
  ("Scripting.FileSystemObject");
var foldr = fs.DeleteFolder
  (pmenu + "\\Work Files")
``` |

Adding and Removing Startup Applications

You specify applications that should be started after a user logs on by creating shortcuts in the AllUsersStartup and Startup folders. The AllUsersStartup folder sets startup applications for all users that log onto a system. The Startup folder sets startup applications for the current user.

Adding startup options

Because these shortcuts are used for automatic startup, the only option you need to set in most cases is the target path. Occasionally you may also want to set a working directory for the application. The following example shows how you can set Internet Explorer as a startup application for all users:

VBScript	JScript
```Set ws = WScript.CreateObject ("WScript.Shell")smenu = ws.SpecialFolders ("AllUsersStartup")Set scut = ws.CreateShortcut (smenu & "\Internet Explorer.LNK")scut.TargetPath = "C:\Program Files \Plus!\Microsoft Internet \IEXPLORE.EXE"scut.Save```	```var ws = WScript.CreateObject ("WScript.Shell")smenu = ws.SpecialFolders ("AllUsersStartup")var scut = ws.CreateShortcut (smenu + "\\Internet Explorer.LNK")scut.TargetPath = "C:\\Program Files \\Plus!\\Microsoft Internet \\IEXPLORE.EXE"scut.Save()```

Removing startup options

If you later want to remove Internet Explorer as a startup application, you delete its related shortcut, like this:

VBScript	JScript
```Dim ws, fs, f, smenuSet ws = WScript.CreateObject ("WScript.Shell")Set smenu = ws.SpecialFolders ("AllUsersStartup")Set fs = CreateObject ("Scripting.FileSystemObject")Set f = fs.GetFile(smenu & "\Internet Explorer.LNK")f.Delete```	```var ws = WScript.CreateObject ("WScript.Shell")smenu = ws.SpecialFolders ("AllUsersStartup")fs = new ActiveXObject ("Scripting.FileSystemObject");f = fs.GetFile(smenu + "\\Internet Explorer.LNK")f.Delete();```

Moving startup options

You may want to move it to the Startup folder so that only the current user (rather than all users) runs the application on startup. To do this, you need to obtain a reference to the original folder and the destination folder, and then move the shortcut with the MoveFile method. Listing 10-12 shows how this can be handled.

Listing 10-12: **Moving a shortcut to a new location**

VBScript	JScript
moveoption.vbs	**moveoption.js**

```
Set ws = WScript.CreateObject
  ("WScript.Shell")
m1 = ws.SpecialFolders("AllUsersStartup")

m2 = ws.SpecialFolders("Startup")
orig = m1 & "\Internet Explorer.LNK"
dest = m2 & "\Internet Explorer.LNK"

Set fs = WScript.CreateObject
  ("Scripting.FileSystemObject")
fs.MoveFile orig, dest
```

```
var ws = WScript.CreateObject
  ("WScript.Shell")
m1 = ws.SpecialFolders
  ("AllUsersStartup")
m2 = ws.SpecialFolders("Startup")
orig = m1 + "\\Internet Explorer.LNK"
dest = m2 + "\\Internet Explorer.LNK"

var fs = WScript.CreateObject
  ("Scripting.FileSystemObject")
fs.MoveFile(orig, dest)
```

Summary

Use the techniques examined in this chapter any time you want to work with short-cuts, menus, and startup applications. Windows Script Host makes it possible to create and manage shortcuts in many different ways. Through shortcuts, you can manage menu options and startup applications as well.

✦   ✦   ✦

Working with the Windows Registry and Event Logs

Through Windows Script Host, you can manage the Windows Registry and the Windows event logs. The registry stores configuration information for the operating system, applications, services, and more. By examining and changing registry information in scripts, you can reconfigure a system so that it runs exactly the way you want it to. The event logs track essential processes on a system and can also be used in auditing system activity. By examining event logs through scripts, you can analyze system activity and monitor a system for problems.

Working with the Windows Registry

The Windows Registry stores configuration settings. Through Windows scripts, you can read, write, and delete registry entries. Because the registry is essential to the proper operation of the operating system, you should only make changes to the registry when you know how these changes will affect the system. Improperly modifying the Windows Registry can cause serious problems and if the registry gets corrupted, you may have to reinstall the operating system. Always double-check registry scripts before running them, and make sure that they do exactly what you intend.

Note Before you edit the registry in any way, you should create or update the system's existing emergency repair disk. This way, if you make a mistake, you can recover the registry and the system. In Windows 2000, you create emergency repair disks through the Backup utility. Start Backup, click Emergency Repair Disk on the Welcome tab and then follow the prompts. Be sure to select the checkbox labeled *Also Backup The Registry To The Repair Directory*.

Understanding the registry structure

The registry stores configuration values for the operating system, applications, user settings, and more. Registry settings are stored as keys and values. These keys and values are placed under a specific root key, which controls when and how the keys and values are used.

The root keys are summarized in Table 11-1. This table also shows the short name by which you can reference the root key in a script. The three keys with short names are the ones you'll work with most often.

Table 11-1
Registry Root Keys

Short Name	Long Name	Description
HKCU	HKEY_CURRENT_USER	Controls configuration settings for the current user.
HKLM	HKEY_LOCAL_MACHINE	Controls system-level configuration settings.
HKCR	HKEY_CLASSES_ROOT	Configuration settings for applications and files. Ensures the correct application is opened when a file is started through Windows Explorer or OLE.
-	HKEY_USERS	Stores default-user and other-user settings by profile.
-	HKEY_CURRENT_CONFIG	Contains information about the hardware profile being used.

Under the root keys, you'll find the main keys that control system, user, and application settings. These keys are organized into a tree structure where folders represent keys. For example, under HKEY_CURRENT_USER\Software\Microsoft, you'll find folders for all Microsoft applications installed by the current user. Under `HKEY_LOCAL_MACHINE\ SYSTEM\CurrentControlSet\Services`, you'll find folders for all services installed on the computer. These folders are officially referenced as keys.

Through Windows scripts, you change the values of existing keys or you can assign values to new keys. Keys are designated by a folder path; for example:

```
HKEY_LOCAL_MACHINE
    \SYSTEM
        \CurrentControlSet
            \Services
                \WINS
                    \Parameters
```

Here, the key is Parameters. This key has values associated with it. Key values have three components: a value name, a value type, and the actual value. In the following example, the value name is `DbFileNm`, the type is `REG_EXPAND_SZ`, and the actual value is `%windir%\system32\wins\wins.mdb`:

```
DbFileNm : REG_EXPAND_SZ : %windir%\system32\wins\wins.mdb
```

Cross-Reference

The `DbFileNm` value controls the location of the WINS database on a Windows 2000 server. Another useful value for controlling WINS is `LogFilePath`, which controls the location of WINS log files on a Windows 2000 server. This value is written as:

```
LogFilePath : REG_EXPAND_SZ : %windir%\system32\wins
```

For more information, see the section titled, "Managing WINS through Windows scripts".

Key values are written by default as normal string values (type `REG_SZ`), but you can assign any of these data types:

✦ `REG_BINARY`—Identifies a binary value. Binary values must be entered using base-2 (0 or 1 only).

✦ `REG_SZ`—Identifies a string value containing a sequence of characters.

✦ `REG_DWORD`—Identifies a `DWORD` value, which is composed of hexadecimal data with a maximum length of four bytes.

✦ `REG_MULTI_SZ`—Identifies a multiple string value.

✦ `REG_EXPAND_SZ`—Identifies an expandable string value, which is usually used with directory paths.

Reading registry keys and values

You can read registry values by passing the full path and name of a key to the RegRead method of the WshShell object. RegRead then returns the value associated with the key. Listing 11-1 shows how you can read the DbFileNm value.

Listing 11-1: **Reading the Windows registry**

VBScript

readkey.vbs
```
Set ws = WScript.CreateObject("WScript.Shell")
v=ws.RegRead("HKLM\SYSTEM\CurrentControlSet\Services\WINS\Parameters\DbFileNm")
WScript.Echo v
```

JScript

readkey.js
```
var ws = WScript.CreateObject ("WScript.Shell")
v=ws.RegRead("HKLM\\SYSTEM\\CurrentControlSet\\Services\\WINS\\Parameters\\DbFileNm")
WScript.Echo(v)
```

The RegRead method only supports the standard data types: REG_SZ, REG_EXPAND_SZ, REG_MULTI_SZ, REG_DWORD, and REG_BINARY. If the value contains another data type, the method returns DISP_E_TYPEMISMATCH.

Writing registry keys and values

Creating keys and writing registry values is a bit different than reading key values. To write keys and value entries to the registry, use the RegWrite method of the WshShell object. This method expects to be passed the key name as well as the value you want to set. You can also set an optional parameter that specifies the value type. If you don't set the type parameter, the value is set as a string of type REG_SZ. If you set the value type, the type must be one of the following: REG_SZ, REG_EXPAND_SZ, REG_DWORD, or REG_BINARY.

Some value types are converted automatically to the appropriate format. With REG_SZ and REG_EXPAND_SZ, RegWrite automatically converts values to strings. With REG_DWORD, values are converted to integers in hexadecimal format. However, REG_BINARY must be set as integers. If you set an incorrect data type or an incorrect value, RegWrite returns E_INVALIDARG.

You can use RegWrite to update existing registry keys and values as well as to create new keys and values. If the path ends with a slash (or double slash for JScript), the entry is written as a key. Otherwise, the entry is written as a value entry. Listing 11-2 changes the value entry for the DbFileNm key and then confirms the change by reading the new value.

Listing 11-2: **Modifying an existing key**

VBScript

modkey.vbs
```
Dim Path
Path = "HKLM\SYSTEM\CurrentControlSet\Services\WINS\Parameters\"
Set ws = WScript.CreateObject("WScript.Shell")
o=ws.RegWrite(Path & "DbFileNm", "%windir%\system32\wins.mdb", "REG_EXPAND_SZ")
v=ws.RegRead(Path & "DbFileNm")
WScript.Echo v
```

JScript

modkey.js
```
var Path
Path = "HKLM\\SYSTEM\\CurrentControlSet\\Services\\WINS\\Parameters\\"
var ws = WScript.CreateObject("WScript.Shell")
o=ws.RegWrite(Path + "DbFileNm","%windir%\\system32\\wins.mdb",
  "REG_EXPAND_SZ")
v=ws.RegRead(Path + "DbFileNm")
WScript.Echo(v)
```

Tip

If you change the settings of a Windows service, you will need to restart the service before the changes take effect. If the service won't start after you've made changes, you should change the key values back to their original settings.

Creating new keys

When you create new keys, you don't have to worry about creating the tree structure that may be associated with the key. The registry automatically creates additional folders as necessary.

Usually, you'll want to add new keys to the HKEY_CURRENT_USER root key. For example, you can create a new key for Windows scripts called HKEY_CURRENT_USER\ WSHBible and then add values to it. Because these values are stored in the current user's profile, they are persistent and aren't destroyed when the user logs out. This makes it possible to retain values across multiple user sessions.

Listing 11-3 shows an example of creating registry keys and assigning values to the keys. The key created is HKEY_CURRENT_USER\WSHBible. The values associated with the key are named Author and Comments.

Listing 11-3: **Creating registry keys and values**

VBScript	**JScript**
Createregkey.vbs	**createregkey.js**

```
Set ws = WScript.CreateObject
   ("WScript.Shell")
val = ws.RegWrite
   ("HKCU\WSHBible\Author",
   "William Stanek")
val = ws.RegWrite
   ("HKCU\WSHBible\Comments",
   "Covers Windows Script Host")
```

```
var ws = WScript.CreateObject
   ("WScript.Shell")
val = ws.RegWrite
   ("HKCU\\WSHBible\\Author",
   "William Stanek")
val = ws.RegWrite
   ("HKCU\\WSHBible\\Comments",
   "Covers Windows Script Host")
```

Deleting registry keys and values

You delete registry keys using the RegDelete method of the WshShell object. The only argument for the method is the full path for the key or the value you want to delete. When you delete a key, the path should end with a slash, like this HKCU\WSHBible\. When you delete a key value, the slash isn't necessary. For example, you can delete the Author value using HKCU\WSHBible\Author as the argument to RegDelete.

Listing 11-4 shows an example of how you can delete the Author and Comment values created in the previous section. The example doesn't delete the HKEY_CURRENT_ USER\WSHBible key.

Listing 11-4: **Deleting registry values**

VBScript	JScript
deleteregkey.vbs	**deleteregkey.js**

```
Set ws = WScript.CreateObject
  ("WScript.Shell")
val = ws.RegDel
("HKCU\WSHBible\Author")
val = ws.RegDel
("HKCU\WSHBible\Comments")
```

```
var ws = WScript.CreateObject
  ("WScript.Shell")
val = ws.RegDel
  ("HKCU\\WSHBible\\Author")
val = ws.RegDel
  ("HKCU\\WSHBible\\Comments")
```

If you want to delete the HKEY_CURRENT_USER\WSHBible key, you change the listing as follows:

```
Set ws = WScript.CreateObject
  ("WScript.Shell")
val = ws.RegDel("HKCU\WSHBible\")
```

```
var ws = WScript.CreateObject
  ("WScript.Shell")
val = ws.RegDel("HKCU\\WSHBible\\")
```

Note   When you delete a key, you permanently delete all of the values associated with the key as well.

Reconfiguring network services through the registry

To better understand how the registry controls system and network settings, let's take a detailed look at how you can manage WINS and DHCP through the Windows Registry.

Managing WINS through Windows scripts

WINS is the Windows Internet Name Service and it is used to resolve computer names to IP addresses. If you log on to a domain using Windows 95, Windows 98, or Windows NT 4.0, your computer may use WINS to access resources on the network.

The Parameters key is the primary key that controls WINS configuration. This key is located in the folder:

```
HKEY_LOCAL_MACHINE
    \SYSTEM
        \CurrentControlSet
            \Services
                \WINS
                    \Parameters
```

Table 11-2 summarizes the main values that you'll use to configure WINS.

Table 11-2
Key Values for Configuring WINS

Key Value	Value Type	Value Description
BackUpDirPath	REG_EXPAND_SZ	Sets the location for WINS backup files. You can change this location to any valid folder path on the local system.
BurstHandling	REG_DWORD	Determines whether WINS uses burst handling mode. Set to 1 to turn the mode on. Set to 0 to turn the mode off.
BurstQueSize	REG_DWORD	Sets the size of the burst queue threshold. The default value is 500, but you can use any value from 50 to 5,000. When the threshold you've set is reached, WINS switches to burst handling mode.
DbFileNm	REG_EXPAND_SZ	Sets the full file path to the WINS database, for example, %windir%\system32\wins.mdb.
DoBackupOnTerm	REG_DWORD	Determines whether the WINS database is backed up when the WINS server is stopped. Set to 1 to turn backups on. Set to 0 to turn backups off.
LogDetailedEvents	REG_DWORD	Determines whether detailed logging of WINS activity is used. All WINS events are logged in the System event log automatically and usually you will want to turn on detailed logging only for troubleshooting. Set to 1 to turn on detailed logging. Set to 0 to turn off detailed logging.
LogFilePath	REG_EXPAND_SZ	Sets an alternative log file path.
LoggingOn	REG_DWORD	Determines whether logging is enabled. Set to 1 to turn on logging. Set to 0 to turn off logging. If you turn off logging, WINS events are not logged in the System event log.
RefreshInterval	REG_DWORD	Sets the interval during which a WINS client must renew its computer name. The minimum value is 2,400 seconds and the default value is 518,400 seconds (six days).

Key Value	Value Type	Value Description
TombstoneInterval	REG_DWORD	Sets the interval during which a computer name can be marked for removal. The value must be equal to or greater than the renewal interval or 345,600 seconds (4 days), whichever is smaller.
TombstoneTimeout	REG_DWORD	Sets the interval during which a computer name can be removed from the WINS database. The value must be greater than or equal to the refresh interval.
VerifyInterval	REG_DWORD	Sets the interval after which a WINS server must verify computer names originating from other WINS servers. This allows inactive names to be removed. The minimum value is 2,073,600 seconds (24 days).

Now that you know the key values and how they are used, you can create a script that manages the WINS configuration. You can then use this script on other WINS servers to ensure that the configurations are exactly the same, which is usually what you want. An example script is shown as Listing 11-5.

Listing 11-5: **Configuring WINS**

VBScript

updatewins.vbs

```
Dim Path
Path = "HKLM\SYSTEM\CurrentControlSet\Services\WINS\Parameters\"
Set ws = WScript.CreateObject("WScript.Shell")
ws.RegWrite Path & "BackUpDirPath","%windir%\system32", "REG_EXPAND_SZ"
ws.RegWrite Path & "BurstHandling",1, "REG_DWORD"
ws.RegWrite Path & "BurstQueSize",500, "REG_DWORD"
ws.RegWrite Path & "DbFileNm","%windir%\system32\wins.mdb", "REG_EXPAND_SZ"
ws.RegWrite Path & "DoBackupOnTerm",1, "REG_DWORD"
ws.RegWrite Path & "LogDetailedEvents",0, "REG_DWORD"
ws.RegWrite Path & "LogFilePath","%windir%\system32", "REG_EXPAND_SZ"
ws.RegWrite Path & "LoggingOn",1, "REG_DWORD"
ws.RegWrite Path & "RefreshInterval",518400, "REG_DWORD"
ws.RegWrite Path & "TombstoneInterval",518400, "REG_DWORD"
ws.RegWrite Path & "TombstoneTimeout",518400, "REG_DWORD"
ws.RegWrite Path & "VerifyInterval",2073600, "REG_DWORD"
```

Continued

> ### Listing 11-5 *(continued)*

JScript

---

updatewins.js

```
var Path
Path = "HKLM\\SYSTEM\\CurrentControlSet\\Services\\WINS\\Parameters\\"
var ws = WScript.CreateObject("WScript.Shell")
ws.RegWrite(Path + "BackUpDirPath","%windir%\\system32", "REG_EXPAND_SZ")
ws.RegWrite(Path + "BurstHandling",1, "REG_DWORD")
ws.RegWrite(Path + "BurstQueSize",500, "REG_DWORD")
ws.RegWrite(Path + "DbFileNm","%windir%\\system32\\wins.mdb", "REG_EXPAND_SZ")
ws.RegWrite(Path + "DoBackupOnTerm",1, "REG_DWORD")
ws.RegWrite(Path + "LogDetailedEvents",0, "REG_DWORD")
ws.RegWrite(Path + "LogFilePath","%windir%\\system32", "REG_EXPAND_SZ")
ws.RegWrite(Path + "LoggingOn",1, "REG_DWORD")
ws.RegWrite(Path + "RefreshInterval",518400, "REG_DWORD")
ws.RegWrite(Path + "TombstoneInterval",518400, "REG_DWORD")
ws.RegWrite(Path + "TombstoneTimeout",518400, "REG_DWORD")
ws.RegWrite(Path + "VerifyInterval",2073600, "REG_DWORD")
```

Managing DHCP through Windows scripts

DHCP is the Dynamic Host Configuration Protocol and it is used to dynamically assign network configuration settings to computers. If you log on to a workstation in an Active Directory domain, your computer probably uses DHCP to obtain the settings it needs to access the network.

DHCP configuration is located in the folder:

```
HKEY_LOCAL_MACHINE
    \SYSTEM
        \CurrentControlSet
            \Services
                \DHCPServer
                    \Parameters
```

The main values that you'll want to work with to configure DHCP are summarized in Table 11-3.

Table 11-3
Key Values for Configuring DHCP

Key Value	Value Type	Value Description
BackupDatabasePath	REG_EXPAND_SZ	Sets the location for DHCP backup files. You can change this location to any valid folder path on the local system.
BackupInterval	REG_DWORD	Sets the interval for automatic backups. The default value is 60 minutes.
DatabaseCleanupInterval	REG_DWORD	Sets the interval for cleaning up old records in the DHCP database. The default value is 1,440 minutes (24 hours).
DatabaseLoggingFlag	REG_DWORD	Determines whether audit logging is enabled. Audit logs track DHCP processes and requests. Set to 1 to turn on. Set to 0 to turn off.
DatabaseName	REG_SZ	Sets the filename for the DHCP database, for example, dhcp.mdb.
DatabasePath	REG_EXPAND_SZ	Sets the directory path for the DHCP database, for example, %SystemRoot%\System32\dhcp.
DebugFlag	REG_DWORD	Determines whether debugging is enabled. If debugging is enabled, detailed events are created in the event logs. Set to 1 to turn on. Set to 0 to turn off.
DetectConflictRetries	REG_DWORD	Sets the number of times DHCP checks to see if an IP address is in use before assigning. Generally, you'll want to check IP addresses at least once before assigning them, which helps to prevent IP address conflicts.
DhcpLogDiskSpace CheckInterval	REG_DWORD	Determines how often DHCP checks the amount of disk space used by DHCP. The default interval is 50 minutes.
DhcpLogFilePath	REG_SZ	Sets the file path for audit log, for example, %windir%\system32\dhcp.
DhcpLogFilesMaxSize	REG_DWORD	Sets the maximum file size for all audit logs. The default is 7MB.

Continued

Table 11-3 *(continued)*

Key Value	Value Type	Value Description
DhcpLogMinSpaceOnDisk	REG_DWORD	Sets the free-space threshold for writing to the audit logs. If the disk drive has less free space than the value specified, logging is temporarily disabled. The default value is 20MB.
RestoreFlag	REG_DWORD	Determines whether the DHCP is restored from backup when the DHCP server is started. Set this option to 1 only if you want to restore a previously saved DHCP database.

Using the key values shown in Table 11-3, you can create scripts that help you manage DHCP. Listing 11-6 shows an example script that reconfigures DHCP settings.

Listing 11-6: **Configuring DHCP**

VBScript

updatedhcp.vbs

```
Dim Path
Path = "HKLM\SYSTEM\CurrentControlSet\Services\DHCPServer\Parameters\"
Set ws = WScript.CreateObject("WScript.Shell")
ws.RegWrite Path & "BackupDatabasePath","%windir%\dhcp\backup", "REG_EXPAND_SZ"
ws.RegWrite Path & "BackupInterval",60, "REG_DWORD"
ws.RegWrite Path & "DatabaseCleanupInterval",1440, "REG_DWORD"
ws.RegWrite Path & "DatabaseLoggingFlag",1, "REG_DWORD"
ws.RegWrite Path & "DatabaseName","dhcp.mdb", "REG_SZ"
ws.RegWrite Path & "DatabasePath","%windir%\system32\dhcp", "REG_EXPAND_SZ"
ws.RegWrite Path & "DebugFlag",0, "REG_DWORD"
ws.RegWrite Path & "DetectConflictRetries",2, "REG_DWORD"
ws.RegWrite Path & "DhcpLogDiskSpaceCheckInterval",50, "REG_DWORD"
ws.RegWrite Path & "DhcpLogFilePath","d:\logs\dhcp", "REG_SZ"
ws.RegWrite Path & "DhcpLogFilesMaxSize",7, "REG_DWORD"
ws.RegWrite Path & "DhcpLogMinSpaceOnDisk",20, "REG_DWORD"
ws.RegWrite Path & "RestoreFlag",0, "REG_DWORD"
```

JScript

---

updatedhcp.js

```
var Path
Path = "HKLM\\SYSTEM\\CurrentControlSet\\Services\\DHCPServer\\Parameters\\"
var ws = WScript.CreateObject("WScript.Shell")
ws.RegWrite(Path+"BackupDatabasePath","%windir%\\dhcp\\backup","REG_EXPAND_SZ")
ws.RegWrite(Path + "BackupInterval",60, "REG_DWORD")
ws.RegWrite(Path + "DatabaseCleanupInterval",1440, "REG_DWORD")
ws.RegWrite(Path + "DatabaseLoggingFlag",1, "REG_DWORD")
ws.RegWrite(Path + "DatabaseName","dhcp.mdb", "REG_SZ")
ws.RegWrite(Path + "DatabasePath","%windir%\\system32\\dhcp","REG_EXPAND_SZ")
ws.RegWrite(Path + "DebugFlag",0, "REG_DWORD")
ws.RegWrite(Path + "DetectConflictRetries",2, "REG_DWORD")
ws.RegWrite(Path + "DhcpLogDiskSpaceCheckInterval",50, "REG_DWORD")
ws.RegWrite(Path + "DhcpLogFilePath","d:\\logs\\dhcp", "REG_SZ")
ws.RegWrite(Path + "DhcpLogFilesMaxSize",7, "REG_DWORD")
ws.RegWrite(Path + "DhcpLogMinSpaceOnDisk",20, "REG_DWORD")
ws.RegWrite(Path + "RestoreFlag",0, "REG_DWORD")
```

Using Event Logs

Windows event logs track activity on a particular system. You can use the logs to track system processes, to troubleshoot system problems and to monitor system security. On Windows 2000 servers and workstations, you'll find the following logs:

✦ **Application Log:** Tracks events logged by applications, such as SQL Server.

✦ **Security Log:** Tracks events you've set for auditing with local or global group policies. Only authorized users can access security logs.

✦ **System Log:** Tracks events logged by the operating system or its components, such as WINS or DHCP.

✦ **Directory Service:** Tracks events logged by Active Directory.

✦ **DNS Server:** Tracks DNS queries, responses, and other DNS activities.

✦ **File Replication Service:** Tracks file replication activities on the system.

Viewing event logs

You can view event logs through Event Viewer. This utility is in the Administrative Tools folder and can also be accessed through the System Tools node in the Computer Management console. As shown in Figure 11-1, Event Viewer's main window is divided into two panels. The left panel is called the console tree. The right panel is the view pane. To view a log, click its entry in the console tree and then the selected log is displayed in the right pane.

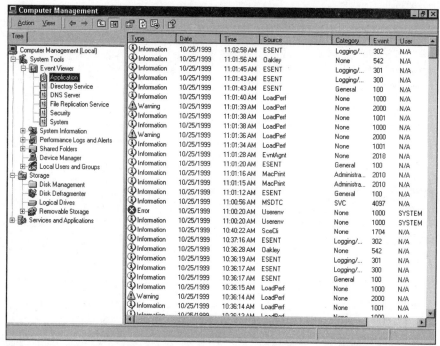

Figure 11-1: Event Viewer displays events on local and remote computers.

When you start Event Viewer, the utility automatically accesses event logs on the local system. You can access event logs on remote computers as well. Right-click Event Viewer in the console tree and then select Connect to Another Computer. You can then use the Select Computer dialog box shown in Figure 11-2 to connect to a remote computer. Choose the Another Computer radio button and then enter the name or IP address of the computer to which you want to connect in the input field provided. Afterward, click OK.

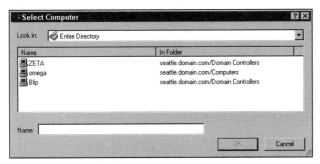

Figure 11-2: To display events on a remote computer, select Another Computer and then enter the computer name or IP address.

Understanding event entries

When you select a log in the console tree, current entries for the log are displayed in the view pane. Each entry provides an overview of why, when, where, and how an event occurred. This information is organized under column headings that provide the following information:

✦ **Type:** The type of event that occurred, such as an error event.

✦ **Date:** The date the event occurred.

✦ **Time:** The time the event occurred.

✦ **Source:** The component that generated the event.

✦ **Category:** The class of the event, such as Online Defragmentation or Logging/Recovery.

✦ **Event:** An identifier for the specific event that occurred.

✦ **User:** The user account that triggered the event.

✦ **Computer:** The computer name where the event occurred.

You can obtain detailed information on an event by double-clicking its entry in the view pane. The additional information provided is:

✦ **Description:** Provides a text description of the event.

✦ **Record Data:** Provides any data or error code output by the event.

Of all the various kinds of information that you can gather from event logs, the most valuable for determining the relevance of an event is the event type. Event types include:

✦ **Error:** An event for an application, component, or service error. You should examine all error events.

✦ **Failure Audit:** An event related to the failed execution of an action. If you are auditing user activities to help you monitor network security, you should keep track of all failed audit events.

✦ **Information:** An information event, which is generally related to a successful action. You don't need to watch information events closely, but may want to track totals on various categories of information events.

✦ **Success Audit:** An event related to the successful execution of an action. You don't need to watch these events closely, but may want to track totals on various categories of these events.

✦ **Warning:** An event that may cause problems on the system, but isn't necessarily the result of an error. You should examine all warning events.

Archiving event logs

On most servers, administrators will archive event logs periodically. When you archive event logs, you store logs for later use. Logs can be archived in three formats:

✦ **Event log format:** This archive type is designed for viewing logs in Event Viewer. You can also access these logs from *Dumpel*, an event log analysis utility. To access an old log in Event Viewer, right-click Event Viewer in the console tree, point to New, and then select Log View. You can now load a previously saved log.

✦ **Text (Tab Delimited):** This archive type works best for viewing in a text editor or word processor. Individual entries are placed on separate lines with each data column representing a field. Tabs are used to separate the fields.

✦ **Text (Comma Delimited):** This archive type works best for importing logs into spreadsheets and databases. You can also work with the logs in Dumpel.

When you save log files to a comma-delimited file, each field in the event entry is separated by a comma. Example event entries look like this:

```
Error,9/4/1999,5:35:07 PM,LicenseService,None,202,N/A,ZETA
Information,9/4/1999,11:25:19 AM,SceCli,None,1704,N/A,ZETA
Information,9/4/1999,11:24:36 AM,ESENT,Logging/Recovery ,302,N/A,ZETA
Information,9/4/1999,11:24:31 AM,Remote Storage,Agent ,1000,N/A,ZETA
```

```
Information,9/4/1999,11:24:19 AM,ESENT,Logging/Recovery ,302,N/A,ZETA
Information,9/4/1999,11:22:49 AM,Oakley,None,542,N/A,ZETA
Information,9/4/1999,11:20:38 AM,ESENT,Logging/Recovery ,301,N/A,ZETA
Information,9/4/1999,11:20:35 AM,EvntAgnt,None,2018,N/A,ZETA
```

The format for the entries is as follows:

```
Type, Date, Time, Source, Category, Event, User, Computer
```

As you can see, the event description and record data is not saved with text-based archives. This saves space and you won't really need the detailed descriptions in most instances. If you do, you can use the event code to find the description. The Windows 2000 Resource Kit has an Event log database that provides detailed information on events and their meaning.

Writing to Event Logs

In Part III of this book, you'll learn how to create scripts that can run automatically, such as scripts that are scheduled to run periodically at a scheduled time, or scripts that run when a user logs on. To help you keep track of the success or failure of these scripts, you can write information related to the scripts directly to the application event log. In this way, when you are browsing or analyzing the logs, you'll know immediately if scripts are running properly or failing.

Event logging basics

When you write events to the application event log, you specify the event ID and the event description. Windows Script Host then directs the event to the event logging service. The event logging service then:

✦ Sets the event type based on the event identifier.

✦ Records the event with the current date and time.

✦ Sets the source as WSH and the category as None.

✦ Sets the event ID based on the event type.

✦ Sets the user to N/A and then sets the computer name.

The results look like this:

```
Type      Date       Time        Source   Category    Event    User    Computer
Warning   9/4/1999   7:24:36 PM   WSH      None          2      N/A     ZETA
Error     9/4/1999   7:13:08 PM   WSH      None          1      N/A     ZETA
```

Windows 95 and Windows 98 systems do not have event logs and for this reason you cannot record events in the application log. Instead, events are logged into a file called wsh.log. This file is located in the Windows installation directory.

The event description is available, but only if you double-click on the event in the Event Viewer. Keep in mind that if you save the event log to a text file, the description is not saved, which will probably mean that you won't be able to determine the meaning of the event.

Working with the LogEvent method

To write events to the application event log, use the `LogEvent` method of the `WshShell` object. The syntax for this method is:

```
LogEvent(eventType, eventDescription [,remoteSystem])
```

in which *eventType* is a numeric identifier for the event type, *eventDescription* is a text description of the event, and *remoteSystem* is an optional value that specifies the system on which you want to log the event. You can only specify remote systems for logging on Windows NT and Windows 2000. Windows 95 and Windows 98 systems ignore the value.

Event types you can specify are summarized in Table 11-4. You set the event type as the first argument for `LogEvent`. If the logging succeeds, `LogEvent` returns `True`. If the logging fails, `LogEvent` returns `False`.

Table 11-4
Specifying Event Types for the LogEvent Method

Event	Value	Event Type
Successful execution	0	Information
Execution error	1	Error
Warning; possible problem	2	Warning
Information	4	Information
Audit of successful action	8	Success Audit
Audit of failed action	16	Failure Audit

Normally, you'll want to use the event log to record the successful or failed execution of the script. For example, if the script is performing nightly backups, you'd want to track the success or failure of the backup process. If you build a `main` function into the script, you can record the outcome of the execution as shown in Listing 11-7. Of course, there are many other ways that you can handle event logging.

Listing 11-7: **Writing to an event log**

VBScript

writelog.vbs

```
Set ws = WScript.CreateObject("WScript.Shell")
ex = main()
If ex Then
 ws.LogEvent 0, "WriteLog.VBS Script Completed Successfully"
Else
 ws.LogEvent 1, "Error executing WriteLog.VBS"
End If

Function main()
 'add main routine
 WScript.Echo "Write log test..."
If err.Number <> 0 Then
 main = 1
Else
 main = 0
End If
End Function
```

JScript

writelog.js

```
var ws = WScript.CreateObject("WScript.Shell")
ex = main()
if (ex == 0) {
 //successful execution
 ws.LogEvent(0, "WriteLog.JS Script Completed Successfully")
 }
else {
 //failed execution
 ws.LogEvent(1, "Error executing WriteLog.JS")
}

function main() {
 //add main routine
 try {
 //add code to try
 WScript.Echo("Write log test...")
 }
 catch(e) {
  return 1
 }
 return 0
}
```

Reading Event Logs

The EventLog method makes writing to event logs fairly easy. Unfortunately, there isn't a simple method that you can use to read event logs. Primarily, this is because event logs have a complex structure and you really need a tool that can search the event logs for relevant information, rather than a tool that simply reads the events. While you can use the built-in capabilities of VBScript and JScript to create log-searching and extraction routines, you don't need to do this. Instead, you can use Dumpel to handle all of the dirty work for you. Dumpel is a resource kit utility designed to help you analyze event logs.

Note

To use the examples in this section, Dumpel must be in a directory that is accessible to the command path. The default installation location for resource kit utilities is Program Files\Resource Kit. This directory is not in the standard command path. You can add this directory to the path or you can move the Dumpel utility to the %SystemRoot% directory. To view the current command path, start a command prompt and then type **path**. To add the resource kit directory to the command path, start a command prompt and then type the following command:

```
set PATH=%PATH%;F:\Program Files\Resource Kit
```

in which F:\Program Files\Resource Kit is the location of the resource kit.

Introducing Dumpel

Dumpel provides many different ways to examine information in event logs. You can dump entire event logs on specific systems and write the logs to files, search the event logs for specific events by ID, or even search event logs for events logged by a specific user. The syntax for Dumpel follows:

```
dumpel [/f <filename>] [/s <servername>] [/l <logname> [/m <source> [/r]]]
       [/e <eventlist>] [/c] [/ns] [/t] [/d <days>]
```

Each of the arguments for Dumpel is summarized in Table 11-5.

Table 11-5
Arguments for Dumpel

Argument	Description
/b	Filters an existing dump log.
/c	Uses commas to separate fields. If not specified, a space is used.
/d <days>	Filters events for the past n days. Value must be greater than 0.

Argument	Description
/e <eventlist>	Filters by event ID. You can specify up to 10 event IDs in a space-separated list. You must use /m to specify a source as well.
/f <filename>	Sets the output filename. If none is specified, the output is sent to the standard output stream.
/format <fmt>	Sets the output format for event fields. Formatting is discussed later in this chapter.
/l <logname>	Examines the specified log, such as system, application, or security.
/m <source>	Filters for events logged by source.
/ns	Specifies that the description should not be dumped.
/r	Reverses the source filtering for /m. All events except those logged by the source are dumped.
/s <servername>	Sets the name of the remote server to use.
/t	Uses a tab to separate fields. If not specified, a space is used.

Using Dumpel

Working with Dumpel is a lot easier than you might imagine, especially after seeing that long list of arguments. With Dumpel, the event log you want to examine is specified with the /l switch. Follow the /l switch with the log type, such as system, application, or security. If you use the /l switch without specifying any other switches, the utility dumps the specified log on the current system to the command line. To dump logs to a file, use the /f switch and specify a filename. The following example dumps the system log to a file on a shared network drive:

```
dumpel /l system /f \\ZETA\DATA\LOG\%computername%.log
```

If the local system is named Gandolf, the result would be a text file named Gandolf.log. The file would contain the entire contents of the system log and each field would be separated with a space. Although Dumpel works with the local system by default, you can access event logs on remote systems as well. Use the /s switch to specify the system name. For example:

```
dumpel /l system /f omega-sys.log /s omega
```

Fields in the event entry are normally separated by spaces, but you can use /t to specify tabs or /c to specify commas as delimiters. You can also use the /format switch to determine which fields to store in the event entries, and their exact order.

To do this, follow the /format switch with any combination of the modifiers shown in Table 11-6. The following example dumps the security log on the local system and restricts output to the date, time, event ID, and event type fields:

```
dumpel /l security /format dtIT
```

Table 11-6
Formatting Modifiers for Dumpel

Modifier	Description
C	Event category
c	Computer name
d	Date
I	Event ID
s	Event comment string
S	Event source
t	Time of day
T	Event type
U	Username

To search the event logs for specified events by identifier, use the /e switch and then enter one to ten event identifiers. Each event must be separated with a space. You must also specify an event source, such as LicenseService or WINS. The following example shows how you can track multiple events in the system log:

```
dumpel /l system /f loc-sys.log /e 401 402 403 404 405 /m netlogon
```

Tip   The Windows 2000 Resource Kit contains a comprehensive database of events and their meaning. If you've installed the resource kit, look for the Windows 2000 Event Log Database in the Tools A to Z listing.

When you use the /m switch, you can search for events logged by specified sources, such as Netlogon or WINS. Unfortunately, you cannot specify multiple sources, but you can use the /r switch with the /m switch to specify that you want to see all events except those for the specified source. In the following example, you search for events logged by the Netlogon service:

```
dumpel /l system /f loc-sys.log /m netlogon
```

In this example, you search for all events *except* those logged by Netlogon:

```
dumpel /l system /f loc-sys.log /m netlogon /r
```

Caution Watch out if you combine /r, /m, and /e, you'll get a list of all events except the designated events for the specified source.

You'll often have existing log files and may not need to create new ones. In this case, use the /b switch to search the existing log file specified with /l. In the following example, you search the loc-sec.log:

```
dumpel /b /l loc-sec.log /e 401
```

In this example, you search the loc-sec.log and write the results to a file:

```
dumpel /b /l loc-sec.log /e 401 /f sec-e401.log
```

So far I've focused on how Dumpel works and how you can use Dumpel from the command line. Now let's look at how you can work with Dumpel in scripts.

Working with Dumpel in scripts

Dumpel is a command-line utility and like other command-line utilities, you can run it within a Windows script using the Run method of the WshShell object. As discussed in Chapter 5, the basic syntax for Run is:

```
object.Run ("command", [winStyle], ["waitOnReturn"])
```

When you use the Run method, you can pass Dumpel any necessary arguments in the command parameter. An example of this is shown as Listing 11-8.

Listing 11-8: **Reading an event log with Dumpel**

VBScript

---

readlog.vbs
```
Set ws = WScript.CreateObject("WScript.Shell")
ret = ws.Run("dumpel /l system /f loc-sys.log /m netlogon",0,"TRUE")

If ret = 0 Then
 ws.LogEvent 0, "ReadLog.VBS Script Completed Successfully"
Else
 ws.LogEvent 1, "Error executing ReadLog.VBS"
End If
```

Continued

Listing 11-8 *(continued)*

JScript

readlog.js

```
var ws = WScript.CreateObject("WScript.Shell");
ret = ws.Run("dumpel /l system /f loc-sys.log /m netlogon",0,"TRUE")

if (ret == 0) {
//successful execution
ws.LogEvent(0, "ReadLog.JS Script Completed Successfully")
}
else {
//failed execution
ws.LogEvent(1, "Error executing ReadLog.JS")
}
```

If you are dumping multiple event logs or event logs on multiple systems, you can enter additional Run statements in the script. Listing 11-9 shows how you can examine the system, security, and application logs on a remote server, and then store the logs on a network drive. Keep in mind that if you run this script as a scheduled task, you'll need to map the drive before you can use it as discussed in Chapter 9.

Listing 11-9: **Working with multiple logs**

VBScript

createlogs.vbs

```
Set ws = WScript.CreateObject("WScript.Shell")
c = ws.ExpandEnvironmentStrings("%computername%")
ret = ws.Run("dumpel /l system /f \\ash\log\" & c & "-sys.log",0,"TRUE")
ret = ret + ws.Run("dumpel /l security /f \\ash\log\" & c & "-sec.log",0,"TRUE")
ret = ret + ws.Run("dumpel /l application /f \\ash\log\" & c & "-app.log",0,"TRUE")

If ret = 0 Then
 ws.LogEvent 0, "CreateLogs.VBS Script Completed Successfully"
Else
 ws.LogEvent 1, "Error executing CreateLogs.VBS"
End If
```

JScript

---

createlogs.js
```
var ws = WScript.CreateObject("WScript.Shell")
c = ws.ExpandEnvironmentStrings("%computername%")
ret = ws.Run("dumpel /l system /f \\\\ash\\log\\" + c + "-sys.log",0,"TRUE")
ret += ws.Run("dumpel /l security /f \\\\ash\\log\\" + c + "-sec.log",0,"TRUE")
ret += ws.Run("dumpel /l application /f \\\\ash\\log\\" + c + "-app.log",0,"TRUE")

if (ret == 0) {
//successful execution
ws.LogEvent(0, "CreateLogs.JS Script Completed Successfully")
}
else {
//failed execution
ws.LogEvent(1, "Error executing CreateLogs.JS")
}
```

Generating Event Log Reports

Event logs are only useful if you can analyze the information they contain. One way to do this is to create a daily event log report for key systems on the network and then publish the results on the corporate intranet. Let's break this process down into a series of steps and then analyze how each step can be implemented.

Step 1: Creating the logs

Step one is to create a script that dumps logs on critical systems and stores the logs on a network drive. If these systems are named Gandolf, Bilbo, and Dragon, the first part of the script would look like Listing 11-10. Each time you run the script, the original logs are overwritten.

Listing 11-10: **Creating logs for the report.**

JScript

---

logstep1.js
```
var ret; ret=0
var ws = WScript.CreateObject("WScript.Shell")

//create array of computers to check from string; no spaces
computers = "gandolf,bilbo,dragon"
```

Continued

Listing 11-10 *(continued)*

JScript

```
sysArray = computers.split(",")

//create array of logs to check from string; no spaces
logs = "system,application,security"
logArray = logs.split(",")

evArray = parseInt(logs.split(","))

//examine each item in the systems array and then the log array
for (s in sysArray) {
 for (l in logArray) {

    ws.Run("dumpel /l " + logArray[l] + " /f \\\\zeta\\corpdatashare\\" +
    sysArray[s] + "-" + logArray[l] + ".log /d 1 /ns /s " +
    sysArray[s],0,"TRUE")
    WScript.Echo("Executing dumpel /l " + logArray[l] + " /f
    \\\\zeta\\corpdatashare\\" + sysArray[s] + "-" + logArray[l] + ".log /d 1
    /ns /s " + sysArray[s],0,"TRUE")


 }
}
```

The output from the script tells you what the script is doing and can really help in understanding the script's logic. The output looks like this:

```
Executing dumpel /l system /f \\zeta\corpdatashare\gandolf-system.log
/d 1 /ns /s gandolf 0 TRUE

Executing dumpel /l application /f \\zeta\corpdatashare\gandolf-application.log
/d 1 /ns /s gandolf 0 TRUE

Executing dumpel /l security /f \\zeta\corpdatashare\gandolf-security.log
/d 1 /ns /s gandolf 0 TRUE

Executing dumpel /l system /f \\zeta\corpdatashare\biblo-system.log
/d 1 /ns /s biblo 0 TRUE

Executing dumpel /l application /f \\zeta\corpdatashare\biblo-application.log
/d 1 /ns /s biblo 0 TRUE

Executing dumpel /l security /f \\zeta\corpdatashare\biblo-security.log
/d 1 /ns /s biblo 0 TRUE

Executing dumpel /l system /f \\zeta\corpdatashare\dragon-system.log
/d 1 /ns /s dragon 0 TRUE
```

```
Executing dumpel /l application /f \\zeta\corpdatashare\dragon-application.log
/d 1 /ns /s dragon 0 TRUE

Executing dumpel /l security /f \\zeta\corpdatashare\dragon-security.log
/d 1 /ns /s dragon 0 TRUE
```

As you can see from the output, the script dumps the logs for the first system specified in the computer's variable, then dumps the logs for the seconds system and so on. The order of the logs is specified in the logs variable. The output contains events for the current day only (/d 1) and does not contain descriptions (/ns).

To dump the log files daily, you can schedule the script to run with the Task Scheduler. Scheduling scripts to run periodically is covered in Chapter 12. Rather than dumping the log to a file and then browsing the file in a text editor, it would be a lot easier if you could browse the file on the corporate intranet. Before you do this, you may want to clean up the files, search for specific events, or format the files at HTML.

Step 2: Formatting the logs for viewing

You can format the logs for viewing in many different ways. If you are running the script manually, the easiest way to do this is to display the contents of each log file in a pop-up dialog box. The code that does this is shown in Listing 11-11. Figure 11-3 shows sample output for a log file.

Listing 11-11: Displaying the log reports in a pop-up dialog box

---

JScript

---

logstep2a.js

```
var ret; ret=0
var ws = WScript.CreateObject("WScript.Shell")

//create array of computers to check from string; no spaces
computers = "gandolf,bilbo,dragon"
sysArray = computers.split(",")

//create array of logs to check from string; no spaces
logs = "system,application,security"
logArray = logs.split(",")

//examine each item in the systems array and then the log array
for (s in sysArray) {
 for (l in logArray) {
```

Continued

Listing 11-11 *(continued)*

JScript

```
    ws.Run("dumpel /l " + logArray[l] + " /f \\\\zeta\\corpdatashare\\" +
¬ sysArray[s] + "-" + logArray[l] + ".log /d 1 /ns /s " +
¬ sysArray[s],0,"TRUE")
    WScript.Echo("Executing dumpel /l " + logArray[l] + " /f
\\\\zeta\\corpdatashare\\" +

sysArray[s] + "-" + logArray[l] + ".log /d 1 /ns /s " + sysArray[s],0,"TRUE")

 }
}

ForReading = 1

for (s in sysArray) {
 for (l in logArray) {

  fname = "\\\\zeta\\corpdatashare\\" + sysArray[s] + "-" +
¬ logArray[l] + ".log"

  var fs = new ActiveXObject ("Scripting.FileSystemObject");
  var f = fs.OpenTextFile (fname, ForReading, "True")
  fContents = f.ReadAll()
  f.Close()

  var w = WScript.CreateObject("WScript.Shell");
  a = w.Popup (fContents,60,"Display File",1)

 }
}
```

As you can see from the listing, For loops are used to display the contents of each log in turn. These For loops are implemented in the same way as the For loops that dump the logs in the first place. The key difference is that instead of dumping logs, you are reading the contents of the logs and displaying them in a pop-up dialog box. You can extend this technique to format the logs as HTML, which then makes the daily log report easier to work with.

Listing 11-12 shows how you can add an HTML header and footer to the log files. Don't worry, I'll analyze the script one step at a time following the listing.

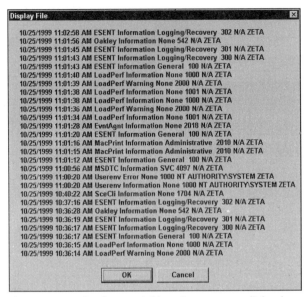

Figure 11-3: Viewing partial logs in a pop-up dialog box

Listing 11-12: **Creating HTML documents for the log reports**

JScript

---

logreports.js

```
// ************************
// Script: The Log Reporter
// Version: 0.9.1
// Creation Date: 9/1/99
// Last Modified: 12/15/99
// Author: William R. Stanek
// Email: winscripting@tvpress.com
// Copyright (c) 1999, 2000 William R. Stanek
// ************************
// Description: Uses the Dumpel utility to dump specified
//              logs on local and remote systems. The script
//              then generates reports formatted as HTML.
//
// Maintenance: When installing this script, you should update
//              computers, logs, netDrive and fname.
//              Computers sets the name of the systems to check.
//              Logs sets the type of event logs to dump
//              netDrive sets the log creation directory.
```

Continued

Listing 11-12 *(continued)*

JScript

```
//              fname sets the full file path to the publishing directory for
//              the HTML reports.
// ************************
theMonth = new Array(12)
theMonth[1] = "January"
theMonth[2] = "February"
theMonth[3] = "March"
theMonth[4] = "April"
theMonth[5] = "May"
theMonth[6] = "June"
theMonth[7] = "July"
theMonth[8] = "August"
theMonth[9] = "September"
theMonth[10] = "October"
theMonth[11] = "November"
theMonth[12] = "December"
theDays = new Array(7)
theDays[1] = "Sunday"
theDays[2] = "Monday"
theDays[3] = "Tuesday"
theDays[4] = "Wednesday"
theDays[5] = "Thursday"
theDays[6] = "Friday"
theDays[7] = "Saturday"

function theDate(aDate) {
   var currentDay = theDays[aDate.getDay() + 1]
   var currentMonth = theMonth[aDate.getMonth() + 1]
   return currentDay + ", " + currentMonth + " " + aDate.getDate()
}

var ret; ret=0
var ws = WScript.CreateObject("WScript.Shell")

//create array of computers to check from string; no spaces
computers = "gandolf,bilbo,dragon"
sysArray = computers.split(",")

//sets the network drive where logs are created
netDrive = "\\\\zeta\\corpdatashare\\"

//create array of logs to check from string; no spaces
logs = "system,application,security"
logArray = logs.split(",")

//examine each item in the systems array and then the log array
for (s in sysArray) {
 for (l in logArray) {
```

```
    ws.Run("dumpel /l " + logArray[l] + " /f " + netDrive + sysArray[s] + "-" +
¬ logArray[l] + ".log /d 1 /ns /s " + sysArray[s],0,"TRUE")
    WScript.Echo("Executing dumpel /l " + logArray[l] + " /f " + netDrive +
¬ sysArray[s] + "-" + logArray[l] + ".log /d 1 /ns /s " +
¬ sysArray[s],0,"TRUE")

 }
}

ForReading = 1
ForAppending = 8

for (s in sysArray) {
 for (l in logArray) {

  fname = "\\\\zeta\\corpdatashare\\" + sysArray[s] + "-" + logArray[l]

  var fs = new ActiveXObject ("Scripting.FileSystemObject");
  var f = fs.OpenTextFile (fname + ".log", ForReading, "True")
  fContents = f.ReadAll()
  f.Close()

  var f = fs.OpenTextFile (fname + ".html", ForAppending, "True")

  fHeader = "<html><head><title>Daily "
  fHeader += logArray[l]
  fHeader += " Log Report for "
  fHeader += sysArray[s]
  fHeader += "</title></head>"
  fHeader += "<body bgcolor='#FFFFFF' text='#000000'>"
  fHeader += "<h1>Daily "
  fHeader += logArray[l]
  fHeader += " Log Report for "
  fHeader += sysArray[s]
  fHeader += "</h1>"
  fHeader += "<h3>"

  today = new Date()
  fHeader += theDate(today)

  fHeader += "</h3>"
  fHeader += "<pre>"

  f.Write(fHeader)
  f.Write(fContents)

  fFooter = "</pre></body></html>"

  f.Write(fFooter)

  f.Close()
 }
}
```

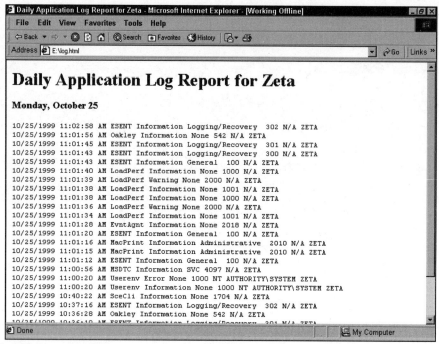

Figure 11-4: Viewing the customized log report in Internet Explorer

The first section of the script sets up a custom Date function. The function looks like this:

```
function theDate(aDate) {
    var currentDay = theDays[aDate.getDay() + 1]
    var currentMonth = theMonth[aDate.getMonth() + 1]
    return currentDay + ", " + currentMonth + " " +
aDate.getDate()
}
```

The purpose of the Date function is to output the date in a custom format. Thus, rather than the standard date format:

```
Sun Sep 5 15:48:52 PDT 1999
```

you get a date that looks like this:

```
Sunday, September 5
```

Another new section of code creates a header for the HTML document you are creating. This code sets a title for the document and sets a level-1 header that will make it easier to work with the log files:

```
fHeader = "<html><head><title>Daily "
  fHeader += logArray[l]
  fHeader += " Log Report for "
  fHeader += sysArray[s]
  fHeader += "</title></head>"
  fHeader += "<body bgcolor='#FFFFFF' text='#000000'>"
  fHeader += "<h1>Daily "
  fHeader += logArray[l]
  fHeader += " Log Report for "
  fHeader += sysArray[s]
  fHeader += "</h1>"
  fHeader += "<h3>"

  today = new Date()
  fHeader += theDate(today)

  fHeader += "</h3>"
```

After creating the header, the code starts a preformatted text element in which the contents of the log file are placed. The code then writes the document header and contents:

```
fHeader += "<pre>"

f.Write(fHeader)
f.Write(fContents)
```

The final steps are to write the document footer and then close the file:

```
fFooter = "</pre></body></html>"

f.Write(fFooter)

f.Close()
```

As shown in Figure 11-4, the result is a customized report that can be viewed on the corporate intranet using any standard Web browser, such as Internet Explorer or Netscape Navigator. The script is designed to append each day's report to the same HTML document. If you don't want historical data, you can open the HTML document's ForWriting rather than ForAppending. Simply replace the lines that read:

```
ForAppending = 8
var f = fs.OpenTextFile (fname + ".html", ForAppending, "True")
```

with these lines:

```
ForWriting = 2
var f = fs.OpenTextFile (fname + ".html", ForWriting, "True")
```

Now, a new HTML document is created each time the script runs. If you plan to publish the reports on the corporate intranet, the network drive you use for the HTML documents should point to an appropriate directory on the intranet server. In the example, the files are written to the network share \\zeta\corpdatashare. This is the same directory where the log files are written. To change this, set the fname variable to the directory you want to use for publishing to the intranet, for example:

```
fname = "\\\\iServer\\webdatashare\\" + sysArray[s] + "-" + logArray[l]
```

Summary

The registry and the event logs are important resources on Windows computers. As you've learned in this chapter, you can manipulate these resources in many different ways. You can read, write, and modify registry keys. You can use the registry to reconfigure network services, such as DHCP and WINS. You can use the event logs to monitor critical systems, and you can create customized reports based on event logs entries as well.

✦   ✦   ✦

Network and Directory Service Scripting

Part III takes you into the heart of scripting Windows 2000: working with network and directory service objects. In Part III, you'll learn to plumb the depths of Active Directory Services Interfaces (ADSI) and master the art of scheduling one-time and recurring network tasks using Startup/Shutdown and login scripts; controlling local and domain resources, services, shared directories, printer queues, and print jobs. By the end of this Part, you'll be an expert Windows 2000 scripter.

Scheduling One-time and Recurring Tasks

One of the most powerful aspects of Windows scripting is the ability to schedule scripts to run automatically. You can schedule scripts to run one time only at 5 PM on Wednesday, every day at 11 PM, every other Monday at 2 AM, and at other times that are convenient. Just as important, you can schedule scripts to run on any network computer and you can manage those scripts through an easy-to-use graphical interface or an equally powerful command-line utility.

Scheduling Local and Remote Jobs

Windows Scripts that run automatically on a periodic or one-time basis are referred to as scheduled jobs or scheduled tasks. While these scheduled jobs can perform any regular scripting duty, there are some important differences in how scheduled jobs are used. So before we dive into job scheduling, let's look at these differences.

Note   Only authorized users can manage services and network time. You may need administrative privileges to perform the tasks in this section.

Scheduling basics

Scheduled jobs are started by a Windows service called Task Scheduler. This service must be running on the local or remote system in order for task scheduling to operate. You can check the status of the Task Scheduler in the Services node of the Computer Management console or through the Services console itself.

Figure 12-1 shows the Services console. You start the Services console by clicking Start ➪ Programs ➪ Administrative Tools ➪ Services. As shown in the figure, the Task Scheduler Status should be Started and the Startup Type should be Automatic. If the service isn't started, right-click its entry and then select Start on the pop-up menu. If the startup type isn't set to automatic, double-click Task Scheduler, choose Automatic on the Startup Type selection list, and then click OK.

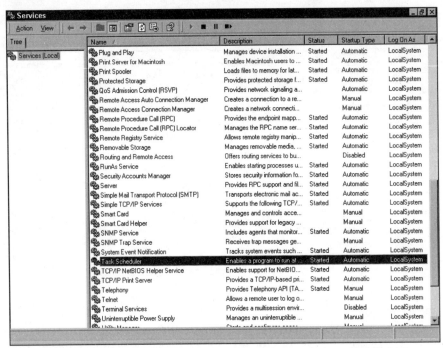

Figure 12-1: The Task Scheduler must be configured properly for scheduled jobs to run.

If you plan to use the command-line scheduler rather than the graphical scheduler, you should configure the logon account for the Task Scheduler. Task Scheduler logs on as the LocalSystem account by default. This account usually doesn't have adequate permissions to perform administrative tasks. Because of this, you should configure Task Scheduler to use a specific user account that has adequate user privileges and access rights to run the tasks you want to schedule. You can change the logon account for Task Scheduler as follows:

1. Double-click Task Scheduler in the Services console.

2. On the Log On tab, choose the This Account radio button as shown in Figure 12-2.

3. Type the name of the authorized account in the field provided, then enter and confirm the password for the account.

4. Click OK.

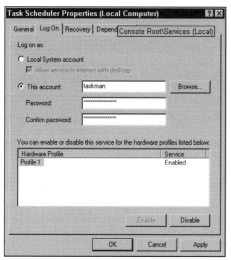

Figure 12-2: Configuring the startup account for Task Scheduler

Synchronizing the system time

Task Scheduler uses the local system time to determine when scripts should run. If the local system time isn't in sync with the rest of the network, scripts may not run when expected. You can specify a timeserver that the computer should synchronize with using the net time command.

The syntax for net time is:

```
net time [\\computername | /domain[:domainname] |
         /rtsdomain[:domainname]] [/set]
net time [\\computername] /querysntp
net time [\\computername] /setsntp[:ntp server list]
```

The options for the net time command are summarized in Table 12-1.

Table 12-1	
Arguments for the net time Command	

Arguments	Description
`\\computername`	Sets the name of the computer you want to check or synchronize with.
`/domain[:domainname]`	Specifies that you want to synchronize with a Primary Domain Controller for `domainname`.
`/rtsdomain[:domainname]`	Specifies that you want to synchronize with a Reliable Timeserver from `domainname`.
`/set`	Sets the computer time on the computer.
`/querysntp`	Displays the DNS name of the currently configured network timeserver for this computer.
`/setsntp[:ntp_server_list]`	Sets the DNS name or IP address of the network timeservers to be used by this computer. If you list multiple timeservers, you must use quotation marks.

In an Active Directory domain, the primary domain controller at the root of the domain tree is designated as the master timeserver. All other computers in the domain can synchronize with this computer or with other designated timeservers. You designate the timeserver that a computer should use with the `/setsntp` command. If you want the Gandolf.tvpress.com server to be the timeserver for a computer, enter the following command:

```
net time /setsntp:gandolf.tvpress.com
```

You can also set the timeserver using its IP address, like this:

```
net time /setsntp:204.67.12.18
```

When you designate a timeserver for a computer, the time is automatically synchronized, provided the timeserver is available. If the timeserver goes off line, the computer won't be able to sync time. You can, however, specify alternative timeservers to use in case of outage. Simply enter the servers in a space-separated list, like this:

```
net time /setsntp:"gandolf.tvpress.com omega.tvpress.com"
```

Here, the server Gandolf.tvpress.com is the primary timeserver and omega.tvpress.com is an alternative timeserver.

Once you designate a timeserver, system time will be synchronized automatically. If you want to determine the current timeserver for a computer, enter the `net time` command with the `/querysntp` option, like this:

```
net time /querysntp
```

The results will look similar to this:

```
The current SNTP value is: gandolf.tvpress.com
omega.tvpress.com
```

Scheduling utilities

As mentioned previously, there are two scheduling utilities: Task Scheduler Wizard and the AT Scheduler. Both utilities are useful.

The Task Scheduler Wizard provides a graphical interface for task assignment. Using this wizard, you can quickly configure tasks without having to worry about syntax issues. The disadvantage is that you don't have a central location for managing scheduled tasks in the enterprise. You access the wizard separately on each individual system that you want to configure and you view the scheduled tasks on each system individually through the related Scheduled Tasks folder.

The AT Scheduler is a command-line utility. Because the AT Scheduler doesn't have a point-and-click interface, you'll have to learn its command syntax, which isn't all that friendly. Still, AT has a definite advantage when it comes to script management. Using AT, you can schedule jobs to run on remote systems without having to access those systems, and you can check the status of jobs in the same way.

Regardless of which scheduling utility you decide to use, you'll need to ensure that the script can access resources with which it needs to work. Scripts don't automatically have access to the environment settings and may not have mapped drives, environment variables, and other necessary resources available. Because of this, you may need to map drives, set environment variables, or perform other preliminary tasks that aren't necessary when you run the script yourself. In fact, if you can run a script from the command line and it operates normally but fails when run as a scheduled task, something in the user environment isn't set properly.

Using the Graphical Task Scheduler

The graphical Task Scheduler makes scheduling and viewing tasks fairly easy. You create new tasks using the Task Scheduler Wizard. You view current tasks and manage their options through the Scheduled Tasks folder.

Note   Group policy and user permissions can affect your ability to schedule tasks with the Task Scheduler Wizard. If you can't run the wizard or you can't access the Scheduled Tasks folder, you don't have the right privileges.

Running the wizard

You can use the Task Scheduler Wizard to create recurring or one-time tasks as follows:

1. Start Windows Explorer, then double-click My Network Places.

2. In My Network Places, access the computer you want to work with and then double-click the Scheduled Tasks folder.

3. Start the Task Scheduler Wizard by double-clicking Add Scheduled Task. A Welcome dialog box is displayed. Click Next.

4. Click Browse to display the *Select Program to Schedule* dialog box shown in Figure 12-3. This dialog box is basically a File Open dialog box that you can use to find the script you want to schedule. When you find the script you want to use, click it and then click Open.

Figure 12-3: Use the Select Program to Schedule dialog box to find the script you want to run as a scheduled task.

5. Type a name for the task as shown in Figure 12-4. The task name should help you determine what the task does. For example, if you are scheduling a script that generates event log reports, type the name **Generate Nightly Log Reports**.

6. Choose a run schedule, then click Next. Tasks can be scheduled to run one time only, daily, weekly, or monthly. They can also be set to run when a specific event occurs, such as when the computer starts or when the current user logs in.

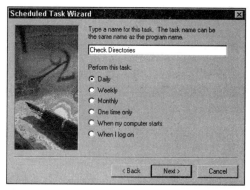

Figure 12-4: Enter a descriptive name for the task and then select a run schedule.

7. The next dialog box you see depends on your previous selection. If you want to run the task daily, the date and time dialog box appears as shown in Figure 12-5. Set a start time and date. Daily scheduled tasks can be configured to run:

   • **Every Day:** Sunday to Saturday.

   • **Weekdays:** Monday to Friday only.

   • **Every ... Day:** Every 2nd, 3rd, ... nth day.

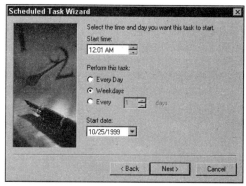

Figure 12-5: Schedule daily tasks using this dialog box.

8. If you want the task to run weekly, the date and time dialog box appears as shown in Figure 12-6. Weekly scheduled tasks can be configured to run using the following fields:

- **Start Time:** Sets the start time of the task.
- **Every ... Week:** Runs the task every week, every other week, or every *n*th week.
- **Day of Week:** Sets the day of the week the task runs, such as on Monday, or on Monday and Friday.

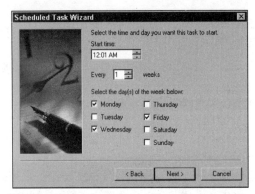

Figure 12-6: Schedule weekly tasks using this dialog box.

9. If you want the task to run monthly, the date and time dialog box appears as shown in Figure 12-7. Monthly scheduled tasks can be configured to run using the following fields:

- **Start Time:** Sets the start time of the task.
- **Day:** Sets the day of the month the task runs. If you select 2, the task runs on the 2nd day of the month.
- **The ... Day:** Sets task to run on the *n*th occurrence of a day in a month, such as the 3rd Monday or the 4th Wednesday of every month.
- **Of the Months:** Sets the months the task runs on.

10. If you want the task to run one time only, the date and time dialog box appears as shown in Figure 12-8. Set the start time and start date.

11. If the task runs when the computer starts or when the current user logs on, you don't have to set a start date and time. The task runs automatically when the startup or logon event occurs.

Figure 12-7: Schedule monthly tasks using this dialog box.

Figure 12-8: Schedule one-time tasks using this dialog box.

12. Once you configure a start date and time, click the Next button to continue. As shown in Figure 12-9, enter a username that can be used when running the scheduled task. This username must have appropriate permissions and privileges to run the scheduled task.

13. Enter and confirm the user's password, then click Next.

Caution

Be careful when running scripts using an account with administrative privileges in the domain. If users have access to the scripts, they may be able to enter malicious code into the script and, in this way, cause problems on the network. If you must use an administrator account to start a script, give the script the same strict security consideration you'd give to the administrator password. Ideally, you place the script in a protected folder on an NTFS volume and then set appropriate NTFS security restrictions on the script.

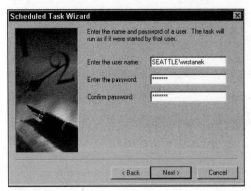

Figure 12-9: When you use the Scheduled Task Wizard, tasks can be run by any designated user. Enter an appropriate username and password.

14. Click Finish to complete the scheduling process. Errors that occur while creating a task don't normally cause failure. Instead, you'll see a prompt telling you something went wrong and you can click OK to continue. After the task is created, double-click the task in Windows Explorer and then correct the problem in the Properties dialog box.

Viewing wizard tasks

All tasks that you create with the Task Scheduler Wizard are accessible through the Scheduled Tasks folder. In Windows Explorer, you can access this folder in the following ways:

✦ On a local system, double-click Control Panel and then click Scheduled Tasks.

✦ On a remote system, double-click My Network Places and then access the computer you want to work with. Afterward, double-click the Scheduled Tasks folder.

Once you access the Scheduled Tasks folder, you can manage tasks in the following ways:

✦ To examine properties for scheduled tasks, double-click the task with which you want to work. Set advanced options through the Settings tab.

✦ To delete a task, click it and then press Delete.

✦ Instead of deleting a task, you may want to temporarily disable it. If you do this, you can start the task at a later date without having to re-create it. You disable a task by double-clicking it and then clearing the Enabled checkbox on the Task tab.

Changing task properties

You can change the properties of a task at any time. Double-click the task's entry in the Scheduled Tasks folder. This displays the properties dialog box shown in Figure 12-10. As shown in the figure, the Properties dialog box has the following tabs:

✦ **Task:** Used to set general task settings. These settings are the same as those set through the Task Scheduler Wizard.

✦ **Scheduled:** Used to set the task's run schedule. These settings are the same as those set through the Task Scheduler Wizard.

✦ **Settings:** Used to set advanced options for the task.

✦ **Security:** Used to restrict access to the task's property settings.

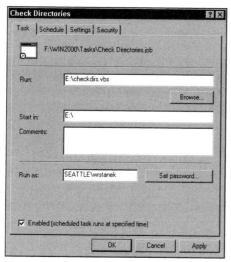

Figure 12-10: You can change the configuration of a scheduled task at any time.

Scheduling Jobs with AT

You can schedule jobs at the command line or within your scripts using the AT utility. With AT, you can schedule tasks anywhere on the network and you don't have to log on to remote systems.

Note   You may need special permissions to schedule tasks on remote systems. If you aren't a member of the local Administrators group, you may not be able to use AT.

Using the AT Scheduler

When you schedule tasks with AT, you use a 24-hour clock on which 00:00 is midnight and 12:00 is 12 PM. When you schedule tasks using AT, you must ensure that:

✦ The Task Scheduler service is running on the local or remote system.

✦ The Task Scheduler service uses an appropriate startup account.

✦ The scripts you want to use are located in directories that can be found along the command path set for the service logon account.

The syntax for the AT utility is:

```
AT [\\computername] [ [id] [/delete] | /delete [/yes]]
AT [\\computername] time [/interactive]
    [ /every:date[,...] | /next:date[,...]] "command"
```

The arguments for the AT utility are summarized in Table 12-2.

Table 12-2
Arguments for the AT Utility

Argument	Description
\\computername	Sets the name of a remote computer on which to schedule the task.
id	Sets the ID number of a task to delete.
/delete	Deletes a scheduled task. If a specific ID isn't set, all scheduled tasks are deleted.
/yes	Cancels scheduled tasks without prompting to confirm the action.
Time	Sets the time when task is to run.
/interactive	Turns on interactive mode, which allows the task to interact with the desktop.
/every:date[,...]	Runs the task on each specified day of the week or month. If date is omitted, the current day of the month is assumed.
/next:date[,...]	Runs the task on the next occurrence of the day. If date is omitted, the current day of the month is assumed.
"command"	Sets the command, program, or script to run.

When you use numeric dates, you can use any value in the range 1-31. Here's how you can schedule a backup script to run every other day at 5 AM:

```
AT 05:00 /every:2,4,6,8,10,12,14,16,18,20,22,24,26,28,30
checkstatus.js
```

Another way to schedule tasks by date is to specify the day of the week. The values are:

- ✦ **M:** Monday
- ✦ **T:** Tuesday
- ✦ **W:** Wednesday
- ✦ **Th:** Thursday
- ✦ **F:** Friday
- ✦ **S:** Saturday
- ✦ **Su:** Sunday

You can schedule tasks to run relative to the current date as well. To do this, specify only a start time, and not a run date. You can start a backup script at 7 PM today as follows:

```
AT 19:00 backup.js
```

You can also schedule tasks to run on the next occurrence of a date. For example, if today is Monday and you want the task to run Wednesday, you can use the following command:

```
AT 07:30 /next:W starttest.js
```

Scheduled tasks usually run as background processes. However, you can specify that tasks run interactively, like this:

```
AT 05:00 /interactive /every:M,W,F copylogs.js
```

So far, all of the examples have assumed that you want to schedule tasks to run on the local system. The local system is the default for the AT Scheduler. If you want to schedule tasks on a remote system, type the UNC name or IP address of the remote system before you specify other parameters, like this:

```
AT \\Bilbo 09:45 /next:Su update.js
```

or, like this:

```
AT \\207.17.12.8 09:45 /every:T,Th backupmainservers.js
```

Viewing scheduled AT jobs

If a task is scheduled with the AT utility, you can view its status and configuration from anywhere on the network. To view scheduled jobs on a local system, type **at** on a line by itself and press Enter. On a remote system, type **at** followed by the UNC name or IP address of the system you want to check, for example:

```
at \\Bilbo
```

When you view tasks, the output you get is similar to the following:

```
Status ID  Day                       Time      Command Line
---------------------------------------------------------------
        1  Each T Th                 7:00 AM   checkstatus.js
        2  Each M F                  9:00 AM   copylogs.js
        3  Each S Su                 8:00 AM   backup.js
```

From the output you can determine the following:

✦ **Status:** Shows the status of a task. A blank entry indicates a normal status. Otherwise, you'll see an error message, such as ERROR.

✦ **ID:** Shows the unique identifier for the task.

✦ **Day:** Shows when the task is scheduled to run. Recurring tasks begin with the keyword Each. One-time tasks begin with the keyword Next.

✦ **Time:** Shows the time the command is scheduled to run.

✦ **Command Line:** Shows the command, program, or script scheduled to run.

If you enter the status ID, you can get information on an individual task, for example:

```
AT 3
```

or

```
AT \\Gandolf 3
```

Deleting scheduled AT jobs

You delete tasks by ID or you can cancel all scheduled tasks. You can delete a specific task like this:

```
AT 3 /delete
```

or

```
AT \\Gandolf 3 /delete
```

You cancel all tasks by typing the */delete* switch without a task ID, like this:

```
AT /delete
```

or

```
AT \\Gandolf /delete
```

When deleting all tasks, you'll be prompted to confirm the action:

```
This operation will delete all scheduled jobs.
Do you want to continue this operation? (Y/N) [N]:
```

Type **y** to confirm that you want to delete all tasks. If you want to delete all tasks without having to confirm the action, use the /yes option:

```
AT /delete /yes
```

or

```
AT \\Gandolf /delete /yes
```

Scheduling with Scripts

The sections that follow show how you can schedule jobs on local and remote systems using scripts. As you'll see, there are many different ways you can schedule jobs in the enterprise.

Using AT in a script

Because the AT Scheduler is a command-line utility, you can access it within scripts using the Run method of the WshShell object. When you use the Run method, you can pass AT arguments as command parameters. An example of this is shown as Listing 12-1.

Listing 12-1: **Scheduling tasks within a script**

VBScript

schedtask.vbs

```
Set ws = WScript.CreateObject("WScript.Shell")
ret = ws.Run("at 5:00 /every:M,W,F copylogs.vbs",0,"TRUE")

If ret = 0 Then
 ws.LogEvent 0, "SchedTask.VBS Script Completed Successfully"
Else
 ws.LogEvent 1, "Error executing SchedTask.VBS"
End If
```

JScript

schedtask.js

```
var ws = WScript.CreateObject("WScript.Shell");
ret = ws.Run("at 5:00 /every:M,W,F copylogs.js",0,"TRUE")

if (ret == 0) {
 //successful execution
 ws.LogEvent(0, "SchedTask.JS Script Completed Successfully")
 }
else {
 //failed execution
 ws.LogEvent(1, "Error executing SchedTask.JS")
 }
```

If you are scheduling multiple tasks, you can enter additional Run statements in the script. Listing 12-2 shows how you could schedule tasks on three different systems.

Listing 12-2: **Scheduling multiple tasks through a script**

VBScript

multitasks.vbs

```
Set ws = WScript.CreateObject("WScript.Shell")
ret = ws.Run("at 5:00 \\Gandolf /every:T,TH log.vbs",0,"TRUE")
```

```
ret = ret + ws.Run("at 5:00 \\Bilbo /every:T,TH log.vbs",0,"TRUE")
ret = ret + ws.Run("at 5:00 \\Dragon /every:T,TH log.vbs",0,"TRUE")
If ret = 0 Then
 ws.LogEvent 0, "SchedTask.VBS Script Completed Successfully"
Else
 ws.LogEvent 1, "Error executing SchedTask.VBS"
End If
```

JScript

multitasks.js

```
var ws = WScript.CreateObject("WScript.Shell");
ret = ws.Run("at 5:00 \\\\Gandolf /every:T,TH log.js",0,"TRUE")
ret += ws.Run("at 5:00 \\\\Bilbo /every:T,TH log.js",0,"TRUE")
ret += ws.Run("at 5:00 \\\\Dragon /every:T,TH log.js",0,"TRUE")

if (ret == 0) {
 //successful execution
 ws.LogEvent(0, "SchedTask.JS Script Completed Successfully")
 }
else {
 //failed execution
 ws.LogEvent(1, "Error executing SchedTask.JS")
 }
```

Automated job creation

In a network environment, you'll often want scheduled tasks to run on multiple computers. Rather than scheduling each script to run manually, you can automate the chore with a script. You'd probably want to use a separate file that the script can read to determine where and how to set up the jobs.

If the text file contains the system names and the jobs to execute, the format can look like this:

```
\\gandolf 00:00 /every:1,5,10,15,20,25,30 cleanup.js
```

You can then create a script that reads the file and executes the necessary commands, such as the one shown in Listing 12-3.

Listing 12-3: **Creating jobs automatically**

schedule.txt

```
\\gandolf 00:00 /every:1,5,10,15,20,25,30 cleanup.js
\\bilbo 00:00 /every:1,5,10,15,20,25,30 cleanup.js
\\dragon 00:00 /every:1,5,10,15,20,25,30 cleanup.js
```

autosched.js

```
var ws = WScript.CreateObject("WScript.Shell")

ForReading = 1
 data = new Array()
 count = 0

 var fs = new ActiveXObject ("Scripting.FileSystemObject");
 var f = fs.OpenTextFile("schedule.txt", ForReading, "True")
 while (!f.AtEndOfStream) {
  data[count] = f.ReadLine()
  count++
 }

for (s in data) {
  ws.Run("at " + data[s],0,"True")
  WScript.Echo("Creating job " + data[s])
 }
```

If you are scheduling the same jobs on multiple computers, you may want to have a file that specifies the computers to use and a script that specifies the jobs to run. If you do this, you don't have to create separate entries when you want to run the same jobs on multiple computers. You can then modify the job creation script as shown in Listing 12-4.

Listing 12-4: **Scheduling the same jobs on multiple systems**

sched-sys.txt

```
gandolf
bilbo
dragon
```

sched-jobs.txt

```
00:00 /every:1,5,10,15,20,25,30 cleanup.js
02:00 /every:M,W,F backup.js
05:00 /every:T,Th copylogs.js
```

autosched2.js

```
var ws = WScript.CreateObject("WScript.Shell")

ForReading = 1
data = new Array()
count = 0

var fs = new ActiveXObject ("Scripting.FileSystemObject");
var f = fs.OpenTextFile("sched-sys.txt", ForReading, "True")
while (!f.AtEndOfStream) {
 data[count] = "\\\\" + f.ReadLine()
 count++
}

ForReading = 1
jobs = new Array()
count = 0

var fs = new ActiveXObject ("Scripting.FileSystemObject");
var f = fs.OpenTextFile("sched-jobs.txt", ForReading, "True")
while (!f.AtEndOfStream) {
 jobs[count] = f.ReadLine()
 count++
}

for (s in data) {
  for (j in jobs) {
    ws.Run("at " + data[s] + " " + jobs [j],0,"True")
    WScript.Echo("Creating job " + jobs [j] + " on " + data[s])
  }
 }
```

Deleting jobs using scripts

You can delete jobs using scripts as well. This is useful if you make a mistake during automated scheduling or simply want to delete jobs that are no longer needed. You can delete jobs using the same techniques that you used to create jobs. The key difference is that instead of specifying jobs to create, you set the job identifiers to delete. You can also delete all scheduled jobs and then re-create them.

Listing 12-5 shows how you can delete all jobs on multiple computers. A text file is again used to specify the names of the systems you want to work with.

Listing 12-5: **Deleting scheduled jobs**

sched-del.txt

```
\\gandolf
\\bilbo
\\dragon
```

deletejobs.js

```
var ws = WScript.CreateObject("WScript.Shell")

ForReading = 1
data = new Array()
count = 0

var fs = new ActiveXObject ("Scripting.FileSystemObject");
var f = fs.OpenTextFile("sched-del.txt", ForReading, "True")
while (!f.AtEndOfStream) {
 data[count] = f.ReadLine()
 count++
}

for (s in data) {
 ws.Run("at " + data[s] + " /delete /yes",0,"True")
 WScript.Echo("Deleting jobs on " + data[s])
}
```

Creating a scheduling manager script

Previous sections outlined several different techniques for creating and deleting scripts. Now let's take this concept a few steps further by developing a script that handles both job creation and job deletion. You'll again use text files to designate where and how jobs should be handled.

A file named sched-svr.txt lists the servers on which you want to create or delete jobs. The file should contain the UNC name of the server, for example:

```
\\Gandolf
\\Bilbo
\\Dragon
\\Goblin
```

A file named sched-repl.txt lists the jobs you want to schedule on the designated servers. The file should only contain the job text:

```
00:00 /every:1,5,10,15,20,25,30 cleanup.js
00:20 /every:M,W,F backup.js
01:00 /every:Su copylogs.js
```

To make the script more dynamic, you'll configure the script to handle arguments. If the user doesn't enter an argument, the script should provide basic instruction on how to use the script. If the user enters an argument, the script should check the value of the argument and determine if the proper value has been entered. These features are implemented as follows:

```
var theArgs = WScript.Arguments

if (theArgs.Count() == 0) {
  WScript.Echo("Configure the text files:")
  WScript.Echo("sched-svr.txt and sched-repl.txt")
  WScript.Echo("Then enter c to copy or d to delete jobs.")
  WScript.Quit(1)
}
else {
  arg1 = theArgs.Item(0)
  WScript.Echo(arg1)
}

if (arg1 == "c") {
  WScript.Echo("Preparing to create Jobs...")
  createJobs()
  WScript.Quit(0)
}

if (arg1 == "d") {
  WScript.Echo("Preparing to delete Jobs...")
  deleteJobs()
  WScript.Quit(0)
}
```

Next, the `createJobs()` and `deleteJobs()` functions should perform the appropriate tasks. Because these functions both read the sched-svr.txt file, there is no reason to code the file-reading functionality twice. Instead, you can call another function that reads the files and returns the data neatly packed away in an array. The functions can then use the array values to configure or delete jobs, for example:

```
function deleteJobs() {

sysArray = getData("sched-svr.txt")

  for (s in sysArray) {
    ws.Run("at " + sysArray[s] + " /delete /yes",0,"True")
    WScript.Echo("Deleting jobs on " + sysArray[s])
  }
}

function createJobs() {

  sysArray = getData("sched-svr.txt")
  jobsArray = getData("sched-repl.txt")
```

```
  for (s in sysArray) {
   for (j in jobsArray) {
    ws.Run("at " + sysArray[s] + " " + jobsArray[j],0,"True")
    WScript.Echo("Creating job " + jobsArray[j] + " on " +
sysArray[s])
   }
  }
 }
```

The getData() function is very similar to the other functions for reading files we've examined. The key difference is that the function expects to be passed the filename to use as the first parameter. In this way, you can call the function to read both sched-svr.txt and sched-repl.txt. This function is implemented using the following code:

```
function getData(fname) {

 ForReading = 1
 data = new Array()
 count = 0

 var fs = new ActiveXObject ("Scripting.FileSystemObject");
 var f = fs.OpenTextFile(fname, ForReading, "True")
 while (!f.AtEndOfStream) {
  data[count] = f.ReadLine()
  count++
 }
 return data
}
```

The complete text for the scheduling manager script is shown in Listing 12-6.

Listing 12-6: **Managing job scheduling**

sched-svr.txt

```
\\Gandolf
\\Bilbo
\\Dragon
\\Goblin
```

sched-repl.txt

```
00:00 /every:1,5,10,15,20,25,30 cleanup.js
00:20 /every:M,W,F backup.js
01:00 /every:Su copylogs.js
```

schedmgr.js

```
// ************************
// Script: Enterprise Scheduling Manager
// Version: 0.9.1
// Creation Date: 9/2/99
// Last Modified: 12/15/99
// Author: William R. Stanek
// Email: winscripting@tvpress.com
//
// Copyright (c) 1999, 2000 William R. Stanek
// ************************
// Description: Manages scheduled tasks on local and
//              remote systems.
// ************************
// Copy jobs to multiple systems
// Enter c at first parameter
// *
// Delete jobs on a group of servers
// Enter d at first parameter
// *
// Server list comes from sched-svr.txt in current directory
// Enter server names on separate lines, such as:
// \\Gandolf
// \\Bilbo
// *
// Scheduled jobs are entered in sched-jobs.txt in the
// current directory. Enter the job information without
// the at or system name, such as:
// 01:00 /every:M,T,W,Th,F,S,Su cleanup.js
// 05:00 /next:1,15 checkstatus.js
// ************************

var ws = WScript.CreateObject("WScript.Shell")

var theArgs = WScript.Arguments

if (theArgs.Count() == 0) {
  WScript.Echo("Configure the text files:")
  WScript.Echo("sched-svr.txt and sched-repl.txt")
  WScript.Echo("Then enter c to copy or d to delete jobs.")
  WScript.Quit(1)
}
else {
  arg1 = theArgs.Item(0)
  WScript.Echo(arg1)
}

if (arg1 == "c") {
```

Continued

Listing 12-6 *(continued)*

```
    WScript.Echo("Preparing to create Jobs...")
    createJobs()
    WScript.Quit(0)
}

if (arg1 == "d") {
   WScript.Echo("Preparing to delete Jobs...")
   deleteJobs()
   WScript.Quit(0)
}

function deleteJobs() {

sysArray = getData("sched-svr.txt")

 for (s in sysArray) {
  ws.Run("at " + sysArray[s] + " /delete /yes",0,"True")
  WScript.Echo("Deleting jobs on " + sysArray[s])
  }
}

function createJobs() {

 sysArray = getData("sched-svr.txt")
 jobsArray = getData("sched-repl.txt")

 for (s in sysArray) {
  for (j in jobsArray) {
   ws.Run("at " + sysArray[s] + " " + jobsArray[j],0,"True")
   WScript.Echo("Creating job " + jobsArray[j] + " on " + sysArray[s])
  }
 }
}

function getData(fname) {

 ForReading = 1
 data = new Array()
 count = 0

 var fs = new ActiveXObject ("Scripting.FileSystemObject");
 var f = fs.OpenTextFile(fname, ForReading, "True")
 while (!f.AtEndOfStream) {
  data[count] = f.ReadLine()
  count++
 }
 return data
}
```

Summary

Task scheduling is one of the primary administrative tasks you'll need to perform in a network environment. As an administrator or a power user with extended permissions, you can use the techniques discussed in this chapter to create and manage scheduled tasks anywhere on the network. When you set out to manage tasks on multiple computers, don't forget that you can use scripts to handle the grunt work. In fact, you can use the scheduling manager script to handle most of your scheduling needs.

✦　　✦　　✦

Managing Computer and User Scripts

Automation is the key to Windows scripting. The previous chapter showed how you can create scripts to run automatically based on the time, day of the week, or date. This chapter focuses on creating scripts that execute based on user logon and logoff, as well as computer startup and shutdown.

Why Use Computer and User Scripts?

Every once in a while, an administrator or user asks me "Why would *I* want to use computer and user scripts?" I always think back to my days in the military when I often needed to log on to a system and be able to immediately begin troubleshooting critical network problems in a real-time environment. I simply didn't have time to start all the tools I needed, run background checks, or perform any other setup tasks; so I automated these processes. When I logged in, the tools I needed to work with started automatically, the background checks initialized and began running, and other configuration tasks were executed as well. The result was that instead of it taking five or six minutes to get ready to troubleshoot, I could start immediately, which helped me earn a reputation as someone who could resolve problems quickly.

While seconds may not count in the environment you work in, you can certainly benefit from automation. Any routine tasks that you or others in your office need to perform on a daily basis can be automated. You can automate these tasks:

✦ After system startup

✦ After logging on to the network

✦ Before logging off

✦ Before shutting down a system

The limits for computer and user scripts are the limits of your imagination. Scripts can run any Windows shell command, work with Windows Script Host, access Windows applications through COM (Component Object Model), and more. You just have to know how to write the script you need. For example, with logon scripts you may want to:

✦ Display a message of the day.

✦ Display a network usage policy or disclaimer.

✦ Start applications or run commands.

✦ Configure default printers and set up other printers.

✦ Map network drives and set default drive paths.

✦ Track the users login and logout times.

✦ Build a daily report from log files and display it in a browser.

So the answer to the question, "Why use computer and user scripts?" is clear. You use computer and user scripts because you want to become more efficient and you want to help others become more efficient.

Note   You'll need special privileges and permissions to manage computer and user scripts. If you aren't an administrator and don't have power user permissions on the local computer, you won't be able to manage startup, shutdown, logon, and logoff scripts.

Introducing Group Policies

In Windows 2000, you normally assign computer and user scripts through group policies. Think of a group policy as a set of rules that help you manage users and computers.

Note   Group policies only apply to systems running Windows 2000. Policies for Windows 95, Windows 98, and Windows NT 4.0 are set with the System Policy Editor (poledit.exe). There are separate policy editors for each operating system.

How are policies used?

Group policies can be applied at various levels in the organization. Policies that apply to individual computers are referred to as *local group policies* and are stored on an individual computer. Other group policies affect multiple computers and are stored in the Active Directory directory service. I'll refer to policies that affect multiple computers as *global group policies*. This will help differentiate between policies that affect individual computers (local group policies) and policies that affect multiple computers (global group policies).

The way policies are applied depends on the structure of the organization. To help you understand the available structures you need to know a bit about Active Directory. Active Directory is the primary directory service for Windows 2000. Active Directory provides the logical and physical structure of the company's network.

Logical structures defined by Active Directory are:

- ✦ **Domains** A domain is a group of computers that share a common directory structure. For example, the computers named Gandolf, Bilbo, and Dragon are all a part of the tvpress.com domain. This means that their full computer names are Gandolf.tvpress.com, Bilbo.tvpress.com, and Dragon.tvpress.com.

- ✦ **Organization units** An organizational unit is a subgroup of domains. Organizational units often mirror the company's functional or business structure. For example, you may have organizational units named Marketing, Engineering, and IS.

- ✦ **Domain trees** A domain tree is one or more domains that share a contiguous namespace. For example, the domains hr.tvpress.com and eng.tvpress.com are all a part of the tvpress.com master domain and are thus a part of the same domain tree.

- ✦ **Domain forests** A domain forest is one or more domain trees that share common directory information. If your company has multiple domains, such as tvpress.com and centraldrive.com, these domains form separate domain trees. However, because they are all defined through your organization's directory, they are a part of the same forest, and can thus share directory information.

The physical structures defined by Active Directory are:

- ✦ **Subnets** A subnet is a network group with a specific IP address range and network mask. For example, the IP addresses for Gandolf, Bilbo, and Dragon are all a part of the 207.19.67 network group. Their IP addresses are 207.19.67.12, 207.19.67.14, and 207.19.67.16, respectively. This means they are all a part of the same subnet.

- ✦ **Sites** A site is a group of one or more subnets. For example, if the company used the network groups 207.19.67 and 204.12.5, they could all be a part of the same site.

Group policies apply to domains, organizational units, and sites. This means you can set group policies based on the physical and logical structure of the network. When multiple policies are in place, they are applied in the following order:

1. Windows NT 4.0 policies (NTConfig.pol)

2. Local group policies

3. Site group policies

4. Domain group policies

5. Organizational unit group policies

6. Child organizational unit group policies

When there are conflicts in policy settings, settings applied later have precedence and overwrite previously set policy settings. For example, site policies have precedence over local group policies.

Note   Windows 2000 does define ways to override and block policy settings. These changes can affect the way policies are inherited and applied.

When are policies applied?

The way policies are applied depends on whether the policies affect computers or users. Computer-related policies are normally applied during system startup. User-related policies are normally applied during logon. The events that take place during startup and logon are as follows:

1. After the network starts, Windows 2000 applies computer policies. The computer policies are applied one at a time as outlined previously. No user interface is displayed while computer policies are being processed.

2. Windows 2000 runs any startup scripts. These scripts are executed one at a time by default. Here, each script must complete or time out before the next starts. Script execution is not displayed to the user unless otherwise specified.

3. When a user logs on, Windows 2000 loads the user profile.

4. Windows 2000 applies user policies. The policies are applied one at a time as outlined previously. The user interface is displayed while user policies are being processed.

5. Windows 2000 runs logon scripts. These scripts are executed simultaneously by default. Normally script execution is not displayed to the user. Scripts in the Netlogon share are run last.

6. Windows 2000 displays the startup interface configured in Group Policy.

How are local group policies managed?

All Windows 2000 computers have a local group policy. You manage local policies on a computer through an extension for the Microsoft Management Console (MMC) called Local Computer Policy. You can access Local Computer Policy as follows:

1. Click the Start menu, then click Run. This displays the Run dialog box.

2. Type **mmc** in the Open field and then click OK. This displays the Microsoft Management Console (MMC).

3. Click Console, then click Add/Remove Snap-in. This displays the Add/Remove Snap-in dialog box shown in Figure 13-1.

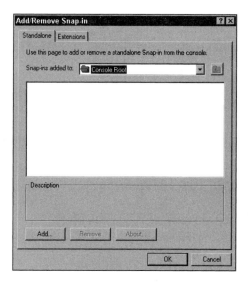

Figure 13-1: Use the Add/Remove Snap-in dialog box to select snap-ins that you want to add to the console.

4. On the Standalone tab, click Add.

5. Next, in the Add Snap-in dialog box, click Group Policy, then click Add. This displays the Select Group Policy Object dialog box.

6. Click Local Computer to edit the local policy on your computer or Browse to find the local policy on another computer.

7. Click Finish in the Group Policy Object dialog box then click Close in the Add Snap-in dialog box.

8. Click OK. As Figure 13-2 shows, the Local Computer Policy snap-in is then added to the console.

Once you've added the Local Computer Policy snap-in to the console, you can manage the local policy on the selected computer.

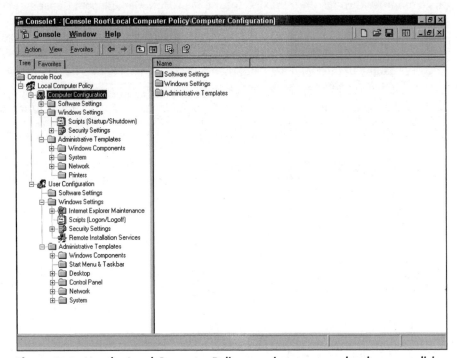

Figure 13-2: Use the Local Computer Policy snap-in to manage local group policies.

How are global group policies managed?

You work with global group policies through the Group Policy snap-in. The way you access this snap-in depends on the type of policy you are working with. For sites, you start the Group Policy snap-in from the Active Directory Sites and Services console. For domains and organizational units, you start the Group Policy snap-in from the Active Directory Users and Computers console.

Once you start the appropriate console, you access the Group Policy snap-in as follows:

1. Right-click on the site, domain, or organizational unit you want to work with in the console root. Then select Properties. This displays a Properties dialog box.

2. In the Properties dialog box, select the Group Policy tab as shown in Figure 13-3. You can now:

- Create a new policy or edit an existing policy by clicking New.

- Edit an existing policy by selecting a policy, then clicking Edit.

- Change the priority of a policy by selecting it and then using the Up/Down buttons to change its position in the Group Policy Object Links list.

- Delete an existing policy by selecting it and then clicking Delete.

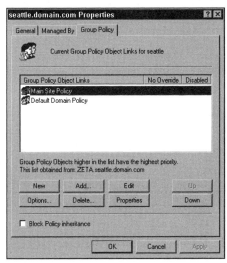

Figure 13-3: Use the Group Policy tab to view, edit, and delete policies.

Using the policy consoles

Figure 13-4 shows the Group Policy snap-in in an MMC console. If you compare this figure to Figure 13-2, you'll see that the Local Computer Policy and the Group Policy snap-ins are configured similarly. These snap-ins have two main nodes:

✦ **Computer Configuration** Used to set computer policies.

✦ **User Configuration** Used to set user policies.

You'll usually find that both Computer Configuration and User Configuration have subnodes for:

✦ Software Settings

✦ Windows Settings

✦ Administrative Templates

You configure user and computer scripts through Windows Settings.

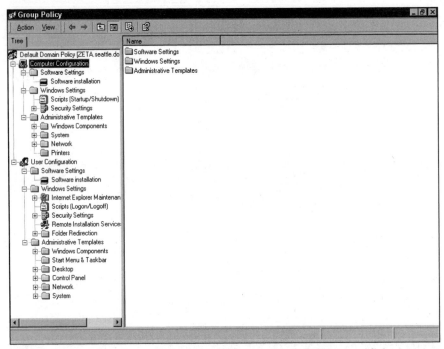

Figure 13-4: Use the Group Policy snap-in to manage global group policies.

Working with Computer and User Scripts

As you've seen, group policies play an important role in the way startup, shutdown, logon, and logoff scripts are assigned. Now let's look at how you can assign these scripts as part of group policies.

Managing startup and shutdown scripts

You assign startup and shutdown scripts to individual computers through local group policy, or to groups of computers through global group policies. By doing this, computers can execute scripts automatically when they are booted or are shut down. You assign a computer a startup or shutdown script by completing the following steps:

1. Access the policy console you want to work with as described previously in the chapter.

2. In the Computer Configuration node, double-click the Windows Settings folder.

3. In the console root, select Scripts. You can now:

   - Specify startup scripts by right-clicking Startup and then selecting Properties.

   - Specify shutdown scripts by right-clicking Shutdown and then selecting Properties.

4. Either technique opens a dialog box similar to the one shown in Figure 13-5. You can now add, delete, or reconfigure script properties.

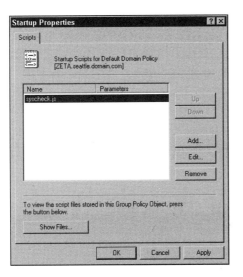

Figure 13-5: Use the Startup Properties dialog box to manage computer scripts.

5. To assign a script, click Add. This displays the Add a Script dialog box. In the Script Name field, type the full file path to the script you want to use, or click Browse to find a script. In the script parameter field, enter any parameters to pass to the scripting host for a Windows script. Repeat this step to add other scripts.

6. During startup or shutdown, scripts are executed in the order that they are listed in the Properties dialog box. Use the Up/Down buttons to change the order of the scripts if necessary.

7. Click OK when you are finished. If you later want to edit the script name or parameters, select the script in the Script For list then click Edit. You can delete a script by selecting it in the Script For list and then clicking Remove.

Managing logon and logoff scripts

Logon and logoff scripts are also managed through local and global group policies. Scripts you assign through local group policies affect all users that log in to that particular computer. Scripts you assign through global group policies affect all computers in the organizational unit, domain, or site. You assign a logon or logoff script by completing the following steps:

1. Access the policy console you want to work with as described previously in the chapter.

2. In the User Configuration node, double-click the Windows Settings folder.

3. In the console root, select Scripts. You can now:

   • Specify logon scripts by right-clicking Logon and then selecting Properties.

   • Specify logoff scripts by right-clicking Logoff and then selecting Properties.

4. Either technique opens a dialog box similar to the one shown in Figure 13-6. You can now add, delete, or reconfigure script properties.

5. To assign a script, click Add. This displays the Add a Script dialog box. In the Script Name field, type the full file path to the script you want to use, or click Browse to find a script. In the script parameter field, enter any parameters to pass to the scripting host for a Windows script. Repeat this step to add other scripts.

6. During logon or logoff, scripts are executed in the order that they are listed in the Properties dialog box. Use the Up/Down buttons to change the order of the scripts if necessary.

7. Click OK when you are finished. If you later want to edit the script name or parameters, select the script in the Script For list then click Edit. You can delete a script by selecting it in the Script For list and then clicking Remove.

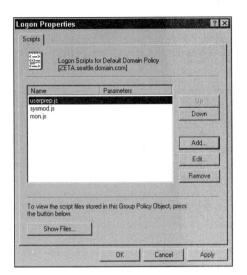

Figure 13-6: Use the Logon Properties dialog box to manage user scripts.

Alternatives to group policy

The sections that follow look at alternatives to assigning scripts through group policy. Group policies only apply to Windows 2000 and do not apply to Windows 95/98 or Windows NT. In a Windows NT 4.0 domain, the key scripts that you'll work with are logon scripts. These scripts are handled by the primary domain controller, which is a Windows NT 4.0 server or a Windows 2000 server acting as a domain controller for the Windows NT domain. Logon scripts must be placed in the domain controller's Netlogon share. Normally, this directory points to %SystemRoot%\System32\ REPL\IMPORT\SCRIPTS on the domain controller.

On Windows 95/98 and Windows NT systems, you normally use command-shell scripts as logon scripts. These scripts must end with the .bat or .cmd extension. Although there is a way to hack the Windows Registry and force the system to allow you to use Windows scripts, I don't recommend this. It is just as easy to use a shell script to call a Windows script containing your logon commands.

Listing 13-1 shows basic logon scripts that are executed through a shell script. The scripting hosts use the user's default working directory and all paths must be set relative to this directory, or you should use a full file path. This example accesses the Netlogon share on the primary domain controller. For logon scripts to be available, you need to configure directory replication or have an administrator do this for you. A good resource to learn about directory replication is *Microsoft Windows NT 4.0 Server Administrator's Pocket Consultant*.

Listing 13-1: **Executing Windows logon scripts through a shell script**

startup.bat

```
cscript \\Gandolf\NETLOGON\start.vbs
cscript \\Gandolf\NETLOGON\start.js
```

start.vbs

```
Set ws = WScript.CreateObject("WScript.Shell")
ws.Run "notepad "  & WScript.ScriptFullName
```

start.js

```
var ws = WScript.CreateObject("WScript.Shell");
ws.Run("notepad "  + WScript.ScriptFullName)
```

Another thing to note is that when you work with Windows 2000 systems, you don't have to assign computer and user scripts through group policy. The following options can be used in addition to, or instead of, group policy:

✦ Assign startup and logon scripts as scheduled tasks. You schedule tasks using the Task Scheduler Wizard.

✦ Assign logon scripts to individual user accounts through the Active Directory Users and Computers console. To do this, access the Profile tab of the User Properties dialog box.

Summary

In this chapter, you learned about the benefits of computer and user scripts. Computer scripts help you automate tasks when a computer is started or shut down. User scripts help you automate tasks when a user logs on or logs off. Both types of scripts can be powerful automation tools if used properly.

✦   ✦   ✦

Introducing Active Directory Service Interfaces

With Active Directory Service Interfaces, you can manage local accounts, domain accounts, Windows services, and other resources through Windows scripts. ADSI is very complex and is designed primarily for programmers that use Visual Basic or C++. Because of this complexity, you'll need to learn a few important concepts before you can start working with ADSI, which are exactly what this chapter covers. Don't worry, I won't try to teach you Visual Basic or C++ programming. I won't try to cover every facet of ADSI either. Instead, I'll focus on the core tasks that you can use time and again to manage network and system resources.

Note　　Rather than provide a ton of background material that you may not need, the focus of this chapter is on using ADSI and not on directory service basics. If you aren't familiar with directory services, you may want to brush up on the basics.

ADSI Essentials

Directory services are an important part of many network operating systems, including Novell NetWare and Microsoft Windows 2000. In Novell NetWare, the directory service is called Novell NetWare Directory Services (NDS). In Microsoft Windows 2000, the directory service is called Active Directory. Some directory services implement a common communication protocol called *the Lightweight Directory Access Protocol (LDAP)*. LDAP is an Internet standard protocol and you use it to access any compliant directory service.

Directory services often use objects to describe and provide access to various network components, such as users and groups. You can access these objects through the Active Directory Service Interfaces. While it's possible to fill several chapters with background material on how ADSI works, you really don't need to know ADSI internals to be able to create Windows scripts that use ADSI. The key concepts you should know are as follows:

✦ ADSI provides access to directory services by exposing their objects as COM objects.

✦ The interfaces of these COM objects provide methods and properties that can be used in Windows Scripts.

✦ You don't manipulate the COM interfaces directly and instead access the interfaces through an ADSI provider.

✦ ADSI uses a multi-tier architecture with clients, routers, and providers.

The sections that follow examine ADSI providers and the ADSI architecture.

Understanding ADSI providers

For Windows scripts, the ADSI provider is the most important aspect of the ADSI model. Each ADSI provider is specific to a particular directory service. You can get ADSI providers from Microsoft and from third-party vendors. ADSI providers from Microsoft include:

✦ ADSI LDAP Provider—A standard provider for LDAP-compliant services and applications. You can use this provider to manage Windows 2000 Active Directory, Microsoft Exchange 5.5/6.0, and more.

✦ ADSI WinNT Provider—A standard provider for accessing Windows NT 4.0 domains, workstations, and servers. You also use this provider to access local resources on Windows 2000 systems, such as local users and local groups.

✦ ADSI NDS Provider—A standard provider for accessing Novell NetWare Directory Services (NDS).

✦ ADSI NWCOMPAT Provider—A standard provider for accessing Novell NetWare 3.

Note   The provider name is case-sensitive and must be used exactly as shown in your scripts.

Providers can be extended at any time by installing new versions, service packs, or other add-ons. As you might expect, many different provider extensions are available. Two extensions that you may want to use are GC and IIS. Both are extensions to the ADSI LDAP Providers.

GC provides access to global catalogs. Global catalogs contain partial replicas of all the domains in a domain forest and are a part of Windows 2000 Active Directory.

You can use the GC extension to search for objects in the enterprise regardless of which domain they are in. For example, if your domain forest contains the domains tvpress.com, centraldrive.com, and weblearningcenter.com, you can search the global catalog for an object without having to know which domain it is in. Once you find the object, you could discover its relative domain and then obtain the object.

IIS provides access to Internet Information Services (IIS). Through IIS, you can create and configure FTP, Web, and SMTP sites. You can also manage logs and the IIS metabase. The *IIS metabase* contains definitions for various aspects of IIS and essentially allows you to read and change the configurations of related sites and services.

Understanding the ADSI architecture

ADSI uses a multi-tier architecture. Without going into all of the unnecessary details, the basic structure of this architecture looks like this:

> Client ⇨ ADSI Router ⇨ ADSI Provider

Following this simple structure, you can see that clients are used to access ADSI and that a middleman called a router is used to access providers. The router implements a core set of objects. These objects present a common set of features and services to providers. Because of this, any feature supported by the ADSI router is also supported by an ADSI provider (unless the provider chooses otherwise).

Any computer that wants to make use of ADSI must have the ADSI client installed. The client is installed automatically with Windows 2000 Professional and Windows 2000 Server. Computers running other operating systems must install the ADSI client. For example, if you run Windows scripts on a Windows 95 or Windows NT 4.0 computer and these scripts use ADSI, you'll need to install the ADSI client prior to running the scripts.

The standard providers distributed with the ADSI Software Developers Kit and in ADSI client distributions are referred to as ADSI system providers. Because ADSI is fully extensible, newer versions of providers are being created all the time. You can take advantage of these extensions by installing the latest version. Most of the features for ADSI providers and the ADSI router are implemented as *Dynamically Linked Libraries (DLLs)*. The key DLLs for system providers include:

✦ Activeds.dll, which implements the ADSI router module

✦ Adsldp.dll, adsldpc.dll, and adsmsext.dll, which implement the ADSI LDAP provider

✦ Adsnt.dll, which implements the ADSI WinNT provider

✦ Adsnds.dll, which implements the ADSI NDS provider

✦ Adsnw.dll, which implements the ADSI NWCompat provider

Note   If a DLL that's needed by a provider isn't installed on a computer, you can't use the provider. You'll need to install the provider.

Binding ADSI objects

You use the ADSI provider interfaces by binding to objects in the related directory service. In WSH, you can bind objects using the WScript.GetObject method. With ADSI, the syntax for the GetObject method is:

VBScript	*JScript*
`Set obj = GetObject("AdsPathString")`	`var obj = GetObject("AdsPathString")`

The AdsPath string identifies the ADSI provider and the object to which you want to bind. The following example obtains an object reference to the organizational unit called IT in the seattle.tvpress.com domain:

VBScript

```
Set ou = GetObject("LDAP://OU=IT,DC=seattle,DC=tvpress,DC=com")
```

JScript

```
var ou = GetObject("LDAP://OU=IT,DC=seattle,DC=tvpress,DC=com")
```

Although the AdsPath string is different for each provider, the basic syntax of the string is summarized in Table 14-1. As you can see from the table, the AdsPath string has two basic elements: special characters and components. Special characters serve primarily as separators but also join class designators and escape special characters. Components identify ADSI providers and designate component classes, such as domain components and organizational units.

Table 14-1
Syntax for AdsPath Strings

String Element Special Characters

Character	Description
Backward slash (\)	Escapes special characters to signify that they should be used as literals.
Forward slash (/)	Separates elements in the AdsPath string.
Semicolon (;)	Separates elements in the AdsPath string.

String Element Special Characters

Character	Description
Comma (,)	Separates elements in the `AdsPath` string.
Equal sign (=)	Joins a class specifier with a component.

Components

Designator	Description
`Provider://`	Designates an ADSI provider, such as `LDAP://`. The provider name is case-sensitive and must be exact.
`OU=`	Designates an organizational unit class, such as `OU=IT`.
`DC=`	Designates a domain component class, such as `DC=tvpress`.
`O=`	Designates an organization, such as `O=Internet`.
`CN=`	Designates a common name, such as `CN=user`.

All directory objects have a unique identifier. The identifier is a representation of each element, from the root of the directory hierarchy to the object you want to work with. When you use commas to separate elements in the hierarchy, you use a reverse order, starting from the object you want to work with and moving to the top-most object. In the previous example, the `AdsPath` string starts in the organizational unit and works up to the top-level of the domain hierarchy. The example could have started with a common name as well, for example:

```
CN=Administrator,OU=IT,DC=seattle,DC=tvpress,DC=com
```

When you use forward slashes to separate objects in the domain hierarchy, you move from the highest-level object to the lowest-level object, like this:

```
DC=com/DC=tvpress/DC=seattle/OU=IT/CN=Administrator
```

When you first start working with the `AdsPath` string, one of the most difficult concepts to understand is how domain names are represented through domain component classes. A technique that is helpful is to remember that domain names, such as `tvpress.com`, represent elements in the domain hierarchy. Here, `tvpress` represents the organizational domain and `com` is the top-level domain. Top-level domains form the root of the domain hierarchy and are also called root domains. *Root domains* are organized by function, organization type, and geographic location.

Normal domains, such as `tvpress.com`, are also referred to as parent domains. Parent domains can be divided into subdomains. These subdomains can be used for divisions or office locations. For example, the fully qualified domains `seattle.tvpress.com`, `portland.tvpress.com`, and `la.tvpress.com` could be used for your company's Seattle, Portland, and, Los Angeles offices respectively.

Each level of the domain hierarchy is represented by a domain component class. In the `portland.tvpress.com` domain:

- ✦ `DC=PORTLAND` represents the subdomain level
- ✦ `DC=TVPRESS` represents the parent level
- ✦ `DC=COM` represents the root level

By specifying these component classes in an `AdsPath`, you gain access to objects within the subdomain container, such as organizational units. If you wanted to work with objects in the parent domain (`tvpress.com`), you reference only the parent level and the root level, for example:

VBScript

```
Set ou = GetObject("LDAP://OU=Marketing,DC=tvpress,DC=com")
```

JScript

```
var ou = GetObject("LDAP://OU=Marketing,DC=tvpress,DC=com")
```

Once you have the object that you want to work with, you can use the available methods and properties to manipulate the object. Through these directory objects you can then:

- ✦ Manage domain accounts for users and groups
- ✦ Manage local accounts for users and groups
- ✦ Administer printers and print jobs
- ✦ Control file services and sharing
- ✦ Manage user sessions and connections
- ✦ Control other system and network resources as well

Taking Advantage of ADSI

Now that you know ADSI essentials, let's look at how you can take advantage of ADSI. ADSI implements dozens of interfaces that can be used in scripts. You access these interfaces through a named provider, such as the ADSI LDAP provider. Each provider implements interfaces for objects that are available through its related directory service. If an object isn't available, the interface isn't implemented. If an object property or method isn't available, the related interface method or property method isn't implemented.

Cross-Reference The sections that follow provide overviews of using the various providers. Later in the chapter and in other chapters in this Part of the book, you'll find more detailed examples.

Working with the ADSI LDAP provider

The *ADSI LDAP provider* is used to manage Windows 2000 Active Directory, Microsoft Exchange 5.5/6.0, and other LDAP-compliant applications. With Active Directory, you use the provider as outlined previously in the section titled, "Binding ADSI objects". As you'll recall, the basic syntax for the AdsPath string is:

```
LDAP://OU=IT,DC=seattle,DC=tvpress,DC=com
```

You can also reference a specific server or domain in the AdsPath. In the following example, you bind to the ADSI object through a server named Zeta:

VBScript

```
Set ou = GetObject("LDAP://Zeta/OU=Marketing,DC=tvpress,DC=com")
```

JScript

```
var ou = GetObject("LDAP://Zeta/OU=Marketing,DC=tvpress,DC=com")
```

In this example, you bind to an ADSI object through a domain on the Internet:

VBScript

```
Set ou = GetObject("LDAP://tvpress.com/OU=Marketing, DC=tvpress,DC=com,O=Internet")
```

JScript

```
var ou = GetObject("LDAP://tvpress.com/OU=Marketing, DC=tvpress,DC=com,O=Internet")
```

Cross-Reference When you access objects outside your local domain, you may need to authenticate yourself. To do this, use the OpenDSObject method. See the section in this chapter titled, "Handling authentication and security" for details.

When you access Microsoft Exchange, you must reference the server name in the AdsPath. Then, instead of referencing domain components, you reference the organization, site, container and mailbox names, for example:

```
LDAP://ServerName/cn=Mailbox,cn=Container,ou=SiteName,o=OrgName
```

In this example, you bind to the `Recipients` container in the mailbox for `wrstanek`:

VBScript

```
Set cont = GetObject("LDAP://qmail/cn=wrstanek,cn=Recipients, ou=Seattle,o=tvpress")
```

JScript

```
var cont = GetObject("LDAP://qmail/cn=wrstanek,cn=Recipients, ou=Seattle,o=tvpress")
```

You can also use forward slashes as shown here:

VBScript

```
Set cont = GetObject("LDAP://qmail/o=tvpress/ou=Seattle/ cn=Recipients/cn=wrstanek")
```

JScript

```
var cont = GetObject("LDAP://qmail/o=tvpress/ou=Seattle/ cn=Recipients/cn=wrstanek")
```

With Microsoft Exchange, common names are mapped to actual display names rather than directory names. This means you access mailboxes and their components using the name displayed in Exchange Administrator, Outlook, or another mail client.

When you use the LDAP provider, you'll use a different set of objects than you'll use with other providers. Table 14-2 lists the objects you'll use most often with the LDAP provider. The table also lists the ADSI interfaces for those objects that are supported by the LDAP provider.

Note   Some LDAP provider objects inherit from `GenObject`, which allows them to access interfaces supported by this object. For example, although the `User` object doesn't support `IADs` directly, the object can use the interface. The reason is that the interface is inherited from `GenObject`.

Table 14-2
Common Objects and Interfaces for the LDAP Provider

ADSI Object	Supported Interfaces	Description
Class	IADs IADsClass	Represents class definitions in the schema.

ADSI Object	Supported Interfaces	Description
GenObject	IADs IADsContainer IADsDeleteOps IADsObjectOptions IADsPropertyList IDirectoryObject IDirectorySearch	Provides common services to most other ADSI objects for the provider.
Group	IADsGroup IADsExtension	Represents a group account.
GroupCollection	IADsMembers	Represents a collection of group accounts.
Locality	IADsLocality IADsExtension	Represents geographical locales of users, organizations, and so forth.
Namespace	IADs IADsContainer IADsOpenDSObject	Represents the LDAP namespace.
Organization	IADsO IADsExtension	Represents an organization.
OrganizationalUnit	IADsOU IADsExtension	Represents an organizational unit.
Pathname	IADsPathname	Represents AdsPath.
PrintQueue	IADsPrintQueue IADsPrintQueueOperations IADsExtension	Represents a print queue.
Property	IADs IADsProperty	Represents attribute definitions in the schema.
RootDSE	IADs IADsPropertyList	Represents the root of the directory tree.
Schema	IADs IADsContainer	Represents the schema container.
Syntax	IADs IADsSyntax	Represents the attribute syntax.
User	IADsUser IADsExtension	Represents a user account.
UserCollection	IADsMembers	Represents a collection of user accounts.

Working with the ADSI WinNT provider

The ADSI WinNT provider is used to access resources in Windows NT 4.0 domains as well as local resources on Windows 2000 systems. With the WinNT provider, the basic syntax for the Ads/Path string is:

```
WinNT://DomainName/ServerName/ObjectName
```

In many ways this syntax makes the WinNT provider easier to work with, but it also limits the reach of the provider. You can access objects in the current NT domain or other accessible NT domains, but you can't access Internet domains. The following example shows how you can access the user account for wrstane in the tvpress domain:

VBScript

```
Set user = GetObject("WinNT://TVPRESS/wrstane")
```

JScript

```
var user = GetObject("WinNT://TVPRESS/wrstane")
```

You can also access a specific server in the domain. In the following example, you access the Primary Domain Controller named Zeta:

VBScript

```
Set user = GetObject("WinNT://TVPRESS/Zeta/wrstane")
```

JScript

```
var user = GetObject("WinNT://TVPRESS/Zeta/wrstane")
```

If a computer named Omega had a local printer named EngPrinter, you could access it as follows:

VBScript

```
Set ptr = GetObject("WinNT://TVPRESS/Omega/EngPrinter")
```

JScript

```
var ptr = GetObject("WinNT://TVPRESS/Omega/EngPrinter")
```

For the WinNT provider, the `AdsPath` can also include the class name of the object to which you want to bind. The main reason to do this is to improve the response time for binding the object. In this example, you specify the user class:

VBScript

```
Set user = GetObject("WinNT://TVPRESS/Zeta/wrstane,user")
```

JScript

```
var user = GetObject("WinNT://TVPRESS/Zeta/wrstane,user")
```

Table 14-3 shows the objects you'll use most often with the WinNT provider. The table also shows the ADSI interfaces for those objects that are supported by the WinNT provider.

Table 14-3
Common Objects and Interfaces for the WinNT Provider

ADSI Object	Supported Interfaces	Description
Class	IADs IADsClass	Represents a class definition.
Computer	IADs IADsComputer IADsComputerOperations IADsContainer IADsPropertyList	Represents a computer account.
Domain	IADs IADsContainer IADsDomain IADsPropertyList	Represents a domain.
FileService	IADs IADsContainer IADsFileService IADsFileServiceOperations IADsPropertyList	Represents a file service.
FileShare	IADs IADsFileShare IADsPropertyList	Represents a file share.

Continued

Table 14-3 *(continued)*

ADSI Object	Supported Interfaces	Description
Group	IADs IADsGroup IADsPropertyList	Represents a group account.
GroupCollection	IADs IADsMembers	Represents a collection of group accounts.
LocalGroup	IADs IADsGroup IADsPropertyList	Represents a local group account.
LocalgroupCollection	IADs IADsMembers	Represents a collection of local group accounts.
Namespace	IADs IADsContainer IADsOpenDSObject	Represents the WinNT namespace.
PrintJob	IADs IADsPrintJob IADsPrintJobOperations IADsPropertyList	Represents a print job.
PrintJobsCollection	IADsCollection	Represents a collection of print jobs.
PrintQueue	IADs IADsPrintQueue IADsPrintQueueOperations IADsPropertyList	Represents a print queue.
Property	IADs IADsProperty	Represents an attribute definition.
Resource	IADs IADsPropertyList IADsResource	Represents a resource.
ResourcesCollection	IADsCollection	Represents a collection of resources.
Schema	IADs IADsContainer	Represents the schema container.
Service	IADs IADsPropertyList IADsService IADsServiceOperations	Represents a service.

ADSI Object	Supported Interfaces	Description
Session	IADs IADsSession IADsPropertyList	Represents a user session.
SessionsCollection	IADsCollection	Represents a collection of user sessions.
Syntax	IADs IADsSyntax	Represents the syntax of an attribute.
User	IADs IADsPropertyList IADsUser	Represents a user account.
UserGroupCollection	IADsMembers	Represents a collection of user groups.

Working with the ADSI NDS provider

When you need to work with Novell NetWare Directory Services, you'll use the ADSI NDS provider. With NDS, you use an AdsPath string that is very similar to the string for the LDAP provider. The key differences are that you use the NDS:// designator and you normally specify the server or domain you want work with, for example:

```
NDS://Goober/CN=Trailer,DC=seattle,DC=tvpress,DC=com,O=Internet
```

or

```
NDS://Goober/O=Internet/DC=com/DC=tvpress/DC=seattle/CN=Trailer
```

In the following example, you bind to the ADSI object through an Internet domain:

VBScript

```
Set cont = GetObject("NDS://seattle.tvpress.com/O=Internet/
DC=com/DC=tvpress/DC=seattle/CN=Trailer ")
```

JScript

```
var cont = GetObject("NDS://seattle.tvpress.com/O=Internet/
DC=com/DC=tvpress/DC=seattle/CN=Trailer ")
```

The objects you'll use most often with the NDS provider are shown in Table 14-4. The table also lists the ADSI interfaces for those objects that are supported by the NDS provider.

Table 14-4
Common Objects and Interfaces for the NDS Provider

ADSI Object	Supported Interfaces	Description
Acl	IADsAcl	Represents an access control list.
BackLink	IADsBackLink	Represents the Back Link attribute.
CaseIgnoreList	IADsCaseIgnoreList	Represents a list of strings that aren't case-sensitive.
Class	IADs IADsClass	Represents a class definition.
Email	IADsEmail	Represents an email account.
FaxNumber	IADsFaxNumber	Represents a fax number.
GenObject	IADs IADsContainer IADsPropertyList IDirectoryObject IDirectorySearch	Provides common services to most of the ADSI objects in the NDS provider.
Group	IADs IADsGroup IADsPropertyList IDirectoryObject IDirectorySearch	Represents a group account.
GroupCollection	IADs IADsMembers	Represents a collection of group accounts.
Hold	IADsHold	Represents the Hold attribute in NDS.
Locality	IADsContainer IADsLocality IADsPropertyList IDirectoryObject IDirectorySearch	Represents the geographical locale of users, organizations, and so forth.
Namespace	IADs IADsContainer IADsOpenDSObject	Represents the namespace.
NetAddress	IADsNetAddress	Represents the NetAddress attribute in NDS.

ADSI Object	Supported Interfaces	Description
OctetList	IADsOctetList	Represents a list of octet strings.
Organization	IADsContainer IADsO IADsPropertyList IDirectoryObject IDirectorySearch	Represents an organization.
OrganizationalUnit	IADsContainer IADsOU IADsPropertyList IDirectoryObject IDirectorySearch	Represents an organizational unit.
Path	IADsPath	Represents the Path attribute in NDS.
PostalAddress	IADsPostalAddress	Represents a postal address.
PrintQueue	IADsPrintQueue IADsPrintQueueOperations IADsPropertyList	Represents a print queue.
Property	IADs IADsProperty	Represents an attribute definition.
ReplicaPointer	IADsReplicaPointer	Represents the ReplicaPointer attribute in NDS.
Schema	IADs IADsContainer	Represents the schema container.
Syntax	IADs IADsSyntax	Represents the syntax of an attribute.
Timestamp	IADsTimestamp	Represents the Timestamp attribute in NDS.
Tree	IADs IADsContainer	Represents a NDS directory tree.
TypedName	IADsTypedName	Represents the TypedName attribute in NDS.

Continued

Table 14-4 (continued)

ADSI Object	Supported Interfaces	Description
User	IADs IADsPropertyList IADsUser IDirectoryObject IDirectorySearch	Represents a user account.
UserCollection	IADs IADsMembers	Represents a collection of user accounts.

Working with the ADSI NWCOMPAT provider

When you need to work with Novell NetWare Directory Services, you use the ADSI NDS provider. With NDS, you use an AdsPath string that is very similar to the string for the LDAP provider. The key differences are that you use the NDS:// designator and you normally specify the server or domain you want work with, for example:

The ADSI NWCOMPAT provider is used to access Novell NetWare 3. The provider designator is NWCOMPAT://. When you use this provider, you should reference the server or domain you want to work with, for example:

```
NWCOMPAT://Goober/CN=Trailer,DC=seattle,DC=tvpress,DC=com,
O=Internet
```

or

```
NWCOMPAT://Goober/O=Internet/DC=com/DC=tvpress/DC=seattle/
CN=Trailer
```

As you can see, the syntax is nearly identical to the syntax for the NDS provider. Table 14-5 shows the objects you'll use most often with the NWCOMPAT provider. The table also shows the ADSI interfaces for those objects that are supported by the NWCOMPAT provider.

Table 14-5
Common Objects and Interfaces for the NWCOMPAT Provider

ADSI Object	Supported Interfaces	Description
Class	IADs IADsClass	Represents a class definition of the schema.

ADSI Object	Supported Interfaces	Description
Computer	IADs IADsComputer IADsComputerOperations IADsContainer IADsPropertyList	Represents a computer on the network.
FileService	IADs IADsContainer IADsFileService IADsFileServiceOperations IADsPropertyList	Represents a file service.
FileShare	IADs IADsFileShare IADsPropertyList	Represents a file share on the network.
Group	IADs IADsGroup IADsPropertyList	Represents a group account.
GroupCollection	IADs IADsMembers	Represents a collection of group accounts.
JobCollection	IADs IADsCollection	Represents a collection of print jobs.
Namespace	IADs IADsContainer	Represents the namespace of the directory.
PrintJob	IADs IADsPrintJob IADsPrintJobOperations IADsPropertyList	Represents a print job.
PrintQueue	IADs IADsPrintQueue IADsPrintQueueOperations IADsPropertyList	Represents a print queue.
Property	IADs IADsProperty	Represents an attribute definition of the schema.
Schema	IADs IADsContainer	Represents the schema container of the provider.
Syntax	IADs IADsSyntax	Represents the syntax of an attribute.
User	IADs IADsPropertyList IADsUser	Represents a user account.
UserCollection	IADs IADsMembers	Represents a collection of users.

ADSI Provider Basics

As you've seen, the ADSI providers make a dizzying array of objects and interfaces available to your Windows scripts. Before going into the specifics of key objects and interfaces, let's look at basic tasks you may need to perform regardless of which provider you use. These basic tasks are:

✦ Generic object binding

✦ Handling authentication and security

✦ Accessing properties and updating objects

Generic object binding

To create effective Windows scripts that use ADSI, you shouldn't make direct assignments in bindings. In most of the previous examples, I created bindings to specific servers, domains, and objects. I did so through a direct assignment, such as:

```
Set user = GetObject("WinNT://TVPRESS/wrstane")
```

Because domain resources can (and frequently do) change, you should be very careful when you bind directly to specific objects. Instead, you should make variable assignments that designate which objects you plan to use and then reference the variables. Ideally, you should make these assignments in the top section of the script so that they are easy to identify and change. You could re-write the previous example and have the outcome look like Listing 14-1.

Listing 14-1: **Setting up the object binding**

VBScript

bind.vbs

```
'Set up NT domain information
NTDomain = "TVPRESS"
NTUser = "wrstane"

'Get user object
Set user = GetObject("WinNT://" & NTDomain & "/" & NTUser)
```

JScript

---

bind.js

```
//Set up NT domain information
NTDomain = "TVPRESS"
NTUser = "wrstane"

//Get user object
var user = GetObject("WinNT://" + NTDomain + "/" + NTUser)
```

You should also use server-less binding whenever possible. So instead of referencing a specific server, such as Zeta or Goober, you reference the domain only. This allows the provider to locate and use the best server. For example, with LDAP and Active Directory, the LDAP provider would locate the best domain controller to work with and then use this domain controller.

Tip

> With LDAP you can bind to the root of the directory tree through the `rootDSE` object. You can then use the `rootDSE` object to access objects in the domain. In this way, you can create scripts that can be used in any domain. For details, see the section of Chapter 16 titled, "Working with Naming Contexts and the rootDSE Object".

Handling authentication and security

When you work with local domains you usually don't have to authenticate yourself to gain access to ADSI objects. If you want to work with objects outside the local domain, or you need to use a controlled account to access objects, you'll need to authenticate yourself through the `OpenDSObject` method of the `IADsOpenDSObject` interface. If you check Tables 14-2 to 14-6, you'll see this interface is supported by the LDAP, NDS, and WinNT providers only.

The `IADsOpenDSObject` interface is accessible when you obtain an object reference to the ADSI provider you want to work with, for example:

VBScript

```
Set prov = GetObject("WinNT:")
```

JScript

```
var prov = GetObject("WinNT:")
```

You can then call the `OpenDSObject` method to obtain the object you want to work with. The basic syntax for this method is:

```
ProvObj.OpenDSObject(ADSPath, UserID, Password, Flags)
```

Here's an example:

```
ProvObj.OpenDSObject("WinNT://TVPRESS/Administrator",
"wrstane", "jiggyPop", ADS_SECURE_CREDENTIALS)
```

When you use this method with other providers, be sure to use the correct syntax. For example, with the LDAP provider and Active Directory, you must specify the user ID in the format:

```
Username@domain
```

Here is an example:

```
wrstanek@seattle.tvpress.com
```

You should also be sure to use the correct flags. Most of the time you'll want to use the `ADS_SECURE_CREDENTIALS` flag, which tells the provider to request secure authentication. Still, there are times when you may want to use a different flag. You may also want to use multiple flags, and you can do this as well.

Table 14-6 provides a summary of the available flags. Because the flags represent constant values, you use multiple flags by adding together the flag values or by adding the constants themselves. While the constants are available in VBScript, they aren't available in JScript. Thus in JScript, you'll have to assign the constant a value, or simply use the expected value. The constant values are specified in octal format and use the 0x prefix.

Table 14-6
Flags for Use with OpenDSObject

Flag	Constant Value	Description
ADS_SECURE_AUTHENTICATION	0x1	Requests secure authentication.
ADS_USE_ENCRYPTION	0x2	Tells ADSI to use SSL (Secure Socket Layer) encryption whenever exchanging data over the network. You must have a Certificate Server installed to use this option.
ADS_USE_SSL	0x2	Tells ADSI to use SSL (Secure Socket Layer) encryption. You must have a Certificate Server installed to use this option.

Flag	Constant Value	Description
ADS_READONLY_SERVER	0x4	Allows the provider to use a read-only connection.
ADS_PROMPT_CREDENTIALS	0x8	Tells ADSI to prompt for user credentials when the authentication is initiated. An interface must be available to display the prompt.
ADS_NO_AUTHENTICATION	0x10	Requests no authentication. The WinNT provider does not support this flag. With Active Directory, the security context is set as "Everyone"
ADS_FAST_BIND	0x20	Requests quick bind with minimum interfaces only (rather than full-interface support).
ADS_USE_SIGNING	0x40	Checks data integrity to ensure the data received is the same as the data sent. To use this flag, you must also set the ADS_SECURE_AUTHENTICATION flag.
ADS_USE_SEALING	0x80	Tells ADSI to use Kerberos encryption. To use this flag, you must also set the ADS_SECURE_AUTHENTICATION flag.

Listing 14-2 shows a more complete example of working with OpenDSObject. Technically, when you obtain a reference to the provider object, you are obtaining a reference to the root of the provider's namespace. You can then work your way through this namespace in a variety of ways. As you examine the listing, compare the VBScript and the JScript code carefully and note the differences. You should also note the output, which demonstrates that the local Administrator account accessed by the WinNT provider is different from the domain Administrator account accessed by the LDAP provider. The accounts have different GUIDs and thus, they are different.

Listing 14-2: **Authenticating your access to the directory**

VBScript

auth.vbs

```
NTDomain = "seattle"
NTUser = "Administrator"

Set prov = GetObject("WinNT:")
Set user = prov.OpenDSObject("WinNT://" & NTDomain & "/" &
  NTUser,"wrstane","jiggyPop", ADS_SECURE_AUTHENTICATION)

'Work with the object
WScript.Echo user.Name
WScript.Echo user.Class
WScript.Echo user.GUID
WScript.Echo ""

Container = "CN=Administrator,CN=Users,DC=SEATTLE,DC=DOMAIN,DC=COM"

Set prov2 = GetObject("LDAP:")
Set user2 = prov2.OpenDSObject("LDAP://" & Container,
"wrstanek@seattle.domain.com","snoreLoud", ADS_SECURE_AUTHENTICATION)

'Work with the object
WScript.Echo user2.Name
WScript.Echo user2.Class
WScript.Echo user2.GUID
WScript.Echo ""
```

JScript

auth.js

```
ADS_SECURE_AUTHENTICATION  = 0x1

NTDomain = "seattle"
NTUser = "Administrator"

var prov = GetObject("WinNT:")
var user = prov.OpenDSObject("WinNT://" + NTDomain + "/" +
  NTUser,"wrstane","jiggyPop", ADS_SECURE_AUTHENTICATION)

//Work with the object
WScript.Echo(user.Name)
WScript.Echo(user.Class)
WScript.Echo(user.GUID)
WScript.Echo("")

Container = "CN=Administrator,CN=Users,DC=SEATTLE,DC=DOMAIN,DC=COM"

var prov2 = GetObject("LDAP:")
```

```
var user2 = prov2.OpenDSObject("LDAP://" + Container,
  "wrstanek@seattle.domain.com","snoreLoud", ADS_SECURE_AUTHENTICATION)

//Work with the object
WScript.Echo(user2.Name)
WScript.Echo(user2.Class)
WScript.Echo(user2.GUID)
WScript.Echo("")
```

Output

```
Administrator
User
{D83F1060-1E71-11CF-B1F3-02608C9E7553}

CN=Administrator
user
21fa96966f2b5341ba91257c73996825
```

Note

> The script returns the local and domain administrators accounts. These accounts are different and the *Globally Unique Identifier (GUID)* associated with the accounts shows this. As you set out to work with the providers, don't forget that local objects are different than domain objects.

Accessing properties and updating objects

Providers access objects through various interfaces. The core interface is IADs. This interface defines a set of properties and methods for working with objects. These properties and methods are examined in the sections that follow.

Working with IADs Properties

IADs properties you'll want to use in Windows scripts are summarized in Table 14-7. These properties allow you to examine (but not set) object properties.

Table 14-7
IADs Properties for Windows Scripts

Properties	Description	Sample Return Value
AdsPath	Retrieves the object's AdsPath.	LDAP://CN=Administrator, CN=Users,DC=SEATTLE, DC=DOMAIN,DC=COM
Class	Retrieves the name of the object's class.	User
GUID	Retrieves the GUID of the object.	21fa96966f2b5341ba91257c73996825

Continued

Table 14-7 *(continued)*

Properties	Description	Sample Return Value
Name	Retrieves the object's relative name.	`CN=Administrator`
Parent	Retrieves the `AdsPath` string for the parent object.	`LDAP://CN=Users,DC=SEATTLE,DC=DOMAIN,DC=COM`
Schema	Retrieves the `AdsPath` string for the related schema class object.	`LDAP://schema/user`

The `AdsPath` strings for the parent and schema are very useful in your Windows scripts. You can use these strings to retrieve the related parent and schema objects. Another useful property is GUID. GUID returns the globally unique identifier that was assigned when the object instance was created. Globally unique identifiers are 128-bit numbers that are guaranteed to be unique in the namespace. Once an object is created, the GUID never changes — even if the object is moved or renamed. Thus, while the `AdsPath` string to the object may change, the GUID won't. Because of this, you may want to use GUIDs to examine and manage objects in scripts.

Listing 14-3 provides a detailed example of how you read property values and display them. You'll also see an example of using the parent and schema properties to retrieve the related objects.

Listing 14-3: **Using IADs properties**

VBScript

iads.vbs

```
Container = "CN=Administrator,CN=Users,DC=SEATTLE,DC=DOMAIN,DC=COM"

Set prov = GetObject("LDAP:")
Set user = prov.OpenDSObject("LDAP://" & Container,
  "wrstanek@seattle.domain.com","lolly", ADS_SECURE_AUTHENTICATION)

'Work with the object
WScript.Echo "Object AdsPath: " & user.AdsPath
WScript.Echo "Object Class: " & user.Class
WScript.Echo "Object GUID: " & user.GUID
WScript.Echo "Object Name: " & user.Name
WScript.Echo "Object Parent: " & user.Parent
WScript.Echo "Object Schema: " & user.Schema
```

```
Set cls = GetObject(user.Schema)
WScript.Echo "Class Name: " & cls.Name

Set parcls = GetObject(user.Parent)
WScript.Echo "Parent Class Name: " & parcls.Name
```

JScript

iads.js

```
ADS_SECURE_AUTHENTICATION  = 0x1
Container = "CN=Administrator,CN=Users,DC=SEATTLE,DC=DOMAIN,DC=COM"

var prov = GetObject("LDAP:")
var user = prov.OpenDSObject("LDAP://" + Container,
"wrstanek@seattle.domain.com","lolly",
  ADS_SECURE_AUTHENTICATION)

//Work with the object
WScript.Echo("Object AdsPath: " + user.AdsPath)
WScript.Echo("Object Class: " + user.Class)
WScript.Echo("Object GUID: " + user.GUID)
WScript.Echo("Object Name: " + user.Name)
WScript.Echo("Object Parent: " + user.Parent)
WScript.Echo("Object Schema: " + user.Schema)

var cls = GetObject(user.Schema)
WScript.Echo("Class Name: " + cls.Name)

var parcls = GetObject(user.Parent)
WScript.Echo("Parent Class Name: " + parcls.Name)
```

Output

```
Object AdsPath: LDAP://CN=Administrator,CN=Users,DC=SEATTLE,DC=DOMAIN,DC=COM
Object Class: user
Object GUID: 21fa96966f2b5341ba91257c73996825
Object Name: CN=Administrator
Object Parent: LDAP://CN=Users,DC=SEATTLE,DC=DOMAIN,DC=COM
Object Schema: LDAP://schema/user
Class Name: user
Parent Class Name: CN=Users
```

You can modify the script to run on your system by changing the following lines to reflect proper settings for your network:

```
Container =
"CN=Administrator,CN=Users,DC=SEATTLE,DC=DOMAIN,DC=COM"
Set user = prov.OpenDSObject("LDAP://" & Container,
  "wrstanek@seattle.domain.com","lolly",
ADS_SECURE_AUTHENTICATION)
```

or

```
Container = "CN=Administrator,CN=Users,DC=SEATTLE,DC=DOMAIN,DC=COM"
var user = prov.OpenDSObject("LDAP://" + Container,
  "wrstanek@seattle.domain.com","lolly",
ADS_SECURE_AUTHENTICATION)
```

Once you do this, you should get a GUID for the Administrator object. Now replace the Container line with the following code:

```
Container = "<GUID=guid>"
```

where *guid* is the actual GUID for the Administrator account. When you run the script again, you should see output similar to the following:

```
Object AdsPath: LDAP://<GUID=21fa96966f2b5341ba91257c73996825>
Object Class: user
Object GUID: 21fa96966f2b5341ba91257c73996825
Object Name: <GUID=21fa96966f2b5341ba91257c73996825>
Object Parent: LDAP:
Object Schema: LDAP://schema/user
Class Name: user
Parent Class Name: LDAP:
```

The output shows the important differences between using a GUID and using a precise object reference. When you access an object by its GUID, you access it directly from the root of the namespace. This is why the parent object and parent class name are `LDAP:`. In your scripts, this difference may cause poorly written scripts to behave differently when you use GUIDs. To prevent problems, ensure that the parent and schema objects you obtain reflect the objects with which you want to work.

Working with IADs methods

As you've seen, the IADs properties are used to obtain standard properties for objects, such as the object name and class. When you want to go beyond standard properties or want to set properties of an object, you'll need to use the methods of the IADs interface. The key methods are:

✦ `Get()` Gets a property value from the property cache.

✦ `Put()` Sets a new value in the property cache.

✦ `GetEx()` Gets an array of cached values.

✦ `PutEx()` Sets an array of cached values.

✦ `GetInfo()` Gets property values for an object from the directory cache.

✦ `GetInfoEx()` Gets property values for an object from the directory cache.

✦ `SetInfo()` Saves the object's cached values to the data store.

Tip   During the testing of VBScript and JScript compatibility with ADSI, I found it difficult to obtain reliable results with `GetEx()`, `GetInfoEx()`, and `PutEx()` in JScript. The reason for this is that ADSI interfaces use safe arrays, which are designed for VBScript. Before you can use safe arrays in JScript, you must convert them to a standard JScript array with the `toArray()` method. Similarly, you can only update a safe array by creating a safe array with the `VBArray()` method.

When you use any of these methods, you obtain the property value by referencing the property name, for example:

```
phone = user.Get("homePhone")
```

or

```
pager = user.Get("pager")
```

You can retrieve any available property with the `Get()` method. Although the `Get()` method is designed to work with single values, it does return two types of values: strings or arrays. This can lead to problems in your scripts. If you are unsure whether a property returns one value or many, you may want to use `GetEx()`. With `GetEx()` you get an array regardless of whether there is one value or multiple values. You can then examine the contents of the array to work with the property values.

You can examine multi-value properties in Listing 14-4. I've used a side-by-side code example so you can make a direct comparison of safe array-handling techniques in VBScript and JScript.

Listing 14-4: **Viewing multi-value properties**

VBScript	JScript
```Set user = GetObject ("LDAP://CN=William R. Stanek, CN=Users, DC=SEATTLE,DC=DOMAIN, DC=COM") Nums = user.GetEx("otherTelephone") For Each a In nums WScript.Echo a Next }```	```var user = GetObject ("LDAP://CN=William R. Stanek, CN=Users, DC=SEATTLE,DC=DOMAIN, DC=COM") nums = user.GetEx("otherTelephone") e = nums.toArray() for (opt in e) { WScript.Echo(e[opt])```

When you use the `Put()` or `PutEx()` methods, you modify property values in the property cache. To set the changes, you call `SetInfo()`. With `Put()`, you can set the home telephone number for a user as shown in Listing 14-5.

Listing 14-5: **Setting property values**

VBScript

```
Set user = GetObject("LDAP://CN=William R. Stanek,CN=Users,
  DC=SEATTLE,DC=DOMAIN,DC=COM")
user.Put "homePhone", "808-555-1212"
user.SetInfo
```

JScript

```
var user = GetObject("LDAP://CN=William R. Stanek,CN=Users,
  DC=SEATTLE,DC=DOMAIN,DC=COM")
user.Put("homePhone", "808-555-1212")
user.SetInfo()
```

The GetInfo() and SetInfo() methods are strongly related. GetInfo() retrieves a snapshot of an object from the directory store and puts it in the cache. When you obtain an object property using Get() or GetEx(), the GetInfo() method is called for you and this is how you are able to obtain a property value. When you check property values later for the same object, these values are retrieved directly from cache and GetInfo() is not called (unless you explicitly call it).

Once you change property values in the cache, you should commit those changes by calling SetInfo(). Keep in mind though, that you shouldn't call SetInfo() each time you change property values. Rather, you should call SetInfo() when you are finished working with the object and want to update the directory store.

The PutEx() method has an interesting syntax that you should know about. When you call PutEx(), you pass in three parameters:

✦ A flag that determines how a property value should be updated

✦ A string containing the property name

✦ An array containing the new value(s) for the property

These parameters give PutEx() the following syntax:

```
Obj.PutEx(Flag, "Property", Array("str1", "str2", ... "strN")
```

Table 14-8 provides an overview of the flags for PutEx().

Table 14-8
Flags for Use with PutEx()

Flag	Constant Value	Description
ADS_PROPERTY_CLEAR	1	Sets the property value to an empty string.
ADS_PROPERTY_UPDATE	2	Replaces the current property value with the array value(s)
ADS_PROPERTY_APPEND	3	Adds the array value(s) to the current property value.
ADS_PROPERTY_DELETE	4	Deletes the specified value(s) in the array from the property.

An example of modifying multi-value properties is shown in Listing 14-6. Note that you normally wouldn't make all of these changes on the same object.

Listing 14-6: **Working with multiple property values**

VBScript

multiprops.vbs

```
Set user = GetObject("LDAP://CN=William R.
Stanek,CN=Users,DC=SEATTLE,DC=DOMAIN,DC=COM")

'Replace current value
Dim r
r = Array("808-555-1212","808-678-1000")
user.PutEx ADS_PROPERTY_UPDATE, "otherTelephone", r
user.SetInfo

'Add another phone number
Dim a
a = Array("206-905-55555")
user.PutEx ADS_PROPERTY_APPEND, "otherTelephone", a
user.SetInfo

'Delete a value while leaving other values
Dim d
d = Array("808-555-1212")
user.PutEx ADS_PROPERTY_DELETE, "otherTelephone", d
user.SetInfo
```

Continued

Listing 14-6: *(continued)*

VBScript

```
'Clear all values
user.PutEx ADS_PROPERTY_CLEAR, "otherTelephone",  vbNullString
user.SetInfo
```

JScript

---

multiprops.js

```
var user = GetObject("LDAP://CN=William R.
Stanek,CN=Users,DC=SEATTLE,DC=DOMAIN,DC=COM")

//Replace current value
r = new VBArray("808-555-1212","808-678-1000")
user.PutEx(ADS_PROPERTY_UPDATE, "otherTelephone", r)
user.SetInfo()

//Add another phone number
a = new VBArray("206-905-55555")
user.PutEx(ADS_PROPERTY_APPEND, "otherTelephone", a)
user.SetInfo()

//Delete a value while leaving other values
d = new VBArray("808-555-1212")
user.PutEx(ADS_PROPERTY_DELETE, "otherTelephone", d)
user.SetInfo()

//Clear all values
user.PutEx(ADS_PROPERTY_CLEAR, "otherTelephone",  "")
user.SetInfo()
```

Summary

ADSI provides a powerful set of interfaces that you can use to manage system and network resources. To work with these interfaces, you use an ADSI provider, such as WinNT or LDAP. Each provider supports an extensible set of objects and these objects implement specific interfaces. The supported interfaces determine the functions you can script. Most objects implement the IADs interface. This interface provides basic functions for reading and writing object properties.

✦   ✦   ✦

Using Schema to Master ADSI

✦ ✦ ✦ ✦

In This Chapter

Understanding ADSI
schema, collections,
and containers

Managing schema
class objects

Viewing property
values and ranges

Viewing automation
data type

✦ ✦ ✦ ✦

One of the most important features of ADSI is its extensibility. ADSI will change and evolve over time, and to adapt to these changes, you'll need to know how to navigate the schema. Schema provides the basic structures that you can script. By examining the schema, you can determine the exact feature set a particular computer supports. You can also determine the acceptable parameters for properties. These elements together provide everything you need to master the provider features and to get detailed information on objects and their properties. As you study this chapter, keep in mind that Appendix B has detailed information on all of the interfaces that this chapter discusses.

Exploring ADSI Schema

In ADSI, you manage groups of objects through collections. You'll encounter collections in a wide variety of circumstances. For example, user sessions are represented through a collection and you use this collection to examine individual `Session` objects. You also manage services, print jobs, and open resources through collections.

Collections are implemented through the `IADsCollection` interface. This interface has methods for obtaining, adding, and removing elements. ADSI defines two special types of collections:

✦ **Containers** Containers contain other objects and are implemented with the `IADsContainer` interface. The `IADsContainer` interface has properties and methods for examining and managing objects.

✦ **Membership groups** Membership groups represent collections of objects belonging to groups and are implemented with the IADsMembers interface. The IADsMembers interface has methods for determining and summarizing group membership. Only users and groups have membership groups.

The Schema object is a top-level container for other objects, and these objects in turn contain other objects. All system providers support a Schema object. Schema is implemented through three interfaces:

✦ IADsClass — Used to manage schema class objects

✦ IADsProperty — Used to view object properties

✦ IADsSyntax — Used to view data types supported by object properties

An object that is not a container is referred to as a leaf element. Only users and groups have membership groups. You can determine this because they implement the IADsMembers interface.

Knowing the object model structure is essential to working with Active Directory schema. So before I cover the schema in depth, I'll map out the object model for WinNT and LDAP. These providers are the ones you'll use the most.

The core WinNT object model

The WinNT provider has the most complex object model. Primarily, this is because WinNT serves a multipurpose role for domains, Windows NT 4.0 computers, and Windows 2000 computers.

With the WinNT provider, the core container objects are Domain, User, and Group. The Domain object represents the top of the domain hierarchy. The User object represents domain user accounts. The Group object represents domain group accounts. While the Domain object holds other containers, the User and Group objects contain individual user and group accounts at the leaf level.

The core hierarchy comes together like this:

```
WinNT:
    - Domain
        - User
        - LocalGroup
            LocalGroupCollection
        - Computer
            - Service
            - FileService
                - FileShare
                - ResourcesCollection
```

```
                    - SessionsCollection
              - PrintQueue
                    - PrintJobsCollection
        - User
        - Group
            UserGroupCollection
            GroupCollection
```

You can use the object model to determine how you can access a specific object. For example, to access the alert service you must go through the `Domain` and `Computer` objects:

VBScript

```
Set service = GetObject("WinNT://tvpress/zeta/alerter,service")
```

JScript

```
var service = GetObject("WinNT://tvpress/zeta/alerter,service")
```

where `tvpress` is the domain name, `zeta` is the computer name, and `alerter` is the name of the service you want to work with.

The core LDAP object model

Compared to the WinNT object model, the LDAP object model is fairly basic. One of the main reasons for this is that the LDAP model seeks to be generic so that it can be used with multiple applications, such as Windows 2000 and Exchange Server. Because of this, the only meaningful way to examine the object models related to the LDAP provider is in the context of a specific implementation. The implementation you'll use the most is the Windows 2000 object model.

The Windows 2000 object model is tied to Active Directory. The root of the Active Directory directory tree is represented with the `RootDSE` object. The `RootDSE` provides information about individual directory servers and is not a part of the standard namespace. Beyond the directory root, you'll find the standard naming contexts for Windows 2000. A naming context is top-level container for the directory tree. The available naming contexts are:

✦ **Domain container** A top-level container for the domain. It contains users, groups, computers, organizational units, and other domain objects.

✦ **Schema container** A top-level container that allows you to access schema objects.

✦ **Configuration container** A top-level container for the entire domain forest. It contains sites, which in turn contain individual sites, subnets, inter-site transports, and other configuration objects.

As you'd expect, these naming contexts hold other containers. You can view other domain containers through Active Directory Users and Computers. As Figure 15-1 shows, the default domain containers are:

✦ **Builtin** — Stores built-in local groups.

✦ **Computers** — Stores computer accounts.

✦ **ForeignSecurityPrincipals** — Stores security identifiers for external objects associated with external, trusted domains.

✦ **Users** — Stores user and group accounts.

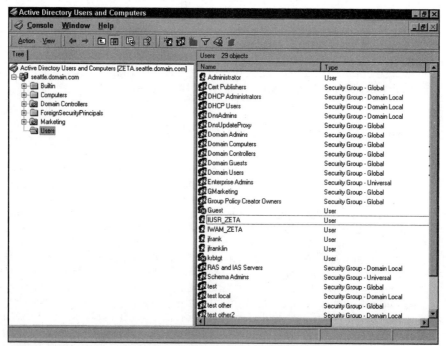

Figure 15-1: You can use Active Directory Users and Computers to view high-level domain containers and their contents.

The default containers are designed to hold specific types of objects. However, you can add just about any type of object to these containers including:

✦ Computers

✦ Contacts

✦ Users

✦ Groups

✦ Printers

✦ Shared Folders

I refer to these types of objects as common-name objects. You access objects in default containers through the *common-name identifier, CN*. For example, if you wanted to access the built-in Administrators group, you could use the following:

VBScript

```
Set acc = GetObject("LDAP://CN=Administrators,CN=Builtin,DC=tvpress,DC=com")
```

JScript

```
var acc = GetObject("LDAP://CN=Administrators,CN=Builtin,DC=tvpress,DC=com")
```

New domain containers can be created as well. To do this, you create organizational units. Organizational units can contain the same objects as the default domain containers. The only default organizational unit is Domain Controllers which is designed to store computer accounts for domain controllers. To access Domain Controllers, you must use the *organizational unit identifier, OU*.

If you create or move objects into the organizational unit container, you access the objects through the organizational unit, for example:

VBScript

```
Set acc = GetObject("LDAP://CN=William R. Stanek,OU=IT,DC=tvpress,DC=com")
```

JScript

```
var acc = GetObject("LDAP://CN=William R. Stanek,OU=IT,DC=tvpress,DC=com")
```

You can view other configuration containers through Active Directory Sites and Services. As Figure 15-2 shows, the default configuration containers are:

✦ **Sites** — A high-level container for subnets, transports, and individual sites.

✦ **Default-First-Site** — The default site for the domain tree.

✦ **Subnets** — A high-level container for subnets in the domain tree.

✦ **Inter-Site Transports** — A high-level container for transports. Transports like IP and SMTP transfer information throughout the domain tree.

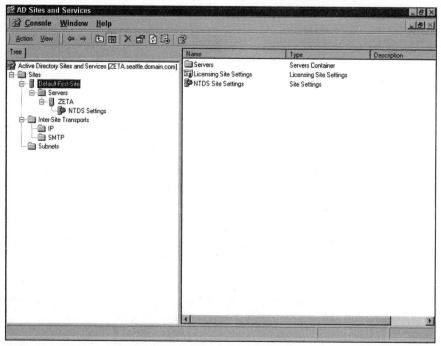

Figure 15-2: You can use Active Directory Sites and Services to view high-level configuration containers and their contents.

Putting all this together, you see that the Windows 2000 object model looks similar to the following:

```
RootDSE
        - Domain Container
            - Default Containers
            - Common Name Objects
            - Organizational Units
```

```
            - Common Name Objects
    - Schema Container
            - Schema Objects
    - Configuration Container
            - Sites Container
                - Site Container
                - Subnets Container
                - Inter-site Transports Container
```

Working with Schema Class Objects

Schema class objects provide a window into the world of the ADSI provider. If you know nothing else about a provider except its name and the core objects it supports, you can—with a bit of trial and error—explore every key feature of the provider. To do this, you access the IADsClass interface of the object you want to work with and then you use the properties of this interface to explore the object.

Accessing an object's schema class

You access an object's schema class through its Schema property. For example, if you want to access the schema for a computer, you can use the following:

VBScript

```
'WinNT Provider
Set obj = GetObject("WinNT://zeta,computer")
Set cls = GetObject(obj.Schema)

'LDAP Provider
Set obj = GetObject("LDAP://CN=Zeta,CN=Computers, DC=tvpress, DC=com")
Set cls = GetObject(obj.Schema)
```

JScript

```
//WinNT Provider
var obj = GetObject("WinNT://zeta,computer")
var cls = GetObject(obj.Schema)

//LDAP Provider
var obj = GetObject("LDAP://CN=Zeta,CN=Computers, DC=tvpress, DC=com")
var cls = GetObject(obj.Schema)
```

Once you've accessed the schema for an object, you can use any of the available properties of IADsClass to work with the schema. These properties are summarized in Table 15-1.

Table 15-1 Properties of IADsClass		
Property	**Status**	**Description**
Abstract	Read/Write	Boolean value that indicates whether the schema class is abstract.
AuxDerivedFrom	Read/Write	Array of AdsPath strings that specify the super Auxiliary classes of this schema class.
Auxiliary	Read/Write	Boolean value that determines whether this schema class is an Auxiliary class.
CLSID	Read/Write	A provider-specific string that identifies the COM object that implements this schema class.
Container	Read/Write	Boolean value that indicates whether this is a Container object.
Containment	Read/Write	Array of strings that identify object types that can be contained within this container.
DerivedFrom	Read/Write	Array of AdsPath strings that indicate which classes this class is derived from.
HelpFileContext	Read/Write	The context identifier for an optional help file.
HelpFileName	Read/Write	The name of an optional help file.
MandatoryProperties	Read/Write	An array of strings that lists the mandatory properties for an ADSI object.
NamingProperties	Read/Write	An array of strings that lists the properties that are used for naming attributes.
OID	Read/Write	A directory-specific object identifier string.
OptionalProperties	Read/Write	An array of strings that lists the optional properties for an ADSI object.
PossibleSuperiors	Read/Write	An array of AdsPath strings that lists classes that can contain instances of this class.
PrimaryInterface	Read Only	A globally unique identifier string for the interface defining this schema class.

Checking to see if an object is a container

Often when you work with objects, you'll want to determine if an object is a container and if so, what objects it contains. You can do this with the `Container` and `Containment` properties. An example is shown as Listing 15-1.

As you examine the listing, note the different VBScript and JScript techniques used to access the `Containment` array. ADSI returns arrays as safe arrays, which are designed to be used with VBScript. To use these arrays in JScript, you can convert the safe array to a normal JScript array.

Listing 15-1: **Checking Containers and Containment**

VBScript	**JScript**
Container.vbs	Container.js

```
Set dom = GetObject("WinNT://tvpress")
Set cls = GetObject(dom.Schema)
If cls.Container = True Then
  WScript.Echo "The domain object
  contains the following objects: "
e = cls.Containment
For each op in e
  WScript.Echo op
Next
End If
```

```
var dom = GetObject("WinNT://tvpress")
var cls = GetObject(dom.Schema)
if (cls.Container == 1) {
  WScript.Echo("The domain object
  contains the following objects: ")
e = cls.Containment.toArray()
for (op in e)
  {
     WScript.Echo(e[op])
  }
}
```

Output

```
The domain object contains the
following children:
Computer
User
Group
```

Output

```
The domain object contains the
following children:
Computer
User
Group
```

Examining mandatory and optional properties

Whether you are creating users, modifying groups, or working with other objects, you often need to be able to determine if a property must be set, or if the property is optional. You can determine mandatory and optional properties using `MandatoryProperties` and `OptionalProperties`, respectively.

Listing 15-2 examines properties of the `Computer` object using both WinNT and LDAP. With WinNT, you can bind directly to the object. With LDAP, you must bind to the object via its container, which in this case is the `Computers` container.

Listing 15-2: **Examining mandatory and optional properties**

VBScript

Checkproperties.vbs

```
Set obj = GetObject("WinNT://zeta,computer")
Set cls = GetObject(obj.Schema)
WScript.Echo obj.AdsPath
displayProps(cls)

Set obj =GetObject("LDAP://CN=Omega,CN=Computers,DC=tvpress,DC=com")
Set cls = GetObject(obj.Schema)
WScript.Echo obj.AdsPath
displayProps(cls)

Sub displayProps(obj)
  For Each p in obj.MandatoryProperties
    WScript.Echo "Mandatory: " & p
  Next
  For Each p in obj.OptionalProperties
    WScript.Echo "Optional: " & p
  Next
End Sub
```

JScript

Checkproperties.js

```
var obj = GetObject("WinNT://zeta,computer")
var cls = GetObject(obj.Schema)
WScript.Echo(obj.AdsPath)
displayProps(cls)

var obj =GetObject("LDAP://CN=Omega,CN=Computers,DC=tvpress,DC=com")
var cls = GetObject(obj.Schema)
WScript.Echo(obj.AdsPath)
displayProps(cls)

function displayProps(obj) {
```

```
  mprop = obj.MandatoryProperties.toArray()
  for ( p in mprop) {
    WScript.Echo("Mandatory: " + mprop[p])
  }

  oprop = obj.OptionalProperties.toArray()
  for ( p in oprop) {
    WScript.Echo("Optional: " + oprop[p])
  }
}
```

Output

```
WinNT://SEATTLE/ZETA
Optional: Owner
Optional: Division
Optional: OperatingSystem
Optional: OperatingSystemVersion
Optional: Processor
Optional: ProcessorCount
LDAP://CN=Omega,CN=Computers,DC=SEATTLE,DC=DOMAIN,DC=com
Mandatory: cn
Mandatory: instanceType
Mandatory: nTSecurityDescriptor
Mandatory: objectCategory
Mandatory: objectClass
Mandatory: objectSid
Mandatory: sAMAccountName
Optional: accountExpires
Optional: accountNameHistory
Optional: aCSPolicyName
Optional: adminCount
...
Optional: x121Address
```

As the output shows, LDAP and Active Directory report many mandatory properties for most objects. Fortunately, some of these properties are set automatically when you create an object instance. The pre-set properties are:

```
instanceType

nTSecurityDescriptor

objectCategory

objectClass

objectSid
```

Because of this, you can create a computer object by setting only the cn and samAccountName properties, for example:

VBScript

```
Set cont = GetObject("LDAP://CN=Computers,DC=tvpress,DC=com")
Set comp = cont.Create("computer", "CN=theta")
comp.Put "samAccountName", "theta"
comp.SetInfo
```

JScript

```
var cont = GetObject("LDAP://CN=Computers,DC=tvpress,DC=com")
var comp = cont.Create("computer", "CN=theta")
comp.Put("samAccountName", "theta")
comp.SetInfo()
```

Viewing Property Syntax, Ranges, and Values

Once you know which properties are available for an object, you may want to take a more detailed look at a particular property. For example, you may want to know the minimum and maximum values the property accepts. You may also want to know which type of values you can pass to the property. You can examine the individual properties of an object using the IADsProperty interface.

Accessing the IADsProperty interface

The IADsProperty interface is designed for managing attributes of schema objects. You gain access to an object's properties by binding to the parent schema object. In this example, you bind to the schema for the Computer object:

VBScript

```
Set cls = GetObject(obj.Schema)
Set par = GetObject(obj.Parent)
```

JScript

```
var cls = GetObject(obj.Schema)
var par = GetObject(obj.Parent)
```

Once you bind to the parent schema object, you can retrieve a specific property using the GetObject() method and the following syntax:

```
SchemaObject.GetObject("Property","PropertyName")
```

where *SchemaObject* is the schema object you obtained and *PropertyName* is the name of the property you want to examine, for example:

VBScript

```
Set prop = cls.GetObject("Property","Owner")
```

JScript

```
var prop = cls.GetObject("Property","Owner")
```

Once you've accessed a property, you can use any of the properties of IADsProperty to work with the schema. These properties are summarized in Table 15-2.

Table 15-2 Properties of IADsProperty		
Property	**Status**	**Description**
MaxRange	Read/Write	Numeric value that sets the upper limit of values for the property.
MinRange	Read/Write	Numeric value that sets the lower limit of values for the property.
MultiValued	Read/Write	Boolean value that indicates whether this property supports multiple values.
OID	Read/Write	The directory-specific object identifier string.
Syntax	Read/Write	A string that specifies the acceptable data type(s) for the property.

Examining object properties

Now that you know the features of IADsProperty that are available to you, you can put these features to use to help you determine syntax, range, and value types for properties. One way to examine this information is to identify a specific property you want to examine and then display its schema. Listing 15-3 examines the OperatingSystem property of the Computer Object.

Listing 15-3: **Examining schema for object properties**

VBScript

viewpropertyschema.vbs

```
Set obj = GetObject("WinNT://zeta,computer")
Set cls = GetObject(obj.Schema)
Set sch = GetObject(cls.Parent)
Set pr = sch.GetObject("Property","OperatingSystem")

WScript.Echo "Property:   " & pr.Name
WScript.Echo "Syntax:     " & pr.Syntax
WScript.Echo "MaxRange:   " & pr.MaxRange
WScript.Echo "MinRange:   " & pr.MinRange
WScript.Echo "Multivalued: " & pr.Multivalued
```

JScript

viewpropertyschema.js

```
var obj = GetObject("WinNT://zeta,computer")
var cls = GetObject(obj.Schema)
var sch = GetObject(cls.Parent)
var pr = sch.GetObject("Property","OperatingSystem")

WScript.Echo("Property:   " + pr.Name)
WScript.Echo("Syntax:     " + pr.Syntax)
WScript.Echo("MaxRange:   " + pr.MaxRange)
WScript.Echo("MinRange:   " + pr.MinRange)
WScript.Echo("Multivalued: " + pr.Multivalued)
```

Output

```
Property:   OperatingSystem
Syntax:     String
MaxRange:   256
MinRange:   0
Multivalued: False
```

If you want to examine all the properties of an object, you can set up a control loop through optional and mandatory object properties (much as you did in Listing 15-2). You'll run into a problem though. While all properties of WinNT objects have maximum and minimum ranges, this isn't necessarily true with objects in other providers. The only properties that are supported for all objects across all providers are `Syntax` and `Multivalued`.

To work around the property-support problem, you'll need to set up error-handling for the script as described in Chapter 6. In Listing 15-4, I've implemented error-handling in a VBScript routine that examines all properties of a given object for WinNT and LDAP. The objects the script examines are `Domain`, `Computer`, `User`, and `Group`. The key to accessing these objects is to obtain a reference to a representative object and then to access the parent schema object.

Listing 15-4: **Examining schema for all object properties**

VBScript

viewall.vbs

```
'Get domain properties for WinNT
Set obj = GetObject("WinNT://seattle")
Set cls = GetObject(obj.Schema)
Set sch = GetObject(cls.Parent)
WScript.Echo obj.AdsPath
displayProps(cls)

'Get computer properties for WinNT
Set obj = GetObject("WinNT://zeta,computer")
Set cls = GetObject(obj.Schema)
Set sch = GetObject(cls.Parent)
WScript.Echo obj.AdsPath
displayProps(cls)

'Get user properties for WinNT
Set obj = GetObject("WinNT://zeta/Administrator,user")
Set cls = GetObject(obj.Schema)
Set sch = GetObject(cls.Parent)
WScript.Echo obj.AdsPath
displayProps(cls)

'Get group properties for WinNT
Set obj = GetObject("WinNT://zeta/administrators,group")
Set cls = GetObject(obj.Schema)
Set sch = GetObject(cls.Parent)
```

Continued

Listing 15-4 *(continued)*

```
WScript.Echo obj.AdsPath
displayProps(cls)

'Get domain properties for LDAP
Set obj = GetObject("LDAP://DC=tvpress,DC=com")
Set cls = GetObject(obj.Schema)
Set sch = GetObject(cls.Parent)
WScript.Echo obj.AdsPath
displayProps(cls)

'Get computer properties for LDAP
Set obj = GetObject("LDAP://CN=Omega,CN=Computers, DC=tvpress,DC=com")
Set cls = GetObject(obj.Schema)
Set sch = GetObject(cls.Parent)
WScript.Echo obj.AdsPath
displayProps(cls)

'Get user properties for LDAP
Set obj = GetObject("LDAP://CN=William R. Stanek,CN=Users,DC=tvpress,DC=com")
Set cls = GetObject(obj.Schema)
Set sch = GetObject(cls.Parent)
WScript.Echo obj.AdsPath
displayProps(cls)

'Get group properties for LDAP
Set obj = GetObject("LDAP://CN=Administrators,CN=Builtin,DC=tvpress,DC=com")
Set cls = GetObject(obj.Schema)
Set sch = GetObject(cls.Parent)
WScript.Echo obj.AdsPath
displayProps(cls)

'Subroutine to display object properties
Sub displayProps(obj)
  On Error Resume Next

  For Each p in obj.MandatoryProperties
    Set prop = sch.GetObject("Property",p)
    WScript.Echo "Property: " & prop.Name
    WScript.Echo "Syntax: " & prop.Syntax
    WScript.Echo "MinRange: " & prop.MinRange
    WScript.Echo "MaxRange: " & prop.MaxRange
    WScript.Echo "Multivalued:" & prop.Multivalued
```

```
      WScript.Echo
    Next

    For Each p in obj.OptionalProperties
      Set prop = sch.GetObject("Property",p)
      WScript.Echo "Property: " & prop.Name
      WScript.Echo "Syntax: " & prop.Syntax
      WScript.Echo "MinRange: " & prop.MinRange
      WScript.Echo "MaxRange: " & prop.MaxRange
      WScript.Echo "Multivalued:" & prop.Multivalued
      WScript.Echo
    Next
End Sub
```

One of the properties that deserves additional discussion is `Multivalued`. If you are unsure whether a property returns a single value or multiple values, use the `Multivalued` property. If you create general-purpose functions for handling properties, you can use this to determine whether you use `Get()`, `GetEx()`, `Put()`, or `PutEx()`, for example:

VBScript	*JScript*

`If prop.Multivalued = True Then`
`  'use GetEx() or PutEx()`
`Else`
`  'use Get() or Put()`
`End If`
	`if (prop.Multivalued == 1) {`
	`  //use GetEx() or PutEx()`
	`else {`
	`  //use Get() or Put()`
	`}`

Summary

As you've seen in this chapter, schema is an important aspect of ADSI scripting. If you know how to access schema, you can examine objects and the properties they support. Some properties are optional when you create a new instance of an object. Other properties are mandatory. You must set mandatory properties when you create an object, such as a user, group, or computer account.

✦   ✦   ✦

Managing Local and Domain Resources with ADSI

✦ ✦ ✦ ✦

In This Chapter

Managing domain settings

Viewing and modifying local computer settings

Local and global user account administration

Local and global group account administration

✦ ✦ ✦ ✦

Windows scripts and ADSI can help you build powerful tools for managing computers and domain resources. The ADSI provider you'll use to manage local resources on Windows NT and Windows 2000 computers is WinNT. You will also use the WinNT provider to manage domain resources. The focus of this chapter is on using WinNT to manage the following:

+ Domain account policies for both Windows NT and Windows 2000

+ Domain user accounts for both Windows NT and Windows 2000

+ Domain group accounts for both Windows NT and Windows 2000

+ Local computer properties for both Windows NT and Windows 2000

+ Local user and group accounts for both Windows NT and Windows 2000

Managing Domain Account Policies

Using the WinNT provider, you can view and set domain account policies for Windows NT and Windows 2000. In Windows NT, you normally access these properties through the *User Manager's Account Policy* dialog box. In Windows 2000, you normally access these properties through Group Policy.

Working with domain objects

Before you can manage domain account policies, you must first obtain a reference to a domain object. In this example, you obtain the domain object for a domain named `tvpress`:

VBScript

```
Set dom = GetObject("WinNT://tvpress")
```

JScript

```
var dom = GetObject("WinNT://tvpress")
```

The domain name you use with WinNT is always the NT domain name whether you are working with Windows NT or Windows 2000. With the domain `seattle.tvpress.com`, the NT equivalent would normally be `seattle`, but with the domain `tvpress.com`, the NT equivalent would normally be `tvpress`.

Once you obtain the `Domain` object, you can get and set the properties of the object, for example:

VBScript   **JScript**

```
dom.Put "MinPasswordLength", 8      dom.Put("MinPasswordLength", 8)
dom.SetInfo                         dom.SetInfo()
```

Table 16-1 summarizes the available `Domain` object properties. A status of RW means that you can set and get the property (i.e. it is readable and writable).

Note Note that if you used the techniques described in Chapter 15 to obtain a summary for the `Domain` object, you'd get slightly different results. The primary reason for this is that the syntax often reports −1 as the highest value when a property restriction can be turned off with a setting of 0. Another interpretation for this is that there isn't an upper range when the property is turned off.

Table 16-1
WinNT Domain Object Summary

Property	Status	Value Type	Min Range	Max Range	Multiple Values
MinPassword Length	RW	Integer	0	14	False
MinPasswordAge	RW	Integer	0	86227200	False
MaxPasswordAge	RW	Integer	86400	86313600	False
MaxBadPasswords Allowed	RW	Integer	0	2147483647	False
PasswordHistory Length	RW	Integer	0	8	False
AutoUnlock Interval	RW	Integer	0	2147483647	False
LockoutObservation Interval	RW	Integer	0	2147483647	False

Preparing to view and set account policies

Before you can manage account policies, you must ensure that the related policies are enabled through group policies. If a policy is disabled or inactive, you won't be able to manipulate the related property. Group policy is discussed in Chapter 13. As discussed in that chapter, you access the domain group policy container through Active Directory Users and Computers. Once you start Active Directory Users and Computers, you can view the group policy for accounts as follows:

1. Right-click on the domain you want to work with in the console root. Then select Properties. This displays a Properties dialog box.

2. In the Properties dialog box, select the Group Policy tab, then click Edit. You can now view and set group policies.

3. Expand Computer Configuration, Windows Settings, and Security Settings. Then click the Account Policies node.

4. Select the Password Policy node and note which policies are enabled or disabled.

5. Select the Account Lockout Policy node and note which policies are enabled or not defined.

6. If you need to enable a policy, double-click it and then select the Define This Policy checkbox or the Enabled radio button as appropriate.

Domain object properties map to password and account lockout policies as follows:

Password Policy:

- ✦ `PasswordHistoryLength` sets Enforce Password History
- ✦ `MaxPasswordAge` sets Maximum Password Age
- ✦ `MinPasswordAge` sets Minimum Password Age
- ✦ `MinPasswordLength` sets Minimum Password Length

Account Lockout Policy:

- ✦ `MaxBadPasswordsAllowed` sets Account Lockout Threshold
- ✦ `AutoUnlockInterval` sets Account Lockout Duration
- ✦ `LockoutObservationInterval` sets Reset Account Lockout Counter After

Viewing and setting account policies

Properties of the domain object can be tricky to use. The key reason for this is that you must set them in a specific way. To help you get around the pitfalls, I'll examine each property briefly.

Using MinPasswordLength

The `MinPasswordLength` property sets the minimum number of characters for passwords. The value must be between 0 and 14. You can view and set the minimum password length as shown in Listing 16-1.

Listing 16-1: **Setting and viewing the minimum password length**

VBScript	JScript
minpass.vbs	minpass.js

```
'Set minimum password length
Set dom = GetObject("WinNT://seattle")
Dom.Put "MinPasswordLength", 8
Dom.SetInfo
'Confirm the change
WScript.Echo dom.Get
  ("MinPasswordLength")
```

```
//Set minimum password length
var dom = GetObject("WinNT://seattle")
dom.Put("MinPasswordLength", 8)
dom.SetInfo()
//Confirm the change
WScript.Echo( dom.Get
  ("MinPasswordLength"))
```

Using MinPasswordAge and MaxPasswordAge

The MinPasswordAge and MaxPasswordAge properties are closely related. MinPasswordAge determines what length of time users must keep a password before they can change it and MaxPasswordAge determines how long users can keep a password before they must change it. The maximum password age must be set to a duration that is longer than the minimum password age. Otherwise, an error occurs when you try to set the property value.

Both MinPasswordAge and MaxPasswordAge have maximum ranges of 998 and 999 days, respectively. You have to set the values in seconds, however, because this is how the Windows Registry handles the values. The easiest way to convert seconds to days is to use 86,400 as a multiplier. This value is the number of seconds in a day. Following this, you can set a minimum password age of 3 days and a maximum password age of 90 days like this:

VBScript	JScript
| ```
Set d = GetObject("WinNT://seattle")
d.Put "MinPasswordAge", 86400*3
d.Put "MaxPasswordAge", 86400*90
d.SetInfo
``` | ```
var d = GetObject("WinNT://seattle")
d.Put("MinPasswordAge", 86400*3)
d.Put("MaxPasswordAge", 86400*90)
d.SetInfo()
``` |

You can then confirm the changes by examining the current property values:

VBScript	JScript
| ```
WScript.Echo d.Get("MinPasswordAge")
WScript.Echo d.Get ("MaxPasswordAge")
``` | ```
WScript.Echo(d.Get ("MinPasswordAge"))
WScript.Echo(d.Get ("MaxPasswordAge"))
``` |

Using PasswordHistoryLength

The password history determines how often a user can reuse an old password. For example, if you set the password history length to 3, the history remembers up to three passwords for each user. If Sally has the passwords coolDays, rainBows, and rubberDuck in the history, she won't be able to re-use those passwords.

You can set and then confirm the password history length as shown in Listing 16-2.

Listing 16-2: Setting and viewing the passwordhistorylength

VBScript	JScript
passhist.vbs	**passhist.js**

```
'Set password history length
Set dom = GetObject("WinNT://seattle")
dom.Put "PasswordHistoryLength", 4
dom.SetInfo

'Confirm the change
WScript.Echo dom.Get
   ("PasswordHistoryLength")
```

```
//Set password history length
var dom = GetObject("WinNT://seattle")
dom.Put ("PasswordHistoryLength", 4)
dom.SetInfo()

//Confirm the change
WScript.Echo(dom.Get
   ("PasswordHistoryLength "))
```

Using MaxBadPasswordsAllowed, AutoUnlockInterval, and LockoutObservationInterval

The MaxBadPasswordsAllowed, AutoUnlockInterval, and LockoutObservation Interval properties all relate to whether accounts get locked out when users enter bad passwords repeatedly. The MaxBadPasswordsAllowed property determines the number of bad passwords a user can enter before they are locked out. The AutoUnlockInterval property determines how long the user is locked out. The LockoutObservationInterval property determines when previously entered bad passwords no longer count toward locking out the account. If the interval is set to 30 minutes, bad passwords entered more than 30 minutes ago don't count.

Both AutoUnlockInterval and LockoutObservationInterval properties have maximum ranges of 99,999 minutes. Again, the value is set in seconds, because this is how the Windows Registry handles the values. To convert seconds to minutes, use 60 as a multiplier. Listing 16-3 shows how you can set unlock and lockout intervals of 50 and 5 minutes, respectively.

Listing 16-3: Setting and viewing the lockout

VBScript	JScript
passlock.vbs	**passlock.js**

```
'Set lockout
Set dom = GetObject("WinNT://seattle")
dom.Put "MaxBadPasswordsAllowed", 4
dom.Put "AutoUnlockInterval", 60*50
```

```
//Set lockout
var dom = GetObject("WinNT://seattle")
dom.Put("MaxBadPasswordsAllowed", 4)
dom.Put("AutoUnlockInterval", 60*50)
```

```
dom.Put "LockoutObservationInterval",      dom.Put( "LockoutObservationInterval",
  60*5                                        60*5)
dom.SetInfo                                 dom.SetInfo()

'Confirm lockout                           //Confirm lockout
WScript.Echo dom.Get                       WScript.Echo(dom.Get
  ("MaxBadPasswordsAllowed")                 ("MaxBadPasswordsAllowed"))
WScript.Echo dom.Get                       WScript.Echo(dom.Get
  ("AutoUnlockInterval")                     ("AutoUnlockInterval"))
WScript.Echo dom.Get                       WScript.Echo(dom.Get
  ("LockoutObservationInterval")             ("LockoutObservationInterval"))
```

Working with Local Computer Properties

The WinNT `Computer` object is used to work with properties of a computer in a Windows NT or Windows 2000 domain. You can't use this object to create computer accounts or to authorize computers in the domain. You can perform these functions with the LDAP provider, however, and this is discussed in Chapter 18.

To work with local computers, you need to obtain an object reference to the computer. In the following example, you obtain the `Computer` object for a local computer named Omega:

VBScript

```
Set dom = GetObject("WinNT://omega,computer")
```

JScript

```
var dom = GetObject("WinNT://omega,computer")
```

Once you obtain the necessary `Computer` object, you can get and set the properties of the object:

VBScript

```
dom.Put "Owner", "William R. Stanek"
dom.SetInfo
```

JScript

```
dom.Put("Owner", "William R. Stanek")
dom.SetInfo()
```

Table 16-2 summarizes the properties of the WinNT `Computer` object. These properties are fairly straightforward so I'm not going to go into each property individually.

Table 16-2
WinNT Computer Object Summary

Property	Status	Value Type	Min Range	Max Range	Multiple Values
Owner	RW	String	0	256	False
Division	RW	String	0	256	False
OperatingSystem	RW	String	0	256	False
OperatingSystemVersion	RW	String	0	256	False
Processor	RW	String	0	256	False
ProcessorCount	RW	String	0	256	False

When you work with the `Computer` object, you may need to examine or update all of the computers on the network. One way you can do this is shown as Listing 16-4.

Note   Note that with JScript, you must create `Enumerator` objects to examine the `Domain` and `Computer` objects. Enumerators are discussed in Chapter 7 in the section entitled "Working with folders". As you examine the sample output, note also that on Windows 2000, the operating system is set to Windows NT, but the OS version is set to 5.0.

Listing 16-4: **Examining all Computer objects in the domain**

VBScript

checkcomp.vbs
```
'Handle Errors
On Error Resume Next
'Get the provider object
Set prov = GetObject("WinNT:")

'Examine the available domains the provider can reach
For each dom in prov

   'Examine the objects in the domain and check for Computer objects
   For each o in dom
```

```
    If o.Class = "Computer" Then

     'Display properties of the Computer
      WScript.Echo o.Class & " " & o.Name
      WScript.Echo " Owner: " & o.Owner
      WScript.Echo " Division: " & o.Division
      WScript.Echo " OperatingSystem: "  & o.OperatingSystem
      WScript.Echo " OS Version: " & o.OperatingSystemVersion
      WScript.Echo " Processor: " & o.Processor
      WScript.Echo " ProcessorCount: " & o.ProcessorCount

    End If

  Next
Next
```

JScript

---

checkcomp.js

```javascript
//Get the provider object
var prov = GetObject("WinNT:")

tlist = new Enumerator(prov)

//Examine the available domains the provider can reach
for (; !tlist.atEnd(); tlist.moveNext())
 {

 s = new Enumerator(tlist.item())

 //Examine the objects in the domain and check for Computer objects
 for (; !s.atEnd(); s.moveNext())
  {

  o = s.item();
  if (o.Class == "Computer") {

    try {
     //Display properties of the Computer
     WScript.Echo(o.Class + " " + o.Name)
     WScript.Echo(" Owner: " + o.Owner)
     WScript.Echo(" Division: " + o.Division)
     WScript.Echo(" OperatingSystem: "  + o.OperatingSystem)
     WScript.Echo(" OS Version: " + o.OperatingSystemVersion)
     WScript.Echo(" Processor: " + o.Processor)
     WScript.Echo(" ProcessorCount: " + o.ProcessorCount)
    }
    catch(e) {
```

Continued

Listing 16-4 *(continued)*

```
        WScript.Echo(" Not online at this time")
    }
  }


  }
}
```

Output

```
Computer OMEGA
 Owner: William Stanek
 Division: Stanek & Associates
 OperatingSystem: Windows NT
 OperatingSystemVersion: 5.0
 Processor: x86 Family 6 Model 6 Stepping 0
 ProcessorCount: Uniprocessor Free
Computer ZETA
 Owner: William R. Stanek
 Division: Stanek & Associates
 OperatingSystem: Windows NT
 OperatingSystemVersion: 5.0
 Processor: x86 Family 6 Model 3 Stepping 3
 ProcessorCount: Uniprocessor Free
```

Creating and Modifying User Accounts

User accounts are represented with the User object. Of all the objects available for WinNT, the User object is the most complex. You can use this object to create, delete, update, and move local user accounts as well as domain accounts. You will also find that WinNT is easier to work with than LDAP in most respects. However, you cannot use WinNT to perform tasks that are specific to Active Directory, such as moving accounts to different containers or organizational units. Beyond this, you also can't manage extended properties for user accounts that are specific to Active Directory. For details on Active Directory and LDAP, see Chapter 18.

User properties for WinNT

Before getting into the specifics of working with user accounts, you should examine Table 16-3. This table provides a brief summary of User object properties. A status of RO means the property is read-only and cannot be updated. A status of RW means the property is read-write and can be updated.

Table 16-3
WinNT User Object Summary

Property	Status	Value Type	Min Range	Max Range	Multiple Values
AccountDisabled	RW	Boolean	0	1	False
AccountExpirationDate	RW	Date String	-	-	False
BadPasswordAttempts	RO	Integer	0	2147483647	False
Description	RW	String	0	257	False
FullName	RW	String	0	257	False
HomeDirDrive	RW	String	0	340	False
HomeDirectory	RW	Path String	0	340	False
IsAccountLocked	RO	Boolean	0	1	False
LastLogin	RO	Date String	-	-	False
LastLogoff	RO	Date String	-	-	False
LoginHours	RW	OctetString	0	0	False
LoginScript	RW	Path String	0	340	False
LoginWorkstations	RW	Safe Array	0	256	True
MaxLogins	RW	Integer	0	2147483647	False
MaxPasswordAge	RW	Integer	86400	86313600	False
MaxStorage	RW	Integer	0	2147483647	False
MinPasswordAge	RW	Integer	0	86227200	False
MinPasswordLength	RW	Integer	0	15	False
ObjectSid	RO	OctetString	0	0	False
Parameters	RO	String	0	340	False
PasswordAge	RO	Date String	-	-	False
PasswordExpired	RO	Integer	0	1	False
PasswordHistoryLength	RO	Integer	0	8	False
PrimaryGroupID	RW	Integer	0	2147483647	False
Profile	RW	Path String	0	340	False
RasPermissions	RW	Integer	0	0	False
UserFlags	RW	Integer	0	0	False

When you work with object properties, you can get them by name or through the Get() method. Listing 16-5 shows an example of working with User object properties by name. As you take a look at the example, note the sample output for each property.

Listing 16-5: **Viewing user properties**

VBScript

viewuser.vbs

```
On Error Resume Next
Set usr = GetObject("WinNT://seattle/omega/tgreen,user")

WScript.Echo "AccountDisabled       " & usr.AccountDisabled
WScript.Echo "AccountExpirationDate " & usr.AccountExpirationDate
WScript.Echo "BadPasswordAttempts   " & usr.BadPasswordAttempts
WScript.Echo "Description            " & usr.Description
WScript.Echo "FullName               " & usr.FullName
WScript.Echo "HomeDirDrive          " & usr.HomeDirDrive
WScript.Echo "HomeDirectory         " & usr.HomeDirectory
WScript.Echo "IsAccountLocked       " & usr.IsAccountLocked
WScript.Echo "LastLogin             " & usr.LastLogin
WScript.Echo "LastLogoff            " & usr.LastLogoff
WScript.Echo "LoginHours            " & usr.LoginHours
WScript.Echo "LoginScript           " & usr.LoginScript
WScript.Echo "LoginWorkstations     " & usr.LoginWorkstations
WScript.Echo "MaxLogins             " & usr.MaxLogins
WScript.Echo "MaxPasswordAge        " & usr.MaxPasswordAge
WScript.Echo "MaxStorage            " & usr.MaxStorage
WScript.Echo "MinPasswordAge        " & usr.MinPasswordAge
WScript.Echo "MinPasswordLength     " & usr.MinPasswordLength
WScript.Echo "Parameters            " & usr.Parameters
WScript.Echo "PasswordAge           " & usr.PasswordAge
WScript.Echo "PasswordExpired       " & usr.PasswordExpired
WScript.Echo "PasswordHistoryLength " & usr.PasswordHistoryLength
WScript.Echo "PrimaryGroupID        " & usr.PrimaryGroupID
WScript.Echo "Profile               " & usr.Profile
WScript.Echo "RasPermissions        " & usr.RasPermissions
WScript.Echo "UserFlags             " & usr.UserFlags
```

Output

```
AccountDisabled       False
AccountExpirationDate 12/31/1999
BadPasswordAttempts   0
Description           Systems Engineer
FullName              Tom Green
HomeDirDrive
HomeDirectory         d:\home
```

```
IsAccountLocked        False
LastLogin              10/3/1999 3:05:55 PM
LoginScript            log.vbs
MaxPasswordAge         432000
MaxStorage             -1
MinPasswordAge         172800
MinPasswordLength      8
Parameters
PasswordAge            1401
PasswordExpired        0
PasswordHistoryLength  3
PrimaryGroupID         513
Profile                d:\data
RasPermissions         1
UserFlags                 66115
```

Working with user account properties

The User object properties are very useful in managing user accounts. Some more so than others, and because of this, several properties deserve special attention. These properties include AccountDisabled, IsAccountLocked, and UserFlags.

You can use AccountDisabled and IsAccountLocked to troubleshoot basic problems with accounts and to track down possible security problems. For example, you may want to schedule a script to run nightly that checks the status of all user accounts to see if they are disabled or locked. You can use this information to help users that are having problems accessing the network and may not want to tell you that they forgot their password for the third time in a row, or to track patterns that may tell you someone is trying to hack into accounts.

Listing 16-6 provides a basic script you can use to check all of the user accounts in a Windows NT or Windows 2000 domain. If an account is disabled or locked, the script writes the account name and status.

Listing 16-6: **Checking for account problems**

VBScript

secuser.vbs
```
'Get the provider object
Set prov = GetObject("WinNT:")
```

Continued

Listing 16-6 *(continued)*

```
'Examine the available domains the provider can reach
For each dom in prov
 'Examine the objects in the domain and check for User objects
  For each o in dom
   If o.Class = "User" Then
     If o.AccountDisabled = "True" Then
       WScript.Echo o.Name & " is disabled"
     End If
     If o.IsAccountLocked = "True" Then
       WScript.Echo o.Name & " is locked"
     End If
   End If
  Next
Next
```

JScript

secuser.js

```
//Get the provider object
var prov = GetObject("WinNT:")

tlist = new Enumerator(prov)

//Examine the available domains the provider can reach
for (; !tlist.atEnd(); tlist.moveNext())
 {
 s = new Enumerator(tlist.item())
 //Examine the objects in the domain and check for User objects
 for (; !s.atEnd(); s.moveNext())
  {
  o = s.item();
   if (o.Class == "User") {
     if (o.AccountDisabled == 1) {
       WScript.Echo(o.Name + " is disabled")
     }
     if (o.IsAccountLocked == 1) {
       WScript.Echo(o.Name + " is locked")
     }
   }
  }
 }
}
```

Output

```
Guest is disabled
testAcc is disabled
Theta is disabled
```

Knowing that an account is disabled or locked isn't very useful if you can't resolve the problem as necessary, and this is where the `UserFlags` property comes into the picture. This property provides an integer value that is the sum of all the flags associated with an account.

Table 16-4 provides a summary of the user flags. Each individual flag represents an account state, such as the password cannot be changed, or the account is disabled, and so forth. By adding the flag value to the total, you can apply the flag. By removing the flag value from the total, you can remove the flag.

Table 16-4
User Flags

Flag	Value	Description
ADS_UF_SCRIPT	0X0001	A logon script will be executed.
ADS_UF_ACCOUNTDISABLE	0X0002	The account is disabled.
ADS_UF_HOMEDIR_REQUIRED	0X0004	A home directory is required.
ADS_UF_LOCKOUT	0X0010	The account is locked out.
ADS_UF_PASSWD_NOTREQD	0X0020	No password is required.
ADS_UF_PASSWD_CANT_CHANGE	0X0040	User cannot change the password.
ADS_UF_ENCRYPTED_TEXT_PASSWORD_ALLOWED	0X0080	User can send an encrypted password.
ADS_UF_TEMP_DUPLICATE_ACCOUNT	0X0100	This is an account for users whose primary account is in another domain.
ADS_UF_NORMAL_ACCOUNT	0X0200	This is a normal account.
ADS_UF_INTERDOMAIN_TRUST_ACCOUNT	0X0800	Trusted account.
ADS_UF_WORKSTATION_TRUST_ACCOUNT	0X1000	This is a computer account that is a member of this domain.
ADS_UF_SERVER_TRUST_ACCOUNT	0X2000	This is a computer account for a backup domain controller that is a member of this domain.

Continued

Table 16-4 *(continued)*		
Flag	**Value**	**Description**
ADS_UF_DONTEXPIREPASSWD	0X10000	The account password doesn't expire.
ADS_UF_MNS_LOGON_ACCOUNT	0X20000	This is an MNS logon account.
ADS_UF_SMARTCARD_REQUIRED	0X40000	Forces the user to log on with a smart card.
ADS_UF_TRUSTED_FOR_DELEGATION	0X80000	The user or computer account under which a service runs is trusted for Kerberos delegation.
ADS_UF_NOT_DELEGATED	0X100000	The security context of the user will not be delegated to a service even if it is trusted.

If you go back to the output of Listing 16-5, you'll see that the sample value for UserFlags is 66115. If you convert that value to hexadecimal format, you get 0×10243. Now if you review the values in Table 16-4, you'll see that the hexadecimal value is the result of the following flags being set on the account:

```
ADS_UF_DONTEXPIREPASSWD      0X10000
ADS_UF_NORMAL_ACCOUNT        0X0200
ADS_UF_PASSWD_CANT_CHANGE    0X0040
ADS_UF_ACCOUNTDISABLE        0X0002
ADS_UF_SCRIPT 0X0001
```

What these flags tell you about the account is:

✦ You are looking at a normal user account that has been assigned a logon script

✦ The account password doesn't expire

✦ The user can't change the password

✦ The account is disabled

If you want to enable the account, you need to remove the related flag. You do this by removing the related value from the UserFlags property. Because you normally wouldn't want to compute flags by hand and then remove flags individually, you need a safe way to remove the flag if it is set, and to leave the UserFlags property alone otherwise. This way you can automate the process and not worry about the details.

The best way to handle this procedure is to use the AccountDisabled and IsLockedOut properties to tell you when an account is disabled or locked, and then to take appropriate corrective action. An example of this is shown as Listing 16-7. In this example, you examine the tgreen account on a computer named omega. If the account is disabled or locked, the code in this listing enables or unlocks the account as appropriate.

Listing 16-7: **Enabling and unlocking a user account**

VBScript

restoreuser.vbs

```
Set usr = GetObject("WinNT://seattle/omega/tgreen,user")

If usr.AccountDisabled = "True" Then
  'ADS_UF_ACCOUNTDISABLE 0X0002

  flag = usr.Get("UserFlags") - 2
  usr.Put "UserFlags", flag
  usr.SetInfo

  WScript.Echo usr.Name & " is now enabled"

End If

If usr.IsAccountLocked = "True" Then

  'ADS_UF_LOCKOUT 0X0010

  flag = usr.Get("UserFlags") - 16
  usr.Put "UserFlags", flag
  usr.SetInfo

  WScript.Echo usr.Name & " is now unlocked"

End If
```

Continued

Listing 16-7 *(continued)*

JScript

---

restoreuser.js

```
var usr = GetObject("WinNT://seattle/omega/tgreen,user")

if (usr.AccountDisabled == 1) {

  //ADS_UF_ACCOUNTDISABLE 0X0002

  flag = usr.Get("UserFlags") - 2
  usr.Put("UserFlags", flag)
  usr.SetInfo()

  WScript.Echo(usr.Name + " is now enabled")

}

if (usr.IsAccountLocked == 1) {

  //ADS_UF_LOCKOUT                    0X0010

  flag = usr.Get("UserFlags") - 16
  usr.Put("UserFlags", flag)
  usr.SetInfo()

  WScript.Echo(usr.Name + " is now unlocked")

}
```

Tip

Actually, the best way to handle this operation is to use a logical XOr. When you perform an XOr comparison of `UserFlags` and the flag you want to remove, you get the desired result. The flag is always removed if set and otherwise the `UserFlags` property is not changed. To set a flag, you can do a logical Or. Unfortunately, this technique works great in Visual Basic, but not in scripts.

With a few simple modifications, you can create a script to enable/unlock or disable/lock any account on the network. An example script is shown as Listing 16-8. In this example, seattle is the NT-equivalent domain name. Replace this with your domain name for the script to work on your network.

Listing 16-8: **Enabling and unlocking a user account**

VBScript

maccounts.vbs

```
lf = Chr(13) + Chr(10)
WScript.Echo "========================================" & lf
WScript.Echo "==       Account Management Script     ==" & lf
WScript.Echo "========================================" & lf

WScript.Echo "Enter account to work with: " & lf

r = WScript.StdIn.ReadLine()


WScript.Echo "Enter R to restore or D to disable: " & lf

n = WScript.StdIn.ReadLine()

WScript.Echo "========================================" & lf
WScript.Echo "==                Working              ==" & lf
WScript.Echo "========================================" & lf

Set usr = GetObject("WinNT://seattle/" & r & ",user")
select case LCase(n)

case "r"

 If usr.AccountDisabled = "True" Then

  'ADS_UF_ACCOUNTDISABLE 0X0002

  flag = usr.Get("UserFlags") - 2
  usr.Put "UserFlags", flag
  usr.SetInfo

  WScript.Echo usr.Name & " is enabled"

 End If

 If usr.IsAccountLocked = "True" Then

  'ADS_UF_LOCKOUT               0X0010

  flag = usr.Get("UserFlags") - 16
  usr.Put "UserFlags", flag
  usr.SetInfo
```

Continued

Listing 16-8 *(continued)*

```
  WScript.Echo usr.Name & " is unlocked"

  End If

case "d"

 If usr.AccountDisabled = "False" Then

  'ADS_UF_ACCOUNTDISABLE 0X0002

  flag = usr.Get("UserFlags") + 2
  usr.Put "UserFlags", flag
  usr.SetInfo

  WScript.Echo usr.Name & " is disabled"

 End If

 If usr.IsAccountLocked = "False" Then

  'ADS_UF_LOCKOUT                    0X0010

  flag = usr.Get("UserFlags") + 16
  usr.Put "UserFlags", flag
  usr.SetInfo

  WScript.Echo usr.Name & " is locked"

  End If

End Select
```

JScript

maccounts.js

```
lf = "\r\n"
WScript.Echo("========================================" + lf)
WScript.Echo("==      Account Management Script     ==" + lf)
WScript.Echo("========================================" + lf)

WScript.Echo("Enter account to work with: " + lf)

r = WScript.StdIn.ReadLine()

WScript.Echo("Enter R to restore or D to disable: " + lf)
```

```
n = WScript.StdIn.ReadLine()

WScript.Echo("=======================================" + lf)
WScript.Echo("==                Working             ==" + lf)
WScript.Echo("=======================================" + lf)

var usr = GetObject("WinNT://seattle/" + r + ",user")

switch (n) {

case "r" :

 if (usr.AccountDisabled == 1) {

  //ADS_UF_ACCOUNTDISABLE 0X0002

  flag = usr.Get("UserFlags") - 2
  usr.Put("UserFlags", flag)
  usr.SetInfo()

  WScript.Echo(usr.Name + " is enabled")

 }

 if (usr.IsAccountLocked == 1) {
  //ADS_UF_LOCKOUT                 0X0010

  flag = usr.Get("UserFlags") - 16
  usr.Put("UserFlags", flag)
  usr.SetInfo()

  WScript.Echo(usr.Name + " is unlocked")

  }

  break

case "d" :

 if (usr.AccountDisabled == 0) {

  //ADS_UF_ACCOUNTDISABLE 0X0002

  flag = usr.Get("UserFlags") + 2
  usr.Put("UserFlags", flag)
  usr.SetInfo()

  WScript.Echo(usr.Name + " is disabled")

 }
```

Continued

Listing 16-8 *(continued)*

```
if (usr.IsAccountLocked == 0) {

//ADS_UF_LOCKOUT                          0X0010

flag = usr.Get("UserFlags") + 16
usr.Put("UserFlags", flag)
usr.SetInfo()

WScript.Echo(usr.Name + " is locked")

}

break
}
```

Output

```
========================================

==        Account Management Script      ==

========================================

Enter account to work with:

tgreen
Enter R to restore or D to disable:

r
========================================

==                Working              ==

========================================

tgreen is enabled
```

 Note   Like many examples in the text, this script is designed to run from the command-line with CScript.exe. If you run the script with WScript.exe, you won't get the results you expect and you'll have a lot of pop-up dialog boxes to deal with.

As you examine the script, you should note the techniques used to display output and handle input. So the output is easy to follow, I added blank lines with Chr(13) and Chr(10) or "\r\n". To read from the command line, the script reads a line from the standard input stream. The code for this is:

```
r = WScript.StdIn.ReadLine()
```

The `StdIn.ReadLine()` method allows you to type in characters and pass the result to a variable when you press Enter. To get the sample output, I typed **tgreen** and then pressed Enter. Afterward, I typed **r** and then pressed Enter.

Managing user accounts with WinNT

With WinNT, you can perform many common user account tasks. You can create and delete accounts. You can also set and change account passwords. Another interesting user-management task is to examine the group membership for users.

Creating user accounts with WinNT

To create user accounts, you use the `Create()` method of the `IADsContainer` interface. This method expects to be passed the two parameters: the class and the relative name of the object to create.

Before you can use the `Create()` method, you must bind to the container in which you will create the account. To create a local account, you bind to the local computer object. To create a domain account, you bind to the domain object. When you create an account with WinNT, you must also set the account password. You do this with the `SetPassword()` method which expects a single string that contains the new password.

The following example binds to the `seattle` domain and creates a user account for jfranklin:

VBScript	**JScript**
| ```
Set obj = GetObject("WinNT://seattle")
Set usr = obj.Create
  ("user", "jfranklin")
usr.SetPassword("gres$#42g")
usr.SetInfo
``` | ```
var obj = GetObject("WinNT://seattle")
var usr = obj.Create
  ("user","jfranklin")
usr.SetPassword("gres$#42g")
usr.SetInfo()
``` |

As stated previously, you can also create local computer accounts. In the next example, you create the same account on a computer named omega:

VBScript	**JScript**
| ```
Set obj = GetObject
  ("WinNT://seattle/omega")
Set usr = obj.Create
  ("user", "jfranklin")
usr.SetPassword("gres$#42g")
usr.SetInfo
``` | ```
var obj = GetObject
  ("WinNT://seattle/omega")
var usr = obj.Create
  ("user", "jfranklin")
usr.SetPassword("gres$#42g")
usr.SetInfo()
``` |

You can of course set other properties for the new account before you create it. You can also set these properties at a later time.

Deleting user accounts with WinNT

You delete accounts with the `Delete()` method of the `IADsContainer` interface. As with `Create()`, this method expects to be passed the two parameters: the class and the relative name of the object to create.

Before you can use the `Delete()` method, you must bind to the container from which you will delete the account. The following example deletes the user account for jfranklin from the `seattle` domain:

VBScript	*JScript*
`Set obj = GetObject("WinNT://seattle")` `obj.Delete "user", "jfranklin"`	`var obj = GetObject("WinNT://seattle")` `obj.Create("user", "jfranklin")`

Setting and changing passwords

You set passwords for new or existing user accounts with the `SetPassword()` method. This method was discussed previously in the chapter. The `User` object also provides a `ChangePassword()` method. To change a password, you can use `ChangePassword()`; however, you must know the old password, which is why this method isn't very practical for day-to-day administration. Instead, you'll usually want to use `SetPassword()`.

Examples of using `SetPassword()` and `ChangePassword()` follow:

VBScript

```
Set usr = GetObject("WinNT://seattle/jsmith,user")
usr.SetPassword "NewPassword"

Set usr = GetObject("WinNT://seattle/omega/hwilder,user")
usr.ChangePassword "OldPassword","NewPassword"
```

JScript

```
var usr = GetObject("WinNT://seattle/jsmith,user")
usr.SetPassword("NewPassword")

var usr = GetObject("WinNT://seattle/omega/hwilder,user")
usr.ChangePassword("OldPassword","NewPassword")
```

Checking group membership

Often you'll need to check group membership for users on the network. One way to do this quickly and efficiently is to use a script that examines group membership on a user-by-user basis with the `Groups()` method of the `User` object. The `Groups()` method returns a collection of group objects to which a user belongs.

You can use `Groups()` to examine all of the groups sjohnson belongs to, as follows:

VBScript	JScript
| ```
Set usr = GetObject
  ("WinNT://seattle/sjohnson,user")

For Each grp In usr.Groups
   WScript.Echo  grp.Name

Next
``` | ```
var usr = GetObject
  ("WinNT://seattle/sjohnson,user")
mList = new Enumerator(usr.Groups());

for (; !mList.atEnd();
mList.moveNext())
{
 s = mList.item()
 WScript.Echo(s.Name)
}
``` |

Output

```
Domain Users
Enterprise Admins
Schema Admins
Domain Admins
Administrators
Backup Operators
```

To make it easier to monitor group membership, you can create a function to check all user accounts in the domain and then create a report. A sample function is shown in Listing 16-9.

Listing 16-9: **Tracking group membership**

VBScript

groupmembership.vbs
```
Set prov = GetObject("WinNT:")
For each dom in prov

 For each o in dom
```

Continued

Listing 16-9 *(continued)*

```
  If o.Class = "User" Then
    WScript.Echo "======================="
    WScript.Echo "Account: " & o.FullName
    For Each grp In o.Groups
      WScript.Echo " " & grp.Name
    Next
  End If

 Next
Next
```

JScript

groupmembership.js

```
//Get the provider object
var prov = GetObject("WinNT:")
tlist = new Enumerator(prov)

for (; !tlist.atEnd(); tlist.moveNext())
 {

 s = new Enumerator(tlist.item())

 for (; !s.atEnd(); s.moveNext())
  {

  o = s.item();
  if (o.Class == "User") {
   WScript.Echo("=======================")
   WScript.Echo("Account: " + o.FullName)

   mList = new Enumerator(o.Groups());

   for (; !mList.atEnd(); mList.moveNext())
    {
     usr = mList.item()
     WScript.Echo(usr.Name)
    }

  }
 }
}
```

Output

```
=======================
Account: Thomas Franklin
  Domain Users
=======================
Account: George Johnson
  Domain Users
=======================
Account: William R. Stanek
  Domain Users
  Enterprise Admins
  Schema Admins
  Domain Admins
  Administrators
  Backup Operators
```

Creating and Modifying Group Accounts

WinNT supports basic functions for managing group accounts. You can create local group accounts on member servers and workstations. You can create domain local and global security groups in domains. You can manipulate any type of group.

Understanding Windows 2000 group types

In Windows 2000, there are several different types of groups and each type of group can have a different scope. The group type affects how the group is used. The three group types are the following:

- ✦ **Local** groups are used only on a local workstation or server.

- ✦ **Security** groups have security controls associated with them and are available in domains.

- ✦ **Distribution** groups are used as email distribution lists and do not have security controls. You define distribution groups in domains.

Group scope further defines the area in which groups are valid. The group scopes are:

- ✦ **Domain local** These groups are used to grant permissions in a single domain. Members of domain local groups can only include user accounts, computer accounts, and groups from the domain in which they are defined.

✦ **Built-in local** These groups are a special group scope that have domain local permissions. Built-in local groups differ from other groups in that they cannot be created or deleted, but you can modify their membership.

✦ **Global** These groups are used to grant permissions to any domain in the domain tree or forest. However, members of global groups can only include user accounts, computer accounts, and groups from the domain in which they are defined.

✦ **Universal** These groups are used to grant wide access throughout a domain tree or forest. Members of global groups include user accounts, computer accounts, and groups from any domain in the domain tree or forest.

Creating groups with WinNT

Creating groups with WinNT is much like creating user accounts. You start by obtaining the domain or local computer container in which you want to create the group. If you obtain a domain container, you create a global domain group by default. If you obtain a local computer container, you create a local group on that computer.

In the following example, you create a local group on a computer named omega and set the group name to myGroup:

VBScript

```
Set obj = GetObject("WinNT://seattle/omega,computer")
Set grp = obj.Create("group", "myGroup")
grp.SetInfo
```

JScript

```
var obj = GetObject("WinNT://seattle/omega,computer")
var grp = obj.Create("group", "myGroup")
grp.SetInfo()
```

Using a similar technique you could create a global domain group as well. If you want to create a domain local group, you must set the groupType property. This property is set with an integer value. The default value of 2 sets the group type to domain local. A value of 4 sets the group type to domain local. Following this, you could create a domain local group called Marketing like this:

VBScript

```
Set obj = GetObject("WinNT://seattle")
Set grp = obj.Create("group", "Marketing")
grp.groupType = 4
grp.SetInfo
```

JScript

```
var obj = GetObject("WinNT://seattle")
var grp = obj.Create("group", "Marketing")
grp.groupType = 4
grp.SetInfo()
```

The only other property that you may want to set for a group is Description, which is used to describe the group. You can set a description for the group when you create it. You can also view or change the value if necessary. In the following example, you add a description to the Marketing group we created previously:

VBScript

```
Set grp = GetObject("WinNT://seattle/Marketing,group")
grp.Description = "Sales and Marketing Group"
grp.SetInfo
```

JScript

```
var grp = GetObject("WinNT://seattle,Marketing,group")
grp.Description = "Sales and Marketing Group"
grp.SetInfo()
```

Checking group membership

Often when you work with groups, you'll want to determine if a particular account or other group is a member. You can do this with the IsMember() method of the Group object. Start by obtaining the group object you want to work with and then passing IsMember the AdsPath string of the member you want to check, for example:

VBScript

```
Set grp = GetObject("WinNT://seattle/Marketing,group")
mem = grp.IsMember("WinNT://seattle/jsmith,user")
WScript.Echo mem
```

JScript

```
var grp = GetObject("WinNT://seattle,Marketing,group")
mem = grp.IsMember("WinNT://seattle/jsmith,user")
WScript.Echo(mem)
```

The IsMember method returns True (or 1) if the member is found and False (or 0) otherwise.

Another way you can work with groups is to obtain a list of current members. You can do this by calling the Members() method, for example:

VBScript

```
Set grp = GetObject("WinNT://seattle/Marketing,group")
mem = grp.Members
```

JScript

```
var grp = GetObject("WinNT://seattle,Marketing,group")
mem = grp.Members()
```

The Members() method returns a collection of members using the IADsMembers interface. You can examine each member using a For loop, for example:

VBScript

```
Set grp = GetObject("WinNT://seattle/Domain Users")
Set mList = grp.members
For Each member In mList
    WScript.Echo member.Name & " " & member.Class
Next
```

JScript

```
var grp = GetObject("WinNT://seattle/Domain Users")
mList = new Enumerator(grp.members());

for (; !mList.atEnd(); mList.moveNext())
{
 s = mList.item()
 WScript.Echo(s.Name)
}
```

Adding and removing group members

You can use the WinNT provider to add and remove members from any type of group. To do this, first obtain the group object you want to work with and then add or remove members using their AdsPath string.

After you add or remove a member, you can use `IsMember()` to confirm the action, for example:

VBScript

```
Set grp = GetObject("WinNT://seattle/Marketing,group")
mem = grp.Add("WinNT://seattle/jsmith,user")
WScript.Echo grp.IsMember("WinNT://seattle/jsmith,user")
```

JScript

```
var grp = GetObject("WinNT://seattle/Marketing,group")
mem = grp.Add("WinNT://seattle/jsmith,user")
WScript.Echo(grp.IsMember("WinNT://seattle/jsmith,user"))
```

Summary

The WinNT provider is very useful when you want to manage basic settings for domains, users, and groups. As you've seen, you can also use WinNT to create, delete, and modify both user and group accounts. When using WinNT with Windows 2000, it's useful to keep in mind the limitations discussed in this chapter. To perform extended functions, such as moving user accounts to different containers or creating organizational units, you'll need to use the LDAP provider.

✦   ✦   ✦

Service and Resource Administration with ADSI

You can use ADSI to control many different aspects of workstations and servers. In this chapter, I look at managing services, opening files, and handling user sessions. When services and resources aren't configured or managed properly, your organization's productivity can grind to a halt. Email messages may not get delivered. Users may get locked out of files and databases. Critical systems may even crash. To help avoid problems with services and resources, you can use scripts to monitor their status, update configuration settings, and more.

Managing Windows Services

Windows services provide essential functions for workstations and servers. Without these services, computers could not perform many important tasks. If you've worked with Windows 2000 for awhile, you know that the operating system has many different features that help you automatically manage services. For example, you can configure the automatic restart of a service and the automatic restart of a computer if a service fails to restart.

With Windows scripts, you gain more control over how and when services are started, stopped, and restarted. You can use scripts to view service status and manage configuration settings as well.

Using and understanding Windows services

The standard utility for managing Windows services is the Services node of the Computer Management console. You can use the entries in the Services node to control and monitor services. When you examine services in the Computer Management console, you find that each service is displayed with summary information. As shown in Figure 17-1, this includes the following fields:

✦ **Name:** Shows the name of the service installed on the system.

✦ **Description:** Shows a brief description of the service.

✦ **Status:** Shows the service status. For example, a stopped service is indicated by a blank entry.

✦ **Startup Type:** Shows the startup setting for the service. Manual services can be started by users or other services. Automatic services are started when the computer boots. Disabled services are configured so that they cannot be started.

✦ **Log On As:** Shows the account the service logs on as. Usually, this is the local system account.

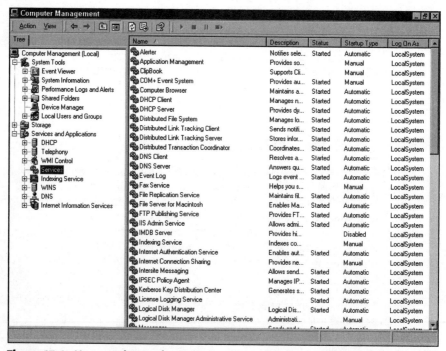

Figure 17-1: You can view and manage services with the Services node in the Computer Management console.

The services that are available on a system depend on the system's configuration. Table 17-1 lists some of the most commonly used services and their default configuration settings.

Table 17-1
Common Windows 2000 Services and Their Default Configuration

Display Name	Description	Startup Type	Log On As
Alerter	Notifies users and computers of administrative alerts.	Automatic	LocalSystem
Application Management	Provides software installation services.	Manual	LocalSystem
ClipBook	Supports the ClipBook Viewer for remote viewing of ClipBooks.	Manual	LocalSystem
COM+ Event System	Provides automatic distribution of COM events.	Manual	LocalSystem
Computer Browser	Maintains an up-to-date list of computers on the network.	Automatic	LocalSystem
DHCP Client	Provides dynamic host configuration information.	Automatic	LocalSystem
DHCP Server	Provides dynamic configuration for DHCP clients.	Automatic	LocalSystem
Distributed File System	Manages distributed file systems.	Automatic	LocalSystem
Distributed Transaction Coordinator	Coordinates distributed transactions.	Automatic	LocalSystem
DNS Client	Resolves and caches Domain Naming System (DNS) names.	Automatic	LocalSystem
DNS Server	Answers DNS requests.	Automatic	LocalSystem
Event Log	Logs event messages.	Automatic	LocalSystem
File Replication Service	Replicates directory data.	Automatic	LocalSystem

Continued

Table 17-1 *(continued)*

Display Name	Description	Startup Type	Log On As
File Server for Macintosh	Enables Macintosh users to work with files on a Windows server.	Automatic	LocalSystem
FTP Publishing Service	Provides FTP connectivity and administration through the Internet Information Services snap-in.	Automatic	LocalSystem
IIS Admin Service	Permits administration of Web and FTP services through the Internet Information Services snap-in.	Automatic	LocalSystem
Indexing Service	Indexes files and provides quick access.	Manual	LocalSystem
Internet Authentication Service	Enables authentication of dial-up and VPN users.	Automatic	LocalSystem
Internet Connection Sharing	Allows computers to share Internet connections.	Manual	LocalSystem
License Logging Service	Logs license-related events.	Automatic	LocalSystem
Logical Disk Manager	Monitors the Logical Disk Manager.	Automatic	LocalSystem
Logical Disk Manager Administrative Service	Used to manage logical disks.	Manual	LocalSystem
Messenger	Sends and receives administrative messages.	Automatic	LocalSystem
Net Logon	Supports authentication of account logon events.	Automatic	LocalSystem
Network DDE	Provides network transport and security for dynamic data exchange (DDE).	Manual	LocalSystem
Network DDE DSDM	Used by Network DDE to manage shared data exchanges.	Manual	LocalSystem
NT LM Security Support Provider	Provides security for remote procedure calls (RPC).	Manual	LocalSystem
Performance Logs and Alerts	Configures performance logs and alerts.	Manual	LocalSystem

Display Name	Description	Startup Type	Log On As
Plug and Play	Manages device installation and configuration.	Automatic	LocalSystem
Print Server for Macintosh	Enables Macintosh users to send print jobs to a spooler on a Windows server.	Automatic	LocalSystem
Print Spooler	Loads files to memory for later printing.	Automatic	LocalSystem
Protected Storage	Provides protected storage for sensitive data.	Automatic	LocalSystem
Remote Registry Service	Allows remote registry manipulation.	Automatic	LocalSystem
Removable Storage	Manages removable media.	Automatic	LocalSystem
Routing and Remote Access	Used to manage routing and remote access.	Disabled	LocalSystem
RunAs Service	Allows users to start process using alternate credentials.	Automatic	LocalSystem
Security Accounts Manager	Stores security information for local user accounts.	Automatic	LocalSystem
Server	Provides essential server services.	Automatic	LocalSystem
Simple Mail Transport Protocol (SMTP)	Transports email across the network.	Automatic	LocalSystem
Smart Card	Manages and controls access to smart cards.	Manual	LocalSystem
Smart Card Helper	Provides support for legacy smart card readers.	Manual	LocalSystem
System Event Notification	Tracks system events.	Automatic	LocalSystem
Task Scheduler	Enables task scheduling.	Automatic	LocalSystem
TCP/IP NetBIOS Helper Service	Supports NetBIOS over TCP/IP (NetBT) service and NetBIOS name resolution.	Automatic	LocalSystem
TCP/IP Print Server	Provides a TCP/IP-based printing.	Automatic	LocalSystem
Telephony	Provides Telephony support.	Manual	LocalSystem
Telnet	Allows a remote user to log on to the system and run console programs.	Manual	LocalSystem

Continued

Table 17-1 *(continued)*

Display Name	Description	Startup Type	Log On As
Windows Installer	Installs, repairs, and removes software using .MSI files.	Manual	LocalSystem
Windows Internet Name Service (WINS)	Provides a NetBIOS name service.	Automatic	LocalSystem
Windows Time	Used to synchronize system time.	Automatic	LocalSystem
Workstation	Provides network connections and communications.	Automatic	LocalSystem
World Wide Web Publishing Service	Provides Web connectivity and administration through the Internet Information Services snap-in.	Automatic	LocalSystem

Windows 2000 has built-in controls for monitoring and restarting services. You configure these recovery features on a per-service basis. To check or manage the recovery settings for a service, follow these steps:

1. Start the Computer Management console. Choose Start, Programs, then Administrative Tools, and then Computer Management.

2. In the Computer Management console, right-click the Computer Management entry in the console tree. Then, select Connect to Another Computer on the shortcut menu. You can now choose the system whose services you want to manage.

3. Click the plus sign (+) next to System Tools and then choose Services.

4. Right-click the service you want to configure and then choose Properties.

5. Choose the Recovery tab as shown in Figure 17-2. Now check or reconfigure recovery options for the first, second, and subsequent recovery attempts.

6. If you choose the Run A File option, you can specify a script that you want to run if the service fails. Enter the full directory path to the script in the File field, or click Browse to find the file. If you want to pass parameters to the script, enter these parameters in the Command Line Parameters field.

7. Click OK.

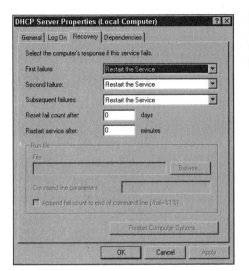

Figure 17-2: You set recovery options on a per-service basis and you can designate scripts to run if the service fails.

Working with service objects

Services are specific to a particular computer. So if you want to manage services, you must do so via the related `Computer` object. You don't access services by their display name. Instead, you access them using the object name for the service. For example, if you want to access the Windows Internet Name Service on a computer called HodgePodge, you would do so as follows:

```
Set service =
GetObject("WinNT://seattle/hodgepodge/wins,service")
```

In this example, `seattle` is the domain name (part of `seattle.tvpress.com`) and `wins` is the actual name of the `Service` object. Table 17-2 provides a detailed mapping of service display names to service object names. When you want to examine a particular service, use the table to help you determine the necessary object name.

<table>
<tr><td colspan="2" align="center">Table 17-2
Service Name Map</td></tr>
<tr><td>*Display Name*</td><td>*Object Name*</td></tr>
<tr><td>Alerter</td><td>Alerter</td></tr>
<tr><td>Application Management</td><td>AppMgmt</td></tr>
<tr><td>ClipBook</td><td>ClipSrv</td></tr>
</table>

Continued

Table 17-2 *(continued)*

Display Name	Object Name
COM+ Event System	EventSystem
Computer Browser	Browser
DHCP Client	Dhcp
DHCP Server	DHCPServer
Distributed File System	Dfs
Distributed Link Tracking Client	TrkWks
Distributed Link Tracking Server	TrkSvr
Distributed Transaction Coordinator	MSDTC
DNS Client	Dnscache
DNS Server	DNS
Event Log	Eventlog
Fax Service	Fax
File Replication Service	NtFrs
File Server for Macintosh	MacFile
FTP Publishing Service	MSFTPSVC
IIS Admin Service	IISADMIN
IMDB Server	ImdbServer
Indexing Service	cisvc
Internet Authentication Service	IAS
Internet Connection Sharing	SharedAccess
Intersite Messaging	IsmServ
IPSEC Policy Agent	PolicyAgent
Kerberos Key Distribution Center	kdc
License Logging Service	LicenseService
Logical Disk Manager	dmserver
Logical Disk Manager Administrative Service	dmadmin
Messenger	Messenger
Net Logon	Netlogon
NetMeeting Remote Desktop Sharing	mnmsrvc

Display Name	Object Name
Network Connections	Netman
Network DDE	NetDDE
Network DDE DSDM	NetDDEdsdm
NT LM Security Support Provider	NtLmSsp
Performance Logs and Alerts	SysmonLog
Plug and Play	PlugPlay
Print Server for Macintosh	MacPrint
Print Spooler	Spooler
Protected Storage	ProtectedStorage
QoS Admission Control (RSVP)	RSVP
Remote Access Auto Connection Manager	RasAuto
Remote Access Connection Manager	RasMan
Remote Procedure Call (RPC)	RpcSs
Remote Procedure Call (RPC) Locator	RpcLocator
Remote Registry Service	RemoteRegistry
Removable Storage	NtmsSvc
Routing and Remote Access	RemoteAccess
RunAs Service	seclogon
Security Accounts Manager	SamSs
Server	lanmanserver
Simple Mail Transport Protocol (SMTP)	SMTPSVC
Simple TCP/IP Services	SimpTcp
Smart Card	SCardSvr
Smart Card Helper	SCardDrv
SNMP Service	SNMP
SNMP Trap Service	SNMPTRAP
System Event Notification	SENS
Task Scheduler	Schedule
TCP/IP NetBIOS Helper Service	LmHosts

Continued

Table 17-2 *(continued)*	
Display Name	*Object Name*
TCP/IP Print Server	LPDSVC
Telephony	TapiSrv
Telnet	TlntSvr
Terminal Services	TermService
Uninterruptible Power Supply	UPS
Utility Manager	UtilMan
Windows Installer	MSIServer
Windows Internet Name Service (WINS)	WINS
Windows Management Instrumentation	WinMgmt
Windows Management Instrumentation Driver Extensions	Wmi
Windows Time	W32Time
Workstation	lanmanworkstation
World Wide Web Publishing Service	W3SVC

If a service you need to work with isn't listed in Table 17-2, you may need to create a list of all services on the computer and then filter this list by the display name. Listing 17-1 shows how you can search for the Windows Internet Name Service (WINS).

Listing 17-1: **Searching for a service object name**

VBScript

servicename.vbs

```
Set comp = GetObject("WinNT://seattle/zeta")

 'Check for Service objects
  For each s in comp

   If s.Class = "Service" Then

     If s.DisplayName = "Windows Internet Name Service (WINS)" Then
```

```
        WScript.Echo s.DisplayName & ": " & s.Name

      End If

    End If


  Next
```

JScript

---

servicename.js
```
var comp = GetObject("WinNT://seattle/zeta")

tlist = new Enumerator(comp)

for (; !tlist.atEnd(); tlist.moveNext())
 {

 s = tlist.item()

 if (s.Class == "Service") {

   if (s.DisplayName == "Windows Internet Name Service (WINS)") {

     WScript.Echo(s.DisplayName + " " + s.Name)

   }
  }
}
```

Output
```
Windows Internet Name Service (WINS): WINS
```

Using service object properties

All service objects have a set of properties that you can work with. These properties are summarized in Table 17-3. (A status of RO means the property is read-only and cannot be updated. A status of RW means the property is read-write and can be updated.)

Table 17-3
Service Object Properties

Property	Status	Value Type	Min Range	Max Range	Multiple Values
Dependencies	RW	Array or String	0	256	True
DisplayName	RW	String	0	256	False
ErrorControl	RW	Integer	-2147483648	2147483647	False
HostComputer	RW	AdsPath String	0	256	False
LoadOrderGroup	RW	String	0	256	False
Path	RW	Path String	0	340	False
ServiceAccountName	RW	String	0	273	False
ServiceType	RW	Integer	-2147483648	2147483647	False
StartType	RW	Integer	-2147483648	2147483647	False
Status	RO	Integer	1	8	False

As with most object properties, you can access property values by name or through the get() method. Listing 17-2 shows how you could examine all of the services running on a particular computer. Services can have multiple dependencies. If they do, these dependencies can be accessed through the Dependencies array. Note the sample values listed in the output, which I'll discuss later in the chapter.

Listing 17-2: **Viewing service settings**

VBScript

viewservices.vbs

```
'Handle Errors
On Error Resume Next

lf = Chr(13) + Chr(10)
'Get the provider object
Set comp = GetObject("WinNT://seattle/zeta")

 'Check for Service objects
  For each s in comp
```

```
   If s.Class = "Service" Then

    'Display service properties
     WScript.Echo s.Class & " " & s.Name
     WScript.Echo "=============================="
     WScript.Echo "StartType: " & s.StartType
     WScript.Echo "ServiceType: " & s.ServiceType
     WScript.Echo "DisplayName: " & s.DisplayName
     WScript.Echo "Path: " & s.Path
     WScript.Echo "ErrorControl: " & s.ErrorControl
     WScript.Echo "HostComputer: " & s.HostComputer
     WScript.Echo "LoadOrderGroup: " & s.LoadOrderGroup
     WScript.Echo "ServiceAccountName: " & s.ServiceAccountName

     'services can have multiple dependencies
     deps = s.Dependencies

     If VarType(deps) = vbString Then
       WScript.Echo "Dependency: " & deps
       Set ds = c.GetObject("Service", deps)

     Else
       For Each a In deps
        WScript.Echo "Dependency: " & a
        Set ds = c.GetObject("Service", a)
       Next
     End If

     WScript.Echo(lf)
   End If

Next
```

JScript

---

viewservices.js

```
lf = "\r\n"

var comp = GetObject("WinNT://seattle/zeta")

tlist = new Enumerator(comp)

for (; !tlist.atEnd(); tlist.moveNext())
 {

 s = tlist.item()
if (s.Class == "Service") {

     //Display service properties
     WScript.Echo(s.Class + " " + s.Name)
```

Continued

Listing 17-2 *(continued)*

JScript

```
WScript.Echo("ServiceType: " + s.ServiceType)
        WScript.Echo("==============================")
        WScript.Echo("StartType: " + s.StartType)
        WScript.Echo("DisplayName: " + s.DisplayName)
        WScript.Echo("Path: " + s.Path)
        WScript.Echo("ErrorControl: " + s.ErrorControl)
        WScript.Echo("HostComputer: " + s.HostComputer)
        WScript.Echo("LoadOrderGroup: " + s.LoadOrderGroup)
        WScript.Echo("ServiceAccountName: " + s.ServiceAccountName)

        try {
         WScript.Echo("Dependencies: " + s.Dependencies)
         }
        catch (e) {
         //property setting not available or is array
         }
        try {
        //services can have multiple dependencies
         e = s.Dependencies.toArray()
          for (opt in e)
          {
            WScript.Echo("Dependencies: " + e[opt])
          }
        }
        catch (e) {
          //property setting not available
        }
        try {
          WScript.Echo("Status: " + s.Get("Status"))
        }
        catch (e) {
          //property setting not available
        }

        WScript.Echo(lf)
        }

    }
```

Output

```
Service WINS
==============================
StartType: 2
ServiceType: 16
DisplayName: Windows Internet Name Service (WINS)
Path: F:\WIN2000\System32\wins.exe
```

```
ErrorControl: 1
HostComputer: WinNT://seattle/zeta
LoadOrderGroup:
ServiceAccountName: LocalSystem
Dependencies: RPCSS
Dependencies: NTLMSSP
Dependencies: SAMSS
Status: 4

Service Wmi
================================
StartType: 3
ServiceType: 32
DisplayName: Windows Management Instrumentation Driver Extensions
Path: F:\WIN2000\system32\Services.exe
ErrorControl: 1
HostComputer: WinNT://seattle/zeta
LoadOrderGroup:
ServiceAccountName: LocalSystem
Dependencies: RPCSS
Dependencies: NTLMSSP
Dependencies: SAMSS
Status: 4
```

Note

I had a problem accessing the `Status` property in JScript on my system. This property wasn't directly accessible by name for some service types. To resolve this problem, I had to use `s.Get("Status")` instead of `s.Status`, in which `s` is the name of the current `Service` object.

Checking Service Status and Dependencies

One of the key properties that you'll use while troubleshooting service problems is `Status`. This property returns a code that indicates the state of the service. The status codes are:

Service Stopped	1	Attempting to Continue Service	5
Attempting to Start Service	2	Attempting to Pause Service	6
Attempting to Stop Service	3	Service Paused	7
Service Running	4	Service Error	8

Another important property that's used in troubleshooting service problems is `Dependencies`. The `Dependencies` property returns an array of services that must be running before the parent service can run. For example, the WINS service can only run if the RPCSS, NTLMSSP, and SAMSS services are running. So if you determine that WINS is a critical service that you want to track or manage through a Windows script, you also want to track and manage these additional services.

Using the `Status` and `Dependencies` properties together, you can determine if a service isn't running because of problems with dependent services. In Listing 17-3, the user is prompted to enter a computer name and service name. The script then checks to see if the service is running normally. If the service isn't running normally, the script checks the status of dependent services.

Listing 17-3: **Resolving service-related problems**

VBScript

trservices.vbs

```
' ************************
' Script: Service Troubleshooter
' Version: 0.9.5
' Creation Date: 10/1/99
' Last Modified: 12/15/99
' Author: William R. Stanek
' Email: winscripting@tvpress.com
' Copyright (c) 1999, 2000 William R. Stanek
' ************************

On Error Resume Next
lf = Chr(13) & Chr(10)

WScript.Echo "========================================" & lf
WScript.Echo "==    Service Troubleshooting Script   ==" & lf
WScript.Echo "========================================" & lf

WScript.Echo "Enter local or remote host name: " & lf

host = WScript.StdIn.ReadLine()

WScript.Echo lf & "Enter service to troubleshoot: " & lf

servName = WScript.StdIn.ReadLine()

Set c = GetObject("WinNT://" & host & ",computer")
Set s = c.GetObject("Service", servName)

WScript.Echo lf & "========================================" & lf
WScript.Echo "Checking Status for " & s.Name
WScript.Echo "========================================" & lf

checkStatus(s)

sub checkStatus(obj)

 Select Case obj.Status
  Case 1
```

```
   WScript.Echo "======================================="
   WScript.Echo "Service not running."
   WScript.Echo "Checking dependent services."
   WScript.Echo "=======================================" & lf

   deps = obj.Dependencies

   If VarType(deps) = vbString Then
      WScript.Echo "Dependency: " & deps & lf

      Set ds = c.GetObject("Service", deps)
      checkStatus(ds)
   Else

    For Each a In deps
      WScript.Echo "Dependency: " & a & lf

      Set ds = c.GetObject("Service", a)
      checkStatus(ds)

    Next
    End If

  Case 4

    WScript.Echo obj.Class & " " & obj.Name & " is running normally"
    WScript.Echo lf

  Case 7

    WScript.Echo obj.Class & " " & obj.Name & " is paused." & lf

  Case 8

    WScript.Echo "======================================="
    WScript.Echo "Service error!"
    WScript.Echo "Checking dependent services."
    WScript.Echo "=======================================" & lf
     deps = obj.Dependencies

    If VarType(deps) = vbString Then
       WScript.Echo "Dependency: " & deps & lf

       Set ds = c.GetObject("Service", deps)
       checkStatus(ds)
    Else

     For Each a In deps
       WScript.Echo "Dependency: " & a & lf
```

Continued

Listing 17-3 *(continued)*

VBScript

```
        Set ds = c.GetObject("Service", a)
        checkStatus(ds)

    Next
    End If


  Case Else

    WScript.Echo obj.Class & " " & obj.Name & " is changing states."
    WScript.Echo lf

 End Select
End Sub
```

Output

```
========================================

==   Service Troubleshooting Script   ==

========================================

Enter local or remote host name:

zeta

Enter service to troubleshoot:

w3svc


========================================

Checking Status for w3svc
========================================


========================================
Service not running or error.
Checking dependent services.
========================================

Dependency: IISADMIN

Service IISADMIN is running normally
```

I've configured the script to use recursive calls to the `checkStatus` subroutine. This enables the script to check the next level of service dependencies in case of service failure. In the previous example, the W3SVC depends on the IISADMIN service. In turn, IISADMIN depends on other services. If both W3SVC and IISADMIN aren't running properly, the script checks the dependent services of IISADMIN. To see how this works, consider the following output from this service troubleshooting script:

```
========================================

==    Service Troubleshooting Script   ==

========================================

Enter local or remote host name:

zeta

Enter service to troubleshoot:

w3svc

========================================

Checking Status for w3svc
========================================

========================================
Service not running or error.
Checking dependent services.
========================================

Dependency: IISADMIN

========================================
Service not running or error.
Checking dependent services.
========================================

Dependency: RPCSS

Service RPCSS is running normally

Dependency: ProtectedStorage

Service ProtectedStorage is running normally
```

In this example, both W3SVC and IISADMIN aren't running normally. Because of this, the script checks the dependencies of both services. The section of code driving most of the script is:

```
deps = obj.Dependencies
```

```
        If VarType(deps) = vbString Then
            WScript.Echo "Dependency: " & deps & lf

            Set ds = c.GetObject("Service", deps)
            checkStatus(ds)
        Else

          For Each a In deps
            WScript.Echo "Dependency: " & a & lf

            Set ds = c.GetObject("Service", a)
            checkStatus(ds)

          Next
        End If
```

This snippet of code is responsible for checking service dependencies. A single
dependency is represented with a string. Multiple dependencies are represented
with an array. Because of this, you need a section of code that checks for a string
value if one is present, and otherwise handles the dependencies as an array.

Viewing and Setting Service Information

These other service object properties let you view and configure service settings:

✦ DisplayName: Specifies the service display name.

✦ ErrorControl: Specifies the actions taken in case of service failure. A value of
0 indicates no recovery settings. A value greater than zero indicates recovery
options have been set.

✦ HostComputer: Displays the AdsPath string of the host computer running
the service.

✦ LoadOrderGroup: Identifies the load order group of which the service is
a member.

✦ Path: Specifies the path and filename of the executable for the service.

✦ ServiceAccountName: Designates the account used by the service at startup.

✦ ServiceType: Specifies the process type in which the service runs.

✦ StartType: Identifies the start type for the service.

Cross-Reference

For detailed information on these properties, see Appendix B. Service properties and
methods are defined in the IADsService and IADsServiceOperations interfaces.

In scripts, you'll often need to view values for the service object properties, and you can do this as shown in Listing 17-2. However, unless you are creating a script to install a service, you won't need to set most of these properties. Because of this, I'll focus on the two properties that you may want to configure: DisplayName and ServiceAccountName.

As you've seen in previous examples, the Service object name isn't tied to the display name. This means you can change the display name without affecting the service. For example, if you want to rename the Windows Management Instrumentation Driver Extensions service as Wmi, you can do so as follows:

VBScript

```
Set s = GetObject("WinNT://seattle/zeta/wmi,service")
s.Put "DisplayName", "Wmi"
s.SetInfo
```

JScript

```
var s = GetObject("WinNT://seattle/zeta/wmi,service")
s.Put("DisplayName", "Wmi")
s.SetInfo()
```

Changing the ServiceAccoutName property, on the other hand, does affect the service. This property controls which domain or system account is used to start the service. If you use a domain account, you must enter the domain name as well as the account name. For example, if the domain is Seattle and the account is Administrator, you enter Seattle/Administration as the account name.

When you set the account name, you must also enter the password for the account. To do this, use the SetPassword() method of the service object. The only parameter for this method is a string containing the account password. You can configure a new service startup account as follows:

VBScript

```
Set s = GetObject("WinNT://seattle/zeta/snmp,service")
s.Put "ServiceAccountName", "Seattle/Administrator"
s.SetPassword "MamboKings"
s.SetInfo
```

JScript

```
var s = GetObject("WinNT://seattle/zeta/snmp,service")
s.Put("ServiceAccountName", "Seattle/Administrator")
s.SetPassword("MamboKings")
s.SetInfo()
```

Starting, Stopping, and Pausing Services

The service object has methods for controlling services in scripts as well. These methods are:

✦ Start() Starts a service.

✦ Stop() Stops a service.

✦ Pause() Pauses a service.

✦ Continue() Resumes a paused service.

Using these methods is rather straightforward. If you want to start the W3SVC, you obtain the related service object and then call Start(), for example:

VBScript

```
Set s = GetObject("WinNT://seattle/zeta/w3svc,service")
s.Start
```

JScript

```
var s = GetObject("WinNT://seattle/zeta/w3svc,service")
s.Start()
```

You can use the other methods in a similar manner. Keep in mind that if you stop a service, you must use Start() to start it, but if you use pause a service, you must use Continue() to resume it.

A problem arises when you want to stop a service that other services depend on. For example, if you want to stop the IISADMIN service and haven't stopped dependent services, you'll get the following error message:

```
A stop control has been sent to a service that other running services are
dependent on.
```

You'll need to stop the dependent services before you can stop this service. Fortunately, if you try to start a service that is dependent on another service that is stopped, Windows 2000 is smart enough to start the dependent service as well. To see how this works, stop the IISADMIN and W3SVC services and then try to start W3SVC. You'll discover that both IISADMIN and W3SVC start.

Listing 17-4 shows a script that you can use to manage services. This script combines some of the techniques I've discussed previously and is not meant to be complete. You'll need to add to the script to suit your needs.

Listing 17-4: **Managing services**

VBScript

---

servicemgr.vbs

```
' ************************
' Script: Service Manager
' Version: 0.9.5
' Creation Date: 10/7/99
' Last Modified: 12/15/99
' Author: William R. Stanek
' Email: winscripting@tvpress.com
' Copyright (c) 1999, 2000 William R. Stanek
' ************************

On Error Resume Next
lf = Chr(13) & Chr(10)

WScript.Echo "========================================" & lf
WScript.Echo "==    Service Manager Script    ==" & lf
WScript.Echo "========================================" & lf

WScript.Echo "Enter local or remote host name: " & lf

host = WScript.StdIn.ReadLine()

WScript.Echo lf & "Enter service to manage: " & lf

servName = WScript.StdIn.ReadLine()

WScript.Echo lf & "G) Start Service" & lf
WScript.Echo "S) Stop Service" & lf

action = WScript.StdIn.ReadLine()

action = LCase(action)

Set c = GetObject("WinNT://" & host & ",computer")
Set s = c.GetObject("Service", servName)

manageService s, action

sub manageService(obj, a)

 On Error Resume Next

 Select Case a
  Case "g"
```

Continued

Listing 17-4 *(continued)*

VBScript

```
If obj.Status = 1 Then

 obj.Start

 WScript.Echo "=========================================="
 WScript.Echo "Starting Service..."
 WScript.Echo "==========================================" & lf

 Else

 WScript.Echo "=========================================="
 WScript.Echo "Service is running already."
 WScript.Echo "=========================================="
 WScript.Echo "Checking dependent services."
 WScript.Echo "==========================================" & lf
 deps = obj.Dependencies

 If VarType(deps) = vbString Then
   WScript.Echo "Dependency: " & deps & lf

   Set ds = c.GetObject("Service", deps)
   checkStatus(ds)
 Else

 For Each a In deps
   WScript.Echo "Dependency: " & a & lf

   Set ds = c.GetObject("Service", a)
   checkStatus(ds)

 Next
 End If
End If

Case "s"

 If obj.Status = 4 Then

 obj.Stop
 WScript.Echo "=========================================="
 WScript.Echo "Stopping Service..."
 WScript.Echo "==========================================" & lf

 Else

 WScript.Echo "=========================================="
 WScript.Echo "Service is already stopped."
```

```
        WScript.Echo "========================================"
        WScript.Echo "Checking dependent services."
        WScript.Echo "========================================" & lf
        deps = obj.Dependencies

        If VarType(deps) = vbString Then
          WScript.Echo "Dependency: " & deps & lf

          Set ds = c.GetObject("Service", deps)
          checkStatus(ds)
        Else

        For Each a In deps
          WScript.Echo "Dependency: " & a & lf

          Set ds = c.GetObject("Service", a)
          checkStatus(ds)

      Next
      End If

    End If

  Case Else

      WScript.Echo "Please re-run script and enter a valid option"

  End Select
End Sub

sub checkStatus(obj)

On Error Resume Next

Select Case obj.Status
  Case 1

    WScript.Echo "========================================"
    WScript.Echo "Service not running."
    WScript.Echo "Checking dependent services."
    WScript.Echo "========================================" & lf
      deps = obj.Dependencies

    If VarType(deps) = vbString Then
      WScript.Echo "Dependency: " & deps & lf

      Set ds = c.GetObject("Service", deps)
      checkStatus(ds)
    Else
      For Each a In deps
```

Continued

Listing 17-4: *(continued)*

VBScript

```
        WScript.Echo "Dependency: " & a & lf
        Set ds = c.GetObject("Service", a)
        checkStatus(ds)

    Next
    End If

  Case 4

    WScript.Echo obj.Class & " " & obj.Name & " is running normally"
    WScript.Echo lf

  Case 7

    WScript.Echo obj.Class & " " & obj.Name & " is paused." & lf

  Case 8

    WScript.Echo "========================================"
    WScript.Echo "Service error!"
    WScript.Echo "Checking dependent services."
    WScript.Echo "========================================" & lf
     deps = obj.Dependencies

    If VarType(deps) = vbString Then
      WScript.Echo "Dependency: " & deps & lf

      Set ds = c.GetObject("Service", deps)
      checkStatus(ds)
    Else

     For Each a In deps
       WScript.Echo "Dependency: " & a & lf

       Set ds = c.GetObject("Service", a)
       checkStatus(ds)

     Next
    End If

  Case Else

    WScript.Echo obj.Class & " " & obj.Name & " is changing states."
    WScript.Echo lf

  End Select
End Sub
```

Output

```
=========================================

==   Service Manager Script   ==

=========================================

Enter local or remote host name:

zeta

Enter service to manage:

w3svc

G) Start Service

S) Stop Service

g
=========================================
Starting Service...
=========================================
```

The script relies on the manageService and checkStatus subroutines to perform most of the work. The manageService subroutine expects to be passed a service object and an action to be performed. For example:

```
sub manageService(obj, a)
  ...
end sub
```

The subroutine then uses these arguments to start or stop services. If the referenced service is already started (or stopped), the script calls checkStatus to display the status of dependent services. You'll find this useful when you want to control services and the services they depend on.

Managing Open Resources and User Sessions

User sessions are created each time users connect to shared resources on a server. If a user opens a file for editing, the file is also listed as an open resource on the server. Problems with open files and user sessions can often affect network operations. If a file is listed as open but no user is actually using it, another user may not be able to access the file. To resolve this problem you need to end the user session causing the problem or close the open file. For this and other reasons, you'll find that you often need to manage user sessions and open resources, especially in a busy network environment.

Viewing open files and user sessions

In Windows 2000, you normally manage open files and user sessions through the Computer Management console. You view connections to shared resources as follows:

1. In the Computer Management console, right-click the Computer Management entry in the console tree. Then select Connect to Another Computer on the shortcut menu. You can now choose the system whose services you want to manage.

2. Click the plus sign (+) next to System Tools and then click the plus sign next to Shared Folders.

3. Select Sessions to view or manage user sessions. The information provided in the Sessions node tells you the following information:

   - **User:** Names of users or computers connected to shared resources. Computer names are shown with a $ suffix to differentiate them from users.

   - **Computer:** IP address of the computer being used.

   - **Type:** Type of computer being used.

   - **Open Files:** Number of files the user has open.

   - **Connected Time:** Elapsed time since the connection was established.

   - **Idle Time:** Elapsed time since the connection was last used.

   - **Guest:** Identifies users accessing the computer through a guest account or default guest access.

4. Select Open Files to view or manage open files. The Open Files node provides the following information about resource usage:

   - **Open File:** File or folder path to the open file on the local system.

   - **File Locks:** Total number of file locks.

   - **Accessed By:** Name of the user accessing the file.

   - **Type:** Type of computer being used.

   - **# Locks:** Number of locks on the resource.

   - **Open Mode:** Access mode used when the resource was opened, such as Read or Write+Read mode.

Figure 17-3 shows Computer Management with the Open Files node selected. As you would expect, you can obtain similar information through Windows scripts. I'll show you how in the next section.

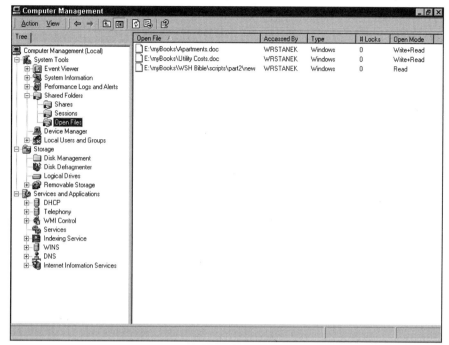

Figure 17-3: You can use Computer Management to get summary information on open files and user sessions.

Viewing resources and sessions in scripts

In scripts, you view open files and user sessions through the `Resource` and `Session` objects. These objects can only be accessed through a `FileService` object. You obtain a `FileService` object through the LanManServer service. The `AdsPath` string should either not state the object type:

```
WinNT://seattle/zeta/lanmanserver
```

or it should state the object type as `FileService`:

```
WinNT://seattle/zeta/lanmanserver,fileservice
```

`FileService` is a special type of object that extends the standard `Service` object, adding several new properties and methods that you can use to work with resources and sessions. If you state the object type as `Service`, as was done in previous examples, you won't get the extended `FileService` interface and instead will get the standard `IADsService` interface.

Additional properties for `FileService` are:

✦ `Description`: A read/write string that describes the file service.

✦ `MaxUserCount`: A read/write integer value that identifies the maximum number of users allowed to run the service concurrently. A value of –1 indicates that no limit is set.

Additional methods for `FileService` are:

✦ `Resources()`: Gets an interface pointer on a collection object that represents current open resources for the file service.

✦ `Sessions()`: Gets an interface pointer on a collection object that represents current open sessions on the file service.

Listing 17-5 shows how you can display the standard and extended features of the `FileService` object. By iterating through each element in the `Resources` and `Sessions` collections, you can display a list of currently open files and active user sessions. You'll use this technique in the next section when you examine `Resource` and `Session` object properties.

Listing 17-5: **Viewing resource and sessions usage**

VBScript

fileservice.vbs

```
On Error Resume Next

Set s = GetObject("WinNT://seattle/zeta/lanmanserver,fileservice")

'Display service properties
WScript.Echo s.Class & " " & s.Name
WScript.Echo "==============================="
WScript.Echo "StartType: " & s.StartType
WScript.Echo "Description: " & s.Description
WScript.Echo "MaxUserCount: " & s.MaxUserCount
WScript.Echo "ServiceType: " & s.ServiceType
WScript.Echo "DisplayName: " & s.DisplayName
WScript.Echo "Path: " & s.Path
WScript.Echo "ErrorControl: " & s.ErrorControl
WScript.Echo "HostComputer: " & s.HostComputer
WScript.Echo "LoadOrderGroup: " & s.LoadOrderGroup
WScript.Echo "ServiceAccountName: " & s.ServiceAccountName
WScript.Echo "Dependencies: " & s.Dependencies
WScript.Echo "Status: " & s.Status
```

```
For Each resource In s.Resources
 WScript.Echo "Resource path: " & resource.Path
Next
For Each session In s.sessions
 WScript.Echo "Session name: " & session.Name
Next
```

JScript

---

fileservice.js

```
var s = GetObject("WinNT://seattle/zeta/lanmanserver,fileservice")

//Display service properties
WScript.Echo(s.Class + " " + s.Name)
WScript.Echo("==============================")
WScript.Echo("StartType: " + s.StartType)
WScript.Echo("Description: " + s.Description)
WScript.Echo("MaxUserCount: " + s.MaxUserCount)
WScript.Echo("ServiceType: " + s.ServiceType)
WScript.Echo("DisplayName: " + s.DisplayName)
WScript.Echo("Path: " + s.Path)
WScript.Echo("ErrorControl: " + s.ErrorControl)
WScript.Echo("HostComputer: " + s.HostComputer)
WScript.Echo("LoadOrderGroup: " + s.LoadOrderGroup)
WScript.Echo("ServiceAccountName: " + s.ServiceAccountName)

try {
 WScript.Echo("Dependencies: " + s.Dependencies)
}
catch (e) {
  //property setting not available
}
try {
 WScript.Echo("Status: " + s.Get("Status"))
}
catch (e) {
  //property setting not available
}

 rList = new Enumerator(s.Resources());
 for (; !rList.atEnd(); rList.moveNext())
 {
  resource = rList.item()
  WScript.Echo("Resource path: " + resource.Path)
 }

 sList = new Enumerator(s.Sessions());
```

Continued

Listing 17-5 *(continued)*

JScript

```
for (; !sList.atEnd(); sList.moveNext())
{
 session = sList.item()
 WScript.Echo("Session name: " + session.Name)
}
```

Output

```
FileService lanmanserver
================================
StartType: 2
Description:
MaxUserCount: -1
ServiceType: 32
DisplayName: Server
Path: F:\WIN2000\System32\services.exe
ErrorControl: 1
HostComputer: WinNT://seattle/zeta
LoadOrderGroup:
ServiceAccountName: LocalSystem
Resource path: E:\myBooks\docs
Resource path: E:\myBooks\docs\chapter1.rtf
Session name: WRSTANEK\127.0.0.1
```

Working with Resource and Session objects

You use Resource objects to view open resources for a file service. The properties for Resource objects are:

- ✦ LockCount: The number of locks on a resource.
- ✦ Path: The file path of the resource.
- ✦ User: The name of the user who opened the resource.
- ✦ UserPath: An AdsPath string of the user object that is accessing the resource.

You use Session objects to view active user sessions for the file service. The properties for Session objects are:

- ✦ Computer: The name of the client workstation from which the session initiated.
- ✦ ComputerPath: The AdsPath of the related computer object.

✦ ConnectTime: The number of minutes since the session started.

✦ IdleTime: The number of minutes the session has been idle.

✦ User: The name of the user that initiated the session.

✦ UserPath: The AdsPath of the related user object.

All properties of Resource and Session objects are read-only. This means you can view them but cannot set them, which makes sense since these values are set automatically by the operating system.

Listing 17-6 shows a script that displays summary information for open files and user sessions on a specified computer. I've written the script in both VBScript and JScript so you can compare the implementation techniques. Note the format of property values in the output. With resources, entries can relate to folder paths and to file paths. Generally, if you have an entry for a file path, you'll also see an entry for the related folder path. With sessions, you'll see that the session name i s a combination of the username and the IP address from which the session originates, such as WRSTANEK\127.0.0.1. You may also see entries that begin with a dollar sign ($), which indicates a computer account rather than a user account.

Listing 17-6: **Viewing resource and sessions usage**

VBScript

shareusage.vbs

```
' ************************
' Script: Share Usage
' Version: 0.9.5
' Creation Date: 10/7/99
' Last Modified: 12/15/99
' Author: William R. Stanek
' Email: winscripting@tvpress.com
' Copyright (c) 1999, 2000 William R. Stanek
' ************************

On Error Resume Next
lf = Chr(13) & Chr(10)
WScript.Echo "======================================" & lf
WScript.Echo "==    Share Usage Script    ==" & lf
WScript.Echo "======================================" & lf

WScript.Echo "Enter local or remote host name: " & lf

host = WScript.StdIn.ReadLine()
```

Continued

Listing 17-6 *(continued)*

VBScript

```
On Error Resume Next

Set s = GetObject("WinNT://" & host & "/lanmanserver,fileservice")

'Display open files
WScript.Echo lf & s.Class & " " & s.Name
WScript.Echo "==============================="
WScript.Echo "Open Files: " & lf

For Each resource In s.Resources
  WScript.Echo "File or Folder Path: " & resource.Path
  WScript.Echo "Number of Locks: " & resource.LockCount
  WScript.Echo "User: " & resource.User & lf
Next

'Display user sessions
WScript.Echo "==============================="
WScript.Echo "User sessions: " & lf

For Each session In s.sessions
  WScript.Echo "Session name: " & session.Name
  WScript.Echo "User: " & session.User
  WScript.Echo "Computer: " & session.Computer
  WScript.Echo "Connect Time: " & session.ConnectTime
  WScript.Echo "Idle Time: " & session.IdleTime & lf
Next
```

JScript

fileservice.js

```
// *************************
// Script: Share Usage
// Version: 0.9.5
// Creation Date: 10/7/99
// Last Modified: 12/15/99
// Author: William R. Stanek
// Email: winscripting@tvpress.com
// Copyright (c) 1999, 2000 William R. Stanek
// *************************

lf = "\r\n"

WScript.Echo("=======================================" + lf)
WScript.Echo("==    Share Usage Script    ==" + lf)
WScript.Echo("=======================================" + lf)
```

```
WScript.Echo("Enter local or remote host name: " + lf)

host = WScript.StdIn.ReadLine()

var s = GetObject("WinNT://" + host + "/lanmanserver,fileservice")

//Display open files
WScript.Echo(lf + s.Class + " " + s.Name)
WScript.Echo("==============================")
WScript.Echo("Open Files: " + lf)


 rList = new Enumerator(s.Resources());

 for (; !rList.atEnd(); rList.moveNext())
 {
  resource = rList.item()
  WScript.Echo("File or Folder Path: " + resource.Path)
  WScript.Echo("Number of Locks: " + resource.LockCount)
  WScript.Echo("User: " + resource.User + lf)
 }

//Display user sessions
WScript.Echo("==============================")
WScript.Echo("User sessions: " + lf)

 sList = new Enumerator(s.Sessions());

 for (; !sList.atEnd(); sList.moveNext())
 {
  session = sList.item()
  WScript.Echo("Session name: " + session.Name)
  WScript.Echo("User: " + session.User)
  WScript.Echo("Computer: " + session.Computer)
  WScript.Echo("Connect Time: " + session.ConnectTime)
  WScript.Echo("Idle Time: " + session.IdleTime + lf)
 }
```

Output

```
==========================================

==   Share Usage Script   ==

==========================================

Enter local or remote host name:

zeta
```

Continued

Listing 17-6 *(continued)*

Output

```
FileService lanmanserver
===============================
Open Files:

File or Folder Path: E:\myBooks\docs
Number of Locks: 0
User: WRSTANEK

File or Folder Path: E:\myBooks\docs\chapter1.rtf
Number of Locks: 0
User: WRSTANEK


===============================
User sessions:

Session name: WRSTANEK\127.0.0.1
User: WRSTANEK
Computer: 127.0.0.1
Connect Time: 7259
Idle Time: 7236
```

In Windows scripts, you can close open files and end user sessions, using the Remove() method of the IADsCollection interface. However, you can only do this if the files or sessions are inactive or erroneously listed. The following example ends all inactive user sessions:

VBScript

```
Set s = GetObject("WinNT://zeta/lanmanserver,fileservice")
Set coll = fso.Sessions

For Each session In coll
 coll.Remove "Session", session.Name
Next
```

JScript

```
var s = GetObject("WinNT://" + host + "/lanmanserver,fileservice")

sList = new Enumerator(s.Sessions());

for (; !sList.atEnd(); sList.moveNext())
```

```
{
  session = sList.item()
  sList.Remove("Session", session.Name)
}
```

Summary

This chapter explored working with services, open resources, and user sessions. Services provide essential functions for Windows computers. You can use scripts to view service settings and to manage service configuration using the properties and methods of the IADsService interface. This interface is extended by IADsFileService and IADsFileServiceOperations, which provide additional features for FileService objects. These additional features enable you to work with open resources and user sessions. Groups of resources and sessions are represented by Resources and Sessions collections, which in turn, contain one or more Resource or Session objects.

✦   ✦   ✦

Maintaining Shared Directories, Printer Queues, and Print Jobs

◆ ◆ ◆ ◆

In This Chapter

Creating shared
folders

Configuring
shared folders

Managing
print queues

Controlling print jobs

◆ ◆ ◆ ◆

In Chapter 9, you learned how to manage network resources, in particular network drives and network printer connections. Now it's time to extend this knowledge so that you can create, control, and configure related resources; namely shared folders, print queues, and print jobs. A key concept on any network is resource sharing; both folders and printers can be shared.

When you share a folder, you make all of its files and subfolders available to network users. Authorized users can then access this shared folder by creating a network drive that points to the folder. Using ADSI, you can create shared folders and set shared folder properties.

When you share printers, you configure a printer for remote access over the network. If a user prints a document, the document is routed to a print queue where it is stored prior to printing. Documents in a print queue are referred to as print jobs. Print jobs can be handled in FIFO (first in, first out) fashion. They can also be printed according to their priority, for example a print job with high priority is printed before a print job with low priority.

Working with Shared Folders

As you know, shared folders are used to make data available over the network. What you may not know is how shared folders generally are managed. Normally, you create and configure shared folders using Windows Explorer or Computer Management. Once you create a shared folder, you can also use Computer Management to view and manage both open resources and user sessions related to the shared folder.

You can also manage shared folders in Windows scripts. Chapter 9 showed you how to map network drives to access shares. Chapter 17 showed you how to view and manage open resources and user sessions for shares. Now let's look at scripting techniques that help you manage the shared folders.

Folder sharing essentials

As with open resources and user sessions, you access shared folders through the `FileService` object of the LanManServer service. After you obtain a pointer to the `FileService` object, you can then create file shares or work with existing file shares through the `FileShare` object. The following example looks at all file shares on a computer called Zeta:

```
Set fs = GetObject("WinNT://zeta/LanmanServer,FileService")
For Each sh In fs
    WScript.Echo sh.name
Next
```

The example returns a list of shares on Zeta, such as:

```
PRINT$
NETLOGON
SYSVOL
CorpDataShare
myBooks
```

The list does not show default shares (other than `PRINT$`). Default shares are shared folders created automatically by the operating system and are also referred to as administrative shares. If you use the `NET SHARE` command-line utility to list the shares on a computer, you'll see all shares (both default and standard). To see a list of all shares, type **net share** at the command line. The resulting output should look similar to the following:

```
Share name    Resource                            Remark
-------------------------------------------------------------------------
-----
I$            I:\                                  Default share
IPC$                                              Remote IPC
```

```
D$              D:\                                   Default share
print$          F:\WIN2000\System32\spool\drivers
                                                      Printer Drivers
ADMIN$          F:\WIN2000                            Remote Admin
C$              C:\                                   Default share
E$              E:\                                   Default share
F$              F:\                                   Default share
CorpDataShare
                F:\CorpData
myBooks         E:\myBooks
NETLOGON
F:\WIN2000\sysvol\sysvol\seattle.domain.com\SCRIPTS
                                                      Logon server share
SYSVOL          F:\WIN2000\sysvol\sysvol              Logon server share
BrotherM        LPT1:                      Spooled    Brother MFC-5550
HPDeskJe        LPT1:                      Spooled    HP DeskJet 890C
The command completed successfully.
```

Note

Note that the last two entries in the list are for shared printers.

Table 18-1 provides an overview of how administrative shares are used.

Table 18-1
Using Administrative Shares

Share Name	Description
ADMIN$	Provides access to the operating system %SystemRoot% during remote administration.
Driveletter$	Allows an administrator to connect to the root folder of a drive. Shares are shown as C$, D$, E$, and so on.
FAX$	Supports network faxes.
IPC$	Supports named pipes during remote access.
Microsoft UAM Volume	User Access Manager volume; provides access control files for non-Windows users.
NETLOGON	Supports the Net Logon service.
PRINT$	Provides access to printer drivers, which are used with network printers.
SYSVOL	Active Directory system volume; used by Active Directory.

Examining shared folders and their properties

When you work with shared folders that already exist, you can obtain their objects directly through the WinNT provider. To do this, you use the following syntax for the AdsPath String:

```
WinNT://ComputerName/lanmanserver/ShareName,FileShare
```

where `ComputerName` is the name of the computer and `ShareName` is the actual name of the share, such as:

```
WinNT://Zeta/lanmanserver/netlogon,FileShare
```

Each shared folder has a set of properties that you can work with. These properties are summarized in Table 18-2.

Table 18-2
FileShare Object Properties

Property	Status	Value Type	Min. Range	Max. Range	Multiple Values
CurrentUserCount	RO	Integer	0	2147483647	False
Description	RW	String	0	257	False
HostComputer	RW	ADsPath String	0	256	False
MaxUserCount	RW	Integer	0	2147483647	False
Path	RW	Path String	0	340	False

Most of these properties are rather straightforward. `CurrentUserCount` returns the current number of users connected to this share. `Description` sets or gets a description of the file share. `HostComputer` sets or gets the AdsPath to the host computer on which the share resides. `Path` sets or gets the file path to shared directory. `MaxUserCount` sets or gets the maximum number of concurrent users for the share. If `MaxUserCount` is set to –1, there is no maximum set for the shared folder.

Listing 18-1 shows how you could display the properties of the Netlogon share and then change the maximum number of users.

Listing 18-1: **Examining properties of shared folders**

VBScript

foldershare.vbs

```
Set fs = GetObject("WinNT://zeta/LanmanServer/netlogon,fileshare")
WScript.Echo fs.Name
WScript.Echo "Current User Count: " & fs.CurrentUserCount
WScript.Echo "Description: " & fs.Description
WScript.Echo "Host Computer: " & fs.HostComputer
WScript.Echo "Maximum User Count: " & fs.MaxUserCount
WScript.Echo "File Path: " & fs.Path
```

JScript

foldershare.js

```
var fs = GetObject("WinNT://zeta/LanmanServer/netlogon,fileshare");
WScript.Echo(fs.Name);
WScript.Echo("Current User Count: " + fs.CurrentUserCount);
WScript.Echo("Description: " + fs.Description);
WScript.Echo("Host Computer: " + fs.HostComputer);
WScript.Echo("Maximum User Count: " + fs.MaxUserCount);
WScript.Echo("File Path: " + fs.Path);
```

Output

```
NETLOGON
Current User Count: 0
Description: Logon server share
Host Computer: WinNT://SEATTLE/zeta
Maximum User Count: -1
File Path: F:\WIN2000\sysvol\sysvol\seattle.domain.com\SCRIPTS
```

Creating and deleting shared folders

As with many other objects, you create and delete shared folders using the `Create()` and `Delete()` methods of the IADsContainer interface. Before you can call either of these methods, you must bind to the container for the LanManServer service, and then you can call `Create()` or `Delete()` as necessary.

The only mandatory properties for creating a shared folder are `Path` and `MaxUserCount`. However, you must also specify the name for the shared folder. Listing 18-2 creates a shared folder called CorpData.

Listing 18-2: **Creating shared folders**

VBScript

---

createshare.vbs

```
Set cont = GetObject("WinNT://seattle/zeta/LanmanServer,FileService")
Set fs = cont.Create("FileShare", "CorpData")
fs.Path = "C:\Data\Users\Docs"
fs.MaxUserCount = -1
fs.SetInfo
```

JScript

---

createshare.js

```
var cont = GetObject("WinNT://seattle/zeta/LanmanServer,FileService");
var fs = cont.Create("FileShare", "CorpData");
fs.Path = "C:\\Data\\Users\\Docs";
fs.MaxUserCount = -1;
fs.SetInfo();
```

You delete shares using a similar technique. First you bind to the container for the `FileService` object. Then you delete the shared folder by name using the `Delete()` method, such as:

VBScript

```
Set cont = GetObject("WinNT://seattle/zeta/LanmanServer,FileService")
cont.Delete "FileShare", "CorpData"
```

JScript

```
var cont = GetObject("WinNT://seattle/zeta/LanmanServer,FileService");
cont.Delete("FileShare", "CorpData");
```

Managing Print Queues

Through print queues, administrators can view and manage printers and pending print jobs. In ADSI, print queues are controlled with the `PrintQueue` object, which is implemented through the `IADsPrintQueue` and `IADsPrintQueueOperations` interfaces.

Examining print queues

Each printer configured for use on the network can have one or more print queues associated with it. For example, you could configure one print queue to handle high-priority printing and another to handle low-priority printing. Both print queues could point to a network-attached printer, and through these print queues you could manage your printing.

In Windows scripts, you access print queues through the Computer object. Each print queue configured on the computer will have a unique object associated with it. The name of this object is the same as the shared printer name, which can be obtained by typing **net share** at the command prompt. If a printer is registered in Active Directory, you can also obtain shared printer names through the Find Printers dialog box. Follow these steps:

1. Click Start, point to Search, and then select For Printers. This displays the Find Printers dialog box.

2. Enter * in the Name field and then click Find Now. The find dialog box will return a list of all printers that are on the network.

3. Right-click on the printer entry that you want to examine and then select Properties.

4. In the Properties dialog box, select the Sharing tab, and then note the shared name of the printer. This is the name you'll use to access the PrintQueue object for this printer.

In a script, you would obtain the name of print queues through the associated Computer object. For example, if a computer named Zeta is a print server and has several print queues attached to it, you could obtain the shared printer name by filtering the related container on the PrintQueue object, such as:

VBScript

```
Set c = GetObject("WinNT://Zeta,computer")
c.Filter = Array("PrintQueue")
n = 0

For Each p In c
 n = n + 1
 Set pq = GetObject(p.ADsPath)
 WScript.Echo "Print Queue " & CStr(n) & ": " & pq.Name
Next
```

Output

```
Print Queue 1: HPEngineering
Print Queue 2: HPMarketing
Print Queue 3: HPTechnology
```

Another way to examine `PrintQueue` objects is to use an `Enumerator` to examine all objects in the `Computer` object's container, searching for the `PrintQueue` class, such as:

JScript

```
var comp = GetObject("WinNT://Zeta,Computer");
n = 0;

tlist = new Enumerator(comp);
for (; !tlist.atEnd(); tlist.moveNext())
  {
  s = tlist.item();
  if (s.Class == "PrintQueue") {
   n += 1;
   WScript.Echo("Print Queue " + n + ": " + s.Name);
  }
  }
```

Output

```
Print Queue 1: HPEngineering
Print Queue 2: HPMarketing
Print Queue 3: HPTechnology
```

You could then manage the `HPEngineering`, `HPMarketing`, and `HPTechnology` print queues on Zeta. To manage the queues individually, you could use any of the following ADsPath strings:

```
WinNT://seattle/zeta/HPEngineering
WinNT://seattle/zeta/HPMarketing
WinNT://seattle/zeta/HPTechnology
```

You could also manipulate the print queues within the For loops, which would allow you to manage all of the print queues on a particular computer.

Using the PrintQueue object

The `PrintQueue` object has many properties associated with it. An overview of properties for the `PrintQueue` object is provided in Table 18-3. You use properties to examine and control configuration of the print queue.

Listing 18-3 shows how you could display properties of print queues on a particular computer. Note the output values for each property. I'll discuss key properties and their uses in the next section.

Table 18-3
PrintQueue Object Properties

Property	Status	Value Type	Min. Range	Max. Range	Multiple Values
Action	RW	Integer	0	2147483647	False
Attributes	RW	Integer	0	2147483647	False
BannerPage	RW	Path String	0	340	False
Datatype	RW	String	0	256	False
DefaultJob Priority	RW	Integer	1	99	False
Description	RW	String	0	257	False
JobCount	RO	Integer	0	2147483647	False
Location	RW	String	0	256	False
Model	RW	String	0	256	False
NetAddresses	RW	String, Array	0	256	True
ObjectGUID	RO	String	0	256	False
PrintDevices	RW	String, Array	0	256	True
PrinterName	RW	String	0	256	False
PrintProcessor	RW	String	0	256	False
Priority	RW	Integer	1	99	False
StartTime	RW	Time String	-	-	False
Status	RO	Integer	0	16777216	False
UntilTime	RW	Time String	-	-	False

Listing 18-3: **Working with print queues**

VBScript

printqueue.vbs

```
On Error Resume Next

Set c = GetObject("WinNT://Zeta,computer")
c.Filter = Array("PrintQueue")
```

Continued

Listing 18-3: *(continued)*

VBScript

```
For Each p In c

  Set pq = GetObject(p.ADsPath)
  WScript.Echo "Shared Printer: " & pq.Name
  WScript.Echo "============================"
  WScript.Echo "Action " & pq.Action
  WScript.Echo "Attributes " & pq.Attributes
  WScript.Echo "Banner Page " & pq.BannerPage
  WScript.Echo "Data Type " & pq.Datatype
  WScript.Echo "Default Job Priority " & pq.DefaultJobPriority
  WScript.Echo "Description " & pq.Description
  WScript.Echo "Host Computer " & pq.HostComputer
  WScript.Echo "Job Count " & pq.JobCount
  WScript.Echo "Location " & pq.Location
  WScript.Echo "Model " & pq.Model
  WScript.Echo "Object GUID " & pq.ObjectGUID
  WScript.Echo "Print Devices " & pq.PrintDevices
  WScript.Echo "Print Processor " & pq.PrintProcessor
  WScript.Echo "Print Queue Name " & pq.PrinterName
  WScript.Echo "Queue Priority " & pq.Priority
  WScript.Echo "Start Time " & pq.StartTime
  WScript.Echo "Until Time " & pq.UntilTime

Next
```

Output

```
Shared Printer: HPEngineering
============================
Action 1
Attributes 8776
Banner Page C:\WIN2000\system32\sysprint.sep
Data Type RAW
Default Job Priority 0
Description Engineering Departmental Printer
Job Count 1
Location 16th Floor
Model HP LaserJet 8000
Object GUID {50DD3D14-25F3-4740-BB87-A1605BE46E95}
Print Devices LPT1:
Print Processor WinPrint
Print Queue Name HP8000Eng
Queue Priority 1
Start Time 4:00:00 PM
Until Time 4:00:00 PM
```

Using a banner page

The `PrintQueue` object properties are helpful in managing printers. One of the most useful properties is `BannerPage`, which lets you view or set the path to a banner-page file used to separate print jobs. Banner pages can be used at the beginning of print jobs in order to clearly identify where one print job starts and another ends. They also can be used to change the print device mode, such as whether the print device uses PostScript or PCL (Printer Control Language).

Windows 2000 provides a default set of banner-page files. These files are saved in the %SystemRoot%\system32 folder with a .SEP file extension. Each file has a different use:

✦ PCL.SEP — switches the printer to PCL mode and prints a banner page before each document

✦ PSCRIPT.SEP — sets the printer to PostScript mode but doesn't print a banner page

✦ SYSPRINT.SEP — sets the printer to PostScript mode and prints a banner page before each document

If you don't like the banner pages provided, you can use the default banner page files as the basis for new ones. You set the banner page for a printer as follows:

VBScript

```
Set pq = GetObject("WinNT://seattle/zeta/HPDeskJe,PrintQueue")

Set WshShell = WScript.CreateObject("WScript.Shell")
sysroot = WshShell.ExpandEnvironmentStrings("%SystemRoot%")

pq.BannerPage = sysroot & "\system32\sysprint.sep"
pq.SetInfo
```

JScript

```
var pq = GetObject("WinNT://seattle/zeta/HPDeskJe,PrintQueue");

var WshShell = WScript.CreateObject("WScript.Shell");
sysroot = WshShell.ExpandEnvironmentStrings("%SystemRoot%");

pq.BannerPage = sysroot + "\\system32\\sysprint.sep";
pq.SetInfo();
```

If you don't want a printer to use a banner page, set the `BannerPage` property to an empty string, such as:

```
Set pq = GetObject("WinNT://seattle/zeta/HPDeskJe,PrintQueue")
pq.BannerPage = ""
pq.SetInfo
```

```
var pq = GetObject("WinNT://seattle/zeta/HPDeskJe,PrintQueue");
pq.BannerPage = "";
pq.SetInfo();
```

Working with general printer information

Many `PrintQueue` properties provide general information, such as the printer model or print device in use. Usually, you'll want to view this information, rather than set it. For example, you could create a script to obtain summary information on all printers on the network. The type of information you might collect could include the printer name, model, description, and location.

More technical information that you may want to gather for administrators includes:

✦ Network Address — Tells you the IP address of a network-attached printer. Printers can have multiple IP addresses.

✦ Print Device — Tells you how the printer is connected to the print server. Printers can be connected through one or more ports, such as LPT1 or LPT1 and LPT2.

✦ Print processor — Creates the raw print data necessary for printing. The format of the data is based on the data type set for the print processor. The primary print processor on Windows 2000 is WinPrint. This print processor supports several different data types.

✦ Data type — Identifies the data type. In most cases, the data type is controlled by the Print Spooler service. Because of this, the data type shown by the `DataType` property is rarely used.

If you move a printer from one location to another, you'll probably need to update the printer's location and description. You may also need to change the print device or network address. An example is shown as Listing 18-4.

Listing 18-4: **Setting print queue information**

VBScript

printinfo.vbs

```
Set pq = GetObject("WinNT://seattle/zeta/HPMarketing,PrintQueue")
pq.Location = "15th Floor SE"
pq.Description = "Color printer for marketing department"
pq.NetAddresses = "192.168.10.5"
pq.SetInfo
```

JScript

printinfo.vbs

```
var pq = GetObject("WinNT://seattle/zeta/HPMarketing,PrintQueue");
pq.Location = "15th Floor SE";
pq.Description = "Color printer for marketing department";
pq.NetAddresses = "192.168.10.5";
pq.SetInfo();
```

Prioritizing print queues and print jobs

Other `PrintQueue` properties control when and how documents are printed. When multiple print queues point to the same physical print device, you may want to control the priority of the print queue. In this way, you could have a high-priority print queue for documents that are needed immediately and a low-priority print queue for all other documents.

You control print queue priority with the `Priority` property. A priority of 1 is the lowest priority. A priority of 99 is the highest priority. If you create two print queues, one with a priority of 1 and the other with a priority of 99, documents in the second queue will always print before documents in the first queue.

Another way to control document printing is to set a default priority for print jobs. Print jobs always print in order of priority. Jobs with higher priority print before jobs with lower priority. Remember that the range of priorities is from 1 to 99.

The following example sets the queue priority to 10 and the default job priority to 1:

VBScript

```
Set pq = GetObject("WinNT://seattle/zeta/HPTechnology,PrintQueue")
pq.Priority = 10
pq.DefaultJobPriority = 1
pq.SetInfo
```

JScript

```
var pq = GetObject("WinNT://seattle/zeta/HPTechnology,PrintQueue");
pq.Priority = 10;
pq.DefaultJobPriority = 1;
pq.SetInfo();
```

Scheduling print queue availability

Print queues are either always available or available only during certain hours. You control print queue availability through the StartTime and UntilTime properties. If these properties are set to the same value, the print queue is always available. If these properties are set to different times, the print queue is only available during the specified time.

You could specify that a print queue is only available after normal business hours by setting StartTime to 5 p.m. and UntilTime to 9 a.m., such as:

VBScript

```
Set pq = GetObject("WinNT://seattle/zeta/HPTechnology2,PrintQueue")
pq.StartTime = "5:00:00 PM"
pq.UntilTime = "9:00:00 AM"
pq.SetInfo
```

JScript

```
var pq = GetObject("WinNT://seattle/zeta/HPTechnology2,PrintQueue");
pq.StartTime = "5:00:00 PM";
pq.UntilTime = "9:00:00 AM";
pq.SetInfo();
```

Checking print queue status

The print queue status tells you the status of the print queue and the physical print device. You can use the status to determine if the printer is jammed, out of paper, and much more.

Checking the status of a print queue is easy; you just obtain the value of the Status property, such as:

```
var pq =
GetObject("WinNT://seattle/zeta/HPEngineering,PrintQueue")
WScript.Echo(pq.Status)
```

Understanding precisely what the status code means is more challenging than merely obtaining the status code because there is a fairly extensive list of status codes. Table 18-4 shows the list.

Table 18-4
Print Queue Status Codes

Constant	Code	Description
-	0	Print is running normally.
ADS_PRINTER_PAUSED	1	Print queue is paused.
ADS_PRINTER_PENDING_DELETION	2	Print queue is being deleted.
ADS_PRINTER_ERROR	3	Printer error.
ADS_PRINTER_PAPER_JAM	4	Paper is jammed in the printer.
ADS_PRINTER_PAPER_OUT	5	Printer is out of paper.
ADS_PRINTER_MANUAL_FEED	6	Printer is set for manual feed.
ADS_PRINTER_PAPER_PROBLEM	7	Printer has a paper problem.
ADS_PRINTER_OFFLINE	8	Printer offline.
ADS_PRINTER_IO_ACTIVE	256	Printer IO active.
ADS_PRINTER_BUSY	512	Printer busy.
ADS_PRINTER_PRINTING	1024	Printer is printing.
ADS_PRINTER_OUTPUT_BIN_FULL	2048	Printer output bin is full.
ADS_PRINTER_NOT_AVAILABLE	4096	Printer not available.
ADS_PRINTER_WAITING	8192	Printer is waiting.
ADS_PRINTER_PROCESSING	16384	Printer is processing.
ADS_PRINTER_INITIALIZING	32768	Printer is initializing.
ADS_PRINTER_WARMING_UP	65536	Printer is warming up.
ADS_PRINTER_TONER_LOW	131072	Printer is low on toner.
ADS_PRINTER_NO_TONER	262144	Printer is out of toner.
ADS_PRINTER_PAGE_PUNT	524288	Printer page punt.
ADS_PRINTER_USER_INTERVENTION	1048576	Printer user intervention.
ADS_PRINTER_OUT_OF_MEMORY	2097152	Printer is out of memory.
ADS_PRINTER_DOOR_OPEN	4194304	Printer door is open.
ADS_PRINTER_SERVER_UNKNOWN	8388608	Printer server has unknown error.
ADS_PRINTER_POWER_SAVE	16777216	Printer is in power save mode.

Rather than trying to handle all possible printer problems in a script, you'll probably want to focus on handling the most common problems. For example, you could create a script that periodically polls all printers on the network, checking for problems and displaying a list of possible ways to resolve these problems.

Listing 18-5 shows a script that monitors printers on a specified print server. The script has two key subroutines: `printMon` and `checkPrinter`. The `printMon` subroutine controls how often the script checks printers. The basic technique is to use `WScript.Sleep` to set a wait interval. This interval is in milliseconds with 300,000 milliseconds equaling 5 minutes. The `checkPrinter` subroutine displays the status of printers. This is handled with a `Select Case` structure that checks the status code.

Listing 18-5: **Monitoring printers**

VBScript

printmonitor.vbs

```
lf = Chr(13) & Chr(10)

WScript.Echo "========================================" & lf
WScript.Echo "==    Printer Monitor    ==" & lf
WScript.Echo "========================================" & lf

WScript.Echo "Enter name of print server to monitor: " & lf
host = WScript.StdIn.ReadLine()
printMon()

'Check printers at 5 minute intervals
sub printMon()

  Set c = GetObject("WinNT://" & host & ",computer")

  c.Filter = Array("PrintQueue")

  WScript.Echo lf & "========================================"
  WScript.Echo "Checking Printers on " & host
  WScript.Echo "========================================"

For Each pq In c
  If pq.Status > 0 Then CheckPrinter(pq)
Next

  'Wait 5 minutes before calling printMon again
  WScript.Sleep(300000)

  printMon()

End Sub
```

```
'Display printer status for non-normal conditions
sub checkPrinter(obj)

WScript.Echo lf
WScript.Echo "Print Queue Name: " & obj.Name
WScript.Echo "Printer Model: " & obj.Model
WScript.Echo "Printer Location: " & obj.Location
WScript.Echo "========================================="

Select Case obj.Status
 Case 1
  WScript.Echo "Print Queue is Paused."

 Case 3
  WScript.Echo "Printer Error!"

 Case 4
  WScript.Echo "Paper Jam!"

 Case 5
  WScript.Echo "Printer is out of paper!"

 Case 6
  WScript.Echo "Printer set to manual paper feed."

 Case 7
  WScript.Echo "Paper problem on printer!"

 Case 8
  WScript.Echo "Printer is offline."

 Case 131072
  WScript.Echo "Printer is low on toner."

 Case 262144
  WScript.Echo "Printer is out of toner!"

 Case Else
   WScript.Echo "Printer is changing states or has error."
   WScript.Echo "Status: " & CStr(pq.Status)

End Select

WScript.Echo "========================================="
WScript.Echo "========================================="

End Sub
```

Continued

Listing 18-5 *(continued)*

Output

```
========================================
==    Printer Monitor    ==
========================================


Enter name of print server to monitor:
Zeta


========================================
Checking Printers on Zeta
========================================


Print Queue Name: HPEngineering
Printer Model: HP LaserJet 8000
Printer Location: 16th Floor SW
========================================
Print Queue is Paused.
========================================
========================================


Print Queue Name: HPMarketing
Printer Model: HP LaserJet 8000
Printer Location: 16th Floor NE
========================================
Print Queue is Paused.
========================================
=========================================
```

Managing print queues

In addition to properties, the PrintQueue object also has methods. These methods
are used to pause, resume, and purge the print queue. You pause a print queue by
invoking its Pause method, such as:

VBScript

```
Set pq = GetObject("WinNT://seattle/zeta/HPEngineering,PrintQueue")
pq.Pause
```

JScript

```
var pq = GetObject("WinNT://seattle/zeta/HPEngineering,PrintQueue");
pq.Pause();
```

To resume printing, the script can invoke the print queue's Resume method. If you want to delete all documents in a print queue, call its Purge method. Here's an example:

VBScript

```
Set pq = GetObject("WinNT://seattle/zeta/HPEngineering,PrintQueue")
pq.Purge
```

JScript

```
var pq = GetObject("WinNT://seattle/zeta/HPEngineering,PrintQueue");
pq.Purge();
```

Note   Any document that has spooled to the printer and is in the printer's memory will continue to print.

Another useful method of the PrintQueue object is PrintJobs. The PrintJobs method retrieves a pointer to a collection of print jobs managed by the print queue. You can then iterate through this collection of print jobs to manage individual documents that are waiting to be printed. Working with print jobs is discussed in the next section.

Controlling Print Jobs

Now that you know how to work with print queues, let's take a look at working with print jobs. A busy print queue can have dozens of documents waiting to be printed. All of these documents are represented as PrintJob objects in the PrintJobs collection.

Examining print job properties

Each PrintJob object has properties that you can view and set. These properties are summarized in Table 18-5.

Table 18-5
Properties of Print Jobs

Property	Status	Value Type	Min. Range	Max. Range	Multiple Values
Description	RW	String	0	256	False
HostPrintQueue	RO	ADsPath String	0	256	False
Notify	RW	String	0	256	False
PagesPrinted	RO	Integer	0	2147483647	False
Position	RW	Integer	0	2147483647	False
Priority	RW	Integer	1	99	False
Size	RO	Integer	0	2147483647	False
StartTime	RW	Time String	-	-	False
Status	RO	Integer	0	256	False
TimeElapsed	RO	Integer	0	2147483647	False
TimeSubmitted	RO	Time String	-	-	False
TotalPages	RO	Integer	0	2147483647	False
UntilTime	RW	Time String	-	-	False
User	RO	String	0	256	False

Listing 18-6 provides a detailed example of working with print job properties. As the listing shows, you access print jobs through the PrintJobs collection.

Listing 18-6: **Monitoring printers**

VBScript

printjobs.vbs
```
On Error Resume Next
Set pq = GetObject("WinNT://zeta/HPDeskJe,PrintQueue")

For Each pj in pq.PrintJobs

   WScript.Echo "Print Job: " & pj.Name
```

```
    WScript.Echo "==============================="
    WScript.Echo "Description: " & pj.Description
    WScript.Echo "Host Print Queue: " & pj.HostPrintQueue
    WScript.Echo "Notify: " & pj.Notify
    WScript.Echo "Notify Path: " & pj.NotifyPath
    WScript.Echo "Pages Printed: " & pj.PagesPrinted
    WScript.Echo "Position: " & pj.Position
    WScript.Echo "Priority: " & pj.Priority
    WScript.Echo "Size: " & pj.Size
    WScript.Echo "Start Time: " & pj.StartTime
    WScript.Echo "Status: " & pj.Status
    WScript.Echo "Time Elapsed: " & pj.TimeElapsed
    WScript.Echo "Time Submitted: " & pj.TimeSubmitted
    WScript.Echo "Total Pages: " & pj.TotalPages
    WScript.Echo "Until Time: " & pj.UntilTime
    WScript.Echo "User: " & pj.User
    WScript.Echo "User Path: " & pj.UserPath
    WScript.Echo "==============================="

Next
```

Output

```
Print Job 2
===============================
Description: Microsoft Word - addresses.doc
Host Print Queue: WinNT://SEATTLE/zeta/HPDeskJet
Notify: Administrator
Pages Printed: 0
Position: 1
Priority: 1
Size: 917328
Start Time: 4:00:00 PM
Status: 0
Time Elapsed: 0
Time Submitted: 11/6/1999 9:25:48 PM
Total Pages: 39
Until Time: 4:00:00 PM
User: Administrator
===============================
```

While most of the print job properties are self-explanatory, a few deserve more attention. These are:

✦ HostPrintQueue—the AdsPath string that names the print queue processing this print job

✦ Notify—the user to be notified when the print job is completed

✦ NotifyPath—the AdsPath string for the user to be notified when the job is completed

✦ PagesPrinted—the total number of pages printed in the current job

✦ `Position`—the numeric position of the print job in the print queue

✦ `Priority`—the priority of the print job from 1 (lowest) to 99 (highest)

✦ `User`—the name of user who submitted the print job

✦ `UserPath`—the `AdsPath` string of the user who submitted the print job

Print jobs can also have a status. A status of zero (0) indicates a normal condition. Any other status indicates a possible problem. Status codes for print jobs are summarized in Table 18-6.

	Table 18-6 Print Job Status Codes	
Constant	**Status Code**	**Description**
-	0	Normal.
ADS_JOB_PAUSED	1	Job is paused.
ADS_JOB_ERROR	2	Job error.
ADS_JOB_DELETING	4	Job is being deleted.
ADS_JOB_PRINTING	8	Job is printing.
ADS_JOB_OFFLINE	16	Job is offline.
ADS_JOB_PAPEROUT	32	Paper is out.
ADS_JOB_PRINTED	64	Job printed.
ADS_JOB_DELETED	256	Job was deleted.

Monitoring print job status

You can check print job status conditions in much the same way as you can check print queue status conditions. In fact, with a few modifications, you can use the print monitor script to monitor print jobs, as well. To see how, examine Listing 18-7.

Listing 18-7: **Monitoring printers and print jobs**

VBScript

printmonitor2.vbs

```
lf = Chr(13) & Chr(10)
```

```
WScript.Echo "======================================" & lf
WScript.Echo "==   Printer Monitor   ==" & lf
WScript.Echo "======================================" & lf

WScript.Echo "Enter name of print server to monitor: " & lf
host = WScript.StdIn.ReadLine()
printMon()

'Check printers at 5 minute intervals
sub printMon()

  Set c = GetObject("WinNT://" & host & ",computer")

  c.Filter = Array("PrintQueue")

  WScript.Echo lf & "======================================"
  WScript.Echo "Checking Printers on " & host
  WScript.Echo "======================================"

  For Each pq In c
   If pq.Status > 0 Then CheckPrinter(pq)

   For Each j in pq.PrintJobs
    checkPrintJobs(j)
   Next
  Next

  'Wait 5 minutes before calling printMon again
  WScript.Sleep(300000)

  printMon()

End Sub

'Display printer status for non-normal conditions
sub checkPrinter(obj)

  WScript.Echo lf
  WScript.Echo "Print Queue Name: " & obj.Name
  WScript.Echo "Printer Model: " & obj.Model
  WScript.Echo "Printer Location: " & obj.Location
  WScript.Echo "======================================"

  Select Case obj.Status
   Case 1
    WScript.Echo "Print Queue is Paused."
   Case 3
    WScript.Echo "Printer Error!"
   Case 4
    WScript.Echo "Paper Jam!"
   Case 5
```

Continued

Listing 18-7 *(continued)*

```
  WScript.Echo "Printer is out of paper!"
 Case 6
  WScript.Echo "Printer set to manual paper feed."
 Case 7
  WScript.Echo "Paper problem on printer!"
 Case 8
  WScript.Echo "Printer is offline."
 Case 131072
  WScript.Echo "Printer is low on toner."
 Case 262144
  WScript.Echo "Printer is out of toner!"
 Case Else
   WScript.Echo "Printer is changing states or has error."
   WScript.Echo "Status: " & CStr(pq.Status)
 End Select

 WScript.Echo "========================================"
 WScript.Echo "========================================"

End Sub

'Display printer job status for non-normal conditions
sub checkPrintJobs(pj)

 Select Case pj.Status
  Case 1

   WScript.Echo lf
   WScript.Echo "Print Job: " & pj.Description
   WScript.Echo "Position: " & pj.Position
   WScript.Echo "Pages Printed: " & pj.PagesPrinted
   WScript.Echo "Total Pages: " & pj.TotalPages
   WScript.Echo "Printed By: " & pj.User
   WScript.Echo "======================================="
   WScript.Echo "Print Job is Paused."
   WScript.Echo "======================================="

  Case 2

   WScript.Echo lf
   WScript.Echo "Print Job: " & pj.Description
   WScript.Echo "Position: " & pj.Position
   WScript.Echo "Pages Printed: " & pj.PagesPrinted
   WScript.Echo "Total Pages: " & pj.TotalPages
   WScript.Echo "Printed By: " & pj.User
   WScript.Echo "======================================="
   WScript.Echo "Print Job error."
   WScript.Echo "======================================="

  End Select
```

End Sub

Output

```
========================================

==    Printer Monitor    ==

========================================

Enter name of print server to monitor:

Zeta

========================================
Checking Printers on Zeta
========================================

Print Queue Name: HPEngineering
Printer Model: HP LaserJet 8000
Printer Location: 16th Floor
========================================
Print Queue is Paused.
========================================
========================================

Print Job: Microsoft Word - listings.doc
Position: 1
Pages Printed: 0
Total Pages: 39
Printed By: Administrator
========================================
Print Job is Paused.
========================================

Print Job: Test Page
Position: 2
Pages Printed: 0
Total Pages: 1
Printed By: Administrator
========================================
Print Job is Paused.
========================================
```

Pausing and resuming print jobs

Like print queues, print jobs can be paused and resumed. You use the Pause
method to pause a print job and the Resume method to resume a print job.
One reason to pause a print job would be to temporarily stop printing a large
document and allow other documents to be printed first.

Listing 18-8 shows an example of how you could control print jobs through Pause and Resume. Anytime there are five or more documents in the print queue and the document being printed has more than 50 pages to print, the active document is paused and other documents are printed. Printing doesn't resume until several of the smaller documents have printed.

Listing 18-8: **Controlling print jobs with Pause and Resume**

VBScript

controlprinting.vbs
```
lf = Chr(13) & Chr(10)

WScript.Echo "=======================================" & lf
WScript.Echo "==    Print Job Monitor    ==" & lf
WScript.Echo "=======================================" & lf

checkJobs()

sub checkJobs()
 Set c = GetObject("WinNT://Zeta,computer")
 c.Filter = Array("PrintQueue")

 'Initialize counter
 n = 0

 For Each pq In c

  For Each j in pq.PrintJobs
    n = n + 1
  Next

  If n > 5 Then
   For Each j in pq.PrintJobs
     If j.Status = 8 And j.TotalPages - j.PagesPrinted > 50 Then
       WScript.Echo "Pausing ... " & j.Description
       j.Pause
     End If
   Next
  End If

  If n < 3 Then
   For Each j in pq.PrintJobs
     If j.Status = 1 Then
       WScript.Echo "Resuming ... " & j.Description
       j.Resume
     End If
```

```
    Next
  End If

Next

'Wait 5 minutes
WScript.Sleep(300000)

'Call self
checkJobs()

end sub
```

Output

```
=======================================

==   Print Job Monitor   ==

=======================================


Pausing ... Microsoft Word - massiveprint.doc
Resuming ... Microsoft Word - massiveprint.doc
```

Summary

Resource sharing is an essential part of any network environment. With Windows scripts, you can manage and maintain many different types of network resources. This chapter focused on working with shared folders, print queues, and print jobs. As you learned, you can create, delete, and modify shared folders. With print queues and print jobs, you can move a few steps beyond normal maintenance by implementing monitoring scripts. These scripts help maintain the healthy status of print queues and print jobs with limited administrator intervention.

✦   ✦   ✦

Managing Active Directory Domain Extensions

As you've seen in previous chapters, many features of Windows 2000 and Active Directory can be scripted with the WinNT ADSI provider. WinNT is useful for managing most core functions, including user, group, and computer accounts. However, when you want to perform more advanced manipulation of Windows 2000 or Active Directory, you'll need to use the LDAP (Lightweight Directory Access Protocol) ADSI provider. With LDAP, you can script the extended features of any Active Directory object.

Working with Naming Contexts and the RootDSE Object

Active Directory uses a multimaster approach for maintaining and replicating directory information. Because of this, you can use any domain controller to view and manage directory information and don't have to specify a specific server when working with Active Directory. In fact, with the LDAP provider you are encouraged not to specify a server in your AdsPaths. Instead, you should bind to the root of the directory tree and then select a naming context that you want to work with. In Active Directory, the RootDSE object represents the root of the directory tree.

Binding to a naming context

A naming context is a top-level container for the directory tree. Three naming contexts are available: domain container, schema container, and configuration container. Domain container contains users, groups, computers, organizational units, and other domain objects. Schema container provides access to schema objects. Configuration container contains sites, which in turn contain individual sites, subnets, intersite transports, and other configuration objects.

As you might expect, the domain container is the one you'll use the most. In most cases, you can bind to the domain container via the `defaultNamingContext` property of the `RootDSE` object, such as:

VBScript

```
Set rootDSE = GetObject("LDAP://rootDSE")
domainContainer = rootDSE.Get("defaultNamingContext")
```

JScript

```
var rootDSE = GetObject("LDAP://rootDSE");
domainContainer = rootDSE.Get("defaultNamingContext");
```

If the domain is `seattle.tvpress.com`, the following is the value of domainContainer:

```
DC=seattle,DC=tvpress,DC=com
```

You can then use the `domainContainer` variable when you work with objects in the domain. For example, instead of specifying the AdsPath:

```
LDAP://OU=Marketing,DC=seattle,DC=tvpress,DC=com
```

you would use the following:

```
LDAP://OU=Marketing," & domainContainer
```

or

```
LDAP://OU=Marketing," + domainContainer
```

Tip   A key reason for binding to `RootDSE` and then to the domain container is to ensure that your scripts work in any domain. For example, you could use the script in the `seattle.tvpress.com`, `newyork.tvpress.com` or `la.tvpress.com` domain. However, if you wanted to access objects in a domain other than the current domain, you must specify the AdsPath. You will also need to authenticate yourself in the domain as discussed in the section of Chapter 14 titled, "Handling Authentication and Security."

Using RootDSE properties

defaultNamingContext is only one of many properties for the RootDSE object. Other properties of this object are summarized in Table 19-1.

Table 19-1
Properties of the RootDSE Object

Property	Description	Value Type	Multi-valued
configuration NamingContext	The distinguished name for the configuration container.	ADsPath String	False
currentTime	The time on the current directory server.	Date Time	False
defaultNamingContext	The distinguished name for the domain of which the current directory server is a member. The value can be changed.	ADsPath String	False
DnsHostName	The DNS address for this directory server.	String	False
dsServiceName	The distinguished name of the NTDS settings object for the current directory server.	ADsPath String	False
HighestCommittedUSN	The Highest Update Sequence Number (USN) used on the current directory server. USNs are used in directory replication.	Integer	False
LdapServiceName	The Service Principal Name (SPN) for the current LDAP server. SPNs are used for mutual authentication.	String	False

Continued

Table 19-1 *(continued)*

Property	Description	Value Type	Multi-valued
namingContexts	The distinguished names for all naming contexts stored on the current directory server.	Array	True
RootDomainNaming Context	The distinguished name for the root domain in the forest that contains the domain of which the current directory server is a member.	ADsPath String	False
schemaNamingContext	The distinguished name of the schema container.	ADsPath String	False
ServerName	The distinguished name of the server object for the current directory server.	ADsPath String	False
subschemaSubentry	The distinguished name of the subSchema object, which exposes supported attributes.	ADsPath String	False
SupportedControl	Object identifiers (OIDs) for the extension controls supported by the current directory server.	Array	True
SupportedLDAPVersion	The major LDAP versions supported by the current directory server.	Array	True
SupportedSASL Mechanisms	The supported security mechanisms for the current server.	Array	True

Listing 19-1 provides a script that displays the values of RootDSE properties. Be sure to examine the output of the script. This output should give you a better understanding of how the RootDSE properties are used.

Listing 19-1: **Working with RootDSE**

VBScript

---

rootdse.vbs

```vbscript
On Error Resume Next
Set obj = GetObject("LDAP://rootDSE")

WScript.Echo "Path: " & obj.AdsPath
WScript.Echo "Subschema: " & obj.subschemaSubentry
WScript.Echo "Service Name: " & obj.dsServiceName
WScript.Echo "Server Name: " & obj.ServerName
WScript.Echo "Default Naming Context: " & obj.defaultNamingContext
WScript.Echo "Schema Naming Context: " & obj.schemaNamingContext
WScript.Echo "Config Naming Context: " & obj.configurationNamingContext
WScript.Echo "Root Domain Naming Context: " & obj.RootDomainNamingContext
WScript.Echo "Highest USN: " & obj.HighestCommittedUSN
WScript.Echo "DNS Host Name: " & obj.DnsHostName
WScript.Echo "LDAP Service Name: " & obj.LdapServiceName

'Examine Multivalued properties
c = obj.namingContexts

For Each a In c
 WScript.Echo "Naming Context: " & a
Next

c = obj.SupportedControl
For Each a In c
 WScript.Echo "Supported Control: " & a
Next

c = obj.SupportedLDAPVersion
For Each a In c
 WScript.Echo "Supported LDAP Version: " & a
Next

c = obj.SupportedSASLMechanisms
For Each a In c
 WScript.Echo "Supported SASL: " & a
Next
```

Output

```
Path: LDAP://rootDSE

Subschema: CN=Aggregate,CN=Schema,CN=Configuration, DC=seattle,DC=tvpress,DC=com
```

Continued

Listing 19-1 *(continued)*

```
Service Name: CN=NTDS Settings,CN=ZETA,CN=Servers,CN=Default-First-
Site,CN=Sites,CN=Configuration,DC=seattle,DC=tvpress,DC=com

Server Name CN=ZETA,CN=Servers,CN=Default-First-Site,
CN=Sites,CN=Configuration,DC=seattle,DC=tvpress,DC=com

Default Naming Context: DC=seattle,DC=tvpress,DC=com

Schema Naming Context: CN=Schema,CN=Configuration,DC=seattle, DC=tvpress,DC=com

Config Naming Context: CN=Configuration,DC=seattle,DC=tvpress,DC=com

Root Domain Naming Context: DC=seattle,DC=tvpress,DC=com

Highest USN: 2055

DNS Host Name: ZETA.seattle.domain.com

LDAP Service Name: seattle.domain.com:zeta$@SEATTLE.DOMAIN.COM

Naming Context: CN=Schema,CN=Configuration,DC=seattle, DC=tvpress,DC=com
Naming Context: CN=Configuration,DC=seattle,DC=tvpress,DC=com
Naming Context: DC=seattle,DC=tvpress,DC=com

Supported Control: 1.2.840.113556.1.4.319
Supported Control: 1.2.840.113556.1.4.801
Supported Control: 1.2.840.113556.1.4.473

Supported LDAP Version: 3
Supported LDAP Version: 2

Supported SASL: GSSAPI
Supported SASL: GSS-SPNEGO
```

Accessing Active Directory Schema

One of the first things you'll notice when you set out to work with Active Directory is that there's an extremely rich feature set and as a result, even the most basic objects can have many properties. To help manage this complexity, Windows 2000 Support Tools includes a utility called ADSI Edit (adsiedit.exe). Using ADSI Edit, you can manage objects in the domain, configuration, and schema containers. The sections that follow provide an overview of installing and using ADSI Edit.

Installing and starting ADSI Edit

ADSI Edit is installed as part of the Windows 2000 Support Tools library. You install the support tools by completing the following steps:

1. Insert the Windows 2000 CD-ROM into the CD-ROM drive. Then when the Autorun screen appears, click Browse This CD. This starts Windows Explorer.

2. In Explorer, click Support, click Support, and then click Setup. This starts the Windows 2000 Support Tools Setup Wizard. Read the Welcome dialog, and then click Next.

3. Enter your user information, and then continue by clicking Next.

4. Select the installation type Typical, and then click Next twice to start the installation.

5. Click Finish.

You can now start ADSI Edit by clicking Start, pointing to Programs, pointing to Windows 2000 Support Tools, pointing to Tools, and then selecting ADSI Edit. As shown in Figure 19-1, ADSI Edit is used to access naming context and their objects. Each naming context has its own node. The node you'll use the most is Domain NC.

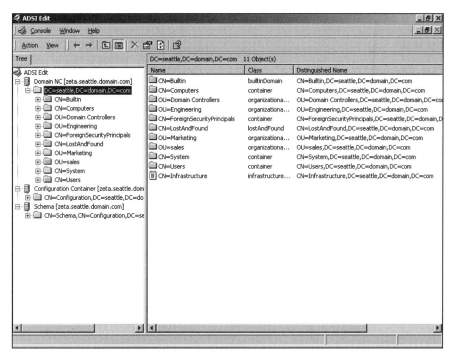

Figure 19-1: Use ADSI Edit to access naming contexts and their related objects.

Examining the domain-naming context

In the Domain NC node, you can access the domain-naming context for each domain in the domain forest. As summarized in Table 19-2, each container stored in this node has an associated object class and distinguished name. Unlike Active Directory Users and Computers, both default and advanced containers are available, which is why you see the additional entries for LostAndFound, System, and Infrastructure.

Table 19-2
Domain NC Node Containers

Name	Object Class	Sample Distinguished Name
CN=Builtin	`builtinDomain`	CN=Builtin,DC=seattle, DC=tvpress,DC=com
CN=Computers	`container`	CN=Computers,DC=seattle, DC=tvpress,DC=com
OU=Domain Controllers	`organizationalUnit`	OU=Domain Controllers, DC=seattle,DC=tvpress, DC=com
CN=ForeignSecurityPrincipals	`container`	CN=ForeignSecurityPrincipals, DC=seattle,DC=tvpress, DC=com
CN=LostAndFound	`lostAndFound`	CN=LostAndFound, DC=seattle,DC=tvpress, DC=com
CN=System	`container`	CN=System,DC=seattle, DC=tvpress,DC=com
CN=Users	`container`	CN=Users,DC=seattle, DC=tvpress,DC=com
CN=Infrastructure	`infrastructureUpdate`	CN=Infrastructure, DC=seattle,DC=tvpress, DC=com

You create an instance of a container object when you bind to the distinguished name for the container. For example, you could bind to the System container using the ADsPath string:

```
CN=System,DC=seattle,DC=tvpress,DC=com
```

You could also access the System container through RootDSE, such as:

VBScript

```
Set rootDSE = GetObject("LDAP://rootDSE")
domainContainer = rootDSE.Get("defaultNamingContext")
Set sysObject = GetObject("LDAP://CN=System," & domainContainer)
```

JScript

```
var rootDSE = GetObject("LDAP://rootDSE");
domainContainer = rootDSE.Get("defaultNamingContext");
var sysObject = GetObject("LDAP://CN=System," + domainContainer);
```

Right-clicking an entry in the Domain NC node displays a menu that allows you to manage the selected container or object. Generally, only advanced administrators should move, rename, or create elements directly in ADSI Edit. More often, you'll use ADSI Edit to examine the properties of containers and objects. To do this, right-click on the element you want to examine, and then select Properties. This displays a dialog box similar to the one shown in Figure 19-2.

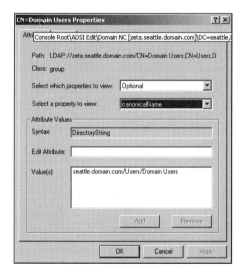

Figure 19-2: The Properties dialog box allows you to view attributes for the selected element.

In the Attributes tab of the Properties dialog box, you can examine mandatory and optional properties of the selected element. The Attribute Values panel displays information for the currently selected property. Being able to view element attributes allows you to explore the properties of Active Directory objects. This is useful if the directory in your domain has been extended or reconfigured.

As you examine attributes, you'll note that the syntax types are a bit different than what you're used to. This is because Active Directory supports different syntax types than we've been working with so far. The mapping between common attribute syntax types and property data types is as follows:

`Boolean`	A Boolean value represented as True/False or 1/0.
`CaseExactString`	A case-sensitive `String`.
`CaseIgnoreString`	A string that isn't case-sensitive.
`DirectoryString`	A string that may contain directory or file path separators, such as `seattle.tvpress.com/Users`.
`DN`	An `AdsPath` string, such as CN=Users, DC=seattle,DC=tvpress, DC=com.
`GeneralizedTime`	A date/time value.
`INTEGER`	An integer value.
`INTEGER8`	An 8-bit integer value.
`OctetString`	A `String` containing hexadecimal values.
`OID`	An object identifier or class.
`ObjectSecurityDescriptor`	An integer value representing the security descriptor of the element.
`Time`	A date/time value.
`UTCTIME`	A UTC (Universal Time Coordinate) date/time value.

Some object attributes are inherited and are not listed as normal object properties. For example, most objects support the mandatory attributes `instanceType`, `objectCategory`, and `objectClass`. These attributes are displayed in ADSI Edit but are not returned as either mandatory or optional attributes when you examine objects through scripts. Still, you usually can call these inherited attributes in scripts, such as:

```
Set cont = GetObject("LDAP://OU=Engineering,DC=seattle,DC=tvpress,DC=com")
c = cont.objectClass
For Each a In c
 WScript.Echo "Object Class: " & a
Next
```

Common Active Directory objects

Active Directory distinguishes between various types of objects using object classes. The top-level object class for domain objects is `domainDNS`. This is the class for domains in the domain-naming context. Domain objects in turn contain other objects. The most commonly used object classes are the following:

- ✦ `computer` — represents computer objects
- ✦ `contact` — represents contacts listed in Active Directory
- ✦ `group` — represents domain security and distribution groups
- ✦ `organizationalUnit` — represents organizational units
- ✦ `user` — represents user accounts

Each of these objects supports a different set of object properties. Because we've examined similar properties in previous chapters, I won't spend a lot of time covering these properties and will instead provide summary tables that you can use as quick references. Afterwards, I'll cover specific techniques for managing these objects.

Managing Computer Objects with LDAP

You can examine computer accounts and set properties that describe a particular computer with the WinNT ADSI provider. You can't, however, manage computer accounts, and this is where the LDAP provider comes in handy. Using the LDAP provider, you can create, rename, move, and delete computer accounts. To do this, you bind to the container or organizational unit that you want to work with and then invoke the appropriate method of the IADsContainer interface on the computer account, such as Create or Delete.

Active Directory computer object properties

Normally, computer objects are stored in the Computers container or the Domain Controllers organizational unit. However, you can store computer objects in any available container or organization unit. Table 19-3 provides a summary of computer object properties for Active Directory.

Table 19-3
Active Directory Computer Object Properties

Property	Status	Value Type	Min. Range	Max. Range	Multiple Values
accountDisabled	RW	Boolean	0	1	False
adminDescription	RW	DirectoryString	0	1024	False
adminDisplayName	RW	DirectoryString	1	256	False
CN	RO	DirectoryString	1	64	False
company	RW	DirectoryString	1	64	False
controlAccessRights	RO	OctetString	16	16	True
department	RW	DirectoryString	1	64	False
description	RW	DirectoryString	0	1024	True
destinationIndicator	RW	PrintableString	1	128	True
displayName	RW	DirectoryString	0	256	False
displayNamePrintable	RW	PrintableString	1	256	False
division	RW	DirectoryString	0	256	False
dNSHostName	RO	DirectoryString	0	2048	False
employeeID	RW	DirectoryString	0	16	False
extensionName	RW	DirectoryString	1	255	True
facsimileTelephone Number	RW	DirectoryString	1	64	False
givenName	RW	DirectoryString	1	64	False
homePhone	RW	DirectoryString	1	64	False
homePostalAddress	RW	DirectoryString	1	4096	False
info	RW	DirectoryString	1	1024	False
initials	RW	DirectoryString	1	6	False
internationalISDN Number	RW	NumericString	1	16	True
location	RW	DirectoryString	0	1024	False
mail	RW	DirectoryString	0	256	False
middleName	RW	DirectoryString	0	64	False
mobile	RW	DirectoryString	1	64	False
mSMQDigests	RW	OctetString	16	16	True

Property	Status	Value Type	Min. Range	Max. Range	Multiple Values
name	RW	DirectoryString	1	255	False
netbootGUID	RO	OctetString	16	16	False
networkAddress	RW	CaseIgnoreString	0	256	True
nTSecurityDescriptor	RO	ObjectSecurity Descriptor	0	132096	False
objectGUID	RO	OctetString	16	16	False
objectSid	RO	OctetString	0	28	False
otherFacsimile TelephoneNumber	RW	DirectoryString	1	64	True
otherHomePhone	RW	DirectoryString	1	64	True
otherLoginWorkstations	RW	DirectoryString	0	1024	True
otherMobile	RW	DirectoryString	1	64	True
otherPager	RW	DirectoryString	1	64	True
otherTelephone	RW	DirectoryString	1	64	True
ou	RW	DirectoryString	1	64	True
pager	RW	DirectoryString	1	64	False
personalTitle	RW	DirectoryString	1	64	False
physicalDelivery OfficeName	RW	DirectoryString	1	128	False
postalAddress	RW	DirectoryString	1	4096	True
postalCode	RW	DirectoryString	1	40	False
postOfficeBox	RW	DirectoryString	1	40	True
primaryInternational ISDNNumber	RW	DirectoryString	1	64	False
primaryTelexNumber	RW	DirectoryString	1	64	False
proxyAddresses	RW	DirectoryString	1	1123	True
registeredAddress	RW	OctetString	1	4096	True
sAMAccountName	RW	DirectoryString	0	256	False
siteGUID	RO	OctetString	16	16	False
street	RW	DirectoryString	1	1024	False
streetAddress	RW	DirectoryString	1	1024	False

Continued

Table 19-3 *(continued)*

Property	Status	Value Type	Min. Range	Max. Range	Multiple Values
telephoneNumber	RW	DirectoryString	1	64	False
telexNumber	RW	OctetString	1	32	True
textEncodedORAddress	RW	DirectoryString	1	1024	False
thumbnailLogo	RW	OctetString	1	32767	False
thumbnailPhoto	RW	OctetString	0	102400	False
title	RW	DirectoryString	1	64	False
userCert	RW	OctetString	0	32767	False
userParameters	RW	DirectoryString	0	32767	False
userPassword	RW	OctetString	1	128	True
userWorkstations	RW	DirectoryString	0	1024	False
wWWHomePage	RW	DirectoryString	1	2048	False
x121Address	RW	NumericString	1	15	True

Creating and deleting computer accounts with LDAP

To create a computer account, you must get the object for the container you want to work with and then invoke the container's `Create` method. The only properties that you must set when creating computer accounts are the common name and the Windows NT SAM account name. You could set these properties when creating an account for a computer called Omega, as shown in Listing 19-2.

Listing 19-2: **Creating a computer account**

VBScript

createcomputer.vbs

```
Set cont = GetObject("LDAP://OU=Engineering,DC=seattle,DC=tvpress,DC=com")
Set comp = cont.Create("computer","CN=Omega")
comp.Put "samAccountName","Omega"
comp.SetInfo
```

JScript

createcomputer.js

```
var cont = GetObject("LDAP://OU=Engineering, DC=seattle,DC=tvpress,DC=com");
var comp = cont.Create("computer","CN=Omega");
comp.Put("samAccountName","Omega");
comp.SetInfo()
```

You can delete a computer account stored in a container by invoking the container's `Delete` method. Here's how you would delete the computer account created in the previous listing:

VBScript

```
Set cont = GetObject("LDAP://OU=Engineering,DC=seattle,DC=tvpress,DC=com")
cont.Delete "computer","CN=Omega"
```

JScript

```
var cont = GetObject("LDAP://OU=Engineering, DC=seattle,DC=tvpress,DC=com");
cont.Delete("computer","CN=Omega");
```

Moving and renaming computer accounts with LDAP

Moving and renaming computer accounts are similar operations. When you move an account, you retrieve the destination container and then invoke the container's `MoveHere` method for the computer account you want to move. Listing 19-3 shows how you could move a computer object from the Computers container to the Engineering organizational unit.

Listing 19-3: **Moving a computer account**

VBScript

movecomputer.vbs

```
'Get rootDSE
Set rootDSE = GetObject("LDAP://rootDSE")
domainCont = rootDSE.Get("defaultNamingContext")
```

Continued

Listing 19-3 *(continued)*

```
'Get the destination container
set cont = GetObject("LDAP://OU=Engineering," & domainCont)

'Move object from original container to the destination
cont.MoveHere "LDAP://CN=Omega,CN=Computers," & domainCont, "CN=Omega"
```

JScript

movecomputer.js

```
//Get rootDSE
var rootDSE = GetObject("LDAP://rootDSE");
domainCont = rootDSE.Get("defaultNamingContext");

//Get the destination container
var cont = GetObject("LDAP://OU=Engineering," + domainCont);

//Move object from original container to the destination
cont.MoveHere("LDAP://CN=Omega,CN=Computers," + domainCont, "CN=Omega");
```

The first parameter for the `MoveHere` method is the current location of the computer object. The second parameter is the object name at the destination. Thus, as Listing 19-4 shows, you could rename a computer object that you are moving simply by specifying a different name as the second parameter.

Listing 19-4: **Moving and renaming a computer account**

VBScript

mrcomputer.vbs

```
'Get rootDSE
Set rootDSE = GetObject("LDAP://rootDSE")
domainCont = rootDSE.Get("defaultNamingContext")

'Get the destination container
set cont = GetObject("LDAP://OU=Marketing," & domainCont)

'Move object and specify new name
cont.MoveHere "LDAP://CN=Omega,CN=Computers," & domainCont, "CN=BobsComputer"
```

JScript

mrcomputer.js

```
//Get rootDSE
var rootDSE = GetObject("LDAP://rootDSE");
domainCont = rootDSE.Get("defaultNamingContext");

//Get the destination container
var cont = GetObject("LDAP://OU=Marketing," + domainCont);

//Move object and specify new name
cont.MoveHere("LDAP://CN=Omega,CN=Computers," + domainCont,
"CN=BobsComputer");
```

If you want to rename an object without changing its container, set the destination container's ADsPath string to be the same as that of the original container. An example is shown as Listing 19-5.

> ### Listing 19-5: **Renaming a computer account** **without moving it**

VBScript

renamecomputer.vbs

```
'Get rootDSE
Set rootDSE = GetObject("LDAP://rootDSE")
domainCont = rootDSE.Get("defaultNamingContext")

'Get the destination container
set cont = GetObject("LDAP://CN=Computers," & domainCont)

'Move object and specify new name
cont.MoveHere "LDAP://CN=Omega,CN=Computers," & domainCont, "CN=Delta"
```

JScript

renamecomputer.js

```
//Get rootDSE
var rootDSE = GetObject("LDAP://rootDSE");
domainCont = rootDSE.Get("defaultNamingContext");
```

Continued

Listing 19-5 *(continued)*

```
//Get the destination container
var cont = GetObject("LDAP://CN=Computers," + domainCont);

//Move object and specify new name
cont.MoveHere("LDAP://CN=Omega,CN=Computers," + domainCont, "CN=Delta");
```

Enabling and disabling computer accounts with LDAP

Computer accounts often need to be enabled or disabled. You enable a computer account to make it active and allow the computer to connect to the domain. To enable a computer account, you set the accountDisabled property to False, such as:

VBScript

```
Set comp = GetObject("LDAP://CN=Omega,OU=Sales,DC=seattle,DC=tvpress,DC=com")
comp.AccountDisabled = "False"
comp.SetInfo
```

JScript

```
var comp = GetObject("LDAP://CN=Omega,OU=Sales,DC=seattle,DC=tvpress,DC=com");
comp.AccountDisabled = "False";
comp.SetInfo();
```

You disable a computer account to deactivate it, which doesn't allow the computer to connect to the domain. However, disabling an account won't forcibly disconnect a computer from a domain. To disable a computer account, you set the accountDisabled property to True, such as:

VBScript

```
Set comp = GetObject("LDAP://CN=Omega,OU=Sales,DC=seattle,DC=tvpress,DC=com")
comp.AccountDisabled = "True"
comp.SetInfo
```

JScript

```
var comp = GetObject("LDAP://CN=Omega,OU=Sales,DC=seattle,DC=tvpress,DC=com");
comp.AccountDisabled = "True";
comp.SetInfo();
```

Managing Contacts with LDAP

In Active Directory, a contact represents an address book entry. Generally, contacts provide names, addresses, and other information needed to contact a person or business. Table 19-4 provides a summary of properties for Active Directory contact objects.

Table 19-4
Active Directory Contact Object Properties

Property	Status	Value Type	Min. Range	Max. Range	Multiple Values
adminDescription	RW	DirectoryString	0	1024	False
adminDisplayName	RW	DirectoryString	1	256	False
cn	RO	DirectoryString	1	64	False
company	RW	DirectoryString	1	64	False
department	RW	DirectoryString	1	64	False
description	RW	DirectoryString	0	1024	True
destinationIndicator	RW	PrintableString	1	128	True
displayName	RW	DirectoryString	0	256	False
displayNamePrintable	RW	PrintableString	1	256	False
division	RW	DirectoryString	0	256	False
employeeID	RW	DirectoryString	0	16	False
extensionName	RW	DirectoryString	1	255	True
facsimileTelephone Number	RW	DirectoryString	1	64	False
givenName	RW	DirectoryString	1	64	False
homePhone	RW	DirectoryString	1	64	False
homePostalAddress	RW	DirectoryString	1	4096	False
info	RW	DirectoryString	1	1024	False
initials	RW	DirectoryString	1	6	False
internationalISDN Number	RW	NumericString	1	16	True
mail	RW	DirectoryString	0	256	False
middleName	RW	DirectoryString	0	64	False

Continued

Table 19-4 *(continued)*

Property	Status	Value Type	Min. Range	Max. Range	Multiple Values
mobile	RW	DirectoryString	1	64	False
name	RW	DirectoryString	1	255	False
nTSecurityDescriptor	RO	ObjectSecurity Descriptor	0	132096	False
objectGUID	RO	OctetString	16	16	False
otherFacsimile TelephoneNumber	RW	DirectoryString	1	64	True
otherHomePhone	RW	DirectoryString	1	64	True
otherMobile	RW	DirectoryString	1	64	True
otherPager	RW	DirectoryString	1	64	True
otherTelephone	RW	DirectoryString	1	64	True
ou	RW	DirectoryString	1	64	True
pager	RW	DirectoryString	1	64	False
personalTitle	RW	DirectoryString	1	64	False
physicalDelivery OfficeName	RW	DirectoryString	1	128	False
postalAddress	RW	DirectoryString	1	4096	True
postalCode	RW	DirectoryString	1	40	False
postOfficeBox	RW	DirectoryString	1	40	True
primaryInternational ISDNNumber	RW	DirectoryString	1	64	False
primaryTelexNumber	RW	DirectoryString	1	64	False
proxyAddresses	RW	DirectoryString	1	1123	True
registeredAddress	RW	OctetString	1	4096	True
sn	RW	DirectoryString	1	64	False
street	RW	DirectoryString	1	1024	False
streetAddress	RW	DirectoryString	1	1024	False
telephoneNumber	RW	DirectoryString	1	64	False
telexNumber	RW	OctetString	1	32	True

Property	Status	Value Type	Min. Range	Max. Range	Multiple Values
textEncodedORAddress	RW	DirectoryString	1	1024	False
thumbnailLogo	RW	OctetString	1	32767	False
thumbnailPhoto	RW	OctetString	0	102400	False
title	RW	DirectoryString	1	64	False
userCert	RW	OctetString	0	32767	False
userPassword	RW	OctetString	1	128	True
wWWHomePage	RW	DirectoryString	1	2048	False
x121Address	RW	NumericString	1	15	True

Using the LDAP provider, you can manage contacts in much the same way as you manage computer accounts. To do this, you bind to the container or organizational unit that you want to work with and then invoke the appropriate container method on the contact. Again, these methods are `Create`, `Delete`, and `MoveHere`.

The only property that you must set when creating a contact is the common name. You may also want to set the following properties:

- ✦ `company` — Company name
- ✦ `department` — Department name
- ✦ `title` — Job title
- ✦ `telephoneNumber` — Business telephone number
- ✦ `homePhone` — Home telephone number
- ✦ `givenName` — First name
- ✦ `initials` — Middle initial
- ✦ `sn` — Last name (surname)
- ✦ `displayName` — Display name in Active Directory
- ✦ `mail` — E-mail address

Listing 19-6 shows how you could create a contact in Active Directory.

Listing 19-6: **Creating a contact**

VBScript

createcontact.vbs
```
Set cont = GetObject("LDAP://OU=Marketing,DC=seattle,DC=tvpress,DC=com")
Set contact = cont.Create("contact","CN=Tony Green")
contact.company = "ABC Enterprises, Ltd."
contact.department = "Sales"
contact.title = "Sales Associate"
contact.telephoneNumber = "206-555-1212"
contact.homePhone = "253-555-1212"
contact.givenName = "Tony"
contact.initials = "R"
contact.sn = "Green"
contact.displayName = "Tony Green"
contact.mail = "tgreen@tvpress.com"
contact.SetInfo
```

JScript

createcontact.js
```
var cont = GetObject("LDAP://OU=Marketing,DC=seattle,DC=tvpress,DC=com");
var contact = cont.Create("contact","CN=Tony Green");
contact.company = "ABC Enterprises, Ltd.";
contact.department = "Sales";
contact.title = "Sales Associate";
contact.telephoneNumber = "206-555-1212";
contact.homePhone = "253-555-1212";
contact.givenName = "Tony";
contact.initials = "R";
contact.sn = "Green";
contact.displayName = "Tony Green";
contact.mail = "tgreen@tvpress.com";
contact.SetInfo();
```

Managing Groups with LDAP

In Chapter 16, you learned the basics for managing groups with the WinNT provider. Now lets look at how you manage groups with the LDAP provider. One of the first things you'll note is that on the surface the administration techniques are similar, but as you delve deeper, you'll find that the LDAP provider supports a richer feature set.

Active Directory group object properties

Table 19-5 provides a summary of properties for Active Directory group objects. Before you can work with a group object, you must bind to the container in which the group object resides, such as:

```
GetObject("LDAP://CN=Users,DC=seattle,DC=tvpress,DC=com")
```

Or you must access the group object directly, such as:

```
GetObject("LDAP://CN=Domain Users,CN=Users, DC=seattle,DC=tvpress,DC=com")
```

<table>
<tr><td colspan="6">Table 19-5
Active Directory Group Object Properties</td></tr>
<tr><td>**Property**</td><td>**Status**</td><td>**Value Type**</td><td>**Min. Range**</td><td>**Max. Range**</td><td>**Multiple Values**</td></tr>
<tr><td>adminDescription</td><td>RW</td><td>DirectoryString</td><td>0</td><td>1024</td><td>False</td></tr>
<tr><td>adminDisplayName</td><td>RW</td><td>DirectoryString</td><td>1</td><td>256</td><td>False</td></tr>
<tr><td>cn</td><td>RO</td><td>DirectoryString</td><td>1</td><td>64</td><td>False</td></tr>
<tr><td>controlAccessRights</td><td>RO</td><td>OctetString</td><td>16</td><td>16</td><td>True</td></tr>
<tr><td>description</td><td>RW</td><td>DirectoryString</td><td>0</td><td>1024</td><td>True</td></tr>
<tr><td>displayName</td><td>RW</td><td>DirectoryString</td><td>0</td><td>256</td><td>False</td></tr>
<tr><td>displayNamePrintable</td><td>RW</td><td>PrintableString</td><td>1</td><td>256</td><td>False</td></tr>
<tr><td>extensionName</td><td>RW</td><td>DirectoryString</td><td>1</td><td>255</td><td>True</td></tr>
<tr><td>groupType</td><td>RW</td><td>Integer</td><td>-2^{31}</td><td>2^{31}</td><td>False</td></tr>
<tr><td>info</td><td>RW</td><td>DirectoryString</td><td>1</td><td>1024</td><td>False</td></tr>
<tr><td>mail</td><td>RW</td><td>DirectoryString</td><td>0</td><td>256</td><td>False</td></tr>
<tr><td>name</td><td>RW</td><td>DirectoryString</td><td>1</td><td>255</td><td>False</td></tr>
<tr><td>nTSecurityDescriptor</td><td>RO</td><td>ObjectSecurity Descriptor</td><td>0</td><td>132096</td><td>False</td></tr>
<tr><td>objectGUID</td><td>RO</td><td>OctetString</td><td>16</td><td>16</td><td>False</td></tr>
<tr><td>objectSid</td><td>RO</td><td>OctetString</td><td>0</td><td>28</td><td>False</td></tr>
<tr><td>proxyAddresses</td><td>RW</td><td>DirectoryString</td><td>1</td><td>1123</td><td>True</td></tr>
<tr><td>sAMAccountName</td><td>RW</td><td>DirectoryString</td><td>0</td><td>256</td><td>False</td></tr>
</table>

Continued

Table 19-5 *(continued)*

Value Property	Min. Status	Max. Type	Multiple Range	Range	Values
telephoneNumber	RW	DirectoryString	1	64	False
textEncodedORAddress	RW	DirectoryString	1	1024	False
userCert	RW	OctetString	0	32767	False
wWWHomePage	RW	DirectoryString	1	2048	False

Creating groups with LDAP

Unlike WinNT, you can only use the LDAP provider to create global group accounts. You cannot use LDAP to create groups stored on local computers. Still, you create groups in much the same way. You access the container in which you want to place the group, and then invoke the container's `Create` method. Afterward, you can set properties for the group.

The only mandatory properties for groups are the common name and the Windows NT SAM account name. This means you could create a group account called Sales as follows:

VBScript

```
Set obj = GetObject("LDAP://CN=Users,DC=seattle,DC=tvpress,DC=com")
Set grp = obj.Create("group", "Sales")
grp.samAccountName = "sales"
grp.SetInfo
```

JScript

```
var obj = GetObject("LDAP://CN=Users,DC=seattle,DC=tvpress,DC=com");
var grp = obj.Create("group", "Sales");
grp.samAccountName = "sales";
grp.SetInfo();
```

You create a global security group by default. If you want to create a different type of group, you must set the `groupType` property when creating the group.

This property is set to an integer value that represents the type of group to create. The following are valid values for groupType:

✦ 2 creates a global distribution group.

✦ 4 creates a domain-local distribution group.

✦ 8 creates a universal distribution group.

✦ -2147483646 creates a global security group.

✦ -2147483644 creates a domain-local security group.

✦ -2147483640 creates a universal security group.

Note　Universal security groups cannot be created when using mixed-mode operations. You must be in native mode operations. In native mode, Active Directory only supports Windows 2000 domains and no longer supports Windows NT domains. So before you change modes, you should ensure that all Windows NT systems in the domain have been upgraded to Windows 2000.

Listing 19-7 shows how you could create these group types in VBScript. You would use similar techniques for JScript.

Listing 19-7: **Creating groups**

VBScript

creategroups.vbs

```
'Create global distribution group
Set obj = GetObject("LDAP://CN=Users,DC=seattle,DC=tvpress,DC=com")
Set grp = obj.Create("group", "CN=MarketingGlobalDist")
grp.groupType = 2
grp.Put "samAccountName", "MarketingGD"
grp.SetInfo

'Create domain local distribution group
Set obj = GetObject("LDAP://CN=Users,DC=seattle,DC=tvpress,DC=com")
Set grp = obj.Create("group", "CN=MarketingDomainLocalDist")
grp.groupType = 4
grp.Put "samAccountName", "MarketingDD"
grp.SetInfo

'Create universal distribution group
Set obj = GetObject("LDAP://CN=Users,DC=seattle,DC=tvpress,DC=com")
Set grp = obj.Create("group", "CN=MarketingUniversalDist")
grp.groupType = 8
grp.Put "samAccountName", "MarketingUD"
grp.SetInfo
```

Continued

Listing 19-7 *(continued)*

```
'Create global security group
Set obj = GetObject("LDAP://CN=Users,DC=seattle,DC=tvpress,DC=com")
Set grp = obj.Create("group", "CN=MarketingGlobal")
grp.groupType = -2147483646
grp.Put "samAccountName", "MarketingG"
grp.SetInfo

'Create domain local security group
Set obj = GetObject("LDAP://CN=Users,DC=seattle,DC=tvpress,DC=com")
Set grp = obj.Create("group", "CN=MarketingDomainLocal")
grp.groupType = -2147483644
grp.Put "samAccountName", "MarketingD"
grp.SetInfo

'Create universal security group
Set obj = GetObject("LDAP://CN=Users,DC=seattle,DC=tvpress,DC=com")
Set grp = obj.Create("group", "CN=MarketingUniversal")
grp.groupType = -2147483640
grp.Put "samAccountName", "MarketingU"
grp.SetInfo
```

Deleting, moving, and renaming groups with LDAP

You can also delete, move, and rename groups. You can delete a group stored in a container by invoking the container's Delete method. Here's how you would delete a group called Marketing:

VBScript

```
Set cont = GetObject("LDAP://OU=Users,DC=seattle,DC=tvpress,DC=com")
cont.Delete "group","CN=Marketing"
```

JScript

```
var cont = GetObject("LDAP://OU=Users,DC=seattle,DC=tvpress,DC=com");
cont.Delete ("group","CN=Marketing");
```

Moving and renaming groups is much like moving and renaming computer accounts. You retrieve the destination container and then invoke the container's MoveHere method for the group you want to move. Listing 19-8 shows how you could move a group called SalesEng from the Users container to the Sales organizational unit.

Listing 19-8: **Moving a group**

VBScript

movegroup.vbs

```
'Get rootDSE
Set rootDSE = GetObject("LDAP://rootDSE")
domainCont = rootDSE.Get("defaultNamingContext")

'Get the destination container
set cont = GetObject("LDAP://OU=Sales," & domainCont)

'Move group from original container to the destination
cont.MoveHere "LDAP://CN=SalesEng,CN=Users," & domainCont, "CN=SalesEng"
```

JScript

movegroup.js

```
//Get rootDSE
var rootDSE = GetObject("LDAP://rootDSE");
domainCont = rootDSE.Get("defaultNamingContext");

//Get the destination container
var cont = GetObject("LDAP://OU=Sales," + domainCont);

//Move group from original container to the destination
cont.MoveHere("LDAP://CN=SalesEng,CN=Users," + domainCont, "CN=SalesEng");
```

To rename a group when you move it, you simply specify a different name as the second parameter for MoveHere. To rename a group and keep it in the same container, use the same value for the original and destination container, as shown in Listing 19-9.

Listing 19-9: **Renaming a group**

VBScript

renamegroup.vbs

```
'Get rootDSE
Set rootDSE = GetObject("LDAP://rootDSE")
domainCont = rootDSE.Get("defaultNamingContext")
```

Continued

Listing 19-9 *(continued)*

```
'Get the destination container
set cont = GetObject("LDAP://OU=Engineering," & domainCont)

'Move group from original container to the destination
cont.MoveHere "LDAP://CN=Coders,OU=Engineering," & domainCont, "CN=Developers"
```

JScript

renamegroup.js

```
//Get rootDSE
var rootDSE = GetObject("LDAP://rootDSE");
domainCont = rootDSE.Get("defaultNamingContext");

//Get the destination container
var cont = GetObject("LDAP://OU=Engineering," + domainCont);

//Move group from original container to the destination
cont.MoveHere("LDAP://CN=Coders,OU=Engineering," + domainCont,
"CN=Developers");
```

Checking group membership with LDAP

One way to work with groups is to obtain a list of current members. You can do this by calling the group object's Members() method. The Members() method returns a collection of members using the IADsMembers interface. You can examine each member using a for loop as shown in Listing 19-10.

Listing 19-10: **Checking group membership**

VBScript

groupmembers.vbs

```
Set grp = GetObject("LDAP://CN=Marketing,CN=Users, DC=seattle,DC=domain,DC=com")

Set mList = grp.members
For Each member In mList
   WScript.Echo member.Name
Next
```

JScript

groupmembers.js

```
var grp = GetObject("LDAP://CN=Marketing,CN=Users, DC=seattle,DC=domain,DC=com");

mList = new Enumerator(grp.members());

for (; !mList.atEnd(); mList.moveNext())
{
 s = mList.item();
 WScript.Echo(s.Name);
}
```

To check for a specific member, you can use the `IsMember ()` method. This method returns True (1) if the user or group is a member of the group and False (0), otherwise. You could use `IsMember` as follows:

VBScript

```
Set grp = GetObject("LDAP://CN=Marketing,CN=Users, DC=seattle,DC=domain,DC=com")

mem = grp.IsMember("CN=William R. Stanek,CN=Users, DC=seattle,DC=domain,DC=com")
WScript.Echo CStr(mem)
```

JScript

```
var grp = GetObject("LDAP://CN=Marketing,CN=Users, DC=seattle,DC=domain,DC=com");

mem = grp.IsMember("CN=William R. Stanek,CN=Users, DC=seattle,DC=domain,DC=com");
WScript.Echo(mem);
```

Adding and removing group members with LDAP

You can use the LDAP provider to add and remove members from a group, as well. First, obtain the group object you want to work with, and then invoke `Add` or `Remove` as appropriate. After you add or remove a member, you can use `IsMember()` to confirm the action, such as:

VBScript

```
Set grp = GetObject("LDAP://CN=Marketing,CN=Users, DC=seattle,DC=domain,DC=com")
grp.Add "CN=William R. Stanek,CN=Users,DC=seattle,DC=domain,DC=com"

WScript.Echo grp.IsMember("CN=William R. Stanek,CN=Users,
DC=seattle,DC=domain,DC=com")
```

JScript

```
var grp = GetObject("LDAP://CN=Marketing,CN=Users, DC=seattle,DC=domain,DC=com");
grp.Add("CN=William R. Stanek,CN=Users,DC=seattle,DC=domain,DC=com");

WScript.Echo(grp.IsMember("CN=William R. Stanek,CN=Users,
DC=seattle,DC=domain,DC=com"));
```

Working with Organizational Units

Organizational units often are used to mirror business or functional structures. For example, if your organization has business groups called Technology, Marketing, and Operations, you may want to have organizational units with the same names. You could then add resources and accounts to these organizational units.

Examining organizational unit properties

Organizational units can be at different physical locations, as well. This is why contact information, such as addresses and telephone numbers, are associated with organizational units. Table 19-6 provides a summary of properties for organizational units.

Table 19-6
Properties for Organizational Units

Property	Status	Value Type	Min. Range	Max. Range	Multiple Values
adminDescription	RW	DirectoryString	0	1024	False
adminDisplayName	RW	DirectoryString	1	256	False
businessCategory	RW	DirectoryString	1	128	True
cn	RW	DirectoryString	1	64	False
description	RW	DirectoryString	0	1024	True
destinationIndicator	RW	PrintableString	1	128	True
displayName	RW	DirectoryString	0	256	False
displayNamePrintable	RW	PrintableString	1	256	False
extensionName	RW	DirectoryString	1	255	True

Property	Status	Value Type	Min. Range	Max. Range	Multiple Values
facsimileTelephone Number	RW	DirectoryString	1	64	False
internationalISDN Number	RW	NumericString	1	16	True
name	RW	DirectoryString	1	255	False
nTSecurityDescriptor	RO	ObjectSecurity Descriptor	0	132096	False
objectGUID	RO	OctetString	16	16	False
ou	RW	DirectoryString	1	64	True
physicalDelivery OfficeName	RW	DirectoryString	1	128	False
postalAddress	RW	DirectoryString	1	4096	True
postalCode	RW	DirectoryString	1	40	False
postOfficeBox	RW	DirectoryString	1	40	True
proxyAddresses	RW	DirectoryString	1	1123	True
registeredAddress	RW	OctetString	1	4096	True
street	RW	DirectoryString	1	1024	False
telephoneNumber	RW	DirectoryString	1	64	False
telexNumber	RW	OctetString	1	32	True
thumbnailLogo	RW	OctetString	1	32767	False
userPassword	RW	OctetString	1	128	True
wWWHomePage	RW	DirectoryString	1	2048	False
x121Address	RW	NumericString	1	15	True

Creating organizational units

Organizational units can be created within the top-level domain container or within existing organizational units. When you create a unit in the top-level domain container, you bind to the domain-naming context and then invoke the `Create` method of this container. Otherwise, you bind to an existing organizational unit and then create a sub unit by invoking the `Create` method.

The only property you must set is OU, which stores the name of the organizational unit. Listing 19-11 creates an organizational unit called Engineering.

Listing 19-11: Creating an organizational unit

VBScript

createou.vbs

```
'Get domain naming context
Set obj = GetObject("LDAP://DC=seattle,DC=domain,DC=com")

'create ou object
Set ou = obj.Create("organizationalUnit","OU=Engineering")

'Set the name of the ou
ou.ou = "Engineering"
ou.SetInfo
```

JScript

createou.js

```
//Get domain naming context
var obj = GetObject("LDAP://DC=seattle,DC=domain,DC=com");

//create ou object
var ou = obj.Create("organizationalUnit","OU=Engineering");

//set the name of the ou
ou.ou = "Engineering";
ou.SetInfo();
```

Modifying organizational units

You can work with existing organizational units in much the same way as you work with other objects. You bind to the `organizationalUnit` object:

```
GetObject("LDAP://OU=Marketing,DC=seattle,DC=tvpress,DC=com")
```

Then you set or get properties. You may also need to examine the objects within the organizational unit. One way to do this would be to obtain a list of all objects that it contains, as shown in Listing 19-12.

Listing 19-12: Accessing objects within an organizational unit

---

VBScript

---

getobjs.vbs

```
Set ou = GetObject("LDAP://OU=Engineering,DC=seattle,DC=domain,DC=com")

For Each member In ou
    WScript.Echo member.Name
Next
```

JScript

---

getobjs.js

```
var ou = GetObject("LDAP://OU=Engineering,DC=seattle,DC=domain,DC=com");

mList = new Enumerator(ou);

for (; !mList.atEnd(); mList.moveNext())
{
 s = mList.item();
 WScript.Echo(s.Name);
}
```

Moving, renaming, and deleting organizational units

The LDAP provider supports the `MoveHere` method for moving and renaming organizational units. The following example moves Developers so that it is a subunit of Engineering:

VBScript

```
Set cont = GetObject("LDAP://OU=Engineering,DC=seattle,DC=domain,DC=com")
cont.MoveHere "LDAP://OU=Developers,DC=seattle,DC=domain,DC=com", "OU=Developers"
```

JScript

```
var cont = GetObject("LDAP://OU=Engineering,DC=seattle,DC=domain,DC=com");
cont.MoveHere("LDAP://OU=Developers,DC=seattle,DC=domain,DC=com", "OU=Developers");
```

You delete organizational units using the `Delete` method. An example follows:

VBScript

```
Set obj = GetObject("LDAP://DC=seattle,DC=domain,DC=com")
obj.Delete "organizationalUnit", "OU=Engineering"
```

JScript

```
var obj = GetObject("LDAP://DC=seattle,DC=domain,DC=com");
obj.Delete("organizationalUnit", "OU=Engineering");
```

Managing User Accounts with LDAP

Just about everything you learned about managing user accounts with WinNT can be applied to managing user accounts with LDAP. There are some important differences, however, and these differences are examined in this section.

Examining user object properties with LDAP

Table 19-7 provides a summary of properties for Active Directory user objects. Before you can work with user objects, you must bind to the container in which the objects reside, such as:

```
GetObject("LDAP://CN=Users,DC=seattle,DC=tvpress,DC=com")
```

Or you must access the user object directly, such as:

```
GetObject("LDAP://CN=William R. Stanek,
OU=Technology,DC=seattle,DC=tvpress,DC=com")
```

Table 19-7
Active Directory User Object Properties

Property	Status	Value Type	Min. Range	Max. Range	Multiple Values
adminDescription	RW	DirectoryString	0	1024	False
adminDisplayName	RW	DirectoryString	1	256	False
cn	RO	DirectoryString	1	64	False

Property	Status	Value Type	Min. Range	Max. Range	Multiple Values
company	RW	DirectoryString	1	64	False
controlAccessRights	RO	OctetString	16	16	True
department	RW	DirectoryString	1	64	False
description	RW	DirectoryString	0	1024	True
destinationIndicator	RW	PrintableString	1	128	True
displayName	RW	DirectoryString	0	256	False
displayNamePrintable	RW	PrintableString	1	256	False
division	RW	DirectoryString	0	256	False
employeeID	RW	DirectoryString	0	16	False
extensionName	RW	DirectoryString	1	255	True
facsimileTelephone Number	RW	DirectoryString	1	64	False
generationQualifier	RW	DirectoryString	1	64	False
givenName	RW	DirectoryString	1	64	False
homePhone	RW	DirectoryString	1	64	False
homePostalAddress	RW	DirectoryString	1	4096	False
info	RW	DirectoryString	1	1024	False
initials	RW	DirectoryString	1	6	False
internationalISDN Number	RW	NumericString	1	16	True
mail	RW	DirectoryString	0	256	False
middleName	RW	DirectoryString	0	64	False
mobile	RW	DirectoryString	1	64	False
mSMQDigests	RW	OctetString	16	16	True
name	RW	DirectoryString	1	255	False
networkAddress	RW	CaseIgnoreString	0	256	True
nTSecurityDescriptor	RO	ObjectSecurity Descriptor	0	132096	False
objectGUID	RO	OctetString	16	16	False
objectSid	RO	OctetString	0	28	False

Continued

Table 19-7 *(continued)*

Property	Status	Value Type	Min. Range	Max. Range	Multiple Values
otherFacsimile TelephoneNumber	RW	DirectoryString	1	64	True
otherHomePhone	RW	DirectoryString	1	64	True
otherLoginWorkstations	RW	DirectoryString	0	1024	True
otherMobile	RW	DirectoryString	1	64	True
otherPager	RW	DirectoryString	1	64	True
otherTelephone	RW	DirectoryString	1	64	True
ou	RW	DirectoryString	1	64	True
pager	RW	DirectoryString	1	64	False
personalTitle	RW	DirectoryString	1	64	False
physicalDelivery OfficeName	RW	DirectoryString	1	128	False
postalAddress	RW	DirectoryString	1	4096	True
postalCode	RW	DirectoryString	1	40	False
postOfficeBox	RW	DirectoryString	1	40	True
primaryInternational ISDNNumber	RW	DirectoryString	1	64	False
primaryTelexNumber	RW	DirectoryString	1	64	False
proxyAddresses	RW	DirectoryString	1	1123	True
registeredAddress	RW	OctetString	1	4096	True
sAMAccountName	RW	DirectoryString	0	256	False
sn	RW	DirectoryString	1	64	False
street	RW	DirectoryString	1	1024	False
streetAddress	RW	DirectoryString	1	1024	False
telephoneNumber	RW	DirectoryString	1	64	False
telexNumber	RW	OctetString	1	32	True
textEncodedORAddress	RW	DirectoryString	1	1024	False
thumbnailLogo	RW	OctetString	1	32767	False

Property	Status	Value Type	Min. Range	Max. Range	Multiple Values
thumbnailPhoto	RW	OctetString	0	102400	False
title	RW	DirectoryString	1	64	False
userCert	RW	OctetString	0	32767	False
userParameters	RW	DirectoryString	0	32767	False
userPassword	RW	OctetString	1	128	True
userWorkstations	RW	DirectoryString	0	1024	False
wWWHomePage	RW	DirectoryString	1	2048	False
x121Address	RW	NumericString	1	15	True

With user objects, the LDAP provider also supports a custom mapping between ADSI properties and Active Directory properties. These customizations only apply to specific properties and are designed to more closely resemble the fields that you'll find in Active Directory Users and Computers dialog boxes.

A partial list of custom mappings is shown in Table 19-8. Because of these custom mappings, your scripts can refer to the givenName property as FirstName, the sn property as LastName, and so on.

Table 19-8
Custom Mappings for User Object Properties

ADSI Properties	Active Directory Property
AccountDisabled	userAccountControl *Mask*
AccountExpirationDate	AccountExpires
BadLoginCount	BadPwdCount
Department	Department
Description	Description
Division	Division
EmailAddress	Mail
EmployeeID	EmployeeID
FaxNumber	FacsimileTelephoneNumber

Continued

Table 19-8 *(continued)*

ADSI Properties	Active Directory Property
FirstName	GivenName
FullName	DisplayName
HomeDirectory	HomeDirectory
HomePage	WWWHomePage
IsAccountLocked	UserAccountControl
Languages	Language
LastFailedLogin	BadPasswordTime
LastLogin	LastLogon
LastLogoff	LastLogoff
LastName	Sn
LoginHours	LogonHours
LoginScript	ScriptPath
LoginWorkstations	UserWorkstations
Manager	Manager
MaxStorage	MaxStorage
NamePrefix	PersonalTitle
NameSuffix	GenerationQualifier
OfficeLocations	PhysicalDeliveryOfficeName
OtherName	MiddleName
PasswordLastChanged	PwdLastSet
PasswordRequired	UserAccountControl
Picture	ThumbnailPhoto
PostalAddresses	PostalAddress
PostalCodes	PostalCode
Profile	ProfilePath
SeeAlso	SeeAlso
TelephoneHome	HomePhone
TelephoneMobile	Mobile
TelephoneNumber	TelephoneNumber
TelephonePager	Pager
Title	Title

Creating user accounts with LDAP

While the WinNT provider allows you to create both local and domain user accounts, the LDAP provider can only create domain user accounts. Yet unlike WinNT, these domain accounts can be placed in any container or organizational unit, giving you additional flexibility.

To create a user account, you must specify the common name and the Windows NT SAM account name. All other properties are optional.

You could create a user account for William R. Stanek and place it in the Technology organizational unit as follows:

VBScript

```
Set obj = GetObject("LDAP://OU=Technology,DC=seattle,DC=domain,DC=com")
Set usr = obj.Create("user", "CN=William R. Stanek")
usr.samAccountName = "wrstanek"
usr.SetInfo
```

JScript

```
var obj = GetObject("LDAP://OU=Technology,DC=seattle,DC=domain,DC=com");
var usr = obj.Create("user", "CN=William R. Stanek");
usr.samAccountName = "wrstanek";
usr.SetInfo();
```

If no additional attributes are specified, the new user account is created with default property settings. These default property settings are as follows:

- ✦ Full Name (displayName) is blank.
- ✦ First Name (givenName) is blank.
- ✦ Last Name (sn) is blank.
- ✦ User Principal Name (UPN) is blank.
- ✦ Password is blank.
- ✦ Primary group is set to Domain Users.

User flags are also set on the account. These flags state that the user must change the password, the account is disabled, and the account never expires. User flags can be set using techniques similar to those discussed in Chapter 16. All of the flags discussed in Table 16-4 apply to LDAP user objects, as well. You set or view these flags through the userAccessControl property.

With LDAP, you must create a user account before you can set or change the password. The related methods are the same, however. You use `SetPassword` to set a password and `ChangePassword` to change a password, such as:

VBScript

```
Set usr = GetObject("LDAP://CN=William R. Stanek,
  OU=Technology,DC=seattle,DC=domain,DC=com")
usr.SetPassword "NewPassword"

Set usr = GetObject("LDAP://CN=William R. Stanek,
  OU=Technology,DC=seattle,DC=domain,DC=com")
usr.ChangePassword "OldPassword","NewPassword"
```

JScript

```
var usr = GetObject("LDAP://CN=William R. Stanek,
  OU=Technology,DC=seattle,DC=domain,DC=com");
usr.SetPassword("NewPassword");

var usr = GetObject("LDAP://CN=William R. Stanek,
  OU=Technology,DC=seattle,DC=domain,DC=com");
usr.ChangePassword("OldPassword","NewPassword");
```

Setting user account flags

The LDAP implementation of the user object provides several advantages over the WinNT implementation, especially when it comes to setting account flags. Unlike WinNT, you can set any of the following properties directly and don't have to use the `userAccessControl` flags:

✦ User must change password

✦ Account disabled

✦ Account lockout

✦ Account expiration

You specify that the user must change his password with the `pwdLastSet` property. A value of zero (0) means the user must change his password at the next logon. A value of –1 clears this setting. In this example, you specify that William R. Stanek must change his password at the next logon:

VBScript

```
Set usr = GetObject("LDAP://CN=William R. Stanek,
OU=Technology,DC=seattle,DC=domain,DC=com")
usr.Put "pwdLastSet", CLng(0)
usr.SetInfo
```

JScript

```
var usr = GetObject("LDAP://CN=William R. Stanek,
OU=Technology,DC=seattle,DC=domain,DC=com");
usr.Put("pwdLastSet", 0);
usr.SetInfo();
```

You can disable a user account by setting the `AccountDisable` property to True (1). Then to enable the account, you would set `AccountDisable` to False (0), such as:

VBScript

```
Set usr = GetObject("LDAP://CN=William R. Stanek,
  OU=Technology,DC=seattle,DC=domain,DC=com")
usr.AccountDisabled = False
usr.SetInfo
```

JScript

```
var usr = GetObject("LDAP://CN=William R. Stanek,
  OU=Technology,DC=seattle,DC=domain,DC=com");
usr.AccountDisabled = 0;
usr.SetInfo();
```

To unlock an account that has been locked out by the operating system, set the `IsAccountLocked` property to False (0), such as:

VBScript

```
Set usr = GetObject("LDAP://CN=William R. Stanek,
  OU=Technology,DC=seattle,DC=domain,DC=com")
usr.IsAccountLocked = False
usr.SetInfo
```

JScript

```
var usr = GetObject("LDAP://CN=William R. Stanek,
  OU=Technology,DC=seattle,DC=domain,DC=com");
usr.IsAccountLocked = 0;
usr.SetInfo();
```

Only Windows 2000 can set IsAccountLocked to True (1). Typically, an account gets locked because a user (or intruder) repeatedly entered a bad password.

Other useful properties for managing user accounts are AccountExpirationDate and AccountExpires. If you want an account to expire on a specific date, set AccountExpirationDate to the desired date, such as:

VBScript

```
Set usr = GetObject("LDAP://CN=William R. Stanek,
  OU=Technology,DC=seattle,DC=domain,DC=com")
usr.AccountExpirationDate = "12/15/2001"
usr.SetInfo
```

JScript

```
var usr = GetObject("LDAP://CN=William R. Stanek,
  OU=Technology,DC=seattle,DC=domain,DC=com");
usr.AccountExpirationDate = "12/15/2001";
usr.SetInfo();
```

To specify that an account should never expire, set AccountExpires to –1, such as:

VBScript

```
Set usr = GetObject("LDAP://CN=William R. Stanek,
  OU=Technology,DC=seattle,DC=domain,DC=com")
usr.AccountExpires = -1
usr.SetInfo
```

JScript

```
var usr = GetObject("LDAP://CN=William R. Stanek,
  OU=Technology,DC=seattle,DC=domain,DC=com");
usr.AccountExpires = -1;
usr.SetInfo();
```

Viewing group membership

As with WinNT, you can use the Groups() method to check group membership for users. The Groups() method returns a collection of group objects to which a user belongs. You could use this method to examine all of the groups William R. Stanek belongs to as follows:

VBScript

```
Set usr = GetObject("LDAP://CN=William R. Stanek,
   OU=Technology,DC=seattle,DC=domain,DC=com")

For Each grp In usr.Groups
   WScript.Echo  grp.Name
Next
```

JScript

```
var usr = GetObject("LDAP://CN=William R. Stanek,
   OU=Technology,DC=seattle,DC=domain,DC=com");

mList = new Enumerator(usr.Groups());

for (; !mList.atEnd(); mList.moveNext())
{
 s = mList.item();
 WScript.Echo(s.Name);
}
```

Output

```
CN=Enterprise Admins
CN=Schema Admins
CN=Domain Admins
CN=Administrators
CN=Backup Operators
```

Moving, renaming, and deleting user accounts with LDAP

The LDAP provider supports the MoveHere method for moving and renaming user accounts, and the Delete method for deleting user accounts. You could move a user account to a different container as follows:

| Listing 19-13: **Moving a user account** |

VBScript

moveuser.vbs

```
'Get rootDSE
Set rootDSE = GetObject("LDAP://rootDSE")
domainCont = rootDSE.Get("defaultNamingContext")
```

Continued

Listing 19-13 *(continued)*

```
'Get the destination container
Set cont = GetObject("LDAP://OU=Engineering," & domainCont)

'Move object from original container to the destination
cont.MoveHere "LDAP://CN=William R. Stanek,OU=Technology," & domainCont,
  "CN=William R. Stanek"
```

JScript

moveuser.js
```
//Get rootDSE
var rootDSE = GetObject("LDAP://rootDSE");
domainCont = rootDSE.Get("defaultNamingContext");

//Get the destination container
var cont = GetObject("LDAP://OU=Engineering," + domainCont);

//Move object from original container to the destination
cont.MoveHere("LDAP://CN=William R. Stanek,OU=Technology," + domainCont,
  "CN=William R. Stanek");
```

Summary

In this chapter, you used the LDAP ADSI provider to manage Active Directory objects. As you learned, many extensions are available for common objects, and you can use these extensions to manipulate objects in many different ways. Because this provider can access other LDAP-compliant technologies, you can apply everything you've learned in this chapter when scripting Exchange Server, as well as other LDAP-compliant servers. For example, you could create, move, and delete Exchange mailboxes using the techniques discussed in this chapter.

✦　　✦　　✦

Where to Go from Here?

Windows 2000 Scripting Bible provides everything you need in order to build powerful solutions for managing systems and networks. As you've seen in this book, anyone can use scripting to automate tasks that would otherwise be handled manually. Not only can automation increase your productivity, it can set you apart as someone who knows how to get the job done. This book has covered many different aspects of scripting. You've learned how to:

+ Read input from the keyboard and display output to files

+ Handle errors and create log files

+ Read and write files

+ Manage registry settings

+ Create and manipulate folders, shortcuts, and menu options

+ Control printers and print queues

+ Map network drives and configure network shares

+ Schedule tasks to be completed at a later date

+ Create logon, logoff, startup, and shutdown scripts

+ Configure and control Windows services

+ Create, view, and modify user accounts

+ Manage security and distribution groups

+ Setup and manage computer accounts

+ Master ADSI schema and learn about new features

+ Lots more

One of the things you quickly learn about Windows scripting is that no single book can ever cover its every facet. This book has focused on scripting the Windows 2000 operating system. Beyond the Windows 2000 operating system, a whole universe of options awaits. These options largely come from Windows Script Host's ability to script ActiveX and COM components.

Working with ActiveX and COM

Microsoft based ActiveX on the Component Object Model (COM). COM allows objects to communicate with each other by using links. Object linking is central to the OLE (Object Linking and Embedding) technology widely used in Windows applications. While both OLE and ActiveX are based on COM, these technologies serve different purposes. OLE is designed for use on PCs. ActiveX trims down COM to make object linking practical for use in distributed network environments.

The ActiveX foundation is built around several core technologies. These technologies include:

✦ ActiveX controls used to extend the capabilities of the scripting hosts

✦ ActiveX documents used to access documents formatted for Word, Excel, PowerPoint, and other applications

You can use ActiveX controls, ActiveX documents, and COM components in your scripts. With VBScript, you use the `GetObject()` or `CreateObject()` to access these elements. When there is a current instance of an object, you call `GetObject()`. Otherwise, if no current instance exists, you use the `CreateObject()` method. With JScript, you normally use `ActiveXObject()` to create an object instance.

Listing 20-1 provides an example of how you could script an Excel spreadsheet using a Windows script. You can script other Microsoft Office Applications, such as Word and Outlook, using similar techniques. Many other applications register COM objects when you install them. You can script these objects, as well.

Listing 20-1: **Scripting an Excel spreadsheet**

VBScript

spreadsheet.vbs

```
' Windows Script Host Sample Script
' This sample will display Windows Scripting Host properties
' in Excel.
```

```
L_Welcome_MsgBox_Message_Text     = "This script will display Windows Scripting Host
properties in Excel."
L_Welcome_MsgBox_Title_Text       = "Windows Scripting Host Sample"
Call Welcome()

' Excel Sample
Dim objXL
Set objXL = WScript.CreateObject("Excel.Application")

objXL.Visible = TRUE

objXL.WorkBooks.Add

objXL.Columns(1).ColumnWidth = 20
objXL.Columns(2).ColumnWidth = 30
objXL.Columns(3).ColumnWidth = 40

objXL.Cells(1, 1).Value = "Property Name"
objXL.Cells(1, 2).Value = "Value"
objXL.Cells(1, 3).Value = "Description"

objXL.Range("A1:C1").Select
objXL.Selection.Font.Bold = True
objXL.Selection.Interior.ColorIndex = 1
objXL.Selection.Interior.Pattern = 1 'xlSolid
objXL.Selection.Font.ColorIndex = 2

objXL.Columns("B:B").Select
objXL.Selection.HorizontalAlignment = &hFFFFEFDD ' xlLeft

Dim intIndex
intIndex = 2

Sub Show(strName, strValue, strDesc)
    objXL.Cells(intIndex, 1).Value = strName
    objXL.Cells(intIndex, 2).Value = strValue
    objXL.Cells(intIndex, 3).Value = strDesc
    intIndex = intIndex + 1
    objXL.Cells(intIndex, 1).Select
End Sub

' Show WScript properties
Call Show("Name",          WScript.Name,          "Application Friendly Name")
Call Show("Version",       WScript.Version,       "Application Version")
Call Show("FullName",      WScript.FullName,      "Application Context: Fully
Qualified Name")
Call Show("Path",          WScript.Path,          "Application Context: Path
Only")
Call Show("Interactive",   WScript.Interactive,   "State of Interactive Mode")
```

Continued

Listing 20-1 *(continued)*

```vbscript
' Show command line arguments.
Dim colArgs
Set colArgs = WScript.Arguments
Call Show("Arguments.Count", colArgs.Count, "Number of command line arguments")

For i = 0 to colArgs.Count - 1
    objXL.Cells(intIndex, 1).Value = "Arguments(" & i & ")"
    objXL.Cells(intIndex, 2).Value = colArgs(i)
    intIndex = intIndex + 1
    objXL.Cells(intIndex, 1).Select
Next

' Welcome
Sub Welcome()
    Dim intDoIt

    intDoIt =  MsgBox(L_Welcome_MsgBox_Message_Text, _
                    vbOKCancel + vbInformation,     _
                    L_Welcome_MsgBox_Title_Text )
    If intDoIt = vbCancel Then
        WScript.Quit
    End If
End Sub
```

JScript

spreadsheet.js

```javascript
// Windows Script Host Sample Script
// This sample will display Windows Scripting Host properties
// in Excel.


var vbOKCancel = 1;
var vbInformation = 64;
var vbCancel = 2;

var L_Welcome_MsgBox_Message_Text    = "This script will display Windows Scripting
Host properties in Excel.";
var L_Welcome_MsgBox_Title_Text      = "Windows Scripting Host Sample";
Welcome();

// Excel Sample
var objXL = WScript.CreateObject("Excel.Application");

objXL.Visible = true;

objXL.WorkBooks.Add;
```

```
objXL.Columns(1).ColumnWidth = 20;
objXL.Columns(2).ColumnWidth = 30;
objXL.Columns(3).ColumnWidth = 40;

objXL.Cells(1, 1).Value = "Property Name";
objXL.Cells(1, 2).Value = "Value";
objXL.Cells(1, 3).Value = "Description";

objXL.Range("A1:C1").Select;
objXL.Selection.Font.Bold = true;
objXL.Selection.Interior.ColorIndex = 1;
objXL.Selection.Interior.Pattern = 1; //xlSolid
objXL.Selection.Font.ColorIndex = 2;

objXL.Columns("B:B").Select;
objXL.Selection.HorizontalAlignment = -4131; // xlLeft

var intIndex = 2;

function Show(strName, strValue, strDesc) {
    objXL.Cells(intIndex, 1).Value = strName;
    objXL.Cells(intIndex, 2).Value = strValue;
    objXL.Cells(intIndex, 3).Value = strDesc;
    intIndex++;
    objXL.Cells(intIndex, 1).Select;
}

// Show WScript properties
Show("Name",        WScript.Name,        "Application Friendly Name");
Show("Version",     WScript.Version,     "Application Version");
Show("FullName",    WScript.FullName,    "Application Context: Fully Qualified
Name");
Show("Path",        WScript.Path,        "Application Context: Path Only");
Show("Interactive", WScript.Interactive, "State of Interactive Mode");

// Show command line arguments.
var colArgs = WScript.Arguments
Show("Arguments.Count", colArgs.length, "Number of command line
arguments");

for (i = 0; i < colArgs.length; i++) {
    objXL.Cells(intIndex, 1).Value = "Arguments(" + i + ")";
    objXL.Cells(intIndex, 2).Value = colArgs(i);
    intIndex++;
    objXL.Cells(intIndex, 1).Select;
}
// Welcome
function Welcome() {
    var WSHShell = WScript.CreateObject("WScript.Shell");
    var intDoIt;
```

Continued

Listing 20-1 *(continued)*

```
    intDoIt =  WSHShell.Popup(L_Welcome_MsgBox_Message_Text,
                              0,
                              L_Welcome_MsgBox_Title_Text,
                              vbOKCancel + vbInformation );
    if (intDoIt == vbCancel) {
        WScript.Quit();
    }
}
```

As you would expect, you can't script all ActiveX and COM components. There are limitations. For example, most components that you use should implement the IDispatch interface. This interface makes a COM component an Automation object, and it is used by Windows Script Host to access component methods and properties.

Looking Ahead

The best resources for learning more are books on VBScript or Visual Basic. You can also use the OLE Viewer or the VBA Editor to browse objects that are available on your system. Both tools are available from Microsoft (www.microsoft.com/com/).

Other technologies you should look at include:

✦ ADO — Active Data Objects allow you to manipulate databases through OLE DB.

✦ ADSI Providers — ADSI Providers allow you to work with other server-based technologies, such as Internet Information Services (IIS). To manage IIS, you use the IIS:// ADSI provider and the set of objects that it provides.

✦ CDO — Collaborative Data Objects provides a set of messaging objects for Exchange, Outlook, and other messaging environments.

✦ SQL-DMO — SQL Distributed Management Objects provide an object model for administering Microsoft SQL Server.

All of these technologies can be accessed in Windows scripts. If you'd like to learn more about these technologies in future editions of Windows 2000 Scripting Bible, please let me know. Send e-mail to win2000scripting@tvpress.com.

✦　　✦　　✦

Windows Scripting Libraries

Now that you've worked through parts I, II, and III, you should be ready to tackle any job using Windows scripting. But rather than start from scratch, it would be good to begin with a set of tools. Part IV provides you those tools. The four chapters in this Part develop a set of script libraries that you can incorporate into your own projects: file system and administration utilities, network and system administration utilities, and account management utilities. With these tools, you're well on your way to creating your one Windows scripting projects. Good luck!

Library: File-System Utilities

◆ ◆ ◆ ◆

In This Chapter

Creating the file-system utility library

Using the file-system utility library

Working with library methods

◆ ◆ ◆ ◆

The file-system utility library provides functions for working with files and folders. Through batch script (.WS) files, you can access these utility functions in any of your scripts. The sections that follow show the source of the library, as well as showing how the library can be used.

Examining the File-System Utility Library

Listing 21-1 shows the file-system utility library script. When calling this script from JScript, be sure to pass path information in JScript format with double slashes as folder separators. You do not need to do this from VBScript. Windows Script Host automatically transforms VBScript paths into JScript paths when you call JScript functions from VBScript.

Listing 21-1: File-system utility library

filesystemlib.js

```
// ************************
// Script: File System Utility Library
// Version: 0.9.5
// Creation Date: 09/15/1999
// Last Modified: 02/05/2000
// Author: William R. Stanek
// Email: win2000scripting@tvpress.com
// ************************
// Description: Provides a utility library for working
//              with files and folders.
// ************************
```

Continued

Listing 21-1: *(continued)*

```
// Copyright (c) 1999-2000 William R. Stanek
// You have a royalty-free right to use these applications, provided
// that you give credit to the author AND agree that the author has
// no warranty, obligations or liability for any of these library
// functions.
// ************************

function GetFolderContents(folderPath, separator)
{
  var contents, fpath, sep;
  fpath = folderPath
  sep = separator

  contents = "";
  contents += "Folders:" + sep
  contents += "==========================" + sep
  contents += GetSubFolders(fpath, sep)
  contents += sep + "Files:" + sep
  contents += "==========================" + sep
  contents += GetFiles(fpath, sep)

  return(contents);
}

function GetSubFolders(folderPath, separator)
{
  var fs, f, fc, s;

  s = "";

  fs = new ActiveXObject("Scripting.FileSystemObject");
  f = fs.GetFolder(folderPath);
  fc = new Enumerator(f.SubFolders);

  for (; !fc.atEnd(); fc.moveNext())
  {
   s += fc.item();
   s += separator
  }

  return(s);
}

function GetFiles(folderPath, separator)
{
  var fs, f, fc, s;

  s = "";
```

```
    fs = new ActiveXObject ("Scripting.FileSystemObject");
    f = fs.GetFolder(folderPath);
    fc = new Enumerator(f.Files);

    for (; !fc.atEnd(); fc.moveNext())
    {
     s += fc.item();
     s += separator
    }

    return(s);
}

function CheckExists(filePath)
{
   var fs, s;

   s = "False";

   fs = new ActiveXObject("Scripting.FileSystemObject");

   if (fs.FolderExists(filePath))
     s = "True";
   else if (fs.FileExists(filePath))
     s = "True";

   return(s);
}

function GetInfo(filePath)
{

   var fs, f, s;

   fs = new ActiveXObject("Scripting.FileSystemObject");

   if (fs.FolderExists(filePath))
     f = fs.GetFolder(filePath);
   else if (fs.FileExists(filePath))
     f = fs.GetFile(filePath);

   s = "Name: " + f.Name + "\r\n";
   s += "Path: " + f.Path + "\r\n";
   s += "Date Created: " + f.DateCreated + "\r\n";
   s += "Date Last Accessed: " + f.DateLastAccessed + "\r\n";
   s += "Date Last Modified: " + f.DateLastModified;

   return(s);
}
```

Continued

Listing 21-1 *(continued)*

```
function GetSize(filePath)
{
  var fs, f, s;

  fs = new ActiveXObject("Scripting.FileSystemObject");
  f = fs.GetFolder(filePath);

  if (fs.FolderExists(filePath))
    f = fs.GetFolder(filePath);
  else if (fs.FileExists(filePath))
    f = fs.GetFile(filePath);

  s = f.size;

  return(s);
}

function GetType(filePath)
{
  var fs, f, s;

  fs = new ActiveXObject("Scripting.FileSystemObject");
  f = fs.GetFolder(filePath);

  if (fs.FolderExists(filePath))
    f = fs.GetFolder(filePath);
  else if (fs.FileExists(filePath))
    f = fs.GetFile(filePath);

  s = f.type;

  return(s);
}

function CheckParentFolder(filePath)
{
  var fs, s = "";

  fs = new ActiveXObject("Scripting.FileSystemObject");
  s += fs.GetParentFolderName(filePath);

  return(s);
}

function SetArchiveAttribute(folderName)
{
  var fs, f, fc, s;
```

```
  fs = new ActiveXObject("Scripting.FileSystemObject");
  f = fs.GetFolder(folderName);
  fc = new Enumerator(f.Files);
  s = "";

  for (; !fc.atEnd(); fc.moveNext())
  {
    theFile = fs.GetFile(fc.item());

    if (!(theFile.attributes && 32))
   {
    theFile.attributes = theFile.attributes + 32;
    }


  }
  return("Finished!");
}

function ClearArchiveAttribute(folderName)
{
  var fs, f, fc, s;

  fs = new ActiveXObject("Scripting.FileSystemObject");
  f = fs.GetFolder(folderName);
  fc = new Enumerator(f.Files);
  s = "";

  for (; !fc.atEnd(); fc.moveNext())
  {

    theFile = fs.GetFile(fc.item());

    if (theFile.attributes && 32)
   {
    theFile.attributes = theFile.attributes - 32;
    }


  }
  return("Finished!");
}

function SetReadOnly(folderName)
{
  var fs, f, fc, s;

  fs = new ActiveXObject("Scripting.FileSystemObject");
  f = fs.GetFolder(folderName);
  fc = new Enumerator(f.Files);
  s = "";
```

Continued

Listing 21-1 *(continued)*

```
  for (; !fc.atEnd(); fc.moveNext())
  {
    theFile = fs.GetFile(fc.item());

    theFile.attributes = 1;
  }
  return("Finished!");
}


function ClearReadOnly(folderName)
{
  var fs, f, fc, s;

  fs = new ActiveXObject("Scripting.FileSystemObject");
  f = fs.GetFolder(folderName);
  fc = new Enumerator(f.Files);
  s = "";

  for (; !fc.atEnd(); fc.moveNext())
  {
    theFile = fs.GetFile(fc.item());

    theFile.attributes = 0;
  }
  return("Finished!");
}

function SetHiddenSystem(folderName)
{
  var fs, f, fc, s;

  fs = new ActiveXObject("Scripting.FileSystemObject");
  f = fs.GetFolder(folderName);
  fc = new Enumerator(f.Files);
  s = "";

  for (; !fc.atEnd(); fc.moveNext())
  {
    theFile = fs.GetFile(fc.item());

    theFile.attributes = 6;

  }
  return("Finished!");
}
```

```
function SetNormal(folderName)
{
  var fs, f, fc, s;

  fs = new ActiveXObject("Scripting.FileSystemObject");
  f = fs.GetFolder(folderName);
  fc = new Enumerator(f.Files);
  s = "";

  for (; !fc.atEnd(); fc.moveNext())
  {
    theFile = fs.GetFile(fc.item());

    theFile.attributes = 0;
  }
  return("Finished!");
}

function ListSpecialFolders(sep)
{
  var s;

  s = "";
  s += "========================================================" + sep;
  s += "Special Folders List" + sep;

  s += "               Windows 2000 Scripting Bible" + sep;
  s += "               by William R. Stanek" + sep;
  s += "========================================================" + sep;
  s += "AllUsersDesktop:   Desktop shortcuts for all users." + sep;
  s += "AllUsersPrograms:  Programs menu options for all users." + sep;
  s += "AllUsersStartMenu: Start menu options for all users." + sep;
  s += "AllUsersStartup:   Startup applications for all users." + sep;
  s += "Desktop:           Desktop shortcuts for the current user." + sep;
  s += "Favorites:         Favorites menu shortcuts for the current user." + sep;
  s += "Fonts:             Fonts folder shortcuts for the current user." + sep;
  s += "MyDocuments:       My Documents menu shortcuts for the current user." +
sep;
  s += "NetHood:           Network Neighborhood shortcuts for the current user." +
sep;
  s += "Printers:          Printers folder shortcuts for the current user." + sep;
  s += "Programs:          Programs menu options for the current user." + sep;
  s += "Recent:            Recently used document shortcuts for the current user."
+ sep;
  s += "SendTo:            SendTo menu shortcuts for the current user." + sep;
  s += "StartMenu:         Start menu shortcuts for the current user." + sep;
  s += "Startup:           Startup applications for the current user." + sep;
  s += "Templates:         Templates folder shortcuts for the current user." + sep;
  s += "========================================================" + sep;
```

Continued

Listing 21-1 *(continued)*

```javascript
  return(s);
}

function NewShortcut(sfolder, sname, stype, starget)
{
  var ws = WScript.CreateObject("WScript.Shell");

  pmenu = ws.SpecialFolders(sfolder);

  var scut = ws.CreateShortcut(pmenu + "\\" + sname + "." + stype);
  scut.TargetPath = starget;

  scut.Save();
}

function CheckMenu(mname)
{
  var fs, f, fc, s;
  fs = new ActiveXObject("Scripting.FileSystemObject");
  var ws = WScript.CreateObject ("WScript.Shell")
  smenu = ws.SpecialFolders(mname)

  f = fs.GetFolder(smenu);
  fc = new Enumerator(f.Files);
  s = "";
  for (; !fc.atEnd(); fc.moveNext())
  {
    theFile = fs.GetFile(fc.item());
    s += theFile + "\r\n"
  }
  return (s)
}

function CheckMenu2(mname)
{
  var fs, f, fc, s;

  var ws = WScript.CreateObject("WScript.Shell");
  smenu = ws.SpecialFolders(mname);

  fs = new ActiveXObject("Scripting.FileSystemObject");
  f = fs.GetFolder(smenu);
  fc = new Enumerator(f.Files);
  s = "";

  for (; !fc.atEnd(); fc.moveNext())
  {
   f1 = fs.GetFile(fc.item());
```

```
    s += fl.name + "\r\n"
    }
    return (s)
}

function NewMenu(sfolder, mname)
{

  var s;
  s = "False"

  var ws = WScript.CreateObject("WScript.Shell");
  pmenu = ws.SpecialFolders(sfolder);

  if (sfolder == "AllUsersPrograms" || sfolder == "AllUsersStart" || sfolder ==
"Programs" || sfolder == "StartMenu") {

    fs = new ActiveXObject("Scripting.FileSystemObject");
    var foldr = fs.CreateFolder(pmenu + "\\" + mname)
    s = "True"

  }
  return(s)
}

function AddMenuOption(sfolder, mname, sname, stype, starget)
{
  var ws = WScript.CreateObject("WScript.Shell");
  pmenu = ws.SpecialFolders(sfolder);

  var scut = ws.CreateShortcut(pmenu + "\\" + mname + "\\" + sname + "." + stype);
  scut.TargetPath = starget;

  scut.Save()
}

function CopyFile2Desktop(filePath)
{
  var fs, test;

  var ws = WScript.CreateObject("WScript.Shell");
  pmenu = ws.SpecialFolders("Desktop");

  fs = new ActiveXObject("Scripting.FileSystemObject");
  fs.CopyFile(filePath, pmenu + "\\");
}
```

Continued

Listing 21-1 *(continued)*

```
function MoveFile2Desktop(filePath)
{
  var ws = WScript.CreateObject("WScript.Shell");
  pmenu = ws.SpecialFolders("Desktop");

  fs = new ActiveXObject("Scripting.FileSystemObject");
  fs.MoveFile(filePath, pmenu + "\\");
}

function CopyFolder2Desktop(filePath)
{
  var fs, test;

  var ws = WScript.CreateObject("WScript.Shell");
  pmenu = ws.SpecialFolders("Desktop");

  fs = new ActiveXObject("Scripting.FileSystemObject");
  fs.CopyFolder(filePath, pmenu + "\\");
}

function MoveFolder2Desktop(filePath)
{
  var ws = WScript.CreateObject("WScript.Shell");
  pmenu = ws.SpecialFolders("Desktop");

  fs = new ActiveXObject("Scripting.FileSystemObject");
  fs.MoveFolder(filePath, pmenu + "\\");
}


function NewFile(filePath)
{
  var fs, s = filePath;
  fs = new ActiveXObject("Scripting.FileSystemObject");

  if (!fs.FileExists(filePath)) {
    var theFile = fs.CreateTextFile(filePath);
    s += " created."
  } else
    s += " already exists.";

  return(s);
}

function NewFolder(folderPath)
{
  var fs, s = folderPath;
  fs = new ActiveXObject("Scripting.FileSystemObject");

  if (!fs.FolderExists(folderPath)) {
```

```
      var foldr = fs.CreateFolder(folderPath);
      s += " created."
   } else
      s += " already exists.";

   return(s);
}

function AddDesktop(sname,trgt)
{

var ws = WScript.CreateObject ("WScript.Shell")
dsktop = ws.SpecialFolders("Desktop")

var scut = ws.CreateShortcut (dsktop + "\\" + sname + ".lnk")
scut.TargetPath = trgt
scut.Save()

}

function AddDesktopURL(sname,trgt)
{

var ws = WScript.CreateObject ("WScript.Shell")
dsktop = ws.SpecialFolders("Desktop")

var scut = ws.CreateShortcut (dsktop + "\\" + sname + ".URL")
scut.TargetPath = trgt
scut.Save()

}

function AddStartMenu(sname,trgt)
{

var ws = WScript.CreateObject ("WScript.Shell")
smenu = ws.SpecialFolders("StartMenu")
var scut = ws.CreateShortcut (smenu + "\\" + sname + ".lnk")
scut.TargetPath = trgt
scut.Save()

}

function AddStartMenuURL(sname,trgt)
{

var ws = WScript.CreateObject ("WScript.Shell")
smenu = ws.SpecialFolders("StartMenu")
var scut = ws.CreateShortcut (smenu + "\\" + sname + ".URL")
scut.TargetPath = trgt
scut.Save()
```

Continued

Listing 21-1 *(continued)*

```
}

function DeleteShortcut(sfolder, sname)
{
  var ws = WScript.CreateObject("WScript.Shell");
  smenu = ws.SpecialFolders(sfolder);

  fs = new ActiveXObject("Scripting.FileSystemObject");
  f = fs.GetFile(smenu + "\\" + sname);

  f.Delete();
}

function DeleteFile(filePath)
{
  var fs;
  fs = new ActiveXObject("Scripting.FileSystemObject");

  fs.DeleteFile(filePath);
}

function DeleteFolder(folderPath)
{
  var fs;
  fs = new ActiveXObject("Scripting.FileSystemObject");

  fs.DeleteFolder(folderPath);
}
```

Using the File-System Utility Library

The file-system utility library has many functions that you can call from other scripts. Most of the functions expect to be passed a folder path, such as:

```
D:\\Working
```

or a file path, such as:

```
D:\\working\\data.txt
```

There are a few exceptions, such as GetFolderContents, GetSubFolders, and GetFiles, that expect additional parameters.

Using GetSubFolders, GetFiles, and GetFolderContents

The GetSubFolders and GetFiles functions return a list of subfolders or files in the referenced folder. These functions expect to be passed a folder path and a character to display as a separator. This separator can be a space, a comma, or a special formatting character, such as \r\n for carriage return and line feed. Here's an example of how you can call GetFiles:

```
theList = GetFiles("C:\\WinnT", "\r\n")
```

If you use a .ws file, you don't have to place the GetFiles function in your script. Instead, you can handle the function like a library call. With a .wsaf file, you can use GetFiles as follows:

```
<Job ID="CreateFolders">
  <Script LANGUAGE="JScript" SRC="filesystemlib.js" />
  <Script LANGUAGE="JScript">
          theList = GetFiles("C:\\WinnT", "\r\n")
          WScript.Echo(theList)
  </Script>
</Job>
```

The GetFolderContents returns a list of all subfolders and files in the referenced folder. The function does this by obtaining the output of both GetSubFolders and GetFiles, and then formatting the output using the separator you've specified, such as:

```
Folders:
=========================
E:\working\data1
E:\working\data2
E:\working\data3
E:\working\samples
E:\working\data_back

Files:
=========================
E:\working\document1.txt
E:\working\document2.txt
E:\working\document3.txt
E:\working\document4.txt
E:\working\document5.txt
E:\working\document6.txt
```

Using CheckExists

You can use the CheckExists function to determine if a resource that you want to work with exists. The function expects to be passed a file or folder path, and returns True if the resource exists and False otherwise. An interesting feature of this function is the If ... Else If construct that tests whether the path you've supplied references a folder of a file:

```
if (fs.FolderExists(filePath))
    s = "True";
else if (fs.FileExists(filePath))
    s = "True";
```

Here, you test for the existence of the file path as a folder and as a file. The If ... Else If construct allows a single function to work with files and folders, and it is used by many other functions in the system utility library, including GetInfo, GetSize, and GetType.

Using GetInfo, GetSize, and GetType

The GetInfo function expects to be passed a file or folder path, and returns summary information for the file or folder. This information is placed on separate lines using \r\n and includes:

✦ File or folder name

✦ File or folder path

✦ Date created

✦ Date last accessed

✦ Date last modified

The GetSize and GetType functions also return file or folder information. GetSize returns the byte size of the file or folder. GetType returns the file or folder type. A similar function is CheckParentFolder. This function returns the name of the parent folder for the specified resource.

Setting and clearing file attributes

The utility library also has functions for working with file attributes. These functions are:

✦ SetReadOnly—Sets the read-only attribute

✦ ClearReadOnly—Clears the read-only attribute

✦ `SetArchiveAttribute`—Sets the archive attribute

✦ `ClearArchiveAttribute`—Clears the archive attribute

✦ `SetHiddenSystem`—Sets the hidden and system attributes

✦ `SetNormalAttribute`—Clears all other attributes and sets the normal attribute

These functions set the attributes on all files in a referenced folder, but they do not go through subfolders. Keep in mind that you can't change the archive attribute on read-only files. Because of this, you may want to call `ClearReadOnly` before calling `SetArchiveAttribute` or `ClearArchiveAttribute`.

You can set the read-only attribute on all files in the D:\working folder as follows:

```
SetReadOnly("D:\\Working")
```

If you use a .wsaf file, you don't have to place the `SetReadOnly` function in your script. Instead, you can handle the function like a library call, such as:

```
<Job ID="CreateFolders">
  <Script LANGUAGE="JScript" SRC="adminlib.js" />
  <Script LANGUAGE="JScript">
          ret = SetReadOnly("D:\\Working")
          WScript.Echo(ret)
  </Script>
</Job>
```

The set and clear functions use an `Enumerator` object to move through each file in the referenced folder. To obtain a file object, the function calls `GetFile` with the name of the current item in the enumerator list. The `file` object is then used to set or clear the appropriate attribute, such as:

```
theFile = fs.GetFile(fc.item());
if (theFile.attributes && 32)
  {
    theFile.attributes = theFile.attributes - 32;
  }
```

Working with special folders, shortcuts, and menus

You can use the `ListSpecialFolders` function to display a formatted list of all the special folders available. This is useful so script users can obtain a list of special folders that they may want to work with. For example, if you prompt users to enter the name of a special folder to manage and they don't know the folder name, they can leave it blank or type "?" to obtain a list of special folders.

The function expects to be passed a line separator, which could be \r\n for output to the command line, a dialog box, or HTML tags, such as <BR>, for display in a browser window. With \r\n, the output of the function looks like this:

```
============================================================
Special Folders List
                    Windows 2000 Scripting Bible
                    by William R. Stanek
============================================================
AllUsersDesktop:     Desktop shortcuts for all users.
AllUsersPrograms:    Programs menu options for all users.
AllUsersStartMenu:   Start menu options for all users.
AllUsersStartup:     Startup applications for all users.
Desktop:             Desktop shortcuts for the current user.
Favorites:           Favorites menu shortcuts for the current
                     user.
Fonts:               Fonts folder shortcuts for the current
                     user.
MyDocuments:         My Documents menu shortcuts for the current
                     user.
NetHood:             Network Neighborhood shortcuts for the
                     current user.
Printers:            Printers folder shortcuts for the current
                     user.
Programs:            Programs menu options for the current user.
Recent:              Recently used document shortcuts for the
                     current user.
SendTo:              SendTo menu shortcuts for the current user.
StartMenu:           Start menu shortcuts for the current user.
Startup:             Startup applications for the current user.
Templates:           Templates folder shortcuts for the current
                     user.
============================================================
```

Once you know which special folder you want to work with, you can add items to the special folder using NewShortcut. The NewShortcut function can be used to create link and URL shortcuts. It can also be used to add start items, menu options, and desktop links. When you use this function, you must pass in the following parameters:

✦ sfolder — The name of the special folder to use, such as Programs

✦ sname — The name of the shortcut, such as My Home Page

✦ stype — The type of the shortcut; either LNK or URL

✦ starget — The target of the shortcut, such as http://www.tvpress.com

The following example creates a URL shortcut on the Programs menu":

```
NewShortcut("Programs", "My Home Page", "URL",
"http://www.tvpress.com/")
```

Other useful functions for working with menus and menu options are NewMenu and AddMenuOption. You use NewMenu to create a new menu and AddMenuOption to add options to the menu.

The NewMenu function expects to be passed the name of a special folder that represents one of the following menus:

✦ AllUsersPrograms

✦ AllUsersStart

✦ Programs

✦ StartMenu

It also expects to be passed the name of the menu to create. With this in mind, you could call NewMenu as follows:

```
NewMenu ("Programs", "Quick Access")
```

You can then use the AddMenuOption function to add options to this menu. You could also use this function to add options to any existing menus, provided they are submenus of Programs or Start. The AddMenuOption function expects to be passed the following arguments:

✦ sfolder — The name of the special folder to use, such as Programs

✦ mname — The name of the submenu to work with, such as Quick Access

✦ sname — The name of the shortcut, such as My Home Page

✦ stype — The type of the shortcut; either LNK or URL

✦ starget — The target of the shortcut, such as http://www.tvpress.com

An example of calling this function follows:

```
AddMenuOption ("Programs", "Quick Access", "My Home Page",
"URL", "http://www.tvpress.com")
```

Managing menu options

The CheckMenu and CheckMenu2 functions are designed to help you track and manage menu options. You can pass the function the name of a special menu and the function returns a list of all options assigned through this menu. The CheckMenu function returns the full file path to the menu options, such as:

```
F:\Documents and Settings\Administrator.ZETA\Start
Menu\Programs\Internet Explorer.lnk
```

```
F:\Documents and Settings\Administrator.ZETA\Start
Menu\Programs\My Home Page.URL

F:\Documents and Settings\Administrator.ZETA\Start
Menu\Programs\Outlook Express.lnk
```

The `CheckMenu2` function returns the option name only, such as:

```
Internet Explorer.lnk
My Home Page.URL
Outlook Express.lnk
```

You can use these functions in several ways. If you are trying to determine whether a particular option is assigned to the current user or all users, you can call `CheckMenu` or `CheckMenu2` once with a current user menu and a second time with an all users menus, such as:

```
WScript.Echo(CheckMenu(StartMenu))
WScript.Echo("=================")
WScript.Echo(CheckMenu(AllUsersStartMenu))
```

Because the `CheckMenu` function returns the complete file path to the options, you can use the function to delete menu options, as well. To see how, let's work through an example. Listing 21-2 obtains a list of options on the Programs menu for the current user and all users on the system. These options are written to a text file (menuoptions.txt). The script uses `WriteChar` from iolib.js and `CheckMenu` from filesystemlib.js.

Listing 21-2: **Getting all menu options**

getoptions.wsaf

```
<Job ID="GetMenuOptions">
  <Script LANGUAGE="JScript" SRC="iolib.js" />
  <Script LANGUAGE="JScript" SRC="filesystemlib.js" />

  <Script LANGUAGE="VBScript">
     theOptions = CheckMenu("Programs")
     ret = WriteChar("d:\\menuoptions.txt", theOptions)
     theOptions = CheckMenu("AllUsersPrograms")
     ret = WriteChar("d:\\menuoptions.txt", theOptions)
  </Script>
</Job>
```

menuoptions.txt

```
D:\WINNT\Profiles\All Users\Start Menu\Programs\Access.lnk
D:\WINNT\Profiles\All Users\Start Menu\Programs\Excel.lnk
D:\WINNT\Profiles\All Users\Start Menu\Programs\FrontPage.lnk
D:\WINNT\Profiles\All Users\Start Menu\Programs\PowerPoint.lnk
D:\WINNT\Profiles\All Users\Start Menu\Programs\Word.lnk
D:\WINNT\Profiles\All Users\Start Menu\Programs\PhotoDraw.lnk
D:\WINNT\Profiles\All Users\Start Menu\Programs\Web Script.LNK
D:\WINNT\Profiles\All Users\Start Menu\Programs\Web Script2.LNK
D:\WINNT\Profiles\All Users\Start Menu\Programs\Web Script3.LNK
```

You then edit the menuoptions.txt file and remove menu options that you don't want to keep. Afterward, you run listing 21-3 to remove the options from the menu. The script uses `ReadLineN` from iolib.js and `DeleteFile` from filesystemlib.js.

Listing 21-3: **Deleting multiple menu options**

deleteoptions.wsaf

```
<Job ID="DeleteOptions">
  <Script LANGUAGE="JScript" SRC="adminlib.js" />
  <Script LANGUAGE="JScript" SRC="filelib.js" />
  <Script LANGUAGE="VBScript">
  Dim numLines, theFile
  numLines = 4

  theFile = "d:\menuoptions.txt"

  For i = 1 to numLines Step 1

    theShortcut = ReadLineN(theFile, i)
    ret = DeleteFile(theShortcut)

  Next
  </Script>
</Job>
```

Note   If you use this script, be sure to update the `numLines` variable so that it reflects the actual number of lines in the menuoptions.txt file.

Adding to the desktop and Start menu

To quickly add shortcuts to the desktop or Start menu for the current user, use the `AddDesktop`, `AddDesktopURL`, `AddStartMenu`, and `AddStartMenuURL` functions. While `AddDesktop` and `AddStartMenu` create link shortcuts, `AddDesktopURL` and `AddStartMenuURL` create URL shortcuts. These functions accept the same parameters: the name of the shortcut (without the .lnk or .url extension) and the target path of the shortcut.

Listing 21-4 shows how you can use these functions in order to add multiple desktop and menu shortcuts. The listing uses the file utility library, as well as the network resource library. The file options.txt contains the shortcuts being added to the desktop. The file adesktop.ws contains a batch script, with the main script written in VBScript.

Listing 21-4: **Adding multiple shortcuts**

options.txt

```
WinScripting Home
http://www.tvpress.com/winscripting/
WinScripting Microsoft
http://msdn.microsoft.com/scripting/
WinScripting for IIS 5.0
http://msdn.microsoft.com/library/sdkdoc/iisref/aore2xpu.htm
```

adesktop.wsaf

```
<Job ID="AddShortcuts">
  <Script LANGUAGE="JScript" SRC="iolib.js" />
  <Script LANGUAGE="JScript" SRC="filesystemlib.js" />

  <Script LANGUAGE="VBScript">
  Dim numLines, theFile
  numLines = 6

  theFile = "D:\datatest.txt"

  For i = 1 to numLines Step 2

    theShortcut = ReadLineN(theFile, i)
    theTarget = ReadLineN(theFile, i+1)
    ret = AddDesktopURL(theShortcut, theTarget)

  Next
  </Script>
</Job>
```

Because this is the first time we've called JScript from VBScript via the utility libraries, let's take a quick look at some key concepts. As the script shows, when you call a JScript function that uses file paths, you don't need to use the JScript syntax. File paths are automatically converted for you, and this is why you can set the file path as:

```
D:\datatest.txt
```

However, you do have to use a slightly different syntax when calling functions that don't return values. The script uses:

```
ret = AddDesktopURL(theShortcut, theTarget)
```

rather than:

```
AddDesktopURL(theShortcut, theTarget)
```

Even though the `AddDesktopURL` function doesn't return a value, you can call the function as though it does return a value. If you don't do this, VBScript thinks the function is a subroutine, and you cannot use parentheses when calling a subroutine.

An interesting feature of the script is the use of a `For Next` loop to read from the file two lines at a time. In the first iteration of the `For` loop, lines 1 and 2 are read from the options.txt file. The value of line 1 is assigned as the shortcut name. The value of line 2 is assigned as the target path. Then the `AddDesktopURL` function is called with these values. In the second iteration of the `For` loop, lines 3 and 4 are read from the options.txt file, and so on.

Other useful desktop functions are `CopyFile2Desktop` and `MoveFile2Desktop`. These functions expect to be passed a file path and then for the file to be either copied or moved to the Windows desktop. You can move a file to the desktop as follows:

```
MoveFile2Desktop("D:\\Working\\document1.txt")
```

Two functions with similar usage are `CopyFolder2Desktop` and `MoveFolder2 Desktop`. These functions expect to be passed a folder path and then for the folder to be either copied or moved to the Windows desktop. You can copy a folder to the desktop as follows:

```
MoveFile2Desktop("D:\\Working\\Data")
```

Using NewFolder and NewFile

You can use the `NewFolder` function to create a new folder, provided the folder doesn't already exist. If you wanted to create a folder at D:\Working\Data, you could use the following call:

```
WScript.Echo(NewFolder("D:\\working\\data"))
```

The value returned from `NewFolder` would either be:

```
D:\working\data created.
```

or

```
D:\working\data already exists.
```

The `NewFile` function can be used in much the same way. The key difference is that you pass `NewFile` the file path you want to create, instead of a folder path, such as:

```
WScript.Echo(NewFile("D:\\working\\data\\document1.txt"))
```

Using DeleteFile, DeleteFolder, and DeleteShortcut

The `DeleteFile` and `DeleteFolder` functions are used to delete files and folders, respectively. You can use wildcards when calling these functions, such as:

```
DeleteFile("D:\\working\\*.txt")
```

 Caution   Be careful when using the delete functions. Never pass a reference to a root folder, such as C:\.

You use `DeleteShortcut` to delete shortcuts. The function expects to be passed the name of a special folder containing the shortcut and the full name of the shortcut. For example, you could delete a shortcut called My Home Page from the Programs menu as follows:

```
DeleteShortcut("Programs", "\My Home Page.URL")
```

If the shortcut is on a submenu, be sure to enter the submenu path as part of the shortcut name, such as:

```
DeleteShortcut("Programs", "Quick Access\\My Home Page.URL")
```

Summary

This chapter developed a utility library for working with file systems. You can call the functions of this library from your own scripts at anytime. The next chapter provides a utility library for handling input and output.

✦   ✦   ✦

◆   ◆   ◆   ◆

In This Chapter

Creating the I/O
utility library

Using the I/O utility
library

Working with library
methods

◆   ◆   ◆   ◆

Library:
I/O Utilities

The I/O utility library provides functions for handling input and output. With these functions, you'll be able to read files, write files, obtain input, and display output. Through batch script (.WS) files, you can access these utility functions in any of your scripts. The sections that follow show the source for the library, as well as how the library can be used.

Examining the I/O Utility Library

The code for the I/O utility library is shown as Listing 22-1. When using this script from JScript, be sure to pass path information in JScript format with double slashes as folder separators. With other scripting languages, you normally don't have to use double slashes.

Listing 22-1: **I/O utility library**

iolib.js

```
// ************************
// Script: I/O Utility Library
// Version: 0.9.5
// Creation Date: 09/20/1999
// Last Modified: 02/15/2000
// Author: William R. Stanek
// Email: winscripting@tvpress.com
// ************************
// Description: Provides a utility library for reading
//              and writing files.
// ************************
// Copyright (c) 1999-2000 William R. Stanek
// You have a royalty-free right to use these applications,
// provided that you give credit to the author AND agree that
```

Continued

Listing 22-1 *(continued)*

```
// the author has no warranty, obligations or liability for
// any of these library functions.
// ************************

function DisplayConsolePrompt(promptText)
{

   lf = "\r\n"
   WScript.Echo(promptText + lf)

   r = WScript.StdIn.ReadLine()

   return(r)
}

function ReadFromKeyboard(scriptname, promptText)
{

   lf = "\r\n"
   WScript.Echo("=======================================" + lf)
   WScript.Echo(scriptname + lf)
   WScript.Echo("=======================================" + lf)

   WScript.Echo(promptText + lf)

   r = WScript.StdIn.ReadLine()

   return(r)
}

function ReadFile(theFile)
{
   var fs, f, r;
   var ForReading = 1;

   fs = new ActiveXObject("Scripting.FileSystemObject");
   f = fs.OpenTextFile(theFile, ForReading);
   r = f.ReadAll();

   return(r);
}

function ReadLineN(theFile,n)
{
   var fs, f, r;
   var ForReading = 1;

   n--
```

```
    fs = new ActiveXObject("Scripting.FileSystemObject");
    f = fs.OpenTextFile(theFile, ForReading);

    for (a = 0; a < n; a++) {
     if (!f.AtEndOfStream) {
      f.SkipLine()
      }
     }
    r =  f.ReadLine();

    return(r);
}

function ReadCharN(theFile,s,n)
{
   var fs, f, r;
   var ForReading = 1;

   fs = new ActiveXObject("Scripting.FileSystemObject");
   f = fs.OpenTextFile(theFile, ForReading);

   f.Skip(s);
   r =  f.Read(n);

   return(r);
}

function WriteLine(theFile,theLine)
{
   var fs, f;
   var ForWriting = 2, ForAppending = 8;

   fs = new ActiveXObject("Scripting.FileSystemObject")

   if (fs.FileExists(theFile))
    var f = fs.OpenTextFile (theFile, ForAppending)
   else
    var f = fs.OpenTextFile (theFile, ForWriting, "True")

   f.WriteLine(theLine);
   f.Close();
}

function WriteChar(theFile,theString)
{
   var fs, f;
   var ForWriting = 2, ForAppending = 8;

   fs = new ActiveXObject("Scripting.FileSystemObject")

   if (fs.FileExists(theFile))
    var f = fs.OpenTextFile (theFile, ForAppending)
```

Continued

Listing 22-1 *(continued)*

```javascript
    else
     var f = fs.OpenTextFile (theFile, ForWriting, "True")

    f.Write(theString);
    f.Close();
}

function DisplayDialog(text, timeout, title, buttonType)
{
    var answ;

    if (timeout == null)
      timeout = 10
    if (title == null)
      title = "Input Required"
    if (buttonType == null)
      buttonType = 3

    var w = WScript.CreateObject("WScript.Shell");
    answ = w.Popup(text, timeout, title, buttonType)
    return(answ)
}

function GetResponse(text, timeout, title, buttonType)
{
    var s, answer;

    answer = DisplayDialog(text, timeout, title, buttonType)

    s = "";

    switch (answer) {
     case 1 :
       s = "ok";
       break;

     case 2 :
       s = "cancel";
       break;

     case 3 :
       s = "abort";
       break;

     case 4 :
       s = "retry";
       break;

     case 5 :
       s = "ignore";
       break;
```

```
    case 6 :
      s = "yes";
      break;

    case 7 :
      s = "no";
      break;

    default :
      s = "none"
      break
      }

    return(s)
}

function GetErrorInfo(e, sep)
{

   var s;
   s = "";

   s += "Error Type:    " + e + sep
   s += "Description: " + e.description + sep;
   s += "Error Code:    "
   s += e.number & 0xFFFF;
   s += sep;

   return(s)
}

function WriteEvent(status)
{
   var s;
   s = ""

   var ws = WScript.CreateObject("WScript.Shell")

   if (status == 0) {
    //successful execution
    s = WScript.ScriptName + " completed successfully."
    ws.LogEvent(0, s)
    }
    else {
    //failed execution
    s = WScript.ScriptName + " did not execute properly."
    s += "\r\n " + WScript.ScriptFullName
    s += "\r\n " + WScript.FullName
    ws.LogEvent(1, s)
    }

}
```

Using the I/O Utility Library

As you examined the source code, you probably noted two general types of functions: those for handling file I/O and those for handling other types of I/O tasks. Let's look at the file I/O functions first and then look at the other I/O functions.

Handling file I/O with the utility library

File I/O tasks make several assumptions. First of all, text files are assumed to be in the default format for the system, which is normally ASCII text. Most of the file I/O functions also expect to be passed a file path, such as:

```
D:\\working\\document1.txt
```

One of the most basic utility functions is `ReadFile`. This function reads an entire file and returns the contents for you to work with. You could use `ReadFile` to display the contents of a file in a pop-up dialog as follows:

```
var w = WScript.CreateObject("WScript.Shell");
w.Popup (ReadFile("D:\\document1.txt"))
```

If you use a .WS file, you don't have to place the `ReadFile` function in your script. Instead, you can handle the function like a library call. With a .WSF file, you could use `ReadFile` as follows:

```
<Job ID="ReadFile">
  <Script LANGUAGE="JScript" SRC="filelib.js" />
  <Script LANGUAGE="JScript">
          theFile = ReadFile("D:\\data.txt")
          WScript.Echo(theFile)
  </Script>
</Job>
```

Other functions in the library can be used in similar ways, as well. Use the `ReadLineN` function to read a specific line in a file, such as the fifth line. If you want to read the fifth line in the file, pass in the file name and then the integer value 5, such as:

```
theLine = ReadLineN("D:\\document.txt",5)
```

The `ReadLineN` function skips four lines in the file and then reads the fifth line. The contents of this line are then returned. To read the first line in the file, you could pass in 1 as the line parameter, such as:

```
theLine = ReadLineN("D:\\document1.txt",1)
```

Note Keep in mind that you cannot try to read a line that doesn't exist. For example, if the file contains 12 lines, you can't try to read the 14th line. If you do, no value is returned.

The `ReadCharN` function is used to read a specific group of characters in a file. For example, if you know that the file contains fixed-length records with each record having 50 characters, you could read in the third record by telling `ReadCharN` to skip 100 characters and then read 50 characters, such as:

```
theRecord = ReadLineN("D:\\data.txt",100,50)
```

The utility library also provides functions for writing to files. The `WriteLine` function writes a line to a file. The `WriteChar` function writes a block of characters to a file. You can use these functions to write onto new files or to append onto existing files. To ensure that existing files are appended, rather then overwritten, the functions make use of the following `If Else` construct:

```
if (fs.FileExists(theFile))
    var f = fs.OpenTextFile (theFile, ForAppending)
else
    var f = fs.OpenTextFile (theFile, ForWriting, "True")
```

Again, this conditional test checks for a file's existence. If the file exists, the file is opened in `ForAppending` mode. Otherwise, the file is opened in `ForWriting` mode. You could use the `WriteLine` function as follows:

```
theFile = "D:\\mydata.txt"
theLine = "William Stanek, wrstane, wrs@tvpress.com, x7789"
WriteLine(theFile,theLine)
```

In a .wsc file you could use `WriteLine` in much the same way:

```
<Job ID="WriteFile">
  <Script LANGUAGE="JScript" SRC="filelib.js" />
  <Script LANGUAGE="JScript">
    theFile = "D:\\mydata.txt"
    theLine = "William Stanek, wrstane, wrs@tvpress.com, x7789"
    WriteLine(theFile,theLine)
  </Script>
</Job>
```

Handling other I/O tasks with the utility library

The I/O utility library also provides functions for handling essential I/O tasks. Two key functions are `DisplayConsolePrompt` and `ReadFromKeyboard`. When called from a script using the CScript host, the `DisplayConsolePrompt` function displays a message at the command prompt and waits for the user to enter a line of information. The function then returns the user's response to the caller. You could use this function anytime you need to obtain input from a user. If you wanted the user to enter the name of a remote system to work with, you could call `DisplayConsolePrompt` like this:

```
response = DisplayConsolePrompt("Please Enter Remote System
Name:")
```

The `ReadFromKeyboard` function takes this idea a bit further. Not only can you supply a prompt to display, but you can also enter banner text to display to the user. For example, if you called `ReadFromKeyboard` as follows:

```
response = ReadFromKeyboard("File Administration Script",
"Please Enter Remote System Name:")
```

the user would see the following output at the command prompt:

```
=========================================

File Administration Script

=========================================

Please Enter Remote System Name:
```

If you would rather display a pop-up dialog, you can use the `DisplayDialog` function, instead. This function provides a quick and easy way to get input from users through pop-up dialogs. To see how this works, you'll need to give the function a test run. Try calling `DisplayDialog` as follows:

```
answ = DisplayDialog("Shall We Continue?")
```

You should see a pop-up dialog with the following default settings:

- ✦ Title set to "Input Required"
- ✦ Timeout set to ten seconds
- ✦ Button type set to Yes/No/Cancel

If necessary, you can override the default settings. Simply enter the parameters you'd like to set, such as:

```
answ = DisplayDialog("Shall We Continue?", 20, "Continue Y/N?")
```

Although the `DisplayDialog` function doesn't analyze the user response, the `GetResponse` function does. Using `GetResponse`, you can determine which button a user pressed and then handle the response appropriately. The text values returned by `GetResponse` are:

✦ ok

✦ cancel

✦ abort

✦ retry

✦ ignore

✦ yes

✦ no

✦ none

You can call `GetResponse` just as you call `DisplayDialog`, but you can do a bit more with the response — and you don't need to worry about which numeric values equate to which answer types. Here's an example:

```
answ = GetResponse("Shall We Continue?")

if (answ = "yes") {
 //answered yes; handle response
} else
 //answered no or didn't respond; handle response
}
```

When you want to handle or track problems with scripts, you'll find that the `GetErrorInfo` and `WriteEvent` functions are very useful. The `GetErrorInfo` function can be used to examine errors that occur during execution, and it normally is used with try catch statements, such as:

```
try {
   x = data
}
catch(e) {
   WScript.Echo(GetErrorInfo(e, "\r\n"))
}
```

If the `data` variable isn't defined, `GetErrorInfo` returns the following results:

```
Error Type:   [object Error]
Description: 'data' is undefined
Error Code:   5009
```

These results could then be displayed to the current user.

The `WriteEvent` function writes events to the Application Log on the local system. The type of event written depends on how a status flag is set when the function is called. If the status is set to 0, the function writes an informational event with the description:

```
ScriptName completed successfully.
```

such as:

```
myscript.ws completed successfully.
```

If the status is set to 1, the function writes an error event with the following description:

```
ScriptName completed successfully.
 ScriptPath
 WSHPath
```

such as:

```
myscript.ws did not execute properly.
 E:\scripts\myscript.ws
 F:\WIN2000\system32\cscript.exe
```

You could use `WriteEvent` in a script as follows:

```
//script body here using a status flag
//to track success or failure

WriteEvent(status)
```

Summary

This chapter developed a utility library for handling input and output. You can call the functions of this library from your own scripts at anytime. The next chapter discusses a network resource library.

✦   ✦   ✦

Library: Network Resource Utilities

The network resource library provides functions for working with drives, network shares, services, open resources, and user sessions. The sections that follow show the source for the script, as well as how the script can be used.

Examining the Network Resource Utility Library

Listing 23-1 shows the source code for the network resource library. Key features implemented in this library are discussed in Chapters 9, 17, and 18.

Listing 23-1: **Managing network resources**

netreslib.js

```
// ************************
// Script: Network Resource Library
// Version: 0.9.8
// Creation Date: 6/30/99
// Last Modified: 2/5/00
// Author: William R. Stanek
// Email: win2000scripting@tvpress.com
// ************************
// Description: Provides a utility library for
//              managing network resources.
// ************************
// Copyright (c) 1999-2000 William R. Stanek
// You have a royalty-free right to use these applications,
provided
```

Continued

Listing 23-1 *(continued)*

```javascript
// that you give credit to the author AND agree that the author has
// no warranty, obligations or liability for any of these library
// functions.
// **************************

function GetDriveInfo()
{
  var fs, d, e, s, t, wnet, cname;

  wNet = WScript.CreateObject("WScript.Network");
  cname = wNet.ComputerName;

  fs = new ActiveXObject ("Scripting.FileSystemObject");
  e = new Enumerator(fs.Drives);
  s = "";
  s += "=========================" + "\r\n";
  s += cname + "\r\n";
  s += "=========================" + "\r\n";

  for (; !e.atEnd(); e.moveNext())
  {

    d = e.item();
    switch (d.DriveType)
    {
    case 0: t = "Unknown"; break;
    case 1: t = "Removable"; break;
    case 2: t = "Fixed"; break;
    case 3: t = "Network"; break;
    case 4: t = "CD-ROM"; break;
    case 5: t = "RAM Disk"; break;
    }
    s += "Drive " + d.DriveLetter + ": - " + t + "\r\n";
    if (d.ShareName)
     s += " Share: " + d.ShareName + "\r\n";
    s += "Total space " + Math.round(d.TotalSize/1048576);
    s += " Mbytes" + "\r\n";
    s += "Free Space: " + Math.round(d.FreeSpace/1048576);
    s += " Mbytes" + "\r\n";
    s += "=========================" + "\r\n";
  }
  return(s);
}

function GetDriveInfo2()
{
  var fs, d, e, s, t, wnet, cname;
```

```
    wNet = WScript.CreateObject("WScript.Network");
    cname = wNet.ComputerName;

    fs = new ActiveXObject ("Scripting.FileSystemObject");
    e = new Enumerator(fs.Drives);
    s = "";
    s += "=========================" + "\r\n";
    s += cname + "\r\n";
    s += "=========================" + "\r\n";

    for (; !e.atEnd(); e.moveNext())
    {

      d = e.item();
    if ((d.DriveType < 2) || (d.DriveType > 3))
        continue;

      switch (d.DriveType)
      {
      case 0: t = "Unknown"; break;
      case 1: t = "Removable"; break;
      case 2: t = "Fixed"; break;
      case 3: t = "Network"; break;
      case 4: t = "CD-ROM"; break;
      case 5: t = "RAM Disk"; break;
      }
      s += "Drive " + d.DriveLetter + ": - " + t + "\r\n";
      if (d.ShareName)
        s += " Share: " + d.ShareName + "\r\n";
      s += "Total space " + Math.round(d.TotalSize/1048576) ;
      s += " Mbytes" + "\r\n";
      s += "Free Space: " + Math.round(d.FreeSpace/1048576);
      s += " Mbytes" + "\r\n";
      s += "=========================" + "\r\n";
      }
      return(s);
}

function CheckFreeSpace()
{
    var fs, d, e, s, tspace, fspace, wnet, cname;

    wnet = WScript.CreateObject("WScript.Network");
    cname = wnet.ComputerName;

    fs = new ActiveXObject ("Scripting.FileSystemObject");
    e = new Enumerator(fs.Drives);
    s = "";
    s += "=========================" + "\r\n";
    s += cname + "\r\n";
    s += "=========================" + "\r\n";
```

Continued

Listing 23-1 *(continued)*

```
 for (; !e.atEnd(); e.moveNext())
 {

  d = e.item();
  if ((d.DriveType < 2) || (d.DriveType > 3))
    continue
  tspace = Math.round(d.TotalSize/1048576);
  fspace = Math.round(d.FreeSpace/1048576);
  if (fspace < (tspace*.1))
   {
    s += "Drive " + d.DriveLetter;
    if (d.VolumName)
     s += "Volume: " + d.VolumName;
    if (d.ShareName)
     s += " Share: " + d.ShareName;
    s += "\r\n!!!" + "\r\n";
    s += "Free Space: " + fspace;
    s += " Mbytes" + "\r\n";
    s += "!!!" + "\r\n";
   }

 }
  return(s);
}

function MapDrive(drv, nshare)
{

  fs = new ActiveXObject("Scripting.FileSystemObject");
  if (fs.DriveExists(drv))
   {
    var wn = WScript.CreateObject ("WScript.Network");
    wn.RemoveNetworkDrive(drv);
   }
  else
   {
    var wn = WScript.CreateObject ("WScript.Network");
    wn.MapNetworkDrive(drv, nshare);
   }
}

function defPrinter(dp)
{
 var wn = WScript.CreateObject("WScript.Network");
 wn.SetDefaultPrinter (dp);
}

function AddPrinter(prntr, pshare)
{
```

```javascript
 var wn = WScript.CreateObject("WScript.Network");
 wn.AddPrinterConnection(prntr, pshare);
}

function RemPrinter(prntr)
{
 var wn = WScript.CreateObject("WScript.Network");
 wn.RemovePrinterConnection (prntr);
}

function getServiceInfo(domain,system)
{
  var lf, ret, tlist;
  lf = "\r\n";
  ret = "";

  var comp = GetObject("WinNT://" + domain + "/" + system);
  tlist = new Enumerator(comp);

  for (; !tlist.atEnd(); tlist.moveNext())
  {

   s = tlist.item();

   if (s.Class == "Service") {

       //Display service properties
       ret += s.Class + " " + s.Name + lf;
       ret += "==============================" + lf;
       ret += "StartType: " + s.StartType + lf;
       ret += "ServiceType: " + s.ServiceType + lf;
       ret += "DisplayName: " + s.DisplayName + lf;
       ret += "Path: " + s.Path + lf;
       ret += "ErrorControl: " + s.ErrorControl + lf;
       ret += "HostComputer: " + s.HostComputer + lf;
       ret += "LoadOrderGroup: " + s.LoadOrderGroup + lf;
       ret += "ServiceAccountName: " + s.ServiceAccountName + lf;

       try {
        ret += "Dependencies: " + s.Dependencies + lf;
       }
       catch (e) {
        //property setting not available or is array
       }
       try {
       //services can have multiple dependencies
        e = s.Dependencies.toArray();
        for (opt in e)
        {
          ret += "Dependencies: " + e[opt] + lf;
        }
```

Continued

Listing 23-1 *(continued)*

```
      }
      catch (e) {
        //property setting not available
      }
      try {
        ret += "Status: " + s.Get("Status") + lf;
      }
      catch (e) {
        //property setting not available
      }

    }

    ret += lf;

  }

  return (ret);
}

function checkService(domain, system, service)
{

  var lf, ret, tlist;
  lf = "\r\n";
  ret = "";

  var comp = GetObject("WinNT://" + domain + "/" + system);
  tlist = new Enumerator(comp);

  for (; !tlist.atEnd(); tlist.moveNext())
  {

    s = tlist.item();

    if (s.Class == "Service") {

      if (s.DisplayName == service || s.Name == service) {

        ret += "=======================================" + lf;
        ret += "Checking status of " + s.Name + lf;

        switch (s.Status) {
         case 1 :
           ret += "=======================================" + lf;
           ret += "Service not running." + lf;
           ret += "=======================================" + lf;
           break;
```

```
        case 2 :
          ret += "=====================================" + lf;
          ret += "Service is starting..." + lf;
          ret += "=====================================" + lf;
          break;
        case 3 :
          ret += "=====================================" + lf;
          ret += "Service is stopping..." + lf;
          ret += "=====================================" + lf;
          break;
        case 4 :
          ret += "=====================================" + lf;
          ret += "Service is running normally." + lf;
          ret += "=====================================" + lf;
          break;
        case 5 :
          ret += "=====================================" + lf;
          ret += "Service is resuming..." + lf;
          ret += "=====================================" + lf;
          break;
        case 6 :
          ret += "=====================================" + lf;
          ret += "Service is pausing." + lf;
          ret += "=====================================" + lf;
          break;
        case 7 :
          ret += "=====================================" + lf;
          ret += "Service is paused." + lf;
          ret += "=====================================" + lf;
          break;
        case 8 :
          ret += "=====================================" + lf;
          ret += "Service error!" + lf;
          ret += "=====================================" + lf;
          break;
        }
      }
    }
  }

  return (ret);

}

function startService(domain, system, service)
{

  var lf, ret;
  lf = "\r\n";
  ret = "";
```

Continued

Listing 23-1 *(continued)*

```
  var s = GetObject("WinNT://" + domain + "/" + system + "/" + service +
",service");

  if (s.Status == 1) {
    s.Start();
    ret += "=========================================" + lf;
    ret += "Starting Service..." + s.Name + lf;
    ret += "=========================================" + lf;

  } else {
    ret += "=========================================" + lf;
    ret += s.Name + " may already be started." +lf;
    ret += "=========================================" + lf;
    ret += checkService(domain, system, service)
  }

  return (ret);

}

function stopService(domain, system, service)
{

  var lf, ret;
  lf = "\r\n";
  ret = "";

  var s = GetObject("WinNT://" + domain + "/" + system + "/" + service +
",service");

  if (s.Status == 4) {
    s.Stop();
    ret += "=========================================" + lf;
    ret += "Stopping Service..." + s.Name + lf;
    ret += "=========================================" + lf;

  } else {
    ret += "=========================================" + lf;
    ret += s.Name + " may already be stopped." +lf;
    ret += "=========================================" + lf;
    ret += checkService(domain, system, service)
  }

  return (ret);

}

function pauseService(domain, system, service)
```

```
{

  var lf, ret;
  lf = "\r\n";
  ret = "";

  var s = GetObject("WinNT://" + domain + "/" + system + "/" + service +
",service");

  if (s.Status == 4) {
    s.Pause();
    ret += "======================================" + lf;
    ret += "Pausing Service..." + s.Name + lf;
    ret += "======================================" + lf;

  } else {
    ret += "======================================" + lf;
    ret += s.Name + " may already be paused." +lf;
    ret += "======================================" + lf;
    ret += checkService(domain, system, service)
  }

  return (ret);

}

function resumeService(domain, system, service)
{

  var lf, ret;
  lf = "\r\n";
  ret = "";

  var s = GetObject("WinNT://" + domain + "/" + system + "/" + service +
",service");

  if (s.Status == 7) {
    s.Continue();
    ret += "======================================" + lf;
    ret += "Resuming Service..." + s.Name + lf;
    ret += "======================================" + lf;

  } else {
    ret += "======================================" + lf;
    ret += s.Name + " may already be running." +lf;
    ret += "======================================" + lf;
    ret += checkService(domain, system, service)
  }

  return (ret);
```

Continued

Listing 23-1 *(continued)*

```
}

function checkRS(domain, system)
{
  var lf, rList, sList, resource, ret, session;

  lf = "\r\n";
  var s = GetObject("WinNT://" + domain + "/" + system +
"/lanmanserver,fileservice");

  ret = "";
  ret += "================================" + lf;
  ret += "Checking Resources and Sessions" + lf;
  ret += lf;
  ret += s.HostComputer + lf;
  ret += "================================" + lf;

  rList = new Enumerator(s.Resources());

   for (; !rList.atEnd(); rList.moveNext())
   {
    resource = rList.item();
    ret += "Resource path: " + resource.Path + lf;
   }

   sList = new Enumerator(s.Sessions());

   for (; !sList.atEnd(); sList.moveNext())
   {
    session = sList.item();
    ret += "Session name: " + session.Name + lf;
   }

  return (ret);
}

function viewDetailedRS(domain, system)
{

  var lf, rList, sList, resource, ret, session;

  lf = "\r\n";
  var s = GetObject("WinNT://" + domain + "/" + system +
"/lanmanserver,fileservice");

  ret = "";
  ret += "================================" + lf;
  ret += "Getting Detailed Information" + lf;
```

```
   ret += "for Resources and Sessions" + lf + lf;
   ret += s.HostComputer + lf;
   ret += "==============================" + lf;

   ret += "==============================" +lf;
   ret += "Open Files: " + lf +lf;

   rList = new Enumerator(s.Resources());

   for (; !rList.atEnd(); rList.moveNext())
   {
    resource = rList.item()
    ret += "File or Folder Path: " + resource.Path +lf;
    ret += "Number of Locks: " + resource.LockCount +lf;
    ret += "User: " + resource.User + lf
   }


   ret += "==============================" +lf;
   ret += "User Sessions: " + lf + lf;

   sList = new Enumerator(s.Sessions());

   for (; !sList.atEnd(); sList.moveNext())
   {
    session = sList.item()
    ret += "Session name: " + session.Name +lf;
    ret += "User: " + session.User +lf;
    ret += "Computer: " + session.Computer +lf;
    ret += "Connect Time: " + session.ConnectTime +lf;
    ret += "Idle Time: " + session.IdleTime +lf;

   }

   ret += "==============================" +lf;
   return (ret);
}

function viewShareInfo(domain, system, share)
{
  var lf, ret;

  lf = "\r\n";
  ret = "";

  var fs = GetObject("WinNT://" + domain + "/" + system + "/LanmanServer/" + share +
",fileshare");
```

Continued

Listing 23-1 *(continued)*

```
  ret += "===============================" +lf;
  ret += fs.Name + " Information " + lf;
  ret += "===============================" +lf;
  ret += "Current User Count: " + fs.CurrentUserCount + lf;
  ret += "Description: " + fs.Description + lf;
  ret += "Host Computer: " + fs.HostComputer + lf;
  ret += "Maximum User Count: " + fs.MaxUserCount + lf;
  ret += "File Path: " + fs.Path + lf;
  ret += "===============================" +lf;

  return (ret);
}

function createShare(domain, system, sharename, path)
{

  var lf;

  lf = "\r\n";
  var s = GetObject("WinNT://" + domain + "/" + system +
"/LanmanServer,fileservice");

  val = "";

  var fs = s.Create("FileShare", sharename);
  fs.Path = path;
  fs.MaxUserCount = -1;
  fs.SetInfo();

}

function deleteShare(domain, system, sharename)
{

  var lf;

  lf = "\r\n";
  var s = GetObject("WinNT://" + domain + "/" + system +
"/LanmanServer,fileservice");

  val = "";

  var fs = s.Delete("FileShare", sharename);

}
```

Using the Network Resource Utility Library

As you've seen from Listing 23-1, the network resource utility library provides many custom functions. Calling these ready-to-use functions from within your own scripts can save you time and effort.

Using GetDriveInfo

The GetDriveInfo function returns a summary of all drives on a system. If you want to run the script as a nightly AT job, you can log the information to a file using the .wsf file shown in Listing 23-2. This script uses the I/O utility library (iolib.js) and the network resource library (netreslib.js).

The results of the script are stored in a file called logfile.txt. Sample output for this file is shown in the listing. Because the WriteChar function appends to existing files, information is added to the log file each time you run the script.

Listing 23-2: **Getting and logging drive information**

logdriveinfo.wsf

```
<Job ID="LogDriveInfo">
  <Script LANGUAGE="JScript" SRC="iolib.js" />
  <Script LANGUAGE="JScript" SRC="netreslib.js" />

  <Script LANGUAGE="JScript">
          checkDrive = GetDriveInfo()
          WriteChar("logfile.txt",checkdrive)
  </Script>
</Job>
```

Output into logfile.txt

```
=========================
ZETA
=========================
Drive C: - Fixed
Total space 2047 Mbytes
Free Space: 564 Mbytes
=========================
Drive G: - Removable
Total space 96 Mbytes
Free Space: 39 Mbytes
=========================
Drive H: - CD-ROM
Total space 584 Mbytes
Free Space: 0 Mbytes
=========================
```

The GetDriveInfo function as currently written checks all drives on the system, including removable drives. These drives must have media. If they don't, you may see a prompt asking you to check the drive. To get a report of fixed and network drives only, use the GetDriveInfo2 function. These statements within the For loop cause the function to skip checks for removable and CD-ROM drives:

```
if ((d.DriveType < 2) || (d.DriveType > 3))
    continue
```

Using CheckFreeSpace

Another useful function for tracking drive info is CheckFreeSpace. CheckFreeSpace returns a warning if a fixed or network drive has less than 10 percent free space available. The code that checks for free space is:

```
tspace = Math.round(d.TotalSize/1048576)
fspace = Math.round(d.FreeSpace/1048576)
if (fspace < (tspace*.1))
```

Here, you take the total free space and multiply by .1 to come up with a value to compare to the amount of free space. The code that checks the free space percentage is easily updated. For example, if you want to report errors when there is 25 percent free space, you can update the function as follows:

```
tspace = Math.round(d.TotalSize/1048576)
fspace = Math.round(d.FreeSpace/1048576)
if (fspace < (tspace*.25))
```

The CheckFreeSpace function can also be run as a nightly AT job. Listing 23-3 shows a sample .wsf file that maps a network share and then updates a central log file. Sample output for this log file is shown.

Listing 23-3: **Examining free space on a system**

checkdriveinfo.wsf

```
<Job ID="DriveInfo">
  <Script LANGUAGE="JScript" SRC="iolib.js" />
  <Script LANGUAGE="JScript" SRC="netreslib.js" />

  <Script LANGUAGE="JScript">
        checkDrive = CheckFreeSpace()
        MapDrive("X:", "\\\\Omega\\data")
        WriteChar("X:\\dspace.log",checkdrive)
        MapDrive("X:")
  </Script>
</Job>
```

Output into dspace.log

```
===========================
ZETA
===========================
Drive C
!!!
Free Space: 8 Mbytes
!!!
===========================
OMEGA
===========================
Drive C
!!!
Free Space: 12 Mbytes
!!!
```

Using MapDrive

MapDrive provides a single function for connecting and disconnecting drives. If the drive referenced in the first parameter exists, the drive is disconnected. Otherwise, the drive is connected to the network share passed in the second parameter. You can use MapDrive to connect a drive as follows:

```
MapDrive("Z:", "\\\\Zeta\\logs")
```

Later, you can disconnect the drive by calling:

```
MapDrive("Z:")
```

Working with printers

The network resource library also has functions for working with printers. These functions are defPrinter for setting a default printer, AddPrinter for adding a printer connection, and RemPrinter for removing a printer connection. The first parameter for all of these functions is the local name of the printer you are working with. AddPrinter expects a second parameter, which is the name of the network printer share you are connecting. You can call AddPrinter in a script as follows:

```
AddPrinter("MarketingPrinter", "\\\\Omega\\Prtrs\\Marketing")
```

Viewing, checking, and managing services

You'll find two key functions for viewing and checking Windows services: getServiceInfo and checkService. The getServiceInfo function provides a detailed summary of all services on a specified computer. For example, you could examine all the services on a computer called Jupiter in the Marketing domain as follows:

```
WScript.Echo(getServiceInfo("Marketing","Jupiter"))
```

The results would look similar to the following:

```
Service Alerter
================================
StartType: 2
ServiceType: 32
DisplayName: Alerter
Path: F:\WINNT\System32\services.exe
ErrorControl: 1
HostComputer: WinNT://marketing/jupiter
LoadOrderGroup:
ServiceAccountName: LocalSystem
Dependencies: LanmanWorkstation

Service AppMgmt
================================
StartType: 3
ServiceType: 32
DisplayName: Application Management
Path: F:\WINNT\system32\services.exe
ErrorControl: 1
HostComputer: WinNT://marketing/jupiter
LoadOrderGroup:
ServiceAccountName: LocalSystem
...
...
Service Wmi
================================
StartType: 3
ServiceType: 32
DisplayName: Windows Management Instrumentation Driver
Extensions
Path: F:\WINNT\system32\Services.exe
ErrorControl: 1
HostComputer: WinNT://marketing/jupiter
LoadOrderGroup:
ServiceAccountName: LocalSystem
```

The checkService function displays the status of a service on a specified system. The service can be referenced by display name or by the actual service name. For example, you could reference the WinMgmt service:

```
WScript.Echo(checkService("seattle", "Zeta", "WinMgmt"))
```

Or the Windows Management Instrumentation service:

```
WScript.Echo(checkService("seattle", "Zeta",
"Windows Management Instrumentation"))
```

If the service is running normally, the output you see is:

```
========================================
Checking status of WinMgmt
========================================
Service is running normally.
========================================
```

If you need to manage services on a remote system, you'll find that the startService, stopService, pauseService, and resumeService functions are very handy. As the names imply, these functions start, stop, pause, or resume services, respectively. Be sure to specify the domain, system, and service name when calling these functions, such as:

```
WScript.Echo(startService("seattle", "Zeta", "WinMgmt"))
```

The return value from the function tells you one of two things. If the service was stopped, you'll get the following message:

```
========================================
Starting Service...WinMgmt
========================================
```

This message tells you that the service is being started. If the service wasn't stopped, however, you'll get this message:

```
========================================
WinMgmt may already be started.
========================================
========================================
Checking status of WinMgmt
========================================
Service is running normally.
========================================
```

The function displays a message that tells you the service may already be started and then calls the checkService function in order to obtain a more precise status.

Using checkRS and viewDetailedRS

The checkRS and viewDetailedRS functions display information about open resources and user sessions. checkRS returns summary information.

`viewDetailedRS` returns detailed information. Both functions expect to be passed a domain and system name to work with, such as:

```
WScript.Echo(checkRS("seattle", "zeta"))
```

The return values from `checkRS` are formatted as follows:

```
==============================
Checking Resources and Sessions

WinNT://seattle/zeta
==============================
Resource path: E:\myBooks
Resource path: E:\myBooks\Apartments.doc
Session name: ADMINISTRATOR\127.0.0.1
```

The return values from `viewDetailedRS` are formatted like this:

```
==============================
Getting Detailed Information
for Resources and Sessions

WinNT://seattle/zeta
==============================
==============================
Open Files:

File or Folder Path: E:\myBooks
Number of Locks: 0
User: ADMINISTRATOR
File or Folder Path: E:\myBooks\Apartments.doc
Number of Locks: 3
User: ADMINISTRATOR
==============================
User Sessions:

Session name: ADMINISTRATOR\127.0.0.1
User: ADMINISTRATOR
Computer: 127.0.0.1
Connect Time: 819
Idle Time: 803
==============================
```

Using viewShareInfo, createShare, and deleteShare

The final set of utility functions is designed to work with network shares. You use `viewShareInfo` to obtain summary information for a named share. Here's how you could examine the netlogon share on a computer called Goldbug in the Gemini domain:

```
WScript.Echo(viewShareInfo("Gemini", "Goldbug", "netlogon"))
```

The return value would look similar to the following:

```
================================
NETLOGON Information
================================
Current User Count: 0
Description: Logon server share
Host Computer: WinNT://gemini/goldbug
Maximum User Count: -1
File Path: F:\WINNT\sysvol\sysvol\gemini.com\SCRIPTS
================================
```

The createShare function provides a quick and easy way to create shared folders on remote computers. Just call the function with the domain name, remote system name, share name, and folder path, such as:

```
createShare("gemini", "goldbug", "UserData", "e:\\Users\\Data")
```

Don't worry if you make a mistake; you can use the deleteShare function to delete the share:

```
deleteShare("gemini", "goldbug", "UserData")
```

Summary

This chapter developed a utility library for managing network resources. Through batch script (.wsf) files, you can access these utility functions in any of your scripts. The next chapter provides a utility library for managing accounts.

✦　　✦　　✦

Library: Account Management Utilities

◆ ◆ ◆ ◆

In This Chapter

Creating the account management library

Using the account management library

Working with library methods

◆ ◆ ◆ ◆

As you set out to manage accounts, you may want to keep the account management library in mind. This library provides functions for managing user, group, and computer accounts, as well as domain account policies. Through batch scripts (.wsf) files, you can access these utility functions in any of your scripts.

Building the Account Management Library

Listing 24-1 provides the source code for the account management library. As you examine the listing, note the function names and how the functions are implemented. If you have specific questions on the techniques used in the listing, you'll find related discussions in Chapters 16 and 19.

Listing 24-1: **Account management utility library**

accountlib.js

```
// ************************
// Script: Account Management Library
// Version: 0.9.5
// Creation Date: 11/01/99
// Last Modified:  2/5/00
// Author: William R. Stanek
// Email: win2000scripting@tvpress.com
// ************************
```

Continued

Listing 24-1 *(continued)*

```
// Description: Provides a utility library for
//              managing Windows 2000 accounts.
// *************************
// Copyright (c) 1999-2000 William R. Stanek
// You have a royalty-free right to use these applications,
// provided that you give credit to the author AND agree that
// the author has no warranty, obligations or liability for any
// of these library functions.
// *************************

//Domain management functions

function setMinPasswordLength(domain, passLength)
{
  var dom = GetObject("WinNT://" + domain);
  dom.Put("MinPasswordLength", passLength);
  dom.SetInfo();

  return ("Minimum Password Length: " + dom.Get("MinPasswordLength"));

}

function setPasswordAge(domain, minAge, maxAge)
{
  var lf, ret, passMinAge, passMaxAge;
  lf = "\r\n";
  ret = "";

  var dom = GetObject("WinNT://" + domain);
  dom.Put("MinPasswordAge", 86400 * minAge);
  dom.Put("MaxPasswordAge", 86400 * maxAge);
  dom.SetInfo();

  passMinAge = dom.Get("MinPasswordAge") / 86400;
  passMaxAge = dom.Get("MaxPasswordAge") / 86400;

  ret += "Minimum Password Age: " + passMinAge + " days" + lf;
  ret += "Maximum Password Age: " + passMaxAge + " days";

  return (ret);
}

function setPasswordHistory(domain, histLength)
{
  var ret;
  ret = "";

  var dom = GetObject("WinNT://" + domain);
  dom.Put("PasswordHistoryLength", histLength);
  dom.SetInfo();
```

```
    return("Password History Length: " + dom.Get("PasswordHistoryLength"));
}

function setAccountLockoutInfo(domain, maxBad, unlockInt, lockoutObs)
{

  var lf, ret, maxBad, autoU, lockO;
  lf = "\r\n";
  ret = "";

  var dom = GetObject("WinNT://" + domain);
  dom.Put("MaxBadPasswordsAllowed", maxBad);
  dom.Put("AutoUnlockInterval", 60 * unlockInt);
  dom.Put("LockoutObservationInterval", 60 * lockoutObs);
  dom.SetInfo();

  maxBad = dom.Get("MaxBadPasswordsAllowed");
  autoU = dom.Get("AutoUnlockInterval") / 60;
  lockO = dom.Get("LockoutObservationInterval") / 60;

  ret += "Maximum Bad Passwords Allowed: " + maxBad + lf;
  ret += "AutoLock Interval: " + autoU + " minutes" + lf;
  ret += "Lockout Observation Interval: " + lockO + " minutes";

  return (ret);
}

//Computer management functions

function getAllComputers() {

  var lf, ret;
  lf = "\r\n";
  ret = "";


  var prov = GetObject("WinNT:");
  tlist = new Enumerator(prov);

  for (; !tlist.atEnd(); tlist.moveNext())
   {

   s = new Enumerator(tlist.item());

   for (; !s.atEnd(); s.moveNext())
    {

    o = s.item();
    if (o.Class == "Computer") {

      try {
       ret += o.Class + " " + o.Name + lf;
```

Continued

Listing 24-1 *(continued)*

```
        ret += " Owner: " + o.Owner + lf;
        ret += " Division: " + o.Division + lf;
        ret += " OperatingSystem: " + o.OperatingSystem + lf;
        ret += " OS Version: " + o.OperatingSystemVersion + lf;
        ret += " Processor: " + o.Processor + lf;
        ret += " ProcessorCount: " + o.ProcessorCount + lf;
      }
    catch(e) {

      ret += " Not online at this time" + lf;
      }
    }
   }
  }

  return (ret);
}

function getDomainComputers(domain) {

  var lf, ret;
  lf = "\r\n";
  ret = "";

  var dom = GetObject("WinNT://" + domain);

  s = new Enumerator(dom);

  for (; !s.atEnd(); s.moveNext())
  {

    o = s.item();
    if (o.Class == "Computer") {

      try {
      ret += o.Class + " " + o.Name + lf;
      ret += " Owner: " + o.Owner + lf;
      ret += " Division: " + o.Division + lf;
      ret += " OperatingSystem: " + o.OperatingSystem + lf;
      ret += " OS Version: " + o.OperatingSystemVersion + lf;
      ret += " Processor: " + o.Processor + lf;
      ret += " ProcessorCount: " + o.ProcessorCount + lf;
      }
    catch(e) {

      ret += " Not online at this time" + lf;
      }
    }
  }
```

```
    return (ret);
}

function createComputerAccount(container, computer) {

  var rootDSE = GetObject("LDAP://rootDSE");
  domainCont = rootDSE.Get("defaultNamingContext");

  try {
    var cont = GetObject("LDAP://OU=" + container + "," + domainCont);
  }
  catch(e) {
    var cont = GetObject("LDAP://CN=" + container + "," + domainCont);
  }

  var comp = cont.Create("computer","CN=" + computer);

  comp.Put("samAccountName",computer);
  comp.SetInfo();

}

function createEnabledComputerAccount(container, computer) {

  var rootDSE = GetObject("LDAP://rootDSE");
  domainCont = rootDSE.Get("defaultNamingContext");

  try {
    var cont = GetObject("LDAP://OU=" + container + "," + domainCont);
  }
  catch(e) {
    var cont = GetObject("LDAP://CN=" + container + "," + domainCont);
  }

  var comp = cont.Create("computer","CN=" + computer);

  comp.Put("samAccountName",computer);
  comp.SetInfo();

  comp.AccountDisabled = "False";
  comp.SetInfo();
}

function deleteComputerAccount(container, computer) {

  var rootDSE = GetObject("LDAP://rootDSE");
  domainCont = rootDSE.Get("defaultNamingContext");

  try {
    var cont = GetObject("LDAP://OU=" + container + "," + domainCont);
  }
  catch(e) {
```

Continued

Listing 24-1 *(continued)*

```
    var cont = GetObject("LDAP://CN=" + container + "," + domainCont);
  }
  cont.Delete("computer","CN=" + computer);

}

function enableComputerAccount(container, computer) {

  var rootDSE = GetObject("LDAP://rootDSE");
  domainCont = rootDSE.Get("defaultNamingContext");

  try {
    var cont = GetObject("LDAP://OU=" + container + "," + domainCont);
  }
  catch(e) {
    var cont = GetObject("LDAP://CN=" + container + "," + domainCont);
  }

  var comp = cont.GetObject("computer","CN=" + computer);

  comp.AccountDisabled = "False";
  comp.SetInfo();
}

function disableComputerAccount(container, computer) {

  var rootDSE = GetObject("LDAP://rootDSE");
  domainCont = rootDSE.Get("defaultNamingContext");

  try {
    var cont = GetObject("LDAP://OU=" + container + "," + domainCont);
  }
  catch(e) {
    var cont = GetObject("LDAP://CN=" + container + "," + domainCont);
  }

  var comp = cont.GetObject("computer","CN=" + computer);

  comp.AccountDisabled = "True";
  comp.SetInfo();
}

//User management functions

function createLocalUser(computer, user, password) {

  var obj = GetObject("WinNT://" + computer)
  var usr = obj.Create("user", user)
  usr.SetPassword(password)
  usr.SetInfo()
```

```
}

function deleteLocalUser(computer, user) {

  var obj = GetObject("WinNT://" + computer)
  obj.Delete("user", user)

}


function createUser(container, fullName, first, last, samName, password) {

  var rootDSE = GetObject("LDAP://rootDSE");
  domainCont = rootDSE.Get("defaultNamingContext");

  try {
    var cont = GetObject("LDAP://OU=" + container + "," + domainCont);
  }
  catch(e) {
    var cont = GetObject("LDAP://CN=" + container + "," + domainCont);
  }

  var usr = cont.Create("user", "CN=" + fullName);
  usr.samAccountName = samName;
  usr.displayName = fullName;
  usr.givenName = first;
  usr.sn = last;
  usr.userPrincipalName = samName

  usr.SetInfo();

  usr.AccountDisabled = 0;
  usr.SetPassword(password);
  usr.SetInfo();

}

function deleteUser(container, displayName) {

  var rootDSE = GetObject("LDAP://rootDSE");
  domainCont = rootDSE.Get("defaultNamingContext");

  try {
    var cont = GetObject("LDAP://OU=" + container + "," + domainCont);
  }
  catch(e) {
    var cont = GetObject("LDAP://CN=" + container + "," + domainCont);
  }

  cont.Delete("User", "CN=" + displayName);
```

Continued

Listing 24-1 *(continued)*

```
}

function userMustChangePassword(container, displayName) {
  var rootDSE = GetObject("LDAP://rootDSE");
  domainCont = rootDSE.Get("defaultNamingContext");

  try {
    var cont = GetObject("LDAP://OU=" + container + "," + domainCont);
  }
  catch(e) {
    var cont = GetObject("LDAP://CN=" + container + "," + domainCont);
  }

  var usr = cont.GetObject("User", "CN=" + displayName);

  usr.Put("pwdLastSet", 0)
  usr.SetInfo()

}

function enableUserAccount(displayName) {

  var rootDSE = GetObject("LDAP://rootDSE");
  domainCont = rootDSE.Get("defaultNamingContext");

  try {
    var cont = GetObject("LDAP://" + domainCont);
  }
  catch(e) {
    var cont = GetObject("LDAP://" + domainCont);
  }

  var usr = cont.GetObject("User", "CN=" + displayName);

  usr.AccountDisabled = 0
  usr.SetInfo()

}

function enableUserAccount(container, displayName) {

  var rootDSE = GetObject("LDAP://rootDSE");
  domainCont = rootDSE.Get("defaultNamingContext");

  try {
    var cont = GetObject("LDAP://OU=" + container + "," + domainCont);
  }
  catch(e) {
    var cont = GetObject("LDAP://CN=" + container + "," + domainCont);
  }
```

```
    var usr = cont.GetObject("User", "CN=" + displayName);

  usr.AccountDisabled = 0
  usr.SetInfo()

}

function disableUserAccount(container, displayName) {

  var rootDSE = GetObject("LDAP://rootDSE");
  domainCont = rootDSE.Get("defaultNamingContext");

  try {
    var cont = GetObject("LDAP://OU=" + container + "," + domainCont);
  }
  catch(e) {
    var cont = GetObject("LDAP://CN=" + container + "," + domainCont);
  }

  var usr = cont.GetObject("User", "CN=" + displayName);

  usr.AccountDisabled = 1
  usr.SetInfo()

}

function unlockUserAccount(container, displayName) {

  var rootDSE = GetObject("LDAP://rootDSE");
  domainCont = rootDSE.Get("defaultNamingContext");

  try {
    var cont = GetObject("LDAP://OU=" + container + "," + domainCont);
  }
  catch(e) {
    var cont = GetObject("LDAP://CN=" + container + "," + domainCont);
  }

  var usr = cont.GetObject("User", "CN=" + displayName);

  usr.IsAccountLocked = 0
  usr.SetInfo()

}

function changePassword(container, displayName, password) {

  var rootDSE = GetObject("LDAP://rootDSE");
  domainCont = rootDSE.Get("defaultNamingContext");
```

Continued

Listing 24-1 *(continued)*

```
  try {
    var cont = GetObject("LDAP://OU=" + container + "," + domainCont);
  }
  catch(e) {
    var cont = GetObject("LDAP://CN=" + container + "," + domainCont);
  }
  var usr = cont.GetObject("User", "CN=" + displayName);

  usr.SetPassword(password)
  usr.SetInfo()

}


function accountExpiration(container, displayName, dateString) {

  var rootDSE = GetObject("LDAP://rootDSE");
  domainCont = rootDSE.Get("defaultNamingContext");

  try {
    var cont = GetObject("LDAP://OU=" + container + "," + domainCont);
  }
  catch(e) {
    var cont = GetObject("LDAP://CN=" + container + "," + domainCont);
  }

  var usr = cont.GetObject("User", "CN=" + displayName);

  usr.AccountExpirationDate = dateString
  usr.SetInfo()

}


//Group management functions

function createGDistGroup (container, groupName, groupSAMName)
{

  var rootDSE = GetObject("LDAP://rootDSE");
  domainCont = rootDSE.Get("defaultNamingContext");

  try {
    var cont = GetObject("LDAP://OU=" + container + "," + domainCont);
  }
  catch(e) {
    var cont = GetObject("LDAP://CN=" + container + "," + domainCont);
  }

  var grp = cont.Create("group", "CN=" + groupName)

  grp.groupType = 2
```

```
    if (groupSAMName == null)
      grp.Put("samAccountName", groupName)
    else
      grp.Put("samAccountName", groupSAMName)

  grp.SetInfo()

}

function createDLDistGroup (container, groupName, groupSAMName)
{

  var rootDSE = GetObject("LDAP://rootDSE");
  domainCont = rootDSE.Get("defaultNamingContext");

  try {
    var cont = GetObject("LDAP://OU=" + container + "," + domainCont);
  }
  catch(e) {
    var cont = GetObject("LDAP://CN=" + container + "," + domainCont);
  }

  var grp = cont.Create("group", "CN=" + groupName)

  grp.groupType = 4

  if (groupSAMName == null)
    grp.Put("samAccountName", groupName)
  else
    grp.Put("samAccountName", groupSAMName)

  grp.SetInfo()

}

function createUDistGroup (container, groupName, groupSAMName)
{

  var rootDSE = GetObject("LDAP://rootDSE");
  domainCont = rootDSE.Get("defaultNamingContext");

  try {
    var cont = GetObject("LDAP://OU=" + container + "," + domainCont);
  }
  catch(e) {
    var cont = GetObject("LDAP://CN=" + container + "," + domainCont);
  }

  var grp = cont.Create("group", "CN=" + groupName)

  grp.groupType = 8
```

Continued

Listing 24-1 *(continued)*

```
  if (groupSAMName == null)
    grp.Put("samAccountName", groupName)
  else
    grp.Put("samAccountName", groupSAMName)

  grp.SetInfo()

}

function createGSecGroup (container, groupName, groupSAMName)
{

  var rootDSE = GetObject("LDAP://rootDSE");
  domainCont = rootDSE.Get("defaultNamingContext");

  try {
    var cont = GetObject("LDAP://OU=" + container + "," + domainCont);
  }
  catch(e) {
    var cont = GetObject("LDAP://CN=" + container + "," + domainCont);
  }

  var grp = cont.Create("group", "CN=" + groupName)

  grp.groupType = -2147483646

  if (groupSAMName == null)
    grp.Put("samAccountName", groupName)
  else
    grp.Put("samAccountName", groupSAMName)

  grp.SetInfo()

}

function createDLSecGroup (container, groupName, groupSAMName)
{

  var rootDSE = GetObject("LDAP://rootDSE");
  domainCont = rootDSE.Get("defaultNamingContext");

  try {
    var cont = GetObject("LDAP://OU=" + container + "," + domainCont);
  }
  catch(e) {
    var cont = GetObject("LDAP://CN=" + container + "," + domainCont);
  }

  var grp = cont.Create("group", "CN=" + groupName)
```

```
  grp.groupType = -2147483644

  if (groupSAMName == null)
    grp.Put("samAccountName", groupName)
  else
    grp.Put("samAccountName", groupSAMName)

  grp.SetInfo()

}

function createUSecGroup (container, groupName, groupSAMName)
{

  var rootDSE = GetObject("LDAP://rootDSE");
  domainCont = rootDSE.Get("defaultNamingContext");

  try {
    var cont = GetObject("LDAP://OU=" + container + "," + domainCont);
  }
  catch(e) {
    var cont = GetObject("LDAP://CN=" + container + "," + domainCont);
  }

  var grp = cont.Create("group", "CN=" + groupName)

  grp.groupType = -2147483640

  if (groupSAMName == null)
    grp.Put("samAccountName", groupName)
  else
    grp.Put("samAccountName", groupSAMName)

  grp.SetInfo()

}

function deleteGroup (container, groupName)
{

  var rootDSE = GetObject("LDAP://rootDSE");
  domainCont = rootDSE.Get("defaultNamingContext");

  try {
    var cont = GetObject("LDAP://OU=" + container + "," + domainCont);
  }
  catch(e) {
    var cont = GetObject("LDAP://CN=" + container + "," + domainCont);
  }

  cont.Delete("group", "CN=" + groupName)
```

Continued

Listing 24-1 *(continued)*

```
}

function createLocalGroup(computer, groupName) {

  var obj = GetObject("WinNT://" + computer)
  var grp = obj.Create("group", groupName)
  grp.SetInfo()

}

function deleteLocalGroup(computer, groupName) {

  var obj = GetObject("WinNT://" + computer)
  obj.Delete("group", groupName)

}

//General computer, group and user functions

function moveAccount(orig, dest, comp) {

  var rootDSE = GetObject("LDAP://rootDSE");
  domainCont = rootDSE.Get("defaultNamingContext");

  try {
    var cont = GetObject("LDAP://OU=" + dest + "," + domainCont);
  }
  catch(e) {
    var cont = GetObject("LDAP://CN=" + dest + "," + domainCont);
  }

  try {
    cont.MoveHere("LDAP://CN=" + comp + ",OU=" + orig + "," + domainCont, "CN=" +
comp);
  }
  catch(e) {
    cont.MoveHere("LDAP://CN=" + comp + ",CN=" + orig + "," + domainCont, "CN=" +
comp);
  }

}

function mrAccount(orig, dest, comp, newcomp) {

  var rootDSE = GetObject("LDAP://rootDSE");
  domainCont = rootDSE.Get("defaultNamingContext");

  try {
    var cont = GetObject("LDAP://OU=" + dest + "," + domainCont);
  }
  catch(e) {
```

```
      var cont = GetObject("LDAP://CN=" + dest + "," + domainCont);
  }

  try {
    cont.MoveHere("LDAP://CN=" + comp + ",OU=" + orig + "," + domainCont, "CN=" +
newcomp);
  }
  catch(e) {
    cont.MoveHere("LDAP://CN=" + comp + ",CN=" + orig + "," + domainCont, "CN=" +
newcomp);
  }

}

function renameAccount(orig, comp, newcomp) {

  var rootDSE = GetObject("LDAP://rootDSE");
  domainCont = rootDSE.Get("defaultNamingContext");

  try {
    var cont = GetObject("LDAP://OU=" + orig + "," + domainCont);
  }
  catch(e) {
    var cont = GetObject("LDAP://CN=" + orig + "," + domainCont);
  }

  try {
    cont.MoveHere("LDAP://CN=" + comp + ",OU=" + orig + "," + domainCont, "CN=" +
newcomp);
  }
  catch(e) {
    cont.MoveHere("LDAP://CN=" + comp + ",CN=" + orig + "," + domainCont, "CN=" +
newcomp);
  }

}

//check functions

function checkUserGroups(domain, userSAMName) {

  var lf, ret;
  lf = "\r\n";
  ret = "";

  var ntusr = GetObject("WinNT://" + domain + "/" + userSAMName)
  ntList = new Enumerator(ntusr.Groups());

  ret += "=================================" + lf;
  ret += userSAMName + " is a member of: " + lf + lf;
```

Continued

Listing 24-1 *(continued)*

```
   for (; !ntList.atEnd(); ntList.moveNext())
   {
    s = ntList.item();
    ret += s.Name + lf;
   }

   return (ret);
}

function checkGroupMembership()
{

   var lf, ret;
   lf = "\r\n";
   ret = "";

   var prov = GetObject("WinNT:")
   tlist = new Enumerator(prov)

   for (; !tlist.atEnd(); tlist.moveNext())
    {

    s = new Enumerator(tlist.item())

    for (; !s.atEnd(); s.moveNext())
     {

     o = s.item();
     if (o.Class == "User") {


       ret += "====================================" + lf;
       if (o.FullName == "")
        ret += "Account: " + o.Name + lf;
       else
        ret += "Account: " + o.FullName + lf;

       mList = new Enumerator(o.Groups());

       for (; !mList.atEnd(); mList.moveNext())
       {
        usr = mList.item();
        ret += usr.Name + lf;
       }

     }
    }
   }
```

```
  return (ret);
}


function checkComputerAccounts() {

  //This function only checks the Computers and Domain Controllers containers
  var lf, ret;
  lf = "\r\n";
  ret = "";

  var prov = GetObject("WinNT:")

  tlist = new Enumerator(prov)

  for (; !tlist.atEnd(); tlist.moveNext())
   {

   s = new Enumerator(tlist.item());

   for (; !s.atEnd(); s.moveNext())
    {

    o = s.item();
     if (o.Class == "Computer") {

      if (o.AccountDisabled == "True") {

        ret += o.Name + " is disabled" + lf;

     }

    }

   }
  }

  return (ret);
}

function checkUserAccounts() {

  //This function checks all containers for users
  var lf, ret;
  lf = "\r\n";
  ret = "";

  var prov = GetObject("WinNT:");
  tlist = new Enumerator(prov);

  for (; !tlist.atEnd(); tlist.moveNext())
   {
```

Continued

Listing 24-1 *(continued)*

```
s = new Enumerator(tlist.item());

for (; !s.atEnd(); s.moveNext())
 {

 o = s.item();
  if (o.Class == "User") {

   if (o.AccountDisabled == 1) {

    ret += o.Name + " is disabled" + lf;

   }

   if (o.IsAccountLocked == 1) {

    ret += o.Name + " is locked" + lf;

   }
  }
 }
}

return (ret);

}
```

Using the Account Management Utilities

The account management library has more than 36 utility functions. After reviewing the source code for the utility library, you are probably ready to put these functions to work on your network. Still, you may need to take a brief look at how the functions are used, and the usage details are exactly what you'll find in the sections that follow.

Configuring domain account policies with the library utilities

The account management library includes four functions for configuring account policies. Each function sets one or more account policies in the designated domain and is used as follows:

✦ `setMinPasswordLength` sets the minimum password length.

✦ setPasswordAge sets the minimum and maximum password age in days.

✦ setAccountLockoutInfo sets the maximum number of bad passwords allowed, the auto unlock interval, and the lockout observation interval. Both intervals are specified in minutes.

✦ setPasswordHistory sets the password history length.

Listing 24-2 shows how you could use these functions in a batch script (.wsf) file.

Listing 24-2: Setting domain account policies with the utility library

logdriveinfo.wsf

```
<Job ID="SetDomainAccountPolicy">
  <Script LANGUAGE="JScript" SRC="accountlib.js" />

  <Script LANGUAGE="JScript">
      WScript.Echo(setMinPasswordLength("seattle", 8))
      WScript.Echo(setPasswordAge("seattle", 5, 60))
      WScript.Echo(setAccountLockoutInfo("seattle", 5, 60, 5))
      WScript.Echo(setPasswordHistory("seattle", 5))
  </Script>
</Job>
```

Output

```
Minimum Password Length: 8
Minimum Password Age: 5 days
Maximum Password Age: 60 days
Maximum Bad Passwords Allowed: 5
AutoLock Interval: 60 minutes
Lockout Observation Interval: 5 minutes
Password History Length: 5
```

Managing groups with the library utilities

In the account management library, you'll find a large section of functions for working with groups. As you know from previous discussions, there are several different types of groups, and each type of group has different characteristics. To manage local groups, you can use the createLocalGroup and deleteLocalGroup functions. When using these functions, be sure to reference the name of the local computer and local group to work with. The following example shows how you could create a local group called LocalMarketing on a computer called Harpo:

```
createLocalGroup("Harpo", "LocalMarketing")
```

If you later wanted to delete the group, you could call `deleteLocalGroup` with the same parameters:

```
deleteLocalGroup("Harpo", "LocalMarketing")
```

You'll also find functions for creating domain security and distribution groups. These functions are:

- ✦ `createDLDistGroup` creates a domain-local distribution group.
- ✦ `createGDistGroup` creates a global distribution group.
- ✦ `createUDistGroup` creates a universal distribution group.
- ✦ `createDLSecGroup` creates a domain-local security group.
- ✦ `createGSecGroup` creates a global security group.
- ✦ `createUSecGroup` creates a universal security group.

You call these functions with the name of the container or organizational unit in which the group should be created and the name of the group, such as:

```
createDLDistGroup ("Engineering", "EngLocalMail")
```

You don't need to specify the CN= or OU= designator. This information is added automatically using the following `try catch` statement:

```
try {
    var cont = GetObject("LDAP://OU=" + container + "," +
    domainCont);
}
catch(e) {
    var cont = GetObject("LDAP://CN=" + container + "," +
    domainCont);
}
```

Note   You'll see similar `try catch` statements used throughout this library. The primary reason for these statements is to make it easier to manage domain resources — you don't need to worry whether you are referencing a container or an organizational unit.

To delete domain groups, use the `deleteGroup` function. Because this function has the same syntax, it can be used as follows:

```
deleteGroup("Engineering", "EngLocalMail")
```

Another useful function for working with groups is `checkGroupMembership`. You can use this function to display or log the group membership of all users in the domain. An example of logging group membership is shown in Listing 24-3.

Listing 24-3: Getting and logging group membership information

logmeminfo.wsf

```
<Job ID="LogMemInfo">
  <Script LANGUAGE="JScript" SRC="accountlib.js" />
  <Script LANGUAGE="JScript" SRC="iolib.js" />

  <Script LANGUAGE="JScript">
        WriteChar("logfile.txt",checkGroupMembership())
  </Script>
</Job>
```

Output into logfile.txt

```
=====================================
Account: Administrator
Enterprise Admins
Schema Admins
Group Policy Creator Owners
Domain Admins
Domain Users
Administrators
=====================================
Account: Guest
Domain Guests
Domain Users
Guests
=====================================
Account: Henry Brown
Domain Users
=====================================
...
...
=====================================
Account: William R. Stanek
Domain Admins
Domain Users
Administrators
=====================================
```

Managing users with the library utilities

Like groups, user accounts can be managed locally and in the domain. To manage local user accounts, you can use the `createLocalUser` and `deleteLocalUser` functions. When creating a local account, pass in the name of the computer on which to create the account, the name of the account, and the account password. The following example creates an account for tjbrown on a computer called Groucho:

```
createLocalUser("Groucho", "tjbrown", "changeMe")
```

Later, you could delete the account using deleteLocalUser:

```
deleteLocalUser("Groucho", "tjbrown")
```

Creating and deleting domain user accounts is a bit different. When you create a domain account with the utility library, you must pass in the following parameters in this order:

✦ Container or organizational unit in which the new account should be created

✦ Full name for the account

✦ First name

✦ Last name

✦ login name (This parameter also sets the SAM account name.)

✦ Password

An example follows:

```
createUser("Engineering", "Henry Brown", "Henry", "Brown",
"hbrown", "radicalmamma")
```

The deleteUser function has only two parameters — the container name and the user display name. Following this, you could delete the previous account with this function call:

```
deleteUser("Engineering", "Henry Brown")
```

Functions are also provided to unlock, enable, disable, and force the user to change passwords on the next login. These functions are unlockUserAccount, enableUserAccount, disableUserAccount, and userMustChangePassword. The syntax for these functions is as follows:

```
unlockUserAccount("Engineering", "Henry Brown")
enableUserAccount("Engineering", "Henry Brown")
disableUserAccount("Engineering", "Henry Brown")
userMustChangePassword("Engineering", "Henry Brown")
```

Additional utility functions are provided, as well. changePassword is used to set a new password for a user. In this example, you set Harold's password to brownBears:

```
changePassword("Engineering", "Harold Brown", "brownBears")
```

`accountExpiration` sets the expiration date on the named account. Use a date string to set a specific expiration date, such as:

```
accountExpiration("Engineering", "Harold Brown", "12/31/99")
```

Or use –1 to specify that the account has no expiration date, such as:

```
accountExpiration("Engineering", "Harold Brown", -1)
```

`checkUserAccounts` returns a list of all accounts that are locked or disabled. You don't need to pass in any parameters when calling this function. Thus, you could call `checkUserAccounts` as follows:

```
WScript.Echo(checkUserAccounts())
```

And you'd then get a list of locked or disabled accounts:

```
Guest is disabled
krbtgt is disabled
```

The final utility function for working with user accounts is `checkUserGroups`. This function displays the group membership of a named user. Because the WinNT provider is used to obtain this list, you should be sure to pass in the SAM account name rather than the display name, as well as the NT domain name. In this example, you check the seattle domain for the group membership of wrstanek:

```
checkUserGroups("seattle", "wrstanek")
```

The result is as follows:

```
================================
wrstanek is a member of:

Enterprise Admins
Domain Admins
Domain Users
Administrators
```

Managing computers with the library utilities

Computer accounts can also be managed with this library. The key functions are the following:

- ✦ `createComputerAccount` is used to create new computer accounts but not enable them.
- ✦ `createEnabledComputerAccount` is used to create and enable new computer accounts.
- ✦ `deleteComputerAccount` is used to delete computer accounts.

✦ `disableComputerAccount` is used to disable computer accounts.

✦ `enableComputerAccount` is used to enable computer accounts.

These functions all have the same syntax. You pass in the name of container or organization units for the computer account, as well as the account name, such as:

```
createComputerAccount("Computers", "Zippo")
createEnabledComputerAccount("Computers", "Zippo")
deleteComputerAccount("Computers", "Zippo")
disableComputerAccount("Engineering", "Jupiter")
enableComputerAccount("Engineering", "Jupiter")
```

You'll find other utility functions for working with computer accounts, as well. Use `getDomainComputers` to obtain information on all active computers in the named domain. You could log information for computers in the seattle domain as shown in Listing 24-4.

Listing 24-4: **Obtaining computer account information**

logmeminfo.wsf

```
<Job ID="LogMemInfo">
  <Script LANGUAGE="JScript" SRC="accountlib.js" />
  <Script LANGUAGE="JScript" SRC="iolib.js" />

  <Script LANGUAGE="JScript">
          WriteChar("logfile.txt", getDomainComputers("seattle"))
  </Script>
</Job>
```

Output into logfile.txt

```
Computer HARPO
 Not online at this time
Computer OMEGA
 Not online at this time
Computer ZETA
 Owner: William Stanek
 Division: Web@Work
 OperatingSystem: Windows NT
 OS Version: 5.0
 Processor: x86 Family 6 Model 3 Stepping 3
 ProcessorCount: Uniprocessor Free
```

`getAllComputers` returns a similar list for all domains in the domain forest. With `checkComputerAccounts`, you can check the status of computer accounts in the domain forest. Simply call the function:

```
WScript.Echo(checkComputerAccounts())
```

You'll obtain a list of all disabled computers, such as:

```
Harpo is disabled
Omega is disabled
```

Functions for renaming and moving accounts

We've taken a look at nearly all of the functions in the utility library. The only remaining functions to discuss are the multipurpose functions:

✦ moveAccount is used to move computer, user, and group accounts.

✦ renameAccount is used to rename computer, user, and group accounts.

✦ mrAccount is used to move and rename computer, user, and group accounts.

These functions are easy to use. You pass moveAccount the original container name, the destination container name, and the name of the object to move, such as:

```
moveAccount("Engineering", "Marketing", "Henry Brown")
```

You pass renameAccount the current container, the current name, and the new name for the account, such as:

```
renameAccount("Engineering", "Henry Brown", "Harold Brown")
```

You pass mrAccount the original container name, the destination container name, the name of the object to move, and the new name, such as:

```
mrAccount("Marketing", "Engineering", "Henry Brown",
"Harold Brown")
```

That's all there is to it. The functions handle the behind the scenes work for you.

Summary

The account management utilities provide a great starting point for managing user, group, and computer accounts. If you want to use these functions in your own scripts, be sure to use batch script (.wsf) files. Remember that you can combine multiple libraries, as well as multiple scripts.

✦   ✦   ✦

Windows Script Host Quick Reference

Use the Windows Script Host Quick Reference to help you quickly find and determine usage for elements you want to work with. The reference is organized by element and by object.

XML Elements

<?job ?>

```
<?job
  [error="flag"]
  [debug="flag"] ?>
```

<?XML ?>

```
<?XML
  version="version"
  [standalone="yes"] ?>
```

<job>

```
<job [id="JobID"]>
 Job code
</job>
```

<object>

```
<object
  id="objectID"
  [classid="clsid:GUID" | progid="programID"]
/>
```

\<package\>

```
<package>
    Code for one or more jobs
</package>
```

\<reference\>

```
<reference
  [object="progID" | guid="typelibGUID"]
  [version="version"] />
```

\<script\>

```
<script
 language="language"
 [src="path"]>
    script code
</script>
```

Drives Collection

Creating: VBScript

```
Set WshNetwork = WScript.CreateObject("WScript.Network")
Set drives = WshNetwork.EnumNetworkDrives
```

Creating: JScript

```
var WshNetwork = WScript.CreateObject("WScript.Network")
var drives = WshNetwork.EnumNetworkDrives
```

Properties

```
object.Count          (Returns: integer)
object.length
object.Item(integer)
```

Printers Collection

Creating: VBScript

```
Set WshNetwork = WScript.CreateObject("WScript.Network")
Set printers = WshNetwork.EnumPrinterConnections
```

Creating: JScript

```
var WshNetwork = WScript.CreateObject("WScript.Network")
var printers = WshNetwork.EnumPrinterConnections
```

Properties

```
object.Count              (Returns: integer)
object.length
object.Item(integer)
```

StdIn Stream*

Creating

```
Set StdIn = WScript.StdIn
var StdIn = WScript.StdIn
```

Methods

```
WScript.StdIn.Close()
WScript.StdIn.Read(characters)
WScript.StdIn.ReadAll()
WScript.StdIn.ReadLine()
WScript.StdIn.Skip(characters)
WScript.StdIn.SkipLine()
```

Properties

```
WScript.StdIn.AtEndOfLine        (Returns: boolean flag)
WScript.StdIn.AtEndOfStream       (Returns: boolean flag)
WScript.StdIn.Column          (Returns: integer)
WScript.StdIn.Line          (Returns: integer)
```

---

*Accessible only in CScript.exe.

StdErr Stream*

Creating

```
Set StdErr = WScript.StdErr
var StdErr = WScript.StdErr
```

Methods

```
WScript.StdErr.Close()
WScript.StdErr.Write("text")
WScript.StdErr.WriteBlankLines(numberOfLines)
WScript.StdErr.WriteLine(["text"])
```

StdOut Stream*

Creating

```
Set StdOut = WScript.StdOut
var StdOut = WScript.StdOut
```

Methods

```
WScript.StdOut.Close()
WScript.StdOut.Write("text")
WScript.StdOut.WriteBlankLines(numberOfLines)
WScript.StdOut.WriteLine(["text"])
```

WshArguments Collection

Creating

```
Set args = WScript.Arguments
var args = WScript.Arguments
```

---

*Accessible only in CScript.exe.

Properties

```
object.Count            (Returns: integer)
object.length
object.Item(integer)
```

WshNetwork Object

Creating

```
Set wn = WScript.CreateObject( "WScript.Network" )
var wn = WScript.CreateObject( "WScript.Network" )
```

Methods

```
object.AddPrinterConnection("localPort",
                            "networkPrinterPath"
                            [,"storeProfileFlag"]
                            [,"userName"]
                            [,"password"])
object.AddWindowsPrinterConnection("networkPrinterPath",
                                   "printerDriverName"
                                   [,"printerPort"])
object.EnumNetworkDrives()
object.EnumPrinterConnections()
object.MapNetworkDrive("driveLetter",
                       "networkShare",
                       [,"storeProfileFlag"]
                       [,"userName"]
                       [,"password"])
object.RemoveNetworkDrive("driveLetterOrNetworkPath"
                          [,"forceFlag"]
                          [,"updateProfileFlag"])
object.RemovePrinterConnection("printerPortOrNetworkPath"
                               [,"forceFlag"]
                               [,"updateProfileFlag"])
object.SetDefaultPrinter("remotePrinterName")
```

Properties

```
object.ComputerName    (Returns: string; current computer
name)
object.UserDomain      (Returns: string; current user domain)
object.UserName        (Returns: string; current user name)
```

WScript Object

Creating

Top-level object; forming the root of the object hierarchy

Methods

```
WScript.ConnectObject(objectName,
                      eventPrefix)
WScript.CreateObject(objectName
                     [,eventPrefix])
WScript.DisconnectObject(objectName)
WScript.Echo([Arg1]
             [,Arg2]
             [,ArgN])
WScript.GetObject(pathToFileContainingAutomationObject
                  [,programID]
                  [,eventPrefix])
WScript.Quit([errorCode])
WScript.Sleep(numberOfMilliseconds)
```

Properties

```
WScript.Application          (Returns: IDispatch interface)
WScript.Arguments        (Returns: WshArguments
collection)
WScript.FullName    (Returns: string; full path to host
executable)
WScript.Name     (Returns: string; name of WScript object)
WScript.Path (Returns: string; directory where script host
resides)
WScript.ScriptFullName(Returns: string; full path to current
script)
WScript.ScriptName      (Returns: string; name of current
script)
WScript.StdErr            (Returns: StdErr stream)
WScript.StdIn          (Returns: StdIn stream)
WScript.StdOut         (Returns: StdOut stream)
WScript.Version        (Returns: script; script host version)
```

WshEnvironment Object

Creating: VBScript

```
Set WshShell = WScript.CreateObject("WScript.Shell")
Set WshEnv = WshShell.Environment("EnvironmentVariableType")
```

Creating: JScript

```
var WshShell = WScript.CreateObject("WScript.Shell")
var WshEnv = WshShell.Environment("EnvironmentVariableType")
```

Methods

```
object.remove("environmentVariableToDelete")
```

Properties

```
object.Count            (Returns: integer)
object.length
object.Item("folderName")
```

WshShell Object

Creating

```
Set ws = WScript.CreateObject("WScript.Shell")
var ws = WScript.CreateObject("WScript.Shell")
```

Methods

```
object.AppActivate("appTitle")
object.CreateShortcut(shortcutNamePath)
object.ExpandEnvironmentStrings(environmentVariableToExpand)
object.LogEvent(eventType,
                "eventDescription"
                [,"targetSystem"])
object.Popup("popupText",
                [secondsToWait]
                [,"popupTitle"]
                [,buttonType])
object.RegDelete("pathToRegistryKeyOrValue")
object.RegRead("pathToRegistryKeyOrValue")
object.RegWrite("pathToRegistryKeyOrValue"
                valueToWrite
                [,dataType])
object.Run("command"
                [,windowStyle]
                ["waitOnReturnFlag"])
object.SendKeys("keysToSend")
```

Properties

```
object.Environment ["environmentVariableType"]
object.SpecialFolders "specialFolderName"
```

WshShortcut Object

Creating: VBScript

```
Set WshShell = WScript.CreateObject("WScript.Shell")
Set linkShortcut = WshShell.CreateShortcut("Name.LNK")
```

Creating: JScript

```
var WshShell = WScript.CreateObject("WScript.Shell")
var linkShortcut = WshShell.CreateShortcut("Name.LNK")
```

Methods

```
object.Save()
```

Properties

```
object.Arguments = "argString"
object.Description = "shortcutDescription"
object.FullName          (Returns: string; full file path to
shortcut)
object.Hotkey = "hotKey"
object.IconLocation = "iconPath, iconIndex"
object.TargetPath = "filePath"
object.WindowStyle = "windowStyle"
object.WorkingDirectory = "workingDirectory"
```

WshSpecialFolders Object

Creating: VBScript

```
Set WshShell = WScript.CreateObject("WScript.Shell")
folder = WshShell.SpecialFolders("SpecialFolderName")
```

Creating: JScript

```
var WshShell = WScript.CreateObject("WScript.Shell")
folder = WshShell.SpecialFolders("SpecialFolderName")
```

Properties

```
object.Count (Returns: integer)
object.length
object.Item("folderName")
```

WshUrlShortcut Object

Creating: VBScript

```
Set WshShell = WScript.CreateObject("WScript.Shell")
Set urlShortcut = WshShell.CreateShortcut("Name.URL")
```

Creating: JScript

```
var WshShell = WScript.CreateObject("WScript.Shell")
var urlShortcut = WshShell.CreateShortcut("Name.URL")
```

Methods

```
object.Save()
```

Properties

```
object.FullName          (Returns: string; full file path to
shortcut)
object.TargetPath = "urlPath"
```

✦   ✦   ✦

Core ADSI Reference

Active Directory Service Interfaces provide the core objects used to script directory services, computer resources, and networks. This appendix provides a quick reference for key interfaces, and their related properties and methods. The reference is not meant to be exhaustive, rather the focus is on the most commonly used features in Windows scripts.

Using This Reference

ADSI providers implement the interfaces examined in this appendix. In Chapter 14, you learned about system providers, specifically WinNT, LDAP, NDS, and NWCOMPAT. These providers implement different subsets of these interfaces. Because each object implements multiple interfaces and there is almost always overlap between objects, it isn't practical to map out each object separately.

Instead, you'll use Tables 14-2 to 14-5 in Chapter 14 and this appendix to map out the core features of an object. For example, if you wanted to determine the complete set of methods and properties that are available for the WinNT Computer object, you would look at Table 14-3 and see that the object implements IADs, IADsComputer, IADsComputerOperations, IADsContainer, and IADsPropertyList. You would then examine each of these interfaces in order to determine available properties and methods that may be available to the WinNT Computer object.

With the LDAP and NDS providers, keep in mind that GenObject provides basic services for most objects. For example, with the LDAP Group object, Table 14-2 shows that Group implements

- ✦ IADsGroup
- ✦ IADsExtension

and GenObject implements

- ✦ IADs
- ✦ IADsContainer
- ✦ IADsDeleteOps
- ✦ IADsObjectOptions
- ✦ IADsPropertyList
- ✦ IDirectoryObject
- ✦ IDirectorySearch

Thus, the combination of features for these interfaces represents the total set of methods and properties that may be available to the Group object.

ADSI Interfaces

The sections that follow provide a quick reference for ADSI interfaces. ADSI providers and ADSI are completely extensible. This means that new versions of providers and ADSI may add or change key features. *Providers don't have to implement all the features of an interface, either.*

IADs

The IADs interface provides the core features for all ADSI objects. You obtain a pointer to this interface when you bind to an object, such as:

```
Set user = GetObject("LDAP://CN=William Stanek,CN=Users
,DC=TVPRESS, DC=Com")
user.Put "givenName", "William"
user.Put "sn", "Stanek"
user.SetInfo
```

Properties

AdsPath
Value: String   **Gettable:** Yes   **Settable:** No
Description: The object's ADsPath that uniquely identifies this object from all others.

Class
Value: String   **Gettable:** Yes   **Settable:** No
Description: The name of the object's class.

GUID
Value: String   **Gettable:** Yes   **Settable:** No
Description: The GUID of the object from the directory store.

Name
Value: String   **Gettable:** Yes   **Settable:** No
Description: The object's relative name.

Parent
Value: String   **Gettable:** Yes   **Settable:** No
Description: The ADsPath string for the parent of the object.

Schema
Value: String   **Gettable:** Yes   **Settable:** No
Description: The ADsPath string to the schema class object for this object.

Methods

Get("*propertyName*")
Returns: String or array
Description: Gets a property value from the property cache.

GetEx("*propertyName*")
Returns: Array
Description: Gets an array of cached property values.

GetInfo()
Returns: Error status
Description: Gets property values for an object from the directory store and loads them into the property cache. Called implicitly the first time you get an object's property. Overwrites any previously cached values for the object.

GetInfoEx("*propertyName*")
Returns: Error status
Description: Gets the values for the select property from the directory store and loads them into the property cache.

Put("*propertyName*", *valueString*)
Returns: Error status
Description: Sets a new value in the property cache.

PutEx(*Flag*, "*propertyName*", *valueArray*)
Returns: Error status
Description: Sets an array of cached values.

SetInfo()
Returns: Error status
Description: Saves the object's cached values to the data store.

IADsAcl

The IADsAcl interface is used to work with ACL attribute values in Novell NetWare Directory Services (NDS).

Properties

Privileges
Value: Number   **Gettable:** Yes   **Settable:** Yes
Description: The privilege setting.

ProtectedAttrName
Value: String   **Gettable:** Yes   **Settable:** Yes
Description: The name of the protected attribute.

SubjectName
Value: String   **Gettable:** Yes   **Settable:** Yes
Description: The name of the subject.

Method

CopyAcl()
Returns: Error status
Description: Makes a copy of an existing ACL.

IADsBackLink

The `IADsBackLink` interface is used to access the Back Link attribute in Novell NetWare Directory Services (NDS).

Properties

ObjectName
Value: String   **Gettable:** Yes   **Settable:** Yes
Description: The name of an object to which the Back Link is attached.

RemoteID
Value: Number   **Gettable:** Yes   **Settable:** Yes
Description: The numeric identifier of a remote server.

IADsCaseIgnoreList

The `IADsCaseIgnoreList` interface is used to access the Case Ignore List attribute in Novell NetWare Directory Services (NDS).

Property

CaseIgnoreList
Value: Array   **Gettable:** Yes   **Settable:** Yes
Description: A sequence of case-insensitive strings.

IADsClass

The `IADsClass` interface is designed for managing schema class objects. You access an object's schema class through its `Schema` property, such as:

```
Set obj = GetObject("WinNT://zeta,computer")
Set cls = GetObject(obj.Schema)

For Each p in cls.MandatoryProperties
    WScript.Echo "Mandatory: " & p
Next
For Each p in cls.OptionalProperties
    WScript.Echo "Optional: " & p
Next
```

Properties

Abstract
Value: Boolean   **Gettable:** Yes   **Settable:** Yes
Description: Boolean value that indicates whether the schema class is abstract.

AuxDerivedFrom
Value: Array   **Gettable:** Yes   **Settable:** Yes
Description: Array of AdsPath strings that specify the super Auxiliary classes of this schema class.

Auxiliary
Value: Boolean   **Gettable:** Yes   **Settable:** Yes
Description: Boolean value that determines whether this schema class is an Auxiliary class.

CLSID
Value: String   **Gettable:** Yes   **Settable:** Yes
Description: A provider-specific string that identifies the COM object that implements this schema class.

Container
Value: Boolean   **Gettable:** Yes   **Settable:** Yes
Description: Boolean value that indicates whether this is a Container object.

Containment
Value: Array   **Gettable:** Yes   **Settable:** Yes
Description: Array of strings that identify object types that can be contained within this container.

DerivedFrom
Value: Array   **Gettable:** Yes   **Settable:** Yes
Description: Array of AdsPath strings that indicate which classes this class is derived from.

HelpFileContext
Value: String   **Gettable:** Yes   **Settable:** Yes
Description: The context identifier for an optional help file.

HelpFileName
Value: String   **Gettable:** Yes   **Settable:** Yes
Description: The name of an optional help file.

MandatoryProperties
Value: Array   **Gettable:** Yes   **Settable:** Yes
Description: An array of strings that lists the mandatory properties for an ADSI object.

NamingProperties
Value: Array   **Gettable:** Yes   **Settable:** Yes
Description: An array of strings that list the properties that are used for naming attributes.

OID
Value: String   **Gettable:** Yes   **Settable:** Yes
Description: The directory-specific object identifier.

OptionalProperties
Value: Array   **Gettable:** Yes   **Settable:** Yes
Description: An array of strings that list the optional properties for an ADSI object.

PossibleSuperiors
Value: Array   **Gettable:** Yes   **Settable:** Yes
Description: An array of `AdsPath` strings that lists classes that can contain instances of this class.

PrimaryInterface
Value: String   **Gettable:** Yes   **Settable:** No
Description: The globally unique identifier of the interface defining this schema class.

Method

Qualifiers()
Returns: Collection of ADSI objects
Description: Method obtains a collection with additional provider-specific limits on the object class. (Not currently implemented)

IADsCollection

The `IADsCollection` interface is used to manage collections. Two special types of collections are `IADsContainer` and `IADsMembers`. You can obtain a collection of session objects as follows:

```
Set fso = GetObject("WinNT://zeta/LanmanServer")
Set coll = fso.Sessions

For Each session In coll
  WScript.Echo "Session name: " & session.Name
Next
```

Methods

Add(Object)
Returns: Error status
Description: Adds an object to the collection. Some collections don't support adding objects.

Remove(*Object*)
Returns: Error status
Description: Removes an object from the collection. Some collections don't support removing objects.

GetObject(*Object*)
Returns: Error status
Description: Gets the specified object. Some collections don't support this method.

IADsComputer

The IADsComputer interface is used to manage computers on a network. You can use this interface when you bind to a computer object, such as:

```
Set comp = GetObject("WinNT://zeta,computer")
If (comp.Class = "Computer") Then
 'Do the following
End If
```

Properties

ComputerID
Value: String   **Gettable:** Yes   **Settable:** No
Description: The globally unique identifier for this machine.

Department
Value: String   **Gettable:** Yes   **Settable:** Yes
Description: The department to which this computer belongs.

Description
Value: String   **Gettable:** Yes   **Settable:** Yes
Description: The description of this computer.

Division
Value: String   **Gettable:** Yes   **Settable:** Yes
Description: The division to which this computer belongs.

Location
Value: String   **Gettable:** Yes   **Settable:** Yes
Description: The physical location of this computer.

MemorySize
Value: Number   **Gettable:** Yes   **Settable:** Yes
Description: The amount of RAM in MB.

Model
Value: String   **Gettable:** Yes   **Settable:** Yes
Description: The model of this computer.

NetAddresses
Value: Array   **Gettable:** Yes   **Settable:** Yes
Description: The network addresses of the computer.

OperatingSystem
Value: String   **Gettable:** Yes   **Settable:** Yes
Description: The installed operating system in use.

OperatingSystemVersion
Value: String   **Gettable:** Yes   **Settable:** Yes
Description: The version of installed operating system in use.

Owner
Value: String   **Gettable:** Yes   **Settable:** Yes
Description: The owner of this computer.

PrimaryUser
Value: String   **Gettable:** Yes   **Settable:** Yes
Description: The contact person for this computer.

Processor
Value: String   **Gettable:** Yes   **Settable:** Yes
Description: The type of CPU.

ProcessorCount
Value: Number   **Gettable:** Yes   **Settable:** Yes
Description: The number of processors installed in this computer.

Role
Value: String   **Gettable:** Yes   **Settable:** Yes
Description: The role of this computer, such as server or workstation.

Site
Value: String   **Gettable:** Yes   **Settable:** No
Description: The globally unique identifier for the site to which the computer belongs.

StorageCapacity
Value: Number   **Gettable:** Yes   **Settable:** Yes
Description: The size of disk space in MB.

IADsComputerOperations

The IADsComputerOperations interface provides extended functions for computers. You can bind to a Computer object and use this interface as follows:

```
Set user =
GetObject("WinNT://domainName/computerName,computer")
```

Methods

Shutdown(*"rebootFlag"*)
Returns: Error status
Description: Executes a remote shutdown of a computer. Set rebootFlag to true for reboot after shutdown.

Status()
Returns: Status code
Description: Returns the current operations status of the computer.

IADsContainer

The IADsContainer interface enables container objects to create, delete, and manage contained ADSI objects. You obtain a pointer to this interface when you bind to a container object, such as:

```
Set obj = GetObject("WinNT://zeta,computer")
Set cls = GetObject(obj.Schema)
If (cls.Container = TRUE) then
    WScript.Echo "The object is a container."
```

```
Else
    WScript.Echo "The object is not a container."
End If
```

Properties

Count
Value: Number   **Gettable:** Yes   **Settable:** No
Description: The number of directory objects in the container or the number of filtered items.

Filter
Value: Array   **Gettable:** Yes   **Settable:** Yes
Description: Items in the array represent object classes.

Hints
Value: Array   **Gettable:** Yes   **Settable:** Yes
Description: Items in the array represent properties found in the schema definition.

Methods

CopyHere("*AdsPath*","*newName*")
Returns: Error status
Description: Creates a copy of an object within a directory.

Create("*objectClass*","*relativeName*")
Returns: Error status
Description: Creates a new object within a container.

Delete("*objectClass*","*relativeName*")
Returns: Error status
Description: Deletes a specified object from a container.

GetObject("*objectClass*","*relativeName*")
Returns: Error status
Description: Gets interface for a named object.

MoveHere("*AdsPathToObject*","*relativeName*")
Returns: Error status
Description: Moves or renames an object within a directory.

IADsDeleteOps

The `IADsDeleteOps` interface provides a method that an object can use to delete itself from the directory store. With container objects, the method also deletes all objects within the container. If the object doesn't implement this interface, you can delete the object via the parent object. You can use `IADsDeleteOps` to delete an object as follows:

```
Set cont = GetObject("LDAP://OU=marketing,DC=tvpress,DC=com")
cont.DeleteObject(0)
```

Method

DeleteObject(*Flag*)
Returns: Error status
Description: Deletes the object from the directory. Set the deletion flag to zero.

IADsDomain

The `IADsDomain` interface is designed for managing resources in domains. You can use this interface when you bind to a domain object, such as:

```
Set comp = GetObject("WinNT://zeta ")
If (comp.Class = "Domain") Then
 'Do the following
End If
```

Properties

AutoUnlockInterval
Value: Number   **Gettable:** Yes   **Settable:** Yes
Description: The minimum time that can elapse before a locked account is automatically re-enabled.

IsWorkgroup
Value: Boolean   **Gettable:** Yes   **Settable:** No
Description: A Boolean that determines whether the computer is a member of a workgroup, rather than a domain.

LockoutObservationInterval
Value: Number   **Gettable:** Yes   **Settable:** Yes
Description: The time interval during which the bad password counter is increased.

MaxBadPasswordsAllowed
Value: Number   **Gettable:** Yes   **Settable:** Yes
Description: The maximum bad password logins before the account is locked out.

MaxPasswordAge
Value: Number   **Gettable:** Yes   **Settable:** Yes
Description: The maximum time that can elapse before a password must be changed.

MinPasswordAge
Value: Number   **Gettable:** Yes   **Settable:** Yes
Description: The minimum time that can elapse before a password can be changed.

MinPasswordLength
Value: Number   **Gettable:** Yes   **Settable:** Yes
Description: The minimum number of characters required in a password.

PasswordAttributes
Value: Number   **Gettable:** Yes   **Settable:** Yes
Description: The restrictions on passwords. Restrictions are set with the following:

✦ `PASSWORD_ATTR_NONE` or 0x00000000

✦ `PASSWORD_ATTR_MIXED_CASE` or 0x00000001

✦ `PASSWORD_ATTR_COMPLEX` or 0x00000002

With `PASSWORD_ATTR_COMPLEX`, the password must include at least one punctuation mark or nonprintable character.

PasswordHistoryLength
Value: Number   **Gettable:** Yes   **Settable:** Yes
Description: The number of passwords saved in the password history. Users cannot reuse a password in the history list.

IADsEmail

The `IADsEmail` interface is used to access the Email Address attribute in Novell NetWare Directory Services (NDS).

Properties

Address
Value: String   **Gettable:** Yes   **Settable:** Yes
Description: The email address of the user.

Type

Value: Number   **Gettable:** Yes   **Settable:** Yes
Description: The type of the email message.

IADsExtension

The IADsExtension interface provides features for extending ADSI. Used with interfaces that extend core ADSI. You won't normally access this interface directly in scripts.

IADsFaxNumber

The IADsFaxNumber interface is used to access the Facsimile Telephone Number attribute in Novell NetWare Directory Services (NDS).

Properties

Parameters

Value: Array   **Gettable:** Yes   **Settable:** Yes
Description: Parameters for the fax machine.

TelephoneNumber

Value: String   **Gettable:** Yes   **Settable:** Yes
Description: The telephone number of the fax machine.

IADsFileService

The IADsFileService interface is used to manage file services. This interface inherits from IADsService, and only additional properties are detailed in this section. You can use this interface when you bind to a file service, such as:

```
Set fs = GetObject("WinNT://zeta/LanmanServer")

fs.Description = "WinNT file service."
n = fs.MaxUserCount
If n = -1 Then
    WScript.Echo "No limit on LanmanServer."
Else
    WScript.Echo n & " users are allowed."
End If
```

To access active sessions or open resources used by the file service, you have to go through the IADsFileServiceOperations interface.

Properties

Description
Value: String   **Gettable:** Yes   **Settable:** Yes
Description: The description of the file service.

MaxUserCount
Value: Number   **Gettable:** Yes   **Settable:** Yes
Description: The maximum number of users allowed to run the service concurrently. A value of –1 indicates no limit is set.

IADsFileServiceOperations

The IADsFileServiceOperations interface provides extended functions for file services. You can bind to a FileService object and use this interface as follows:

```
Set user =
GetObject("WinNT://domainName/computerName/LanmanServer")
```

The IADsFileServiceOperations interface allows you to work with open resources and active sessions of the file service through IADsSession and IADsResource, respectively. You can use these collections as follows:

```
Set fso = GetObject("WinNT://zeta/LanmanServer")
For Each resource In fso.Resources
    WScript.Echo "Resource path: " & resource.Path
Next
For Each session In fso.sessions
    WScript.Echo "Session name: " & session.Name
Next
```

Methods

Resources()
Returns: Resource Collection
Description: Gets an interface pointer on a collection object that represents current open resources for this file service.

Sessions()
Returns: Sessions Collection
Description: Gets an interface pointer on a collection object that represents current open sessions on this file service.

IADsFileShare

The `IADsFileShare` interface is used to manage shared folders. You can use this interface when you bind to the LanmanServer service on the host computer, such as:

```
Set fso = GetObject("WinNT://seattle/zeta/LanmanServer")
Set fs = fso.Create("FileShare", "Test")
WScript.Echo fs.Class
fs.Path = "F:\test"
fs.SetInfo
```

Properties

CurrentUserCount
Value: Number   **Gettable:** Yes   **Settable:** No
Description: The current number of users connected to this share.

Description
Value: String   **Gettable:** Yes   **Settable:** Yes
Description: The description of the file share.

HostComputer
Value: String   **Gettable:** Yes   **Settable:** Yes
Description: The `AdsPath` reference to the host computer.

Path
Value: String   **Gettable:** Yes   **Settable:** Yes
Description: The file system path to a shared directory.

MaxUserCount
Value: Number   **Gettable:** Yes   **Settable:** Yes
Description: The maximum number of concurrent users for the share.

IADsGroup

The `IADsGroup` interface is used to manage group membership. You can use this interface when you bind to a Group object, such as:

```
Set grp = GetObject("LDAP://CN=Backup
Operators,CN=Builtin,DC=seattle,DC=domain,DC=com")
```

```
grp.Add("LDAP://CN=William R.
Stanek,CN=Users,DC=seattle,DC=domain,DC=com")

WScript.Echo grp.IsMember("LDAP://CN=William R.
Stanek,CN=Users,DC=seattle,DC=domain,DC=com")
```

Property

Description
Value: String   **Gettable:** Yes   **Settable:** Yes
Description: The description of the group.

Methods

Add(*"AdsPathString"*)
Returns: Error status
Description: Adds an object to a group.

IsMember(*"AdsPathString"*)
Returns: Membership flag
Description: Determines whether the user or group is a member. A nonzero value indicates that the user is a member of the group.

Members(*"AdsPathString"*)
Returns: Members object collection
Description: Gets the Members object collection that you can use to iterate through group membership.

Remove(*"AdsPathString"*)
Returns: Error status
Description: Removes an object from a group.

IADsHold

The IADsHold interface is used to access the Hold attribute in Novell NetWare Directory Services (NDS).

Properties

Amount
Value: Number   **Gettable:** Yes   **Settable:** Yes
Description: The amount charged against the user for the period on hold.

ObjectName
Value: String   **Gettable:** Yes   **Settable:** Yes
Description: The name of the object on hold.

IADsLargeInteger

The IADsLargeInteger interface is used to manipulate 64-bit integers of the LargeInteger type. Use the formula:

```
largeInt = HighPart * 2^32 + LowPart
```

Properties

HighPart
Value: Number   **Gettable:** Yes   **Settable:** Yes
Description: The high part of the integer.

LowPart
Value: Number   **Gettable:** Yes   **Settable:** Yes
Description: The low part of the integer.

IADsLocality

The IADsLocality interface represents the geographical location of a directory element and is used to manage locality. The interface supports organizing accounts by location, organization, and organizational unit. IADsLocality implements IADsContainer. You can access this interface as follows:

```
Set dom = getObject("LDAP://zeta/DC=tvpress, DC=com")
Set loc = dom.GetObject("locality","L=myLocality")
```

Properties

Description
Value: String   **Gettable:** Yes   **Settable:** Yes
Description: The description of the locality.

LocalityName
Value: String   **Gettable:** Yes   **Settable:** Yes
Description: The name of the locality.

PostalAddress
Value: String   **Gettable:** Yes   **Settable:** Yes
Description: The main post office address of the locality.

SeeAlso
Value: String   **Gettable:** Yes   **Settable:** Yes
Description: Other information relevant to the locality.

IADsMembers

The IADsMembers interface is used to manage a collection of objects that belong to a group. You can use this interface when you get the Members object collection, such as:

```
Set grp = GetObject("LDAP://CN=Administrators,CN=Builtin,
DC=seattle,DC=domain,DC=com")

grp.members.filter = Array("user")
For each usr in grp.members
    WScript.Echo usr.Name & "," & usr.Class & "," & usr.AdsPath
Next
```

Properties

Count
Value: String   **Gettable:** Yes   **Settable:** No
Description: The number of members.

Filter
Value: String   **Gettable:** Yes   **Settable:** Yes
Description: The filter for selection.

IADsNamespaces

The IADsNamespaces interface is used to manage namespace objects. You obtain a pointer to this interface when you bind to the object using the "ADs:" string, such as:

```
Set ns = GetObject("ADs:")
```

Property

DefaultContainer
Value: Array   **Gettable:** Yes   **Settable:** Yes
Description: The default container name for the current user. You can set this property by assigning an AdsPath. You do not need to call SetInfo().

IADsNetAddress

The `IADsNetAddress` interface is used to access the Net Address attribute in Novell NetWare Directory Services (NDS).

Properties

Address
Value: Array   **Gettable:** Yes   **Settable:** Yes
Description: The network addresses supported.

AddressType
Value: Number   **Gettable:** Yes   **Settable:** Yes
Description: The communication protocol supported.

IADsO

The `IADsO` interface is used to manage the organization to which an account belongs. `IADsO` implements `IADsContainer`. You can use this interface when you obtain a pointer to the domain object, such as:

```
Set prov = GetObject("LDAP:")
Set org =
prov.OpenDSObject("LDAP://DC=SEATTLE,DC=DOMAIN,DC=COM",
"wrstanek@seattle.domain.com","stanek",
ADS_SECURE_AUTHENTICATION)

org.Filter = Array("organization")
For each o in org
    WScript.Echo "Fax number of " & o.Name & " : " &
o.Description
Next
```

Properties

Description
Value: String   **Gettable:** Yes   **Settable:** Yes
Description: The description of the organization.

FaxNumber
Value: String   **Gettable:** Yes   **Settable:** Yes
Description: The fax number of the organization.

LocalityName
Value: String   **Gettable:** Yes   **Settable:** Yes
Description: The name of the organization.

PostalAddress
Value: String   **Gettable:** Yes   **Settable:** Yes
Description: The postal address of the organization.

SeeAlso
Value: String   **Gettable:** Yes   **Settable:** Yes
Description: The other information relevant to this organization.

TelephoneNumber
Value: String   **Gettable:** Yes   **Settable:** Yes
Description: The telephone number of the organization.

IADsObjectOptions

The IADsObjectOptions interface for accessing provider-specific options of an ADSI object. These options are primarily used when searching the directory, such as:

```
Set cont = GetObject("LDAP://DC=seattle,DC=domain,DC=com")
srvName = cont.GetOption(ADS_OPTION_SERVERNAME)
WScript.Echo "Server Name for connection: " & srvName
PageSize = cont.GetOption(ADS_OPTION_PAGE_SIZE)
```

Methods

GetOption(*optionConstantOrValue*)
Returns: Error status
Description: Gets an option. Options are:

ADS_OPTION_SERVERNAME or 0

ADS_OPTION_REFERRALS or 1

ADS_OPTION_PAGE_SIZE or 2

ADS_OPTION_SECURITY_MASK or 3

SetOption(*optionConstantOrValue*, *integerValue*)
Returns: Error status
Description: Sets an option.

IADsOctetList

The `IADsOctetList` interface is used to access the OctetList attribute in Novell NetWare Directory Services (NDS).

Property

OctetList
Value: Array   **Gettable:** Yes   **Settable:** Yes
Description: An ordered sequence of byte arrays.

IADsOpenDSObject

The `IADsOpenDSObject` interface is designed to obtain an object reference securely. You obtain a pointer to this interface when you bind to the ADSI provider that you want to work with, such as:

```
Set prov = GetObject("WinNT:")
Set user = prov.OpenDSObject("WinNT://" & NTDomain & "/" &
NTUser,"wrstane","jiggyPop", ADS_SECURE_AUTHENTICATION)
```

Method

OpenDSObject(*ADSPath, UserID, Password, Flags*)
Returns: Pointer to the object
Description: Binds to an ADSI object using the specified credentials.

IADsOU

The `IADsOU` interface is used to manage the organizational unit to which an account belongs. `IADsOU` implements `IADsContainer`. You can use this interface when you obtain a pointer to the domain object, such as:

```
Set prov = GetObject("LDAP:")
Set org =
prov.OpenDSObject("LDAP://DC=SEATTLE,DC=DOMAIN,DC=COM",
"wrstanek@seattle.domain.com","stanek",
ADS_SECURE_AUTHENTICATION)

org.Filter = Array("OrganizationalUnit")
For each o in org
    WScript.Echo "Category " & o.BusinessCategory & " : " &
o.Description
Next
```

Properties

BusinessCategory
Value: String   **Gettable:** Yes   **Settable:** Yes
Description: The business function of the organizational unit.

Description
Value: String   **Gettable:** Yes   **Settable:** Yes
Description: The description of the organizational unit.

FaxNumber
Value: String   **Gettable:** Yes   **Settable:** Yes
Description: The fax number of the unit.

LocalityName
Value: String   **Gettable:** Yes   **Settable:** Yes
Description: The physical location of the unit.

PostalAddress
Value: String   **Gettable:** Yes   **Settable:** Yes
Description: The post office address of the unit.

SeeAlso
Value: String   **Gettable:** Yes   **Settable:** Yes
Description: Other information relevant to the unit.

TelephoneNumber
Value: String   **Gettable:** Yes   **Settable:** Yes
Description: The telephone number of the unit.

IADsPath

The `IADsPath` interface is used to access the Path attribute in Novell NetWare Directory Services (NDS).

Properties

Path
Value: String   **Gettable:** Yes   **Settable:** Yes
Description: The file path for a directory.

Type
Value: Number   **Gettable:** Yes   **Settable:** Yes
Description: The type of file system.

VolumeName
Value: String   **Gettable:** Yes   **Settable:** Yes
Description: The name of the volume.

IADsPathname

The IADsPathname interface is used to examine, extract, and construct paths. You can use this interface with any AdsPath.

Property

EscapedMode
Value: Number   **Gettable:** Yes   **Settable:** Yes
Description: The mode for escaping a path. Valid modes are:

```
ADS_ESCAPEDMODE_DEFAULT or 1
ADS_ESCAPEDMODE_ON or 2
ADS_ESCAPEDMODE_OFF or 3
```

Methods

AddLeafElement("*leafElement*")
Returns: Error status
Description: Adds an element to the end of the object path.

CopyPath()
Returns: Error status
Description: Instantiates an object with the same path as the current AdsPath.

GetElement(*index*)
Returns: Error status
Description: Gets the leaf element stored at the index.

GetEscapedElement(*number,stringToEscape*)
Returns: Escaped string
Description: Takes a path string with special characters and returns the string with escaped values. The *number* parameter is reserved for future use, so just enter 0.

GetNumElements()
Returns: Number
Description: Gets the number of elements in the path.

RemoveLeafElement()
Returns: Error status
Description: Removes the last element from the path.

Retrieve(*formatType*)
Returns: AdsPath String
Description: Retrieves a path with a specific format. Formats are:

ADS_FORMAT_WINDOWS or 1

ADS_FORMAT_WINDOWS_NO_SERVER or 2

ADS_FORMAT_WINDOWS_DN or 3

ADS_FORMAT_WINDOWS_PARENT or 4

ADS_FORMAT_X500 or 5

ADS_FORMAT_X500_NO_SERVER or 6

ADS_FORMAT_X500_DN or 7

ADS_FORMAT_X500_PARENT or 8

ADS_FORMAT_SERVER or 9

ADS_FORMAT_PROVIDER or 10

ADS_FORMAT_NAMESPACE or 10

ADS_FORMAT_LEAF or 11

Set("*AdsPath*",*optionType*)
Returns: Error status
Description: Sets an AdsPath string with specific type. Option types are:

ADS_SETTYPE_FULL or 1

ADS_SETTYPE_PROVIDER or 2

ADS_SETTYPE_NAMESPACE or 2

ADS_SETTYPE_SERVER or 3

ADS_SETTYPE_DN or 4

SetDisplayType(*displayType*)
Returns: Error status
Description: Determines how a path is to be displayed. Display types are:

ADS_DISPLAY_FULL or 1

ADS_DISPLAY_VALUE_ONLY or 2

IADsPostalAddress

The IADsPostalAddress interface is used to access the Postal Address attribute in Novell NetWare Directory Services (NDS).

Properties

PostalAddress
Value: Array   **Gettable:** Yes   **Settable:** Yes
Description: The postal address of the user.

IADsPrintJob

The IADsPrintJob interface represents print jobs. Use the IADsPrintJobOperations interface to manage print jobs. You can access this interface through a PrintQueue object, such as:

```
Set pq = GetObject("WinNT://zeta/HPDeskJe")
Set pqo = pq
For Each pj in pqo.PrintJobs
    WScript.Echo pj.class
    WScript.Echo pj.description
    WScript.Echo pj.HostPrintQueue
    Set pjo = pj
    If Hex(pjo.status) = 10 Then
      ' if document is printing; pause it
        pjo.Pause
    Else
        pjo.Resume
    End If
Next
```

Properties

Description
Value: String   **Gettable:** Yes   **Settable:** Yes
Description: The description of the print job.

HostPrintQueue
Value: String   **Gettable:** Yes   **Settable:** No
Description: An ADsPath string that names the print queue processing this print job.

Notify
Value: String   **Gettable:** Yes   **Settable:** Yes
Description: The user to be notified when the job is completed.

NotifyPath
Value: String   **Gettable:** Yes   **Settable:** Yes
Description: An AdsPath string for the user to be notified when the job is completed.

Priority
Value: Number   **Gettable:** Yes   **Settable:** Yes
Description: The priority of the print job.

Size
Value: Number   **Gettable:** Yes   **Settable:** No
Description: The size of the print job in bytes.

StartTime
Value: Date   **Gettable:** Yes   **Settable:** Yes
Description: The earliest time when the print job should be started.

TimeSubmitted
Value: Date   **Gettable:** Yes   **Settable:** No
Description: The time when the job was submitted to the print queue.

TotalPages
Value: Number   **Gettable:** Yes   **Settable:** No
Description: The total number of pages in the print job.

UntilTime
Value: Date   **Gettable:** Yes   **Settable:** Yes
Description: The time when the print job should be stopped.

User
Value: String   **Gettable:** Yes   **Settable:** No
Description: The name of user who submitted the print job.

UserPath
Value: String   **Gettable:** Yes   **Settable:** No
Description: The AdsPath string for the user who submitted the print job.

IADsPrintJobOperations

The `IADsPrintJobOperations` interface provides extended functions for print jobs. You can use this interface when you obtain a `PrintJob` object, such as:

```
Set pqo = GetObject("WinNT://zeta/HPDeskJe")
For each pj in pqo.PrintJobs
 set pjo = pj
 WScript.Echo "Print job status: " & Hex(pjo.status)
Next
```

Properties

PagesPrinted
Value: Number   **Gettable:** Yes   **Settable:** No
Description: The total number of pages printed for the current job.

Position
Value: Number   **Gettable:** Yes   **Settable:** Yes
Description: The numeric position of print job in the print queue.

Status
Value: Number   **Gettable:** Yes   **Settable:** Yes
Description: The status of print job as a hexadecimal value. The values are:

ADS_JOB_PAUSED or 0x00000001

ADS_JOB_ERROR or 0x00000002

ADS_JOB_DELETING or 0x00000004

ADS_JOB_PRINTING or 0x00000010

ADS_JOB_OFFLINE or 0x00000020

ADS_JOB_PAPEROUT or 0x00000040

ADS_JOB_PRINTED or 0x00000080

ADS_JOB_DELETED or 0x00000100

TimeElapsed
Value: Number   **Gettable:** Yes   **Settable:** No
Description: The elapsed time in seconds since the job started printing.

Methods

Pause()
Returns: Error status
Description: Pauses the print job.

Resume()
Returns: Error status
Description: Resumes the print job.

IADsPrintQueue

The IADsPrintQueue interface represents a printer on a network. You can use the IADsPrintQueueOperations interface to control printer queues. You can use the interface when you obtain a PrintQueue object, such as:

```
Set pq = GetObject("WinNT://zeta/HPDeskJe")
```

You could examine all print queues as follows:

```
Set comp = GetObject("WinNT://zeta,computer")
comp.Filter = Array("PrintQueue")
For Each p In comp
 Set pq = GetObject(p.ADsPath)
 WScript.Echo pq.Name & " is a " & pq.Model
Next
```

Properties

BannerPage
Value: String   **Gettable:** Yes   **Settable:** Yes
Description: The file path to a banner-page file used to separate print jobs.

Datatype
Value: String   **Gettable:** Yes   **Settable:** Yes
Description: The data type that can be processed by the print queue.

DefaultJobPriority
Value: Number or String   **Gettable:** Yes   **Settable:** Yes
Description: The default priority assigned to each print job.

Description
Value: String   **Gettable:** Yes   **Settable:** Yes
Description: The description of the print queue.

Location
Value: String   **Gettable:** Yes   **Settable:** Yes
Description: A description of the print queue location.

Model
Value: String   **Gettable:** Yes   **Settable:** Yes
Description: The name of the driver used by the print queue.

NetAddresses
Value: Array   **Gettable:** Yes   **Settable:** Yes
Description: The network IP addresses for the printer (if applicable).

PrintDevices
Value: Array   **Gettable:** Yes   **Settable:** Yes
Description: The names of print devices that the print queue uses as spooling devices.

PrinterPath
Value: String   **Gettable:** Yes   **Settable:** Yes
Description: The network path (for a shared printer).

PrintProcessor
Value: String   **Gettable:** Yes   **Settable:** Yes
Description: The print processor associated with the print queue.

Priority
Value: Number   **Gettable:** Yes   **Settable:** Yes
Description: The priority of this printer object's job queue.

StartTime
Value: Date   **Gettable:** Yes   **Settable:** Yes
Description: The time when the print queue starts processing jobs.

UntilTime
Value: Date   **Gettable:** Yes   **Settable:** Yes
Description: The time at which the print queue stops processing jobs.

IADsPrintQueueOperations

The IADsPrintQueueOperations interface provides extended features for print queues. You can work with this interface by getting a pointer to a PrintQueue object, such as:

```
Set pqo = GetObject("WinNT://zeta/HPDeskJe")
If pqo.Status = ADS_PRINTER_TONER_LOW Then
  WScript.Echo "The printer is low on toner."
End If
```

Property

Status
Value: Number   **Gettable:** Yes   **Settable:** No
Description: The current status of the print queue. Valid status codes are:

ADS_PRINTER_PAUSED or 0x00000001

ADS_PRINTER_PENDING_DELETION or 0x00000002

ADS_PRINTER_ERROR or 0x00000003

ADS_PRINTER_PAPER_JAM or 0x00000004

ADS_PRINTER_PAPER_OUT or 0x00000005

ADS_PRINTER_MANUAL_FEED or 0x00000006

ADS_PRINTER_PAPER_PROBLEM or 0x00000007

ADS_PRINTER_OFFLINE or 0x00000008

ADS_PRINTER_IO_ACTIVE or 0x00000100

ADS_PRINTER_BUSY or 0x00000200

ADS_PRINTER_PRINTING or 0x00000400

ADS_PRINTER_OUTPUT_BIN_FULL or 0x00000800

ADS_PRINTER_NOT_AVAILABLE or 0x00001000

ADS_PRINTER_WAITING or 0x00002000

ADS_PRINTER_PROCESSING or 0x00004000

ADS_PRINTER_INITIALIZING or 0x00008000

ADS_PRINTER_WARMING_UP or 0x00010000

ADS_PRINTER_TONER_LOW or 0x00020000

ADS_PRINTER_NO_TONER or 0x00040000

ADS_PRINTER_PAGE_PUNT or 0x00080000

ADS_PRINTER_USER_INTERVENTION or 0x00100000

ADS_PRINTER_OUT_OF_MEMORY or 0x00200000

ADS_PRINTER_DOOR_OPEN or 0x00400000

ADS_PRINTER_SERVER_UNKNOWN or 0x00800000

ADS_PRINTER_POWER_SAVE or 0x01000000

Methods

Pause()
Returns: Error status
Description: Pauses the print queue.

PrintJobs()
Returns: Print Job Collection
Description: Retrieves a pointer to a collection of print jobs that are managed by the print queue.

Purge()
Returns: Error status
Description: Deletes all jobs from the print queue.

Resume()
Returns: Error status
Description: Resumes the print queue.

IADsProperty

The `IADsProperty` interface is designed for managing attributes for schema objects. You gain access to an object's properties by binding to the parent schema object, such as:

```
Set obj = GetObject("WinNT://zeta,computer")
Set cl = GetObject(obj.Schema)
Set sc = GetObject(cl.Parent)
Set prop = sc.GetObject("Property","Owner")
WScript.Echo "Attribute: " & prop.Name
WScript.Echo "Syntax: " & prop.Syntax
WScript.Echo "MaxRange: " & prop.MaxRange
WScript.Echo "MinRange: " & prop.MinRange
WScript.Echo "Multivalued:" & prop.Multivalued
```

Properties

MaxRange
Value: Number   **Gettable:** Yes   **Settable:** Yes
Description: The upper limit of values for the property.

MinRange
Value: Number   **Gettable:** Yes   **Settable:** Yes
Description: The lower limit of values for the property.

MultiValued
Value: Boolean　**Gettable:** Yes　**Settable:** Yes
Description: The Boolean value indicates whether this property supports multiple values.

OID
Value: String　**Gettable:** Yes　**Settable:** Yes
Description: The directory-specific object identifier.

Syntax
Value: String　**Gettable:** Yes　**Settable:** Yes
Description: The property type, such as `String`.

Method

Qualifiers()
Returns: Collection of ADSI objects
Description: Method obtains a collection with additional provider-specific limits on the property.

IADsPropertyEntry

The `IADsPropertyEntry` interface allows a user to specify how a property's values can be manipulated. To access a property entry, use the `Item` property or call the `GetPropertyItem` method on the `IADsPropertyList` interface, such as:

```
Set plist = GetObject("LDAP://zeta/DC=TVPRESS,DC=com")
plist.GetInfo
Set pentry = plist.GetPropertyItem("dc",
ADSTYPE_CASE_IGNORE_STRING)
```

Properties

ADS_Type
Value: String　**Gettable:** Yes　**Settable:** Yes
Description: The data type of the property.

ControlCode
Value: String　**Gettable:** Yes　**Settable:** Yes
Description: A constant that specifies the operation to be performed on the property. These constants are `ADS_PROPERTY_CLEAR`, `ADS_PROPERTY_UPDATE`, `ADS_PROPERTY_APPEND`, and `ADS_PROPERTY_DELETE`.

Name
Value: String   **Gettable:** Yes   **Settable:** Yes
Description: The name of the property entry.

Values
Value: Array   **Gettable:** Yes   **Settable:** Yes
Description: Array representing the values of the property.

IADsPropertyList

The IADsPropertyList interface is used to manage property entries in the property cache. You gain access to this interface when you load an object's properties into the property cache, such as:

```
Set plist = GetObject("LDAP://zeta/DC=TVPRESS,DC=com")
plist.GetInfo
```

Property

PropertyCount
Value: String   **Gettable:** Yes   **Settable:** No
Description: The number of properties in the property list.

Methods

GetPropertyItem("*propertyName*",*propertyTypeConstant*)
Returns: Property entry
Description: Use this method to obtain a property entry. The normal constant is ADSTYPE_CASE_IGNORE_STRING.

Item(*propertyNameOrIndex*)
Returns: Property entry
Description: Obtains a property entry by name or index.

Next()
Returns: Property entry
Description: Obtains the next item in the cached property list.

PurgePropertyList()
Returns: Error status
Description: Deletes the cached property list for the object.

PutPropertyItem(*propertyEntry*)
Returns: Error status
Description: Updates a value in the cached property list.

Reset()
Returns: Error status
Description: Moves back to the start of the cached property list.

ResetPropertyItem(*propertyNameOrIndex*)
Returns: Error status
Description: Removes a property from the cached property list by name or by index.

Skip(*numberToSkip*)
Returns: Error status
Description: Skips a specified number of items in the cached property list.

IADsPropertyValue

The IADsPropertyValue interface represents a property value in a property entry. You can obtain this interface through the Values property of IADsPropertyEntry, such as:

```
Set plist =
GetObject("WinNT://tvpress/zeta/administrator,user")
plist.GetInfo

Set pentry = plist.GetPropertyItem("description",
ADSTYPE_CASE_IGNORE_STRING)

For Each v In pentry.Values
    Set pval = v
    WScript.Echo pval.CaseIgnoreString
    pval.Clear
Next
```

Properties

ADsType
Value: Number   **Gettable:** Yes   **Settable:** Yes
Description: A constant representing a property's data type.

Boolean
Value: Boolean   **Gettable:** Yes   **Settable:** Yes
Description: A Boolean value.

CaseExactString
Value: String   **Gettable:** Yes   **Settable:** Yes
Description: A case-sensitive string.

CaseIgnoreString
Value: String   **Gettable:** Yes   **Settable:** Yes
Description: A case-insensitive string.

DNString
Value: String   **Gettable:** Yes   **Settable:** Yes
Description: An object's distinguished name.

Integer
Value: Number   **Gettable:** Yes   **Settable:** Yes
Description: An integer value.

LargeInteger
Value: Number   **Gettable:** Yes   **Settable:** Yes
Description: A large integer value.

NumericString
Value: String   **Gettable:** Yes   **Settable:** Yes
Description: A string to be treated as a number.

OctetString
Value: String   **Gettable:** Yes   **Settable:** Yes
Description: A string of eight-bit characters.

PrintableString
Value: String   **Gettable:** Yes   **Settable:** Yes
Description: A printable string.

SecurityDescriptor
Value: Interface Pointer   **Gettable:** Yes   **Settable:** Yes
Description: A security descriptor of type `IADsSecurityDescriptor`.

UTCTime
Value: String   **Gettable:** Yes   **Settable:** Yes
Description: A date in Coordinated Universal Time format.

Method

Clear()
Returns: Error status
Description: Clears the current values of the `PropertyValue` object.

IADsReplicaPointer

The `IADsReplicaPointer` interface is used to access the Replica Pointer attribute in Novell NetWare Directory Services (NDS).

Properties

Count
Value: Number   **Gettable:** Yes   **Settable:** Yes
Description: The number of existing replicas.

ReplicaAddressHints
Value: Array   **Gettable:** Yes   **Settable:** Yes
Description: A network address suggested as a node where a name server might be located.

ReplicaNumber
Value: Number   **Gettable:** Yes   **Settable:** Yes
Description: The ID number of the replica.

ReplicaType
Value: Number   **Gettable:** Yes   **Settable:** Yes
Description: A value indicating the type of replica as master, secondary, or read-only.

ServerName
Value: String   **Gettable:** Yes   **Settable:** Yes
Description: The name of the server holding the replica.

IADsResource

The `IADsResource` interface is used to manage open resources for a file service. You can obtain a collection of resources through the `FileService` object, such as:

```
Set fso = GetObject("WinNT://zeta/LanmanServer")
If (IsEmpty(fso) = False) Then
    For Each resource In fso.resources
        WScript.Echo "Resource name: " & resource.name
        WScript.Echo "Resource path: " & resource.path
    Next
End If
```

Properties

LockCount
Value: Number   **Gettable:** Yes   **Settable:** No
Description: The number of locks on a resource.

Path
Value: String   **Gettable:** Yes   **Settable:** No
Description: The file path of the resource.

User
Value: String   **Gettable:** Yes   **Settable:** No
Description: The name of the user who opened the resource.

UserPath
Value: String   **Gettable:** Yes   **Settable:** No
Description: The AdsPath string of the user object that is accessing the resource.

IADsSession

The `IADsSession` interface is used to manage active user sessions for the file service. You can access this interface through the `FileService` object, such as:

```
Set fso = GetObject("WinNT://zeta/LanmanServer")
Set s = fso.Sessions
```

Properties

Computer
Value: String   **Gettable:** Yes   **Settable:** No
Description: The name of the client workstation from which the session initiated.

ComputerPath
Value: String   **Gettable:** Yes   **Settable:** No
Description: The `ADsPath` of the related computer object.

ConnectTime
Value: Number   **Gettable:** Yes   **Settable:** No
Description: The number of minutes since the session began.

IdleTime
Value: Number   **Gettable:** Yes   **Settable:** No
Description: The number of minutes that the session has been idle.

User
Value: String   **Gettable:** Yes   **Settable:** No
Description: The name of user who initiated the session.

UserPath
Value: String   **Gettable:** Yes   **Settable:** No
Description: The ADsPath of the related user object.

IADsService

The IADsService interface is used to manage services on a computer. Services are accessed through the IADsComputer interface, such as:

```
Set comp = GetObject("WinNT://seattle/zeta/alerter,service")
```

The IADsFileService and IADsFileServiceOperations interfaces provide additional features for file services.

Properties

Dependencies
Value: Array   **Gettable:** Yes   **Settable:** Yes
Description: An array of services that must be running before this service can run.

DisplayName
Value: String   **Gettable:** Yes   **Settable:** Yes
Description: The display name of this service.

ErrorControl
Value: Number   **Gettable:** Yes   **Settable:** Yes
Description: The actions taken in case of service failure. Permissible actions are:

- ✦ ADS_SERVICE_ERROR_IGNORE or 0x00000000
- ✦ ADS_SERVICE_ERROR_NORMAL or 0x00000001
- ✦ ADS_SERVICE_ERROR_SEVERE or 0x00000002
- ✦ ADS_SERVICE_ERROR_CRITICAL or 0x00000003

HostComputer
Value: String   **Gettable:** Yes   **Settable:** Yes
Description: The AdsPath string of the host computer running the service.

LoadOrderGroup
Value: String   **Gettable:** Yes   **Settable:** Yes
Description: The load order group of which the service is a member.

Path
Value: String   **Gettable:** Yes   **Settable:** Yes
Description: The path and filename of the executable for the service.

ServiceAccountName
Value: String   **Gettable:** Yes   **Settable:** Yes
Description: The name of the account used by the service at startup.

ServiceAccountPath
Value: String   **Gettable:** Yes   **Settable:** Yes
Description: The `AdsPath` string of the startup account.

ServiceType
Value: Number   **Gettable:** Yes   **Settable:** Yes
Description: The process type in which the service runs. Valid types are:

- ✦ `ADS_SERVICE_KERNEL_DRIVER` or 0x00000001
- ✦ `ADS_SERVICE_FILE_SYSTEM_DRIVER` or 0x00000002
- ✦ `ADS_SERVICE_OWN_PROCESS` or 0x00000010
- ✦ `ADS_SERVICE_SHARE_PROCESS` or 0x00000020

StartType
Value: Number   **Gettable:** Yes   **Settable:** Yes
Description: The start type for the service. Valid types are:

ADSI Service Start Type
```
ADS_SERVICE_BOOT_START
ADS_SERVICE_SYSTEM_START
ADS_SERVICE_AUTO_START
ADS_SERVICE_DEMAND_START
ADS_SERVICE_DISABLED
```

Win32 Service Start Type
```
ADS_SERVICE_BOOT_START
ADS_SERVICE_SYSTEM_START
ADS_SERVICE_AUTO_START
ADS_SERVICE_DEMAND_START
ADS_SERVICE_DISABLED
```

StartupParameters
Value: String   **Gettable:** Yes   **Settable:** Yes
Description: Parameters passed to the service at startup.

Version
Value: String   **Gettable:** Yes   **Settable:** Yes
Description: The version of the service.

IADsServiceOperations

The IADsServiceOperations interface provides extended features for services.
File service and file-service operations are managed through IADsFileService
and IADsFileServiceOperations. You can access this interface through the
Services object, such as:

```
Set comp = GetObject("WinNT://zeta,computer")
Set serv = comp.GetObject("Service", "alerter")
```

Property

Status
Value: Number   **Gettable:** Yes   **Settable:** No
Description: The current status of the service. Valid status codes are:

ADS_SERVICE_STOPPED or 0x00000001

ADS_SERVICE_START_PENDING or 0x00000002

ADS_SERVICE_STOP_PENDING or 0x00000003

ADS_SERVICE_RUNNING or 0x00000004

ADS_SERVICE_CONTINUE_PENDING or 0x00000005

ADS_SERVICE_PAUSE_PENDING or 0x00000006

ADS_SERVICE_PAUSED or 0x00000007

ADS_SERVICE_ERROR or 0x00000008

Methods

Start()
Returns: Error status
Description: Starts the service.

Stop()
Returns: Error status
Description: Stops the service.

Pause()
Returns: Error status
Description: Pauses the service.

Continue()
Returns: Error status
Description: Resumes a paused service.

SetPassword("*newPassword*")
Returns: Error status
Description: Sets a new password to be used with the service startup account.

IADsSyntax

The IADsSyntax interface is designed for managing syntax in the schema. You obtain a pointer to this interface when you bind to a property of a schema object, such as:

```
Set obj = GetObject("WinNT://zeta,computer")
Set cl = GetObject(obj.Schema)
Set sc = GetObject(cl.Parent)
Set prop = sc.GetObject("Property","Owner")
Set synt = GetObject(sc.ADsPath & "/" & prop.Syntax)
WScript.Echo "Automation data type: " & synt.OleAutoDataType
```

Property

OleAutoDataType
Value: Number   **Gettable:** Yes   **Settable:** Yes
Description: Indicates the virtual type constant for the property.

IADsTimestamp

The IADsTimestamp interface is used to access the Timestamp attribute in Novell NetWare Directory Services (NDS).

EventID
Value: Number   **Gettable:** Yes   **Settable:** Yes
Description: An event identifier.

WholeSeconds
Value: Number   **Gettable:** Yes   **Settable:** Yes
Description: The number of whole seconds relative to 12:00 a.m., 1 January, 1970, Universal Time Coordinate (UTC).

IADsTypedName

The IADsTypedName interface is used to access the Typed Name attribute in Novell NetWare Directory Services (NDS).

Properties

Interval
Value: Number   **Gettable:** Yes   **Settable:** Yes
Description: The frequency of object references.

Level
Value: Number   **Gettable:** Yes   **Settable:** Yes
Description: The priority level of the object.

ObjectName
Value: String   **Gettable:** Yes   **Settable:** Yes
Description: The name of the object.

IADsUser

The IADsUser interface is used to manage user accounts. You can bind to local and domain accounts. To bind to local accounts, use the following syntax:

```
Set user = GetObject("WinNT://computerName/userName,user")
```

To bind to domain accounts, use:

```
Set user = GetObject("WinNT://domainName/userName,user")
```

or use:

```
Set user = GetObject("LDAP://CN=userName,CN=Users,
DC=ChildDomain,DC=Domain,DC=RootDomain")
```

Properties

AccountDisabled
Value: Boolean   **Gettable:** Yes   **Settable:** Yes
Description: Boolean that indicates whether the account is disabled.

AccountExpirationDate
Value: Date   **Gettable:** Yes   **Settable:** Yes
Description: The expiration date and time of the user account.

BadLoginAddress
Value: String   **Gettable:** Yes   **Settable:** No
Description: The address that last caused a bad login for the account.

BadLoginCount
Value: Number   **Gettable:** Yes   **Settable:** No
Description: The number of the bad login attempts since login count was last reset.

Department
Value: String   **Gettable:** Yes   **Settable:** Yes
Description: The organizational unit associated with the account.

Description
Value: String   **Gettable:** Yes   **Settable:** Yes
Description: The description of the account.

Division
Value: String   **Gettable:** Yes   **Settable:** Yes
Description: The division associated with the account.

E-mailAddress
Value: String   **Gettable:** Yes   **Settable:** Yes
Description: The e-mail address of the account.

EmployeeID
Value: String   **Gettable:** Yes   **Settable:** Yes
Description: The employee ID number associated with the account.

FaxNumber
Value: String or Array   **Gettable:** Yes   **Settable:** Yes
Description: The list of fax numbers associated with the account.

FirstName
Value: String   **Gettable:** Yes   **Settable:** Yes
Description: The first name of the user.

FullName
Value: String   **Gettable:** Yes   **Settable:** Yes
Description: The full name of the user.

GraceLoginsAllowed
Value: Number **Gettable:** Yes **Settable:** Yes
Description: The number of times the user can log on after the password has expired.

GraceLoginsRemaining
Value: Number **Gettable:** Yes **Settable:** Yes
Description: The number of grace logins remaining.

HomeDirectory
Value: String **Gettable:** Yes **Settable:** Yes
Description: The home directory of the user.

HomePage
Value: String **Gettable:** Yes **Settable:** Yes
Description: The URL of the user's home page.

IsAccountLocked
Value: Boolean **Gettable:** Yes **Settable:** Yes
Description: A Boolean that indicates whether the account is locked.

Languages
Value: Array **Gettable:** Yes **Settable:** Yes
Description: An array of acceptable natural languages.

LastFailedLogin
Value: Date **Gettable:** Yes **Settable:** No
Description: The date and time of the last failed login.

LastLogin
Value: Date **Gettable:** Yes **Settable:** No
Description: The date and time of the last login.

LastLogoff
Value: Date **Gettable:** Yes **Settable:** No
Description: The date and time of the last logoff.

LastName
Value: String **Gettable:** Yes **Settable:** Yes
Description: The last name of the user.

LoginHours
Value: Array   **Gettable:** Yes   **Settable:** Yes
Description: An array of values that indicate the time periods during each day of the week that the user can log on.

LoginScript
Value: String   **Gettable:** Yes   **Settable:** Yes
Description: The login script path for the account.

LoginWorkstations
Value: Array   **Gettable:** Yes   **Settable:** Yes
Description: An array of computer names or IP addresses from which the user can log on.

Manager
Value: String   **Gettable:** Yes   **Settable:** Yes
Description: The manager of the user.

MaxLogins
Value: Number   **Gettable:** Yes   **Settable:** Yes
Description: The maximum number of simultaneous login sessions allowed for the account.

MaxStorage
Value: Number   **Gettable:** Yes   **Settable:** Yes
Description: The maximum amount of disk space allowed for the user.

NamePrefix
Value: String   **Gettable:** Yes   **Settable:** Yes
Description: The name prefix of the user, such as Mr. or Mrs.

NameSuffix
Value: String   **Gettable:** Yes   **Settable:** Yes
Description: The name suffix of the user, such as Jr.

OfficeLocations
Value: Array or String   **Gettable:** Yes   **Settable:** Yes
Description: Office locations for the user.

OtherName
Value: String   **Gettable:** Yes   **Settable:** Yes
Description: An additional name of the user, such as a middle name.

PasswordExpirationDate
Value: Date   **Gettable:** Yes   **Settable:** Yes
Description: The date and time when the account password expires.

PasswordLastChanged
Value: Date   **Gettable:** Yes   **Settable:** No
Description: The date and time when the password was last changed.

PasswordMinimumLength
Value: Number   **Gettable:** Yes   **Settable:** Yes
Description: The minimum number of characters allowed in a password.

PasswordRequired
Value: Boolean   **Gettable:** Yes   **Settable:** Yes
Description: Boolean value that indicates whether a password is required.

Picture
Value: Array   **Gettable:** Yes   **Settable:** Yes
Description: An octet string array of bytes that hold a picture of the user.

PostalAddresses
Value: Array   **Gettable:** Yes   **Settable:** Yes
Description: An array that holds addresses associated with the account.

PostalCodes
Value: Array   **Gettable:** Yes   **Settable:** Yes
Description: An array of zip codes for the Postal Addresses.

Profile
Value: String   **Gettable:** Yes   **Settable:** Yes
Description: The path to the user's profile.

RequireUniquePassword
Value: Boolean   **Gettable:** Yes   **Settable:** Yes
Description: Boolean value that indicates whether a new password must be different from ones in the password history.

SeeAlso
Value: Array   **Gettable:** Yes   **Settable:** Yes
Description: Array of `AdsPath` strings for other objects related to this user.

TelephoneHome
Value: Array or String   **Gettable:** Yes   **Settable:** Yes
Description: An array of home phone numbers for the user.

TelephoneMobile
Value: Array or String   **Gettable:** Yes   **Settable:** Yes
Description: An array of mobile phone numbers for the user.

TelephoneNumber
Value: Array or String   **Gettable:** Yes   **Settable:** Yes
Description: An array of work-related phone numbers for the user.

TelephonePager
Value: Array   **Gettable:** Yes   **Settable:** Yes
Description: An array of pager numbers for the user.

Title
Value: String   **Gettable:** Yes   **Settable:** Yes
Description: The user's job title.

Methods

ChangePassword(*"oldPassword","newPassword"*)
Returns: Error status
Description: Changes the password for the account.

Groups()
Returns: Error status
Description: Obtains a collection of groups (`IADsMembers`) to which the user account belongs.

SetPassword(*"password"*)
Returns: Error status
Description: Sets the password for a new account.

IDirectoryObject

The `IDirectoryObject` interface provides non-Automation clients with direct access to directory service objects. Only non-Automation clients can call the methods of `IDirectoryObject`. Automation clients cannot use `IDirectoryObject` and instead use the `IADs` interface.

IDirectorySearch

The `IDirectorySearch` interface allows non-Automation clients to query the directory. Only non-Automation clients can call the methods of `IDirectorySearch`. Automation clients cannot use `IDirectorySearch` and instead use the `IADs` interface.

ADSI Error Codes

As you've seen in this reference, many methods return an error code. The type of error code you see depends on the ADSI provider that you are using. With WinNT, NDS, and NWCOMPAT, you normally see error codes in the form:

0x80005xxx E_ADS_* for standard errors

0x00005xxx S_ADS_* for severe errors

The LDAP provider, on the other hand, maps all errors to Win32 errors. Because of this, you'll normally see error codes in the form:

0x8007xxxx LDAP_* for LDAP errors

0x8007xxxx ERROR_* for Win32 errors

Table B-1 summarizes standard error codes.

Table B-1 Standard ADSI Error Codes		
Error Code	**Error Message**	**Description**
0x00005011	S_ADS_ERRORSOCCURRED	One or more errors occurred.
0x00005012	S_ADS_NOMORE_ROWS	Search operation reached the last row.
0x00005013	S_ADS_NOMORE_COLUMNS	Search operation reached the last column for the current row.
0x80005000	E_ADS_BAD_PATHNAME	An invalid ADSI pathname was passed.
0x80005001	E_ADS_INVALID_DOMAIN_OBJECT	An unknown ADSI domain object was requested.

Continued

Table B-1 *(continued)*

Error Code	Error Message	Description
0x80005002	E_ADS_INVALID_USER_OBJECT	An unknown ADSI user object was requested.
0x80005003	E_ADS_INVALID_COMPUTER_OBJECT	An unknown ADSI computer object was requested.
0x80005004	E_ADS_UNKNOWN_OBJECT	An unknown ADSI object was requested.
0x80005005	E_ADS_PROPERTY_NOT_SET	The specified ADSI property was not set.
0x80005006	E_ADS_PROPERTY_NOT_SUPPORTED	The specified ADSI property is not supported.
0x80005007	E_ADS_PROPERTY_INVALID	The specified ADSI property is invalid
0x80005008	E_ADS_BAD_PARAMETER	One or more input parameters are invalid.
0x80005009	E_ADS_OBJECT_UNBOUND	The specified ADSI object is not bound to the remote resource.
0x8000500A	E_ADS_PROPERTY_NOT_MODIFIED	The specified ADSI object has not been modified.
0x8000500B	E_ADS_PROPERTY_MODIFIED	The specified ADSI object has been modified.
0x8000500C	E_ADS_CANT_CONVERT_DATATYPE	The data type cannot be converted.
0x8000500D	E_ADS_PROPERTY_NOT_FOUND	The property cannot be found in the cache.
0x8000500E	E_ADS_OBJECT_EXISTS	The ADSI object exists.
0x8000500F	E_ADS_SCHEMA_VIOLATION	The action violates the directory service schema rules.
0x80005010	E_ADS_COLUMN_NOT_SET	The specified column in the ADSI was not set.
0x80005014	E_ADS_INVALID_FILTER	The specified search filter is invalid.

Table B-2 summarizes LDAP error codes and provides the corresponding Win32 error codes.

<table>
<tr><td colspan="4">Table B-2
LDAP Error Codes with Win32</td></tr>
<tr><td>**ADSI Error Code**</td><td>**LDAP Error Message**</td><td>**Win32 Error Message**</td><td>**Description**</td></tr>
<tr><td>0</td><td>LDAP_SUCCESS</td><td>NO_ERROR</td><td>Operation succeeded.</td></tr>
<tr><td>0x80070005</td><td>LDAP_INSUFFICIENT_ RIGHTS</td><td>ERROR_ACCESS_ DENIED</td><td>User doesn't have sufficient access rights.</td></tr>
<tr><td>0x80070008</td><td>LDAP_NO_MEMORY</td><td>ERROR_NOT_ENOUGH_ MEMORY</td><td>System is out of memory.</td></tr>
<tr><td>0x8007001f</td><td>LDAP_OTHER</td><td>ERROR_GEN_FAILURE</td><td>Unknown error occurred.</td></tr>
<tr><td>0x800700ea</td><td>LDAP_PARTIAL_ RESULTS</td><td>ERROR_MORE_DATA</td><td>Partial results received.</td></tr>
<tr><td>0x800700ea</td><td>LDAP_MORE_RESULTS_ TO_RETURN</td><td>ERROR_MORE_DATA</td><td>More results are to be returned.</td></tr>
<tr><td>0x800704c7</td><td>LDAP_USER_ CANCELLED</td><td>ERROR_CANCELLED</td><td>User cancelled the operation.</td></tr>
<tr><td>0x800704c9</td><td>LDAP_CONNECT_ERROR</td><td>ERROR_CONNECTION_ REFUSED</td><td>Cannot establish the connection.</td></tr>
<tr><td>0x8007052e</td><td>LDAP_INVALID_ CREDENTIALS</td><td>ERROR_LOGON_ FAILURE</td><td>Logon failure.</td></tr>
<tr><td>0x800705b4</td><td>LDAP_TIMEOUT</td><td>ERROR_TIMEOUT</td><td>The search timed out.</td></tr>
<tr><td>0x80071392</td><td>LDAP_ALREADY_ EXISTS</td><td>ERROR_OBJECT_ ALREADY_EXISTS</td><td>The object already exists.</td></tr>
<tr><td>0x8007200a</td><td>LDAP_NO_SUCH_ ATTRIBUTE</td><td>ERROR_DS_NO_ ATTRIBUTE_ OR_VALUE</td><td>Requested attribute does not exist.</td></tr>
<tr><td>0x8007200b</td><td>LDAP_INVALID_ SYNTAX</td><td>ERROR_DS_INVALID_ ATTRIBUTE_SYNTAX</td><td>The syntax is invalid.</td></tr>
<tr><td>0x8007200c</td><td>LDAP_UNDEFINED_ TYPE</td><td>ERROR_DS_ ATTRIBUTE_TYPE_ UNDEFINED</td><td>Type is not defined.</td></tr>
<tr><td>0x8007200d</td><td>LDAP_ATTRIBUTE_OR_ VALUE_EXISTS</td><td>ERROR_DS_ ATTRIBUTE_OR_ VALUE_EXISTS</td><td>The attribute exists or value has been assigned.</td></tr>
</table>

Continued

Table B-2 *(continued)*

ADSI Error Code	LDAP Error Message	Win32 Error Message	Description
0x8007200e	LDAP_BUSY	ERROR_DS_BUSY	The server is busy.
0x8007200f	LDAP_UNAVAILABLE	ERROR_DS_ UNAVAILABLE	The server is not available.
0x80072014	LDAP_OBJECT_CLASS_ VIOLATION	ERROR_DS_OBJ_ CLASS_VIOLATION	Object class violation
0x80072015	LDAP_NOT_ALLOWED_ ON_NONLEAF	ERROR_DS_CANT_ON_ NON_LEAF	Operation is not allowed on a non-leaf object
0x80072016	LDAP_NOT_ALLOWED_ ON_RDN	ERROR_DS_CANT_ ON_RDN	Operation is not allowed on relative name.
0x80072017	LDAP_NO_OBJECT_ CLASS_MODS	ERROR_DS_CANT_ MOD_OBJ_CLASS	Cannot modify object class
0x80072020	LDAP_OPERATIONS_ ERROR	ERROR_DS_ OPERATIONS_ERROR	Operations error occurred.
0x80072021	LDAP_PROTOCOL_ ERROR	ERROR_DS_ PROTOCOL_ERROR	Protocol error occurred.
0x80072022	LDAP_TIMELIMIT_ EXCEEDED	ERROR_DS_ TIMELIMIT_ EXCEEDED	Time limit exceeded.
0x80072023	LDAP_SIZELIMIT_ EXCEEDED	ERROR_DS_ SIZELIMIT_ EXCEEDED	Size limit exceeded.
0x80072024	LDAP_ADMIN_LIMIT_ EXCEEDED	ERROR_DS_ADMIN_ LIMIT_EXCEEDED	Administration limit on the server exceeded.
0x80072025	LDAP_COMPARE_FALSE	ERROR_DS_COMPARE_ FALSE	Compare yielded FALSE.
0x80072026	LDAP_COMPARE_TRUE	ERROR_DS_COMPARE_ TRUE	Compare yielded TRUE.
0x80072027	LDAP_AUTH_METHOD_ NOT_SUPPORTED	ERROR_DS_AUTH_ METHOD_NOT_ SUPPORTED	Authentication method is not supported.
0x80072028	LDAP_STRONG_AUTH_ REQUIRED	ERROR_DS_STRONG_ AUTH_REQUIRED	Strong authentica-tion is required.

ADSI Error Code	LDAP Error Message	Win32 Error Message	Description
0x80072029	LDAP_INAPPROPRIATE_AUTH	ERROR_DS_INAPPROPRIATE_AUTH	Authentication is inappropriate.
0x8007202a	LDAP_AUTH_UNKNOWN	ERROR_DS_AUTH_UNKNOWN	Unknown authentication error occurred.
0x8007202b	LDAP_REFERRAL	ERROR_DS_REFERRAL	Referral error.
0x8007202c	LDAP_UNAVAILABLE_CRIT_EXTENSION	ERROR_DS_UNAVAILABLE_CRIT_EXTENSION	Critical extension is unavailable.
0x8007202d	LDAP_CONFIDENTIALITY_REQUIRED	ERROR_DS_CONFIDENTIALITY_REQUIRED	Confidentiality is required.
0x8007202e	LDAP_INAPPROPRIATE_MATCHING	ERROR_DS_INAPPROPRIATE_MATCHING	Inappropriate matching error.
0x8007202f	LDAP_CONSTRAINT_VIOLATION	ERROR_DS_CONSTRAINT_VIOLATION	Constraint violation.
0x80072030	LDAP_NO_SUCH_OBJECT	ERROR_DS_NO_SUCH_OBJECT	Object does not exist.
0x80072031	LDAP_ALIAS_PROBLEM	ERROR_DS_ALIAS_PROBLEM	Alias is invalid.
0x80072032	LDAP_INVALID_DN_SYNTAX	ERROR_DS_INVALID_DN_SYNTAX	Distinguished name has an invalid syntax.
0x80072033	LDAP_IS_LEAF	ERROR_DS_IS_LEAF	Object is a leaf.
0x80072034	LDAP_ALIAS_DEREF_PROBLEM	ERROR_DS_ALIAS_DEREF_PROBLEM	Cannot remove reference for the alias.
0x80072035	LDAP_UNWILLING_TO_PERFORM	ERROR_DS_UNWILLING_TO_PERFORM	Invalid operation.
0x80072036	LDAP_LOOP_DETECT	ERROR_DS_LOOP_DETECT	Loop was detected.
0x80072037	LDAP_NAMING_VIOLATION	ERROR_DS_NAMING_VIOLATION	Naming violation.

Continued

Table B-2 *(continued)*

ADSI Error Code	LDAP Error Message	Win32 Error Message	Description
0x80072038	LDAP_RESULTS_ TOO_LARGE	ERROR_DS_OBJECT_ RESULTS_TOO_LARGE	Results returned are too large.
0x80072039	LDAP_AFFECTS_ MULTIPLE_DSAS	ERROR_DS_AFFECTS_ MULTIPLE_DSAS	Multiple directory service agents are affected.
0x8007203a	LDAP_SERVER_DOWN	ERROR_DS_SERVER_ DOWN	Cannot contact the LDAP server.
0x8007203b	LDAP_LOCAL_ERROR	ERROR_DS_LOCAL_ ERROR	Local error occurred.
0x8007203c	LDAP_ENCODING_ ERROR	ERROR_DS_ ENCODING_ERROR	Encoding error occurred.
0x8007203d	LDAP_DECODING_ ERROR	ERROR_DS_ DECODING_ERROR	Decoding error occurred.
0x8007203e	LDAP_FILTER_ERROR	ERROR_DS_FILTER_ UNKNOWN	Search filter is bad.
0x8007203f	LDAP_PARAM_ERROR	ERROR_DS_PARAM_ ERROR	A bad parameter was passed.
0x80072040	LDAP_NOT_SUPPORTED	ERROR_DS_NOT_ SUPPORTED	Feature is not supported.
0x80072041	LDAP_NO_RESULTS_ RETURNED	ERROR_DS_NO_ RESULTS_RETURNED	Results are not returned.
0x80072042	LDAP_CONTROL_NOT_ FOUND	ERROR_DS_CONTROL_ NOT_FOUND	Control was not found.
0x80072043	LDAP_CLIENT_LOOP	ERROR_DS_CLIENT_ LOOP	Client loop was detected.
0x80072044	LDAP_REFERRAL_ LIMIT_EXCEEDED	ERROR_DS_ REFERRAL_LIMIT_ EXCEEDED	Referral limit has been exceeded.

✦   ✦   ✦

Essential Command-Line Utilities for Use with Windows Scripts

Command-line utilities provide some of the most powerful and useful features you'll find anywhere. Using command-line utilities, you often can replace dozens of lines of code with a few simple statements. As you explore Windows 2000 you'll find that hundreds of utilities are available and all of them can be run within your Windows scripts.

In this appendix, I've selected the top 50 utilities that you may want to use. You'll find a quick reference for commands as well as detailed entries on command usage and syntax. All examples show command-line and Windows script syntax.

ARP

```
ARP -a [inet_addr] [-N if_addr]
ARP -d inet_addr [if_addr]
ARP -s inet_addr eth_addr [if_addr]
```

eth_addr   Sets the physical MAC address in hexadecimal format, such as HH-HH-HH-HH-HH-HH where H is a hexadecimal value from 0 to F. Each network adapter card has a built-in MAC address.

if_addr	Sets the IP address of the interface whose address translation table should be modified. If you don't specify an address, the first available interface is used.
inet_addr	Sets an internet address.
-a	Displays current ARP entries.
-d	Deletes the specified entry.
-g	Same as -a.
-N *if_addr*	Displays the ARP entries for the network interface specified by *if_addr*.
-s	Adds the host and associates the Internet address *inet_addr* with the physical address *eth_addr*. The physical address is given as six hexadecimal bytes separated by hyphens. The entry is permanent.

Details:

ARP displays and modifies the IP-to-Physical address translation tables used by the address resolution protocol (ARP). Address Resolution Protocol (ARP) cache is maintained by Windows 2000 workstations and servers. Use the ARP command to view and manage this cache.

Use IPCONFIG to get a list of MAC addresses for a system's network adapter cards. If you PING an IP address on the LAN, the address is automatically added to the ARP cache.

Command Shell
```
arp -d 192.168.15.25
```

VBScript
```
Set ws = WScript.CreateObject("WScript.Shell")
ret = ws.Run("arp -d 192.168.15.25",0,"True")
```

JScript
```
var ws = WScript.CreateObject("WScript.Shell");
ws.Run("arp -d 192.168.15.25",0,"True")
```

AT

```
AT [\\computername] [ [id] [/DELETE] | /DELETE [/YES]]
AT [\\computername] time [/INTERACTIVE]
AT [ /EVERY:date[,...] | /NEXT:date[,...]] "command"
```

`"command"`	Sets the command or script to run at the designated time.
`/delete`	Cancels a scheduled task. If `id` is omitted, all scheduled commands on the system are canceled.
`/every:date[,...]`	Runs the command on a recurring basis on each weekday or day of the month specified. Valid values are M, T, W, Th, F, S, Su, or 1 through 31. Separate consecutive days with dashes. Separate non-consecutive days with commas.
`/interactive`	Allows the job to interact with the desktop.
`/next:date[,...]`	Runs the task on a specific weekday or day of month. This is a non-recurring task.
`/yes`	Forces a confirmation prompt before deleting scheduled tasks.
`\\computername`	Sets a remote computer on which the task should run. If omitted, tasks are scheduled on the local computer.
`id`	The identification number assigned to a scheduled task.
`time`	Sets the time when command is to run in the format HH:MM. Time is set on a 24-hour clock (00:00 – 23:59).

Details:

AT schedules commands and programs to execute at a specific date and time. Tasks can be scheduled to run on a one time or recurring basis. To list currently scheduled tasks, enter the AT command on a line by itself.

Command Shell

```
at 00:15 /every:M "backup.vbs"
at 01:00 /next:Su "rm c:\temp\*.tmp"
at 1 /delete
```

VBScript

```
Set ws = WScript.CreateObject("WScript.Shell")
ret = ws.Run("at 00:15 /every:M 'backup.vbs'",0,"True")
```

JScript

```
var ws = WScript.CreateObject("WScript.Shell");
ws.Run("at 00:15 /every:M 'backup.vbs'",0,"True")
```

CHKDSK

CHKDSK [*drive:*][[*path*]*filename*][/F][/V][/R][/X][/I][/C][/L[:*size*]]

[*drive:*]	Sets the drive to check.
[*path*]*filename*	Sets the files and directories to check for fragmentation (FAT only).
/C	Skips checking cycles in folder structure.
/F	Fixes errors on the disk.
/I	On NTFS, performs basic index checks instead of extended checks.
/L:*size*	On NTFS, changes size of the check disk log (in KB). If size is not specified, the current size is displayed.
/R	Finds bad sectors and recovers readable information.
/V	Lists each file as it is checked.
/X	Forces the drive to dismount if necessary before performing CHKDSK. This option also fixes errors.

Details:
CHKDSK checks a disk for errors and displays a report.

Command Shell
```
chkdsk /F /R c:
chkdsk c: d:
```

VBScript
```
Set ws = WScript.CreateObject("WScript.Shell")
ret = ws.Run("chkdsk /F /R c:",0,"True")
```

JScript
```
var ws = WScript.CreateObject("WScript.Shell");
ws.Run("chkdsk /F /R c:",0,"True")
```

COMPACT

COMPACT [/C | /U] [/S[:*dir*]] [/A] [/I] [/F] [/Q] [*filename* [...]]

filename	Sets the files or directories to compress.
/A	Displays or compresses files with the hidden or system attributes. These files are omitted by default.

/C	Compresses the specified files, directories, and/or drives. Directories will be marked so that files added afterward will be compressed.
/F	Forces compression or decompression on all specified files and directories, even those which are already flagged as compressed. Otherwise, flagged files and directories are skipped by default.
/I	Ignores errors. By default, COMPACT stops when an error is encountered.
/Q	Sets quiet mode so only essential information is reported.
/S	Includes subdirectories.
/U	Decompresses the specified files, directories, and/or drives. Directories will be marked so that files added afterward will not be compressed.

Details:
COMPACT displays or alters the compression of files on NTFS partitions. If you use COMPACT without parameters, you can view the compression state of the current directory and any files it contains. You can use multiple filenames and wildcards.

Command Shell
```
compact /I /C c:\working\scripts
compact /F /U d:\
```

VBScript
```
Set ws = WScript.CreateObject("WScript.Shell")
ret = ws.Run("compact /I /C c:\working\scripts",0,"True")
```

JScript
```
var ws = WScript.CreateObject("WScript.Shell");
ws.Run("compact /I /C c:\\working\\scripts",0,"True")
```

CONVERT

```
CONVERT drive: /FS:NTFS [/V]
```

drive:	Sets the drive to convert to NTFS.
/FS:NTFS	Switch needed to convert the volume to NTFS.
/V	Run in verbose mode.

Details:
CONVERT converts FAT volumes to NTFS. If you try to convert the current drive or any drive being used by the operating system, the command prompts you to convert the drive on reboot. If you accept, a flag is set and the drive is converted the next time you reboot the system. If you decline, the operation is cancelled.

Command Shell
```
convert d: /FS:NTFS
convert d: /FS:NTFS /V
```

VBScript
```
Set ws = WScript.CreateObject("WScript.Shell")
ret = ws.Run("convert d: /FS:NTFS",0,"True")
```

JScript
```
var ws = WScript.CreateObject("WScript.Shell");
ws.Run("convert d: /FS:NTFS",0,"True")
```

DATE

```
DATE [/T | mm-dd-yy]
```

mm-dd-yy	Sets the date in MM-DD-YYYY format. *mm* can be 1-2. *dd* can be 1-31. *yy* can be 80-99 or 1980-2079.
/T	Displays current date.

Details:
DATE displays or sets the date. Type in **date** and press Enter to set the date interactively.

Command Shell
```
date
date 04-11-2002
```

VBScript
```
Set ws = WScript.CreateObject("WScript.Shell")
ret = ws.Run("date 04-11-2002",0,"True")
```

JScript
```
var ws = WScript.CreateObject("WScript.Shell");
ws.Run("date 04-11-2002",0,"True")
```

EXPAND

```
EXPAND [-r] source destination
EXPAND -r source [destination]
EXPAND -D source.cab [-f:files]
EXPAND source.cab -F:files destination
```

-D	Displays list of source files.
-F:files	List of files to expand from a .CAB file.
-r	Rename expanded files.
source	Source files to be expanded.
destination	Destination file path.

Details:

EXPAND decompresses files compressed with the Microsoft distribution format or files stored in .CAB files. You can use wildcards when specifying the source files. Also, if you don't specify a destination path, the current directory is used.

Command Shell

```
expand -r setup.ex_
expand *.ex_ d:\working\distro\
```

VBScript

```
Set ws = WScript.CreateObject("WScript.Shell")
ret = ws.Run("expand -r setup.ex_",0,"True")
```

JScript

```
var ws = WScript.CreateObject("WScript.Shell");
ws.Run("expand -r setup.ex_",0,"True")
```

FC

```
FC [/A] [/C] [/L] [/LBn] [/N] [/T] [/U] [/W] [/nnnn]
   [drive1:][path1]filename1 [drive2:][path2]filename2
FC /B [drive1:][path1]filename1 [drive2:][path2]filename2
```

[drive1:][path1]filename1	Source file for comparison.
[drive2:][path2]filename2	Target file to use in comparison.
/nnnn	When attempting to resync ASCII text files, this specifies the number of lines that must match before the command considers an area to be identical. By default, two lines must match before the command considers an area to be identical.

/A	Displays only the first and last lines for each set of differences.
/B	Performs a binary comparison.
/C	Disregards whether letters in the comparison are upper- or lowercase.
/L	Compares files as ASCII text.
/LBn	Sets the maximum consecutive mismatches before FC cancels the operation.
/N	Displays the line numbers on an ASCII comparison.
/T	FC can compare tabs within files to spacing to detect differences. By default, FC converts tabs to spaces for comparisons. To turn this feature off, use this switch.
/U	Compare files as Unicode rather than ASCII.
/W	Ignores white space (tabs and spaces) for comparison. Multiple spaces and tabs are converted to a single space for the comparison.

Details:

FC compares two files and displays the differences between them. In binary mode, FC displays all differences. In ASCII/Unicode mode, FC looks for differences area by area. The size of these areas are set with /*nnnn*, /0050 for example.

Command Shell

```
fc /A /LB50 /0004 attitude.txt changes.txt
fc /B cr.bin cr2.bin
```

Windows Script

compare.bat

```
fc /A /LB50 /0004 attitude.txt changes.txt > log.txt
fc /B cr.bin cr2.bin > log.txt
```

compare.vbs

```
Set ws = WScript.CreateObject("WScript.Shell")
ret = ws.Run("compare.bat",0,"True")
```

compare.js

```
var ws = WScript.CreateObject("WScript.Shell");
ws.Run("compare.bat",0,"True")
```

FORMAT

```
FORMAT drive: [/FS:file-system] [/V:label] [/Q] [/A:size] [/C]
[/X]
FORMAT drive: [/V:label] [/Q] [/F:size]
FORMAT drive: [/V:label] [/Q] [/T:tracks /N:sectors]
FORMAT drive: [/V:label] [/Q] [/1] [/4]
FORMAT drive: [/Q] [/1] [/4] [/8]
```

`drive:`	Sets the letter of the drive to format.
`/1`	Formats a single side of a floppy disk.
`/4`	Formats a 5.25-inch, 360KB, floppy disk in a high-density drive.
`/8`	Formats a 5.25-inch disk with eight sectors per track.
`/A:size`	Overrides the default allocation unit size. NTFS supports 512, 1024, 2048, 4096, 8192, 16K, 32K, and 64K. FAT supports 8192, 16K, 32K, 64K, 128K, and 256K. NTFS compression is not supported for allocation unit sizes above 4096K.
`/C`	Turn on file compression.
`/F:size`	Sets the size of the floppy disk to format. Common sizes are 360 or 1.2 for 5.25-inch disks, and 1.44 or 2.88 for 3.5-inch disks.
`/FS:file-system`	Sets the type of the file system as FAT or NTFS.
`/N:sectors`	Sets the number of sectors per track. Used with `/T` and cannot be used with `/F`.
`/Q`	Performs a quick format.
`/T:tracks`	Sets the number of tracks per disk side.
`/V:label`	Sets the volume label.
`/X`	Forces the drive to dismount before formatting if necessary.

Details:

FORMAT formats a floppy disk or hard drive for use with Windows 2000.

Command Shell
```
format e: /FS:NTFS /C /V:Secondary
format a: /Q
```

VBScript
```
Set ws = WScript.CreateObject("WScript.Shell")
ret = ws.Run("format e: /FS:NTFS /C /V:Secondary",0,"True")
```

JScript
```
var ws = WScript.CreateObject("WScript.Shell");
ws.Run("format e: /FS:NTFS /C /V:Secondary",0,"True")
```

FTP

```
FTP [-v] [-d] [-i] [-n] [-g] [-s:filename] [-a]
    [-w:windowsize] [host]
```

host	Sets the hostname or IP address of the remote host to which you want to connect.
-a	Uses any available local interface to bind data connection. Can sometimes resolve connectivity problems.
-d	Sets debug mode, which displays all messages sent between the client and the server.
-g	Allows you to use wildcards when setting file and path names.
-i	Turns off interactive mode when you are transferring multiple file. Used to perform unattended transfers.
-n	Turns off auto-login during the initial connection.
-s:*filename*	Designates a text file containing FTP commands; the commands will automatically run after FTP starts.
-v	Turns off display of remote server responses.
-w:*buffersize*	Sets a new transfer buffer size, overriding the default buffer size of 4096 bytes.

Details:
FTP transfers files using FTP (File Transfer Protocol). When you transfer files in scripts using FTP, be sure to use a transfer file which can contain any available FTP commands and to turn off interactive prompts for transferring multiple file. The following FTP commands are available once you start the utility:

!	Exits to the command shell.
?	Gets command help

append	Starts a download in the current directory and appends to an existing file (if available) rather than overwriting the file.
ascii	Sets transfers mode to ASCII text. Use this with text file transfers to preserve end-of-line designators.
bell	Turns beep on/off for confirmation of command completion. Default setting is off.
binary	Sets transfer mode to binary. Use with executables and other binary file types.
bye	Exits to the Command Shell.
cd	Changes the remote working directory.
close	Closes FTP session, but doesn't exit the FTP utility.
debug	Turns debug mode on/off. Default setting is off.
delete	Deletes a file .
dir	Lists contents of directory on the system you are connected to for transfers
disconnect	Closes the connection to the remote system.
get	Downloads a file from the remote system.
glob	Allows you to use wildcards when naming files and directories.
hash	Turns hash mark printing on/off. If this property is set, the # character prints each time the buffer is transferred, providing a visual cue for progress.
lcd	Changes the working directory on the local system, such as lcd c:\winnt\system32.
literal	Sends arbitrary FTP command.
ls	Lists contents of remote directory. Because the command is designed after the Unix ls, all normal ls flags are available, such as ls -l or ls -lsa.
mdelete	Deletes multiple files on the remote system.
mdir	Lists contents of multiple remote directories.
mget	Downloads multiple files from the remote system.
mkdir	Creates a directory on the remote system.
mls	Lists contents of multiple remote directories.
mput	Sends multiple files to the remote system.

open	Opens a connection to a remote system specified following the command, such as `open idg.com`.
prompt	Turns prompt mode on/off for `mget`, `mput`, and `mdelete`. Default mode is off.
put	Sends a file to the remote system.
pwd	Prints working directory on remote machine.
quit	Quits FTP sessions and exits to the command shell.
quote	Sends arbitrary FTP command.
recv	Downloads a file from the remote system.
remotehelp	Gets help from remote server.
rename	Renames a file on the remote system.
rmdir	Removes a directory on the remote system.
send	Sends a file to the remote system.
trace	Traces the IP route of the file transfer.
type	Sets the transfer type and toggles between ASCII and binary.
user	Starts logon procedure to change users while connected to a remote host.
verbose	Turns verbose mode on/off. Default is off.

Command Shell
```
ftp -i -g -s:tranf.txt idg.com
ftp -i idg.com
```
VBScript
```
Set ws = WScript.CreateObject("WScript.Shell")
ret = ws.Run("ftp -i -g -s:tranf.txt idg.com",0,"True")
```
JScript
```
var ws = WScript.CreateObject("WScript.Shell");
ws.Run("ftp -i -g -s:tranf.txt idg.com",0,"True")
```

FTYPE

```
FTYPE [fileType[=[command]]]
```

fileType	Sets the file type to examine or change.
command	Sets the launch command to use when opening files of this type.

Details:
FTYPE displays or modifies file types used in file extension associations. To display the current file types, enter FTYPE without any parameters. To delete an existing file type, set its launch command to an empty string, such as:

```
ftype perl=
```

If passing arguments, %0 or %1 is substituted with the filename being launched through the association. %* gets all the parameters and %2 gets the 1st parameter, %3 the second, etc. %~n gets all the remaining parameters starting with the nth parameter, where n may be between 2 and 9.

Command Shell
```
ASSOC .pl=Perl
FTYPE Perl=c:\winnt\system32\perl.exe %1 %*
```

VBScript
```
Set ws = WScript.CreateObject("WScript.Shell")
ret = ws.Run("ASSOC .pl=Perl",0,"True")
ret = ws.Run("FTYPE Perl=c:\winnt\system32\perl.exe %1
%*",0,"True")
```

JScript
```
var ws = WScript.CreateObject("WScript.Shell");
ws.Run("ASSOC .pl=Perl",0,"True")
ws.Run("FTYPE Perl=c:\\winnt\\system32\\perl.exe %1
%*",0,"True")
```

IPCONFIG

```
ipconfig [/all | /release [adapter] | /renew [adapter]
            | /flushdns | /registerdns
            | /showclassid adapter
            | /setclassid adapter [classidtoset]
  | /displaydns ]
```

adapter	Name of the adapter or pattern with * to match any character and ? to match one character.
classidtoset	Sets the DHCP class ID.
/all	Displays full configuration information.
/displaydns	Displays the contents of the DNS resolve cache.
/flushdns	Flushes the DNS resolve cache.
/registerdns	Refreshes all DHCP leases and re-registers DNS names.
/release	Releases the IP address for the specified adapter.
/renew	Renews the IP address for the specified adapter.

/setclassid	Modifies the DHCP class ID.
/showclassid	Shows all the DHCP class IDs for the adapter.

Details:
IPCONFIG displays TCP/IP configuration values. The /release and /renew switches are useful when your network uses DHCP. /renew forces the computer to request new address information from the DHCP server. /release forces the computer to release the dynamic IP address assigned by the DHCP server.

Command Shell
```
ipconfig /renew
ipconfig /release
```
VBScript
```
Set ws = WScript.CreateObject("WScript.Shell")
ret = ws.Run("ipconfig /renew",0,"True")
```
JScript
```
var ws = WScript.CreateObject("WScript.Shell");
ws.Run("ipconfig /renew",0,"True")
```

NBTSTAT

```
NBTSTAT [-a remotename] [-A IP_address] [-c] [-n]
        [-r] [-R] [-RR] [-s] [-S] [interval] ]
```

interval	Redisplays selected statistics, pausing interval seconds between each display. Press Ctrl+C to stop redisplaying statistics.
-A IP_address	Displays a remote computer's statistics by IP address.
-a remotename	Displays a remote computer's statistics by NetBIOS name.
-c	Displays the local computer's name cache including IP addresses.
-n	Displays local NetBIOS names.
-RR	Sends release to WINS and then starts WINS refresh.
-R	Reloads LMHOSTS after deleting the names from the NetBIOS name cache.
-r	Displays statistics for names resolved by broadcast and via WINS.
-S	Displays all client and server sessions by IP addresses.

-s	Displays all client and server sessions, converting destination IP addresses to hostnames via the local HOSTS file.

Details:

NBTSTAT displays status of NetBIOS over TCP/IP. NBTSTAT is useful for obtaining local and remote system NetBIOS information.

Command Shell

```
nbtstat -a mars1
nbtstat -A 192.152.16.8
nbtstat -c
```

VBScript

```
Set ws = WScript.CreateObject("WScript.Shell")
ret = ws.Run("nbtstat -A 192.152.16.8",0,"True")
```

JScript

```
var ws = WScript.CreateObject("WScript.Shell");
ws.Run("nbtstat -A 192.152.16.8",0,"True")
```

NET ACCOUNTS

```
NET ACCOUNTS [/FORCELOGOFF:{minutes | NO}] [/MINPWLEN:length]
             [/MAXPWAGE:{days | UNLIMITED}] [/MINPWAGE:days]
             [/UNIQUEPW:number] [/DOMAIN]
```

/DOMAIN	Specifies that the operation should be performed on the primary domain controller of the current domain. Otherwise, the operation is performed on the local computer. (Applies only to Windows 2000 workstations that are members of an NT domain. By default, Windows 2000 servers perform operations on the primary domain controller.)
/FORCELOGOFF:{minutes	NO}	Sets the time, in minutes, before a user is forced to log off when the account expires or valid logon hours expire. Users receive a warning prior to being logged off. By default, the option is set to NO, which prevents forced log off.
/MAXPWAGE:{days	UNLIMITED}	Sets the number of days that a password is valid. The default is 90 days and the range is 1 – 49,710 days.

/MINPWAGE:*days*	Sets the minimum number of days before a user can change a password. The default is 0, which sets no minimum time. The range is 0 – 49710.
/MINPWLEN:*length*	Sets the minimum number of characters for a password. The default is 6 characters and the range is 0 – 14.
/UNIQUEPW:*number*	Specifies the number of unique passwords a user must use before being able to reuse a password. The default is 5 and the range is 0 – 24.

Details:
NET ACCOUNTS manages user account and password policies. Use NET ACCOUNTS to manage user and password policies. To manage the accounts themselves, use NET USER, NET GROUP, or NET LOCALGROUP.

Command Shell
```
net accounts /domain /minpwlen:8 /maxpwage:45 /minpwage:10
```
VBScript
```
Set ws = WScript.CreateObject("WScript.Shell")
ret = ws.Run("net accounts /domain /minpwlen:8 /maxpwage:45
/minpwage:10",0,"True")
```
JScript
```
var ws = WScript.CreateObject("WScript.Shell");
ws.Run("net accounts /domain /minpwlen:8 /maxpwage:45
/minpwage:10",0,"True")
```

NET COMPUTER

```
NET COMPUTER \\computername {/ADD | /DEL}
```

computername	Sets the computer to add or delete from the domain.
/ADD	Adds the specified computer to the domain.
/DEL	Removes the specified computer from the domain.

Details:
NET COMPUTER adds or removes computers from a domain. The command is available only on Windows 2000 servers and is only applicable to the default domain.

Command Shell

```
net computer \\pluto8 /del
net computer \\saturn /add
```

VBScript

```
Set ws = WScript.CreateObject("WScript.Shell")
ret = ws.Run("net computer \\saturn /add",0,"True")
```

JScript

```
var ws = WScript.CreateObject("WScript.Shell");
ws.Run("net computer \\\\saturn /add",0,"True")
```

NET CONFIG SERVER

```
NET CONFIG SERVER [/AUTODISCONNECT:time] [/SRVCOMMENT:"text"]
                  [/HIDDEN:{YES | NO}]
```

/AUTODISCONNECT:*time*	Sets the number of minutes a user's session can be inactive before it is disconnected. The default is 15 minutes. The range is –1 to 65535 minutes. Use –1 to have the service never disconnect user sessions.
/SRVCOMMENT:"*text*"	Adds a comment for the server that is displayed in browse lists such as in Server Manager or NET VIEW. Enclose the comments in quotation marks and use up to 48 characters.
/HIDDEN:{YES | NO}	Allows you to prevent the server from being displayed in browser lists. The default is NO. Although a server is hidden from view, it is still accessible.

Details:

NET CONFIG SERVER displays or modifies configuration information for the server service. Enter **NET CONFIG SERVER** on a line by itself to see the current configuration of the server service.

Command Shell

```
net config server
net config server /autodisconnect:10 /hidden:yes
```

VBScript

```
Set ws = WScript.CreateObject("WScript.Shell")
ret = ws.Run("net config server /autodisconnect:10
/hidden:yes",0,"True")
```

JScript
```
var ws = WScript.CreateObject("WScript.Shell");
ws.Run("net config server /autodisconnect:10
/hidden:yes",0,"True")
```

NET CONFIG WORKSTATION

```
NET CONFIG WORKSTATION [/CHARCOUNT:bytes]
                       [/CHARTIME:msec]
                       [/CHARWAIT:sec]
```

/CHARCOUNT:*bytes*   Sets the number of bytes Windows 2000 collects before sending the data to a communication device. The default is 16 bytes and the range is 0 – 65535 bytes. If /CHARTIME:*msec* is also set, Windows 2000 acts on whichever condition is satisfied first.

/CHARTIME:*msec*   Sets the amount of time in milliseconds that Windows 2000 collects data before sending the data to a communication device. The default is 250 milliseconds and the range is 0 – 65535000 milliseconds. If /CHARCOUNT:*bytes* is also set, Windows 2000 acts on whichever condition is satisfied first.

/CHARWAIT:*sec*   Sets the number of seconds that Windows 2000 waits for a communication device to become available. The default is 3600 seconds and the range is 0 – 65535 seconds.

Details:
NET CONFIG WORKSTATION displays or modifies configuration information for the workstation service. Enter **NET CONFIG WORKSTATION** on a line by itself to see the current configuration of the workstation service.

Command Shell
```
net config workstation
net config workstation /charcount:32
```
VBScript
```
Set ws = WScript.CreateObject("WScript.Shell")
ret = ws.Run("net config workstation /charcount:32",0,"True")
```
JScript
```
var ws = WScript.CreateObject("WScript.Shell");
ws.Run("net config workstation /charcount:32",0,"True")
```

NET CONTINUE

```
NET CONTINUE service
```

    service   The service to resume.

Details:

Use `NET CONTINUE` to resume a paused service. Services that can be paused and resumed include: File Server For Macintosh, Lpdsvc, Net Logon, Network DDE, Network DDE DSDM, NT LM Security Support Provider, Remote Access Server, Server, Simple TCP/IP Services, Task Scheduler, and Workstation.

Command Shell
```
net continue "file server for macintosh"
```

VBScript
```
Set ws = WScript.CreateObject("WScript.Shell")
ret = ws.Run("net continue 'file server for
macintosh'",0,"True")
```

JScript
```
var ws = WScript.CreateObject("WScript.Shell");
ws.Run("net continue 'file server for macintosh'",0,"True")
```

NET FILE

```
NET FILE [id [/CLOSE]]
```

    id   The open file's identification number.

    /CLOSE   Closes an open file and releases locked records.

Details:

`NET FILE` manages open files on a server. Enter **NET FILE** by itself to display a complete listing of open files, which includes the name of the user who has the file open and the number of file locks (if applicable).

Command Shell
```
net file
net file 0001 /CLOSE
```

VBScript
```
Set ws = WScript.CreateObject("WScript.Shell")
ret = ws.Run("net file 0001 /CLOSE",0,"True")
```

JScript

```
var ws = WScript.CreateObject("WScript.Shell");
ws.Run("net file 0001 /CLOSE",0,"True")
```

NET GROUP

```
NET GROUP [groupname [/COMMENT:"text"]] [/DOMAIN]
NET GROUP groupname {/ADD [/COMMENT:"text"] | /DELETE}
         [/DOMAIN]
NET GROUP groupname username [...] {/ADD | /DELETE} [/DOMAIN]
```

groupname	Sets the name of the global group to work with. To view a list of users in the global group, specify only the group name.
username[...]	Lists one or more usernames to add to or remove from a global group. Use spaces to separate multiple usernames.
/ADD	Creates a global group, or adds a username to an existing global group.
/COMMENT:"*text*"	Adds an optional description for the global group. The comment can have up to 48 characters and must be enclosed in quotation marks.
/DELETE	Removes a global group, or removes a username from a global group.
/DOMAIN	Specifies that the operation should be performed on the primary domain controller of the current domain. Otherwise, the operation is performed on the local computer. (Applies only to Windows 2000 workstations that are members of an NT domain. By default, Windows 2000 servers perform operations on the primary domain controller.)

Details:

NET GROUP manages global groups. Enter **NET GROUP** by itself to see a list of all global groups. Be sure to use quotation marks in group or usernames that have spaces.

Command Shell

```
net group "domain admins"
net group "domain admins" wrstanek /add
```

VBScript
```
Set ws = WScript.CreateObject("WScript.Shell")
ret = ws.Run("net group 'domain admins' wrstanek
/add",0,"True")
```
JScript
```
var ws = WScript.CreateObject("WScript.Shell");
ws.Run("net group 'domain admins' wrstanek /add",0,"True")
```

NET LOCALGROUP

```
NET LOCALGROUP [groupname [/COMMENT:"text"]] [/DOMAIN]
NET LOCALGROUP groupname {/ADD [/COMMENT:"text"] | /DELETE}
              [/DOMAIN]
NET LOCALGROUP groupname name [...] {/ADD | /DELETE} [/DOMAIN]
```

groupname	Sets the name of the local group to work with. To view a list of users in the local group, specify only the group name.
username[...]	Lists one or more usernames to add to or remove from a local group. Use spaces to separate multiple usernames.
/ADD	Creates a local group, or adds a username to an existing local group.
/COMMENT:"text"	Adds an optional description for the local group. The comment can have up to 48 characters and must be enclosed in quotation marks.
/DELETE	Removes a local group, or removes a username from a local group.
/DOMAIN	Specifies that the operation should be performed on the primary domain controller of the current domain. Otherwise, the operation is performed on the local computer. (Applies only to Windows 2000 workstations that are members of an NT domain. By default, Windows 2000 servers perform operations on the primary domain controller.)

Details:
NET LOCALGROUP manages local groups. Enter **NET LOCALGROUP** by itself to see a list of all local groups. Be sure to use quotation marks in group or usernames that have spaces.

Command Shell

```
net localgroup "account operators"
net localgroup "account operators" wrstanek /add
```

VBScript

```
Set ws = WScript.CreateObject("WScript.Shell")
ret = ws.Run("net localgroup 'account operators' wrstanek
/add",0,"True")
```

JScript

```
var ws = WScript.CreateObject("WScript.Shell");
ws.Run("net localgroup 'account operators' wrstanek
/add",0,"True")
```

NET NAME

```
NET NAME [name [/ADD | /DELETE]]
```

name	The message name designated to receive messages. You can use up to 15 characters.
/ADD	Adds a messaging name alias to a computer.
/DELETE	Removes a messaging name from a computer.

Details:

NET NAME controls the list of recipients for messenger service messages. Use this command to set names of users who should receive messages for the computer. Enter **NET NAME** by itself to display the current list of names. You cannot delete the current computer's name or the currently logged-on user from the list. These name entries are set to receive messages by default. See NET SEND for details on sending messages.

Command Shell

```
net name wrstanek
net name wrstanek /DELETE
```

VBScript

```
Set ws = WScript.CreateObject("WScript.Shell")
ret = ws.Run("net name wrstanek /DELETE",0,"True")
```

JScript

```
var ws = WScript.CreateObject("WScript.Shell");
ws.Run("net name wrstanek /DELETE",0,"True")
```

NET PAUSE

```
NET PAUSE service
```

service   The service to put on hold.

Details:

NET PAUSE suspends a service and puts it on hold. When you use NET PAUSE to pause a service, you can use NET CONTINUE to resume it. Services that can be paused and resumed include File Server For Macintosh, Lpdsvc, Net Logon, Network DDE, Network DDE DSDM, NT LM Security Support Provider, Remoteboot, Remote Access Server, Server, Simple TCP/IP Services, Task Scheduler, and Workstation.

Command Shell

```
net pause "task scheduler"
```

VBScript

```
Set ws = WScript.CreateObject("WScript.Shell")
ret = ws.Run("net pause 'task scheduler'",0,"True")
```

JScript

```
var ws = WScript.CreateObject("WScript.Shell");
ws.Run("net pause 'task scheduler'",0,"True")
```

NET PRINT

```
NET PRINT \\computername\sharename
NET PRINT [\computername] job# [/HOLD | /RELEASE | /DELETE]
```

\\computername	The name of the computer sharing the printer queue.
sharename	The name of the shared printer queue.
job#	The number assigned to the print job in the print queue.
/DELETE	Removes a job from a queue.
/HOLD	Pauses the print job.
/RELEASE	Releases a print job that is held.

Details:

NET PRINT displays print jobs and shared queues. Use NET PRINT to manage shared printer queues and display queue status. To manage the shared printers themselves, use NET SHARE.

Command Shell
```
net print \\zeta\eng1
net print 0043 /delete
```

VBScript
```
Set ws = WScript.CreateObject("WScript.Shell")
ret = ws.Run("net print 0043 /delete",0,"True")
```

JScript
```
var ws = WScript.CreateObject("WScript.Shell");
ws.Run("net print 0043 /delete",0,"True")
```

NET SEND

```
NET SEND {name | * | /DOMAIN[:name] | /USERS} message
```

name	The username, computer name, or messaging name to send a message to. If a name has spaces, enclose it in quotation marks.
*	Sends the message to all of the names in your work-group or domain.
message	The message to send. Quotation marks aren't needed.
/DOMAIN[:name]	Sends the message to all of the names in the current domain. Use name to set an alternative domain or workgroup name.
/USERS	Sends the message to all users connected to the server.

Details:

NET SEND sends a messenger service message. Use NET SEND to send messages to other users, computers, or messaging names on the network. If you send a message to a specific user, the user must be logged on and running the Messenger service to receive the message.

Command Shell
```
net send wrstanek "What are you working on?"
net send /domain "Please log off Opus. System maintenance."
```

VBScript
```
Set ws = WScript.CreateObject("WScript.Shell")
ret = ws.Run("net send wrstanek 'What are you working
on?'",0,"True")
```

JScript
```
var ws = WScript.CreateObject("WScript.Shell");
ws.Run("net send wrstanek 'What are you working on?'",0,"True")
```

NET SESSION

```
NET SESSION [\\computername] [/DELETE]
```

computername	The name of the Windows 2000 server you want to examine.
/DELETE	Disconnects the local computer and the designated workstation or server, closing all open files for the session. If you don't specify a computer name, all sessions are ended.

Details:

NET SESSION lists or disconnects sessions between the local computer and other computers on the network. Enter NET SESSION to examine the local computer's sessions. Enter **NET SESSION** *computername* to examine sessions on another computer. This command only works on servers.

Command Shell
```
net session \\pluto
net session \\jupiter /delete
```

VBScript
```
Set ws = WScript.CreateObject("WScript.Shell")
ret = ws.Run("net session \\jupiter /delete",0,"True")
```

JScript
```
var ws = WScript.CreateObject("WScript.Shell");
ws.Run("net session \\\\jupiter /delete",0,"True")
```

NET SHARE

```
NET SHARE sharename
NET SHARE sharename=drive:path [/USERS:number | /UNLIMITED]
                              [/REMARK:"text"]
                              [/CACHE:Manual | Automatic | No]
NET SHARE sharename [/USERS:number | /UNLIMITED]
                    [/REMARK:"text"]
                    [/CACHE:Manual | Automatic | No]
NET SHARE {sharename | devicename | drive:path} /DELETE
```

devicename	Sets one or more printers shared by *sharename*. You can use LPT1: through LPT9:.
drive:path	Sets the complete path of the directory to be shared.
sharename	Sets the network name of the shared resource.
/CACHE:Automatic	Enables offline client caching with automatic updates.
/CACHE:Manual	Enables offline client caching with manual updates.
/CACHE:No	Disables offline client caching.
/DELETE	Stops sharing the specified resource.
/REMARK:"*text*"	Adds an optional comment about the shared resource. Quotation marks are mandatory.
/UNLIMITED	Specifies that an unlimited number of users can simultaneously access the shared resource.
/USERS:*number*	Sets the maximum number of users who can simultaneously access the shared resource.

Details:

NET SHARE manages shared printers and directories. Enter **NET SHARE** with a share name only to display information about the specified share.

Command Shell

```
net share netdata="r:\network\data\" /unlimited
net share netdata /delete
```

VBScript

```
Set ws = WScript.CreateObject("WScript.Shell")
ret = ws.Run("net share netdata /delete",0,"True")
```

JScript

```
var ws = WScript.CreateObject("WScript.Shell");
ws.Run("net share netdata /delete",0,"True")
```

NET START

```
NET START [service]
```

service	The service to start. Enclose service names that have spaces in quotation marks.

Details:

NET START starts network services or lists network services that are running. Enter **NET START** by itself to list running services. Services you can start on workstations and servers include Alerter, Client Service For Netware, Clipbook Server, Computer Browser, DHCP Client, Directory Replicator, Eventlog, LPDSVC, Messenger, Net Logon, Network DDE, Network DDE DSDM, Network Monitoring Agent, NT LM Security Support Provider, Plug and Play, Remote Access Connection Manager, Remote Access ISNSAP Service, Remote Access Server, Remote Procedure Call (RPC) Locator, Remote Procedure Call (RPC) Service, Server, Simple TCP/IP Services, SNMP, Spooler, Task Scheduler, TCPIP NetBIOS Helper, Ups, and Workstation

These additional services are available only on Windows 2000 servers: File Server For Macintosh, Gateway Service For Netware, Microsoft DHCP Server, Print Server For Macintosh, and Windows Internet Name Service.

NET START can also start network services not provided with the Windows 2000 operating system.

Command Shell

```
net start "Microsoft DHCP Server"
net start "Windows Internet Name Service"
```

VBScript

```
Set ws = WScript.CreateObject("WScript.Shell")
ret = ws.Run("net start 'Windows Internet Name
Service'",0,"True")
```

JScript

```
var ws = WScript.CreateObject("WScript.Shell");
ws.Run("net start 'Windows Internet Name Service'",0,"True")
```

NET STATISTICS

```
NET STATISTICS [WORKSTATION | SERVER]
```

SERVER   Displays Server service statistics.

WORKSTATION   Displays Workstation service statistics.

Details:

NET STATISTICS displays workstation and server statistics. Enter **NET STATISTICS** by itself to list the services for which statistics are currently available.

Command Shell

```
net statistics workstation
net statistics server
```

Windows Script

stats.bat

```
net statistics workstation > log.txt
net statistics server > log.txt
```

compare.vbs

```
Set ws = WScript.CreateObject("WScript.Shell")
ret = ws.Run("stats.bat",0,"True")
```

compare.js

```
var ws = WScript.CreateObject("WScript.Shell");
ws.Run("stats.bat",0,"True")
```

NET STOP

```
NET STOP service
```

service   The service to stop. Enclose service names with spaces in quotation marks.

Details:

NET STOP stops network services. Stopping a service cancels any network connections the service is running. You must have administrator privileges to stop services. The EventLog service cannot be stopped.

Services you can stop on workstations and servers include: Alerter, Client Service For Netware, Clipbook Server, Computer Browser, DHCP Client, Directory Replicator, LPDSVC, Messenger, Net Logon, Network DDE, Network DDE DSDM, Network Monitoring Agent, NT LM Security Support Provider, Plug and Play, Remote Access Connection Manager, Remote Access ISNSAP Service, Remote Access Server, Remote Procedure Call (RPC) Locator, Remote Procedure Call (RPC) Service, Server, Simple TCP/IP Services, SNMP, Spooler, Task Scheduler, TCPIP NetBIOS Helper, Ups, and Workstation

These additional services are available only on Windows 2000 servers: File Server For Macintosh, Gateway Service For NetWare, Microsoft DHCP Server, Print Server For Macintosh, and Windows Internet Name Service.

NET STOP can also start network services not provided with Windows 2000.

Command Shell

```
net stop "Microsoft DHCP Server"
net stop "Windows Internet Name Service"
```

VBScript

```
Set ws = WScript.CreateObject("WScript.Shell")
ret = ws.Run("net stop 'Windows Internet Name
Service'",0,"True")
```

JScript

```
var ws = WScript.CreateObject("WScript.Shell");
ws.Run("net stop 'Windows Internet Name Service'",0,"True")
```

NET TIME

```
NET TIME [\\computername | /DOMAIN[:domainname] |
         /RTSDOMAIN[:domainname]] [/SET]
         [\\computername] /QUERYSNTP
         [\\computername] /SETSNTP[:server_list]
```

\\computername	The name of a server with which you want to check or synchronize.
/DOMAIN[:domainname]	Specifies that the computer should synchronize with the Primary Domain Controller for the designated domain.
/RTSDOMAIN[:domainname]	Specifies that the computer should synchronize with a Reliable Time Server for the designated domain.
/SET	Synchronizes the computer's time with the time on the specified server or domain.
/QUERYSNTP	Displays the currently configured NTP server for the computer.
/SETSNTP: server_list	Sets the NTP time servers the computer should use. Enter DNS names or IP addresses separated by spaces.

Details:

NET TIME displays time and synchronizes time with remote computers. Enter **NET TIME** by itself to display the current date and time on the network's timeserver (which is normally the primary domain controller).

Command Shell

```
net time /SETSNTP:pluto.tvpress.com
```

VBScript

```
Set ws = WScript.CreateObject("WScript.Shell")
ret = ws.Run("net time /SETSNTP:pluto.tvpress.com",0,"True")
```

JScript
```
var ws = WScript.CreateObject("WScript.Shell");
ws.Run("net time /SETSNTP:pluto.tvpress.com",0,"True")
```

NET USE

```
NET USE [devicename | *] [\\computername\sharename[\volume]
        [password | *]] [/USER:[domainname\]username]
        [/USER:[username@domainname]
        [[/DELETE] | [/PERSISTENT:{YES | NO}]]
NET USE [devicename | *] [password | *]] [/HOME]
NET USE [/PERSISTENT:{YES | NO}]
```

*	Prompts for a required password.
\\computername	The UNC name of the server to connect to. If the computer name contains blank characters, enclose the double backslash (\\) and the computer name and enclose the share in quotation marks, such as "\\PLUTO\NETDATA"
devicename	Assigns a device to connect to or disconnect from. A device name is either a disk drive (lettered D: through Z:) or a printer (LPT1: through LPT9:). Type an asterisk instead of a specific device name to assign the next available device name.
domainname	Sets a domain. Otherwise, the current domain is used.
password	The password needed to access the shared resource.
username	The username with which to log on.
/DELETE	Disconnects the specified connection.
/HOME	Connects a user to their home directory.
/PERSISTENT	Determines whether the connection is persistent. The default is the last setting used.
\sharename	The network name of the shared resource.
/USER	Used to set the username for the connection (if it is different than the currently logged in user's name).
\volume	Sets a NetWare volume on the server. Client Services for Netware or Gateway Service for Netware must be running.
YES	Makes connections persistent, which saves connections as they are made and restores them at next logon.
NO	Makes a temporary connection, which is disconnected when the user logs off.

Details:

NET USE manages remote connections. Enter **NET USE** by itself to display a list of network connections.

Command Shell
```
net use \\pluto\netdata * /persistent
net use \\pluto\netdata /delete
```

VBScript
```
Set ws = WScript.CreateObject("WScript.Shell")
ret = ws.Run("net use \\pluto\netdata /delete",0,"True")
```

JScript
```
var ws = WScript.CreateObject("WScript.Shell");
ws.Run("net use \\\\pluto\\netdata /delete",0,"True")
```

NET USER

```
NET USER [username [password | *] [options]] [/DOMAIN]
NET USER username {password | *} /ADD [options] [/DOMAIN]
NET USER username [/DELETE] [/DOMAIN]
```

*	Prompts for the password.
password	Assigns or changes a password for a user account.
username	Sets the name of the user account to create, view, or modify.
/ADD	Adds a user account.
/DELETE	Removes a user account.
/DOMAIN	Specifies that the operation should be performed on the primary domain controller of the current domain. Otherwise, the operation is performed on the local computer. (Applies only to Windows 2000 workstations that are members of an NT domain. By default, Windows 2000 servers perform operations on the primary domain controller.)

Options:

/ACTIVE:{YES | NO}	Enables or disables a user account. If the account is not active, the user cannot log on. The default is YES.
/COMMENT:"text"	Sets a description of up to 48 characters for the account. Enclose the text in quotation marks.

/COUNTRYCODE:*nnn*	Sets the operating system country code for the user's help and error messages. A value of 0 is the default.
/EXPIRES:{*date* | NEVER}	Determines whether the user's account expires. The default is never. Expiration dates can be in mm/dd/yy or dd/mm/yy, depending on the country code.
/FULLNAME:"*name*"	Sets the user's full name. Enclose the name in quotation marks.
/HOMEDIR:*pathname*	Sets the path of the user's home directory. The path must exist before you can use it.
/PASSWORDCHG:{YES | NO}	Determines whether users can change their own password. The default is YES.
/PASSWORDREQ:{YES | NO}	Determines whether a user account must have a password. The default is YES.
/PROFILEPATH[:path]	Sets a path for the user's logon profile.
/SCRIPTPATH:pathname	Sets the location of the user's logon script.
/TIMES:{*times* | ALL}	Specifies the times and days a user is allowed to log on. Times are expressed as day[-day][,day[-day]],time[-time][,time [-time]] and limited to 1-hour increments. Days can be spelled out or abbreviated (M, T, W, Th, F, Sa, Su). Hours can be 12- or 24-hour notation. For 12-hour notation, use AM or PM. The value ALL means a user can always log on. A null value (blank) means a user can never log on. Separate day and time entries with commas, and units of time with semicolons.
/USERCOMMENT:"*text*"	Allows a user comment to be added or changed.
/WORKSTATIONS: {*computername*[,...] | *}	Lists as many as eight workstations from which a user can log on to the network. If /WORKSTATIONS has no list, or if the list is *, the user can log on from any computer.

Details:

NET USER manages user accounts. Enter **NET USER** by itself to list the user accounts for the server. The command works only on servers.

When you want to create or modify domain accounts, be sure to enter **/DOMAIN**.

Command Shell
```
net user wrstanek happydayz /ADD
net user wrstanek /DELETE
```

VBScript
```
Set ws = WScript.CreateObject("WScript.Shell")
ret = ws.Run("net user wrstanek /DELETE",0,"True")
```

JScript
```
var ws = WScript.CreateObject("WScript.Shell");
ws.Run("net user wrstanek /DELETE",0,"True")
```

NET VIEW

```
NET VIEW [\\computername | /DOMAIN[:domainname]]
NET VIEW /NETWORK:NW [\\computername]
```

\\computername	Specifies the computer whose shared resources you want to view.
/DOMAIN:domainname	Sets the domain for which you want to view computers that have resources available. If the domain name is omitted, all domains on the network are listed.
/NETWORK:NW	Displays all the servers on a NetWare network. If a computer name is specified, only the resources available on that computer are displayed.

Details:
NET VIEW displays available network resources. Enter **NET VIEW** without options to display a list of computers in the current domain or network.

Command Shell
```
net view \\delta
net view /domain:engineering
```

Windows Script
---

view.bat
```
net view \\delta > log.txt
net view /domain:engineering > log.txt
```

compare.vbs
```
Set ws = WScript.CreateObject("WScript.Shell")
ret = ws.Run("view.bat",0,"True")
```

compare.js

```
var ws = WScript.CreateObject("WScript.Shell");
ws.Run("view.bat",0,"True")
```

NETSTAT

```
NETSTAT [-a] [-e] [-n] [-s] [-p protocol] [-r] [interval]
```

interval	Redisplays selected statistics, pausing between each display. Press CTRL+C to stop redisplaying statistics. If this option is omitted, information is only displayed once.
-a	Displays connections and listening ports.
-e	Displays Ethernet statistics. This may be combined with -s to obtain additional details.
-n	Displays IP addresses and port numbers rather than computer names.
-p *protocol*	Shows connections for the specified protocol (TCP or UDP). If the -s option is used with -p, you can view protocol information for TCP, UDP, ICMP, or IP.
-r	Displays the contents of the routing table.
-s	Displays per-protocol statistics. By default, statistics are shown for TCP, UDP, ICMP, and IP. Use with -p to examine a specific protocol.

Details:

NETSTAT displays status of network connections as well as protocol statistics. Unlike most other commands, most options provide completely different types of information. TCP/IP networking must be installed.

Command Shell

```
netstat -a
netstat -s -p TCP
```

Windows Script

nstats.bat

```
netstat -a > log.txt
netstat -s -p TCP > log.txt
```

compare.vbs

```
Set ws = WScript.CreateObject("WScript.Shell")
ret = ws.Run("nstats.bat",0,"True")
```

compare.js

```
var ws = WScript.CreateObject("WScript.Shell");
ws.Run("nstats.bat",0,"True")
```

NSLOOKUP

```
NSLOOKUP [-option] [computer | server]
```

`-option`	An option to perform a query with; in the form `-command=value` or `-command`. The most commonly used command is `querytype`, which sets the type of record you want to examine. Record types include A, CNAME, MX, NS, PTR, and SOA.
`computer`	The hostname or IP address you want to look up in DNS.
`server`	The DNS server to use for the lookup. If you don't specify a server, the default name server is used.

Details:

`NSLOOKUP` shows the status of Domain Name System (DNS) for servers and workstations with DNS resolution. To use this command, TCP/IP networking must be configured. DNS lookup can be performed interactively or non-interactively. DNS lookups are most useful if you need to look up the IP address of a known host or examine DNS entries. If you want to see if a particular Internet host is available, `PING` is a better command to use.

Command Shell

```
nslookup www.tvpress.com
nslookup -querytype=mx tvpress.com
```

Windows Script

---

ns.bat

```
nslookup www.tvpress.com > log.txt
nslookup -querytype=mx tvpress.com > log.txt
```

compare.vbs

```
Set ws = WScript.CreateObject("WScript.Shell")
ret = ws.Run("ns.bat",0,"True")
```

compare.js

```
var ws = WScript.CreateObject("WScript.Shell");
ws.Run("ns.bat",0,"True")
```

NTBACKUP

```
ntbackup backup [systemstate] "bks file name" /J {"job name"}
                [/P {"pool name"}] [/T { "tape name"}]
                [/N {"media name"}] [/F {"file name"}]
                [/D {"set description"}] [/DS {"server name"}]
                [/IS {"server name"}] [/A] [/V:{yes|no}]
                [/R:{yes|no}] [/L:{f|s|n}] [/M {backup type}]
                [/RS:{yes|no}] [/HC:{on|off}]
```

bks file name	Sets the name of the backup selection file (.bks file) to be used for this backup operation. This file contains information on the files and folders selected for backup. You have to create the file using the graphical user interface (GUI) version of Windows 2000 Backup.
systemstate	Specifies that you want to back up the System State data. Additionally, the backup type will be forced to normal or copy.
/A	Performs an append operation. You must use /G or /T with this option. Do not use /P.
/D {"set description"}	Specifies a label for each backup set.
/DS {"server name"}	Backs up the directory service file for the specified Microsoft Exchange Server.
/F {"file name"}	Sets the logical disk path and file name. Do not use /P, /G, or /T with this option.
/HC:{on|off}	Specifies whether to use hardware compression, if available, on the tape drive.
/IS {"server name"}	Backs up the Information Store file for the specified Microsoft Exchange Server.
/J {"job name"}	Sets the job name to be used in the log file.
/L:{f|s|n}	Specifies the type of log file: f = full, s = summary, n = none.
/M {backup type}	Specifies the backup type. It must be one of the following: normal, copy, differential, incremental, or daily.

`/N {"media name"}`	Specifies the media name for the backup. Do not use /A with this switch.
`/P {"pool name"}`	Sets the name of the media pool to use. This is usually the Backup media pool. If you select this option you must not use these switches: /A, /G, /F, and /T.
`/R:{yes|no}`	Specifies whether to restrict access to this tape to the owner or members of the Administrators group.
`/RS:{yes|no}`	Specifies whether to back up the Removable Storage database.
`/T {"tape name"}`	Sets the tape name, which overwrites the existing tape label. Do not use this switch in conjunction with /P.
`/V:{yes|no}`	Specifies whether data should be verified after the backup is complete.

Details:

NTBACKUP is used to backup files on Windows 2000 computers. You cannot restore files from the command line using NTBACKUP. Some switches default to the options you've set in the graphical version of Backup unless they are changed by a command-line switch. These switches are /V, /R, /L, /M, /RS, and /HC.

You can only back up the system state on a local computer. You cannot back up the system state on a remote computer. Before you can back up Windows Media Services files, you should read the online help file titled "Running Backup with Windows Media Services".

Command Shell

```
ntbackup backup \\pluto\c$ /j "Backup Set 1" /f "D:\backup.bkf"
ntbackup backup \\pluto\d$ /m normal /j "My Jobs" /p "NTBackup"
/n "Set 1" /v:yes /r:no /l:s /rs:no /hc:on
```

VBScript

```
Set ws = WScript.CreateObject("WScript.Shell")
ret = ws.Run("ntbackup backup \\pluto\c$ /j 'Backup Set 1' /f
'D:\backup.bkf'",0,"True")
```

JScript

```
var ws = WScript.CreateObject("WScript.Shell");
ws.Run("ntbackup backup \\\\pluto\\c$ /j 'Backup Set 1' /f
'D:\\backup.bkf'",0,"True")
```

PATH

```
PATH [[drive:]path[;...][;%PATH%]
PATH ;
```

`[drive:]`	Sets the drive to check.
`path`	Sets the directory path.

Details:

PATH displays or sets a search path for executable files. The command path is set during logon using system and user environment variables, namely the %PATH% variable. To view current path setting, type **PATH** on a line by itself and press Enter. The directory order in the command path indicates the search order used by the command shell when looking for executables and scripts.

Update existing path information by appending a new path to the %PATH% environment variable, for example:

```
path %PATH%;c:\scripts\networking
```

Clear the path by entering:

```
path ;
```

Command Shell

```
path
path c:\scripts\networking;%PATH%
```

VBScript

```
Set ws = WScript.CreateObject("WScript.Shell")
ret = ws.Run("path c:\scripts\networking;%PATH%",0,"True")
```

JScript

```
var ws = WScript.CreateObject("WScript.Shell");
ws.Run("path c:\\scripts\\networking;%PATH%",0,"True")
```

PING

```
PING [-t] [-a] [-n count] [-l size] [-f] [-i TTL] [-v TOS]
     [-r count] [-s count] [[-j host-list] | [-k host-list]]
     [-w timeout] destination-list
```

`destination-list`	A list of computers to ping; specified by hostname or IP address. If NetBIOS resolution is enabled for the computer/domain, you can also use NetBIOS names (the computer name is an NT domain).

-a	Resolve IP addresses to hostnames when pinging.
-f	Specifies that the ping packet shouldn't be fragmented when it goes through gateways.
-i *TTL*	Sets a Time To Live value.
-j *host-list*	Sets the packet route using the host list. The route doesn't have to include all potential gateways. Use spaces to separate hostnames.
-k *host-list*	Sets a strict packet route using the host list. The route must be inclusive of all gateways. Use spaces to separate hostnames.
-l *size*	The number of bytes to send in the ping. The default is 64 and the maximum is 8192.
-n *count*	Number of times to ping the specified computer. The default is 4.
-r *count*	Displays the route taken by the ping packets. *Count* determines the number of hops to count from 1 to 9.
-s *count*	The timestamp for the number of hops set by *count*.
-t	Ping repeatedly until interrupted.
-v *TOS*	Sets the type of service.
-w *timeout*	A timeout set in milliseconds.

Details:
PING sends data to a computer to determine if a network connection can be established. TCP/IP networking must be configured. PING is a good command to use before trying to work with an Internet resource. If the ping returns a bad IP address or host unreachable, it means the computer you want to work with isn't available.

Command Shell
```
ping -t www.idg.com
ping -n 50 www.idg.com
```

VBScript
```
Set ws = WScript.CreateObject("WScript.Shell")
ret = ws.Run("ping www.idg.com",0,"True")
if ret <> 0 Then
  WScript.Echo "Error!"
Else
  WScript.Echo "Success"
End If
```

JScript

```
var ws = WScript.CreateObject("WScript.Shell")
ret = ws.Run("ping www.idg.com",0,"True")
if (ret != 0)
  WScript.Echo("Error!")
else
  WScript.Echo("Success")
```

RECOVER

```
RECOVER [drive:][path]filename
```

[drive:][path]filename	Sets the drive, directory, or file to recover.

Details:

RECOVER recovers readable information from a bad or defective disk.

Command Shell

```
recover a:
```

VBScript

```
Set ws = WScript.CreateObject("WScript.Shell")
ret = ws.Run("recover a:",0,"True")
```

JScript

```
var ws = WScript.CreateObject("WScript.Shell");
ws.Run("recover a:",0,"True")
```

ROUTE

```
ROUTE [-f] [-p] [command [destination] [MASK netmask] [gateway]
      [METRIC metric]]
```

-f	Clears the routing tables of gateway entries. This option is executed before running any of the available route commands.
-p	When used with the ADD command, makes the route persistent so it continues to exist when the system is restarted. When used with the PRINT command, prints a list of persistent routes.

command	Allows you to specify one of these route commands:
	PRINT: **Prints a route.**
	ADD: **Adds a route.**
	DELETE: **Deletes a route.**
	CHANGE: **Modifies a route.**
destination	Sets the route destination host.
MASK *netmask*	A subnet mask to associate with the route entry. The default network mask is 255.255.255.255.
gateway	The gateway for the route.
METRIC *costmetric*	Sets a numeric cost metric for the route. Valid values are from 1 to 9999.

Details:

ROUTE manages network routing tables. If you use a hostname for the destination rather than an IP address, ROUTE looks in the NETWORKS file to resolve the destination to an IP address. If you use a hostname for a gateway, ROUTE looks in the HOSTS file to resolve the host to an IP address. If the command is PRINT or DELETE, you can use wildcards for the destination and gateway.

The cost metric is useful in determining which route the local computer attempts to use first. Routes with a metric of 1 are always attempted before routes with higher-cost metrics.

Command Shell
```
route -p add mail.idg.com 255.255.255.0 214.15.8.2 1
route delete mail.idg.com 214.*
```

VBScript
```
Set ws = WScript.CreateObject("WScript.Shell")
ret = ws.Run("route delete mail.idg.com 214.*",0,"True")
```

JScript
```
var ws = WScript.CreateObject("WScript.Shell");
ws.Run("route delete mail.idg.com 214.*",0,"True")
```

TIME

```
TIME [time | /T]
```

time	Sets the time in [HH:[MM:[SS.[hh]]]][A|P] format.
/T	Displays the current time without a prompt.

Details:

TIME displays or sets the system time. TIME is normally set on a 24-hour clock. You can also set an a.m. or p.m. value if you use the A or P modifiers. Valid values are:

+ Hours: 0 to 23

+ Minutes: 0 to 59

+ Seconds: 0 to 59

+ Hundredths: 0 to 99

Command Shell
```
time /t
time 22:50
```
VBScript
```
Set ws = WScript.CreateObject("WScript.Shell")
ret = ws.Run("time 22:50",0,"True")
```
JScript
```
var ws = WScript.CreateObject("WScript.Shell");
ws.Run("time 22:50",0,"True")
```

TRACERT

```
TRACERT [-d] [-h maximum_hops] [-j host-list]
        [-w timeout] target_name
```

target_name	The remote computer to locate.
-d	Does not convert IP addresses for hops.
-h maximum_hops	The maximum number of hops between the local computer and the target.
-j host-list	Sets the trace route using the host list. The route doesn't have to include all potential gateways. Use spaces to separate hostnames.
-w timeout	Waits the specified number of milliseconds before timing out.

Details:

TRACERT displays the path between the local computer and a remote computer. Tracing the route between two computers is extremely helpful in troubleshooting network routing problems.

Command Shell

```
tracert tvpress.com
tracert -d tvpress.com
```

Windows Script

---

trace.bat

```
tracert tvpress.com > log.txt
tracert -d tvpress.com > log.txt
```

compare.vbs

```
Set ws = WScript.CreateObject("WScript.Shell")
ret = ws.Run("trace.bat",0,"True")
```

compare.js

```
var ws = WScript.CreateObject("WScript.Shell");
ws.Run("trace.bat",0,"True")
```

✦　　✦　　✦

Index

SYMBOLS

A

Continued

N

Name property
    Computer objects, 415
    Contact objects, 422
    File objects, 128
    Folder objects, 118
    Group objects, 425
    IADs, 280
    OrganizationalUnit objects, 433
    User objects, 437
NamePrefix, 440
Namespace objects
    LDAP provider, 265
    NDS provider, 270
    NWCOMPAT provider, 273
    WinNT provider, 268
NameSuffix, 440
naming contexts
    accessing using ADSI Edit, 404
    described, 403
    domain-naming context, 410–413
namingContexts, 406
NamingProperties, 294
NDS (Novell NetWare Directory Services)
    provider, 258, 269–272
NET SHARE, 376
net time command, 221–223
NetAddress, 270
NetAddresses, 383
netbootGUID, 415
NetDDE, 345
NetDDEdsdm, 345
NetHood folder, 166
NETLOGON (administrative share), 377
Netlogon (service object name), 344
Netman, 345

network resource library
    checking free space, 500–501
    drive mapping, 501
    getting drive info, 499–500
    printer operations, 501
    source, 487
    Windows services operations, 501–503
network services reconfiguration using
    Registry, 189–195
networkAddress, 415, 437
NewFile, 476
NewFolder, 475
NewMenu, 471
NewShortcut, 470
Normal file/folder attribute, 129
Nothing keyword, 114
Notify, 394, 395
NotifyPath, 395
Novell NetWare 3 provider, 258, 272–273
Novell NetWare Directory Services (NDS)
    provider, 258, 269–272
NtFrs, 344
NtLmSsp, 345
NtmsSvc, 345
nTSecurityDescriptor property
    Computer objects, 415
    Contact objects, 422
    Group objects, 425
    OrganizationalUnit objects, 433
    User objects, 437
Null
    data type, 36
    variable subtype, 14
Number data type, 36
NUMBER_OF_PROCESSORS, 78
numseconds, 52
NWCOMPAT provider, 258, 272–273

Continued

Continued

Notes

Notes

Notes

Notes

Notes